Till Patrik Holterhus (ed.)

The Law Behind Rule of Law Transfers

On Rule Based Interactions of Legal Orders in a Globalized World

Nomos

The Deutsche Nationalbibliothek lists this publication in the Deutsche Nationalbibliografie; detailed bibliographic data are available on the Internet at http://dnb.d-nb.de

ISBN 978-3-8487-5716-9 (Print)
978-3-8452-9848-1 (ePDF)

British Library Cataloguing-in-Publication Data
A catalogue record for this book is available from the British Library.

ISBN 978-3-8487-5716-9 (Print)
978-3-8452-9848-1 (ePDF)

Library of Congress Cataloging-in-Publication Data
Holterhus, Till Patrik
The Law Behind Rule of Law Transfers
On Rule Based Interactions of Legal Orders in a Globalized World
Till Patrik Holterhus (ed.)
296 p.

ISBN 978-3-8487-5716-9 (Print)
978-3-8452-9848-1 (ePDF)

1st Edition 2019

Preface

The present volume undertakes to explore *The Law Behind Rule of Law Transfers*. Rule of law transfers have already been studied extensively in academia. Yet, it is my impression that thus far scholarship has predominantly centered around the socio-political dimensions of such transfers. This volume, therefore, departs from such common paths and intends to assess rule of law transfers in their particular *legal* dimensions. Such perspective assumes that rule of law transfers do not only *consider* the rule of law as a legal concept, but hold a legal dimension *themselves*. It is particularly concerned with understanding what positive legal norms impel and drive the promotion of the rule of law abroad. It strives to explore which legal instruments and mechanisms govern and organize the actual transfer processes. And, furthermore, it asks which legal structures enable and facilitate the implementation of rule of law transfers within recipient legal orders.

The contributions included in this volume have been selected through a call for papers for a Special Issue of the Goettingen Journal of International Law (GoJIL Vol. 9, No. 1, 2018) for which I acted as a Special Issue Editor. All contributions underwent a process of double-blind peer review, not only with respect to their overall scholarly quality, but also with respect to their compatibility with this volume's particular approach as described above.

I would like to sincerely thank *Prof. Dr. Peter-Tobias Stoll* and *BVR Prof. Dr. Andreas L. Paulus* as well as The Goettingen Association for the Promotion of International Law for their generous support which enabled the publication of this volume in print. Furthermore, for an excellent collaboration I wish to express my gratitude to the Goettingen Journal of International Law and in particular its Editor-in-Chief *Maximilian Heinze* who took upon himself the efforts of overseeing the organizational aspects of the project. Last but not least, I would like to thank *Agata Daszko* and *Jasmin Evers* for their valuable assistance with the final editing.

Göttingen/Berlin, February 2019 *Till Patrik Holterhus*

Table of Contents

A Theoretical Introduction and Legal Perspective on Rule of Law Transfers

Till Patrik Holterhus[*]

Table of Contents

* Dr. Till Patrik Holterhus, MLE., LL.M. (Yale), Assistant Professor at the Institute for International Law and European Law at the Georg-August-University Göttingen and Professeur Invité at the Pantheon-Sorbonne University Paris (in 2018 and 2019).

This volume deals with the theme of *The Law Behind Rule of Law Transfers*. Transfers of the rule of law between legal orders have been studied extensively in academia. Yet, so far scholarship has, in this regard, predominantly centered around the socio-political questions.

There is, however, more to explore. The volume, therefore, departs from common scholarly paths and intends to assess and explain rule of law transfers as a *legal* phenomenon. Such an analytical perspective is based on the assumption that rule of law transfers do not only *consider* the rule of law as a legal concept but encompass a legal dimension *themselves*.

The following introduction will establish the theoretical basis on which such a legal approach shall be carried out. Four arguments will be developed: First, that there exists a plurality of state and non-state legal orders which interact on a global scale (A.). Second, that one particular way of such interaction is the transfer of legal items between legal orders (B.). Third, that the *rule of law*, as a fundamental legal concept, is such an item and subject to legal transfers (C.). And fourth, that – without doubting the influence of many social and political factors – the law itself plays an underestimated role with respect to rule of law transfers in the global plurality of legal orders (D.). Subsequently, the wide range of legal perspectives on the topic of rule of law transfers contained in this volume shall briefly be outlined (E.).

A. Interactions of Legal Orders in a Globalized World

I. The Plurality of Legal Orders

We live in a world of numerous legal orders – the phrase *legal orders* to be understood as unitary and therefore distinguishable sets of positive legal norms and their (demanded) sphere of authority and application. The plurality of such legal orders exists for different reasons.

1. *Multiple National Legal Orders*

First and foremost, the legal plurality derives from the (still dominant legal axiom of the) territorial divide into (legal) communities – since the 17th century and until today, in the form of the Westphalian nation state.[1] Based on early concepts of internal and external independence as well as exclusive sovereignty, each nation state, in the course of time, has developed its specific legal order. Although comparative legal scholarship tends to sometimes group these various national legal orders into a few overall legal families or systems (*Rechtskreise*),[2] national legal orders (at least in theory) exist distinctively and independently.

2. *Further Pluralization Through Globalization*

This (traditional) plurality of national legal orders has experienced and continues to experience further pluralization through the contemporary phenomenon of globalization. This phenomenon can best be described as the present process of a steady increase in worldwide human communication, interrelation, interdependence and integration in numerous fields, including economic, political, social, cultural, technical, but also legal aspects, predominantly caused by new technological means of communication and advanced ways of transportation, but also the rise of shared global challenges.[3] Although such ever-closer and accelerated global exchange

---

1 See E. C. Ip, 'Globalization and the Future of the Law of the Sovereign State', 8 *International Journal of Constitutional Law* (2010) 3, 636; M. Mann, 'Has Globalization Ended the Rise and Rise of the Nation-state?', 4 *Review of International Political Economy* (1997) 3, 472.

2 For an overview see H. P. Glenn, 'Comparative Legal Families and Comparative Legal Traditions', in M. Reimann & R. Zimmermann (eds), *The Oxford Handbook of Comparative Law* (2006), 421.

3 For an introductory discussion see D. Held & A. McGrew, 'The Great Globalization Debate: An Introduction', in D. Held & A. McGrew (eds), *The Global Transformations Reader: An Introduction to the Globalization Debate*, 2nd ed. (2003), 1; see also W. Twining, 'Implications of 'Globalisation' for Law as a Discipline', in A. Halpin & V. Roeben (eds), *Theorising the Global Legal Order* (2009), 39, 40-42 [Twining, Globalisation].

and integration actually appears to bear the potential to result in a certain global harmonization (and therefore ultimately in the reduction of the plurality) of legal orders, so far, it is the contrary that has happened. Correspondingly, *Horatia Muir Watt* cites and expounds:

> "'Despite a world with globalizing pretensions, [comparatists] would discover that intensity of contact actually emphasizes a sense of difference, not of sameness.' It may be that accelerated exchange actually accentuates local particularisms; it does not appear, at any rate, that the world is becoming more homogeneous."[4]

This accurate observation stems from two reasons. First, although globalization has undeniably caused a certain decline of the nation state's supremacy within the logic of legal orders,[5] it has not (yet) accomplished an actual conversion from the overall paradigm of the nation state to a paradigm of a global community or even a single cosmopolitan society[6] (including the idea of one, or at least only a few valid (constitutionalized[7]) global legal orders).[8]

Second, in such a continuingly nation-state-oriented global order, the globalization-caused effects and challenges naturally exceed national spheres of influence. This creates a demand for legal organization above and beyond the nation state resulting in the development of not *other* but *further* distinct levels of legal orders that add to the national legal plurality. These additional levels comprise various polycentric, sometimes competing and fragmented,[9] as well as steadily diversifying, legal orders (and their

---

4 H. M. Watt, 'Globalization and Comparative Law,' in M. Reimann & R. Zimmermann (eds), *The Oxford Handbook of Comparative Law* (2006), 579, 587 citing R. Munday, 'Accounting for an Encounter,' in P. Legrand & R. Munday (eds), *Comparative Legal Studies: Traditions and Transitions* (2003), 3, 21; D. Nelken, 'Comparatists and Transferability,' in *ibid.*, 437, 460 [Nelken, Comparatists and Transferability].

5 See R. Michaels, 'Globalisation and Law: Law Beyond the State,' in R. Banakar & M. Travers (eds), *Law and Social Theory* (2013), 287, 293-299 [Michaels, Globalisation].

6 On the paradigm of a global community in general see e.g. R. Domingo, *The New Global Law* (2010).

7 For an overview on the concept of constitutionalization in international law see A. Peters, 'Fragmentation and Constitutionalization,' in A. Orford & F. Hoffmann (eds), *The Oxford Handbook of the Theory of International Law* (2016), 1011, 1015-1019.

8 See Michaels, 'Globalisation,' *supra* note 5, 287, 287.

9 For an overview on the concept of fragmentation in international law see Peters, *supra* note 7, 1012-1015.

institutions[10]) – be they regional, supranational, international or transnational legal (sub)orders (the legal order of the *Council of Europe*, the legal order of the *United Nations* (UN), the legal order of the *World Trade Organisation* (WTO), the legal order of the *European Union* (EU), or various legal orders created by particular international treaties such as for human rights or international investment, the *lex mercatoria*, or the *lex sportiva*, to name but a few).

Although still predominantly created by or derived from the sovereign authority of nation states, these legal orders are no longer restricted to claims of national territorial authority but do cover and overlay multiple national territories at once, demand application in spheres beyond the nation state or even assume their universality.[11] One may in this respect be inclined to agree with *Paul Schiff Berman*'s statement:

> "[...] one does not need to believe in the death of the nation-state to recognize both that physical location can no longer be the sole criterion for conceptualizing legal authority and that nation-states must work within a framework of multiple overlapping jurisdictional assertions by state, international, and even nonstate communities."[12]

II. Intensification of Legal Order Interactions Through Globalization

It does not come as a surprise that these various overlapping legal orders interact (and collide[13]) in multiple ways.[14] Accordingly, as observed by *William Twining*:

> "[T]he possible kinds of relations between co-existing legal orders can be extraordinarily diverse: they may complement each other; the relationship may be one of co-operation, co-optation, competition, subor-

---

10 For example, *The Project on International Courts and Tribunals* (PICT) has identified over 120 non-state international bodies and mechanisms that are vested with the power to make legal determinations with respect to international law (see http://www.pict-pcti.org, last visited 13 December 2018).

11 See Watt, *supra* note 4, 582-583; P. S. Berman, *Global Legal Pluralism – A Jurisprudence of Law beyond Borders* (2012), 3-22; R. Michaels, 'The True Lex Mercatoria: Law Beyond the State', 14 *Indiana Journal of Global Legal Studies* (2007) 2, 447.

12 Berman, *supra* note 11, 5.

13 For a particular focus on conflicts between legal orders see *ibid.*, 23-57.

14 W. Twining, 'Diffusion of Law – A Global Perspective', 36 *The Journal of Legal Pluralism and Unofficial Law* (2004) 49, 1, 10-15 [Twining, Diffusion of Law].

> dination, or stable symbiosis; the orders may converge, assimilate, merge, repress, imitate, echo, or avoid each other."[15]

Although such interactions of legal orders are by no means a solely modern occurrence,[16] today's state of interactions can, however, be considered a particularly extensive and dynamic one. This is, again, due to the phenomenon of globalization, which intensifies the interaction of legal orders in two ways. First, the above-described circumstances of globalization particularly allow for and facilitate the interaction between legal orders *independent* of their geographical or jurisdictional proximity or overlap. Second, the globalization-caused increase of legal orders above and beyond the nation state also leads to a structural diversification of interactions. In today's multilevel legal plurality, interactions are no longer confined to horizontal interactions between nation states, but now also comprise horizontal interactions between legal orders above or beyond the nation states, as well as vertical or diagonal cross-level interactions.[17]

B. Legal Transfers

A distinct type of interaction in this plurality of legal orders is the legal transfer.

I. Defining Legal Transfer

The notion *legal transfer* exists in various, slightly differing, connotations (a multiplicity sometimes even referred to as a "battle of metaphors"[18]). These connotations include "legal transplant", "legal migration", "diffusion of laws", "legal borrowing", "legal reception", "legal adaptation", "adoption of laws", "legal influence", "legal inspiration", "legal imitation", "legal irritation" or "legal cross-fertilization". However, at least at their core, they all describe a similar process.[19]

---

15 Twining, 'Diffusion of Law', *supra* note 14, 1, 15.

16 See Twining, 'Globalisation', *supra* note 3, 52.

17 See Twining, 'Diffusion of Law', *supra* note 14, 13.

18 V. F. Perju, 'Constitutional Transplants, Borrowing, and Migrations', in M. Rosenfeld & A. Sajó (eds), *The Oxford Handbook of Comparative Constitutional Law* (2012), 1304, 1306.

19 See *ibid.*, 1306-1308.

Here, *legal transfer* shall be used.[20] It shall simply be understood as the interactive process of the intentional[21] dissemination of legal rules, institutions, regimes, concepts, theories, ideas or other legal phenomena (legal items[22]) from a donating legal order (donor order) to a receiving legal order (recipient order).[23]

Since the interactions in the above-described plurality of legal orders are no longer confined to interactions between nation states, the same holds true for legal transfers. The intentional dissemination of legal items, therefore, needs to be conceived as happening in various directions – be it the *classic* transfers between nation states, but also horizontal transfers between legal orders above or beyond the nation states, as well as vertical or diagonal cross-level transfers.[24]

II. *The (Im)Possibility of Legal Transfers and the Starting Point of Scholarly Interest*

Although it seems quite obvious that such transfers take place, it has been argued that legal transfers are, in fact, impossible. The argument stands that legal items are to such an extent inseparably linked to the (cultural) characteristics and realities of their original legal order that they cannot be implemented into other legal orders without necessarily losing their particular character and could, therefore, never actually be considered trans-

---

20 For an interesting description of slight differences between the notions "legal transplantation", "legal translation" and "legal transfer" see J. Hendry, 'Legal Pluralism and Normative Transfer', in G. Frankenberg (ed.), *Order from Transfer – Comparative Constitutional Design and Legal Culture* (2013), 153, 165-170 [Frankenberg (ed.), Order from Transfer].

21 *Intentional* here to be understood as the deliberate induction of the dissemination solely by the donor order, solely by the recipient order, mutually by donor and recipient order, or even by third orders or actors independent of donor and recipient order.

22 The term "legal items" is inspired by *Günter Frankenberg*'s use of the term "constitutional items", G. Frankenberg, 'Constitutions as Commodities: Notes on a Theory of Transfer', in Frankenberg (ed.), Order from Transfer, *supra* note 20, 1, 1 [Frankenberg, Constitutions].

23 See Hendry, *supra* note 20, 165, 168-169; Perju, *supra* note 18, 1313-1315; J. M. Miller, 'A Typology of Legal Transplants: Using Sociology, Legal History and Argentine Examples to Explain the Transplant Process', 51 *American Journal of Comparative Law* (2003) 4, 839.

24 See Perju, *supra* note 18, 1319-1321.

ferred ("at best, what can be displaced from one jurisdiction to another is, literally, a meaningless form of words"[25]).[26]

This argument can be quite easily refuted: The concept of legal transfers is by no means to be understood as assuming (the possibility of) the transplantation of an identical and unchanged legal structure from one legal order to another[27] – a conception that would indeed appear quite impossible, especially with respect to culturally deeply imbedded legal items of the sphere of public law. It rather describes situations in which the intended dissemination of a legal item *in its essence* has taken place (in *Günter Frankenberg*'s terms a "de- and recontextualization"[28]). *Uwe Kischel*, therefore, rightly points out that the cognition of a change or development of a legal rule in the course of its transfer from donor order to recipient order, is not to be considered the end, but rather the starting point of scholarly interest.[29]

C. *Rule of Law Transfers*

Legal transfers take place (or have done so) with respect to a variety of legal items for quite some time – the rule of law being such a typical item.[30] Interestingly, the scholarly assessment of the rule of law as a subject of transfer has, however, emerged only fairly recently. Traditionally, (compara-

---

25 P. Legrand, 'The Impossibility of 'Legal Transplants'', 4 *Maastricht Journal of European and Comparative Law* (1997) 2, 111, 120.

26 For an overview on the scholarly debate, particularly known for the controversy between the two opponents *Alan Watson* and *Pierre Legrand*, see Frankenberg, 'Constitutions', *supra* note 22, 4-7 or M. Graziadei, 'Comparative Law as the Study of Transplants and receptions', in Reimann & Zimmermann (eds), *supra* note 4, 441, 465-470.

27 See Twining, 'Diffusion of Law', *supra* note 14, 24-25.

28 On the so-called IKEA Theory see Frankenberg, 'Constitutions', *supra* note 22, 1 and G. Frankenberg, 'Constitutional Transfer: The IKEA Theory Revisited', 8 *International Journal of Constitutional Law* (2010) 3, 563 [Frankenberg, IKEA Theory Revisited].

29 U. Kischel, *Rechtsvergleichung* (2015), 67.

30 See M. Zürn, A. Nollkaemper & R. Peerenboom, 'Introduction', in M. Zürn, A. Nollkaemper & R. Peerenboom (eds), *Rule of Law Dynamics – In an Era of International and Transnational Governance* (2012), 1, 1-8 or J. Kokott, 'From Reception and Transplantation to Convergence of Constitutional Models in the Age of Globalization – with Special Reference to the German Basic Law', in C. Starck (ed.), *Constitutionalism, Universalism and Democracy – A Comparative Analysis* (1999), 71, 97-102, 124-127.

tive) legal scholarship tended to have a certain preference for the assessment of the (historical) dissemination of legal items ascribed to the sphere of private law – ranging from singular legal provisions (e.g. the land registration and transfer system of *Ulrich Hübbe* in the 19th century), to entire legal codes (e.g. the *[Napoleonic] French Civil Code of 1804*).[31] Only with the emergence of comparative constitutional law as an academic discipline following World War II and, with an even stronger impetus, after the beginning of post-soviet transitions in Eastern Europe as well as the end of apartheid in South Africa in the early 1990's,[32] also the analysis of transfers in the sphere of public and constitutional law advanced into the focus of scholarly attention, including, in particular, the concept of the rule of law.[33]

I. *The Rule of Law as a General Concept*

For the purpose of this introduction, the (highly debated) concept of the rule of law shall be described as a set of principles organizing the public governance of a certain community by subjecting (public) power to law and legal constraints.[34]

In its traditional (state-centered) form, the rule of law can conceptually be divided into six core principles. First, a community must be organized by general, clear, public and accessible, prospective, and predictive laws, being equally applied, instead of being ruled arbitrarily, in the sense of random individual decisions prone to bias, prejudice etc. (legality). Second, the right and power to enforce compliance with the law must lie with the public governing institutions and not with private actors (public monopoly of power). Third, the governing institutions themselves must be bound by the law (supremacy of the law). Fourth, the power of the governing institutions must be separated into independent branches, establishing

31 On this particular private law focus see Graziadei, *supra* note 26, 444-455; Watt, *supra* note 4, 590-592.

32 M. Tushnet, 'Comparative Constitutional Law', in Reimann & Zimmermann (eds), *supra* note 4, 1225, 1226-1228.

33 See Perju, *supra* note 18, 1305-1306.

34 See M. Krygier & A. Winchester, 'Arbitrary Power and the Ideal of the Rule of Law', in C. May & A. Winchester (eds), *Handbook on the Rule of Law* (2018), 75, 76-78; M. Krygier, 'Rule of Law (and Rechtsstaat)', in J. R. Silkenat, J. E. Hickey Jr. & P. D. Barenboim (eds), *The Legal Doctrines of the Rule of Law and the Legal State (Rechtsstaat)* (2014) 45, 46.

checks and balances among them (separation of powers). Fifth, accessible, independent, effective and fair mechanisms to settle legal disputes must exist, in particular allowing the governed community to review the exercise of governmental power (effective judicial remedies). Sixth, the governing institutions, in particular with respect to the making, applying, enforcing and interpreting of the law, must be legitimized by the governed community itself (legitimacy).[35]

Mainly developed in the course of the struggle over the establishment of governmental powers in the Westphalian Nation-States of the 18th, 19th and 20th centuries,[36] the rule of law is today understood as being conceptually applicable to any legal (sub)order, above or beyond the State that features public governance functions.[37] Furthermore, even the public international legal order as such – essentially not functioning by typical means of public governance (in the sense of a delegation of powers), but rather as an organizational governance tool to arrange the legal relationships within a community of equal sovereign actors (states) and international organizations – is conceived as being measurable against the rule of law's principles with respect to e.g. legality, legal certainty, or the existence of effective legal dispute settlement mechanisms.[38]

---

35 See T. P. Holterhus, 'The History of the Rule of Law', in F. Lachenmann & R. Wolfrum (eds), 21 *Max Planck Yearbook of United Nations Law* (2018), 430, 432-433 with further references. However, much theoretical dispute over the rule of law's further content needs to be considered unsettled: Definitions range from purely formal to quite substantive approaches; formal definitions again being separated into thinner (demanding governance by general, clear, prospective, predictive, and equally applied laws) and thicker (additionally requiring the governing institutions to be bound (and limited) by the law as well as by a separation of powers and a certain level of participation of the governed community) versions. Substantive definitions again add features such as individual rights, dignity, justice, substantive equality, and other moral values or welfare. For an overview of the theoretical dispute see B. Z. Tamanaha, *On the Rule of Law: History, Politics, Theory* (2004), 91-113; J. Møller, 'The Advantages of a Thin View' in May & Winchester (eds), *supra* note 24, 21; A. Bedner, 'The Promise of a Thick View' in May & Winchester (eds), *supra* note 24, 34.

36 On the rule of law's historical origins and development see Holterhus, *supra* note 35, 430 with further references.

37 See C. May, 'The Rule of Law as the *Grundnorm* of the New Constitutionalism', in S. Gill and A. C. Cutler (eds), *New Constitutionalism and World Order* (2014), 63.

38 On this general aspect see e.g. R. McCorquodale, 'Defining the International Rule of Law: Defying Gravity?', 65 *International & Comparative Law Quarterly* (2016) 2, 277; A. Watts, 'The International Rule of Law', 36 *German Yearbook of International Law* (1993), 15; J. Waldron, 'The Rule of International Law', 30 *Harvard*

II. The Rule of Law as a Subject of Transfer

This fundamental concept of the rule of law is subject to legal transfer, meaning subject to the intentional dissemination from donating to receiving legal orders. However, when considering the rule of law as a subject of legal transfer, one does not find such transfers to be identical or even similar in nature. In light of the above-described global plurality of legal orders and the resulting variations and directions of legal transfers, the dissemination of the rule of law does not follow a standard formula but happens in quite diverse ways.[39]

1. The Diverse Substance and Form of Rule of Law Transfers

Accordingly, when speaking of the rule of law as an item of transfer this necessarily denotes a different subject in every particular constellation. *Michele Graziadei*, on legal transfers in general, fittingly refers to this as follows:

> "When we recognize this multiplicity, we can see that what crosses boundaries is highly diverse in both substance and form, even though it may simply be 'the law' to the untrained eye."[40]

This diversity in substance and form particularly applies to the rule of law as a subject of legal transfer.

With respect to legal substance, depending on the constellation, it is more often a particular principle or even fragments thereof that are transferred rather than the concept of the rule of law as a whole (meaning the entire set of the above-described legal principles). Such variations of the transferred item are not solely a result of the (sometimes limited) intentions of the respective donors and/or recipients but are often also caused by structural particularities of the involved legal orders.[41] While, for example,

---

Journal of Law & Public Policy (2006) 1, 15; S. Chesterman, 'An International Rule of Law?', 56 *American Journal of Comparative Law* (2003) 2, 331.

39 For a general perspective on the diversity of legal transfers see Twining, 'Diffusion of Law', *supra* note 14, 16-17.

40 Graziadei, *supra* note 26, 471.

41 See R. Kleinfeld, 'Competing Definitions of the Rule of Law', in T. Carothers (ed.), *Promoting the Rule of Law Abroad – In Search of Knowledge* (2006), 31, 54-65; P. C. Westerman, 'The Rule of Law as Export Product', 5 *The Theory and Practice of Legislation* (2017) 2, 1, 2-7; Zürn, Nollkaemper & Peerenboom, *supra* note 30, 5; J.

typical organizational structures within Nation States might be quite receptive to implementing a thorough separation of powers, this would (even in the form of checks and balances) not apply to the current institutional structures of the UN as a legal order.[42]

Another diversification of what is subject to the respective rule of law transfers derives from the possible variations of the transferred item's legal form. Although transferring the rule of law's principles in the form of constitutional provisions (e.g. from one constitutional structure into another (existing or newly adopted) constitutional structure) often appears to be the most practical and actually is the most commonly chosen way, this again might not fit the intentions and/or particularities of the involved donor and recipient orders (e.g. because of the absence or impossibility of a constitutional structure in the recipient order). Rule of law transfers therefore also happen in various other forms – be it the adoption or inclusion of statutes, institutional structures, lines of adjudication, particular judicial decisions, or even established doctrine as well as jurisprudential scholarly thought and concepts, to name but a few.[43]

2. *A Broad Categorization by Recipient Orders*

Despite these variations in legal substance and form, an assessment of the more recent processes of rule of law transfers however allows for a broad distinction between two categories.

a. Nation States as Recipient Orders

The first category would comprise such rule of law transfers which address nation states as the recipient legal orders. A quite important example for many (attempted) rule of law transfers in this category, are the multiple waves of the so-called law and development initiatives of the post-World

---

C. Reitz, 'Export of the Rule of Law,' 13 *Transnational Law & Contemporary Problems* (2003) 2, 429, 442-444.

42 On the particularities of applying the rule of law to the UN generally see A. Nollkaemper, 'The Internationalized Rule of Law,' 1 *Hague Journal on the Rule of Law* (2009) 1, 74, 74-75.

43 See Twining, 'Diffusion of Law,' *supra* note 14, 20; Zürn, Nollkaemper & Peerenboom, *supra* note 30, 5; for the context of constitutional law see Kokott, *supra* note 30, 76-77.

War II era – peaking in the now ongoing fourth wave which started with the end of the Cold War and the downfall of the Soviet Union. Based on the belief that States organized under the rule of law were more likely to become or remain stable, and by that would serve the overall good of a peaceful global (economic) community, Western States (with the US on the early forefront), the *Bretton Woods* institutions and multiple further actors, showed and continue to show tremendous efforts to *export* the concept of the rule of law to national legal orders around the globe. To this end the law and development initiatives continue to be predominantly aimed at post-colonialist, transitional (conflict and post-conflict) and developing countries, after the end of the Cold War with a particular focus on former Soviet States, using first and foremost financial and technical foreign assistance and development aid as means of influence to develop rule of law structures in the respective recipient States.[44]

With the end of the Cold War and the downfall of the Soviet Union, it is also the EU as a supranational entity that became a significant actor and began to provide a relevant framework in the field of rule of law promotion in third States – provoking transfers not only by making the implementation of rule of law structures a precondition in its accession and enlargement policy (so-called *Copenhagen Criteria*, now laid down in Article 49 TEU), but also by making rule of law promotion an essential principle of its foreign and security policy, its neighboring policy, its development cooperation policy and its foreign common commercial policy.[45]

Furthermore, today more than ever, various international legal orders (with their respective institutions, administrative bodies, courts and tribunals), such as the UN, the *World Bank*, the *Council of Europe* or the conglomerate legal orders in the fields of international human rights law or international investment law, to name but a few examples, play an active role in the rule of law promotion on the nation state level – be it by functioning as donor orders themselves or as catalyzing intermediaries for the

44 For an overview see e.g. D. M. Trubek, 'The 'Rule of Law' in Development Assistance: Past, Present and Future', in D. M. Trubek, & A. Santos (eds), *The New Law and Economic Development* (2006), 74; A. Magen, 'The Rule of Law and Its Promotion Abroad: Three Problems of Scope', 45 *Stanford Journal of International Law* (2009), 51, 77-83; F. Schimmelfennig, 'A Comparison of the Rule of Law Promotion Policies of Major Western Powers', in Zürn, Nollkaemper & Peerenboom (eds), *supra* note 30, 111.

45 For an overview see e.g. W. Schroeder (ed.), *Strengthening the Rule of Law in Europe* (2016), chap. 10, 11, 12; M. Kmezić, *EU Rule of Law Promotion* (2016), 1-27; L. Pech, 'Rule of Law as a Guiding Principle of the European Union's External Action', CLEER Working Papers 2012/3.

respective dominating donor (State) orders behind these international regimes.[46]

b. Recipient Orders Above and Beyond the Nation State

The second category would consist of rule of law transfers which do not address nation states as the recipient orders but legal orders above and beyond them.[47] Such a category necessarily requires the above-discussed assumption of the possible conceptual extension and application of the rule of law to non-state legal orders featuring public governance functions.[48] On that basis, few, but quite significant transfer processes to recipient orders above and beyond the nation state take place.

An illustrative example of such a rule of law transfer to a legal order above the nation state would be the introduction of a legal review mechanism for targeted sanctions within the UN, in particular, the *UN Security Council* (UNSC). When the UN started to adopt resolutions which included so-called targeted sanctions (meaning specific economic sanctions under Chapter VII, Article 41 UN-Charter, which did not target states but individuals by ordering the freezing of their assets or banning them from travelling) in the 1990's, there was no (effective) mechanism to enable the affected individuals to review their listing for such sanctions. However, in response to political pressure from the EU (the donor order in this example) – caused by the *European Court of Justice*'s (ECJ) famous *Kadi*-adjudication, which essentially decided that the enforcement and implementation of targeted sanctions by and within the EU was precluded under EU law, as long as the UNSC would not establish an effective individual review mechanism (beyond the mere possibility of diplomatic protection) – the UNSC

46 See e.g. M. Heupel, 'Rule of Law Promotion through International Organizations and NGOs', in Zürn, Nollkaemper & Peerenboom (eds), *supra* note 30, 133; E. Selous, 'The Rule of Law, Development and the United Nations', in C. A. Feinäugle (ed.), *The Rule of Law and Its Application to the United Nations* (2016), 211; A. Santos, 'The World Bank's Uses of the 'Rule of Law' Promise in Economic Development', in Trubek, & Santos (eds), *supra* note 44, 74.

47 See T. Genkow & M. Zürn, 'Constraining International Authority through the Rule of Law', in Zürn, Nollkaemper & Peerenboom (eds), *supra* note 30, 68; M. Kötter & G. F. Schuppert, 'Applying the Rule of Law to Contexts Beyond the State', in Silkenat, Hickey Jr. & Barenboim (eds), *supra* note 34, 71; Nollkaemper, *supra* note 42, 74.

48 On the United Nations in particular see C. A. Feinäugle (ed.), *The Rule of Law and Its Application to the United Nations* (2016).

in 2009 actually introduced the Office of the Ombudsman which today hears individual complaints of enlisted individuals and holds quite far-reaching delisting powers. Irrespective of the question whether the Office of the Ombudsman adequately fulfills the conceptual requirements of the rule of law core principle of effective judicial remedies, a certain rule of law transfer to the UN (as a recipient order above the Nation State) is apparent.[49]

Another example of a rule of law transfer (or rather a series of continuous transfers) to a legal order above the nation state is the establishment of the rule of law as a fundamental principle within the supranational EU as a recipient order. Essentially starting in the 1960's and 1970's the development of the rule of law as a general principle of EU law – in the sense of a legally binding principle addressing all EU organs and institutions with respect to their exercise of governmental powers, be it in administrative, judicial or legislative matters – was fostered largely by ECJ adjudication. However, the ECJ did not develop the various concretizations, principles and sub-principles of an EU rule of law out of thin air – such as legality of administrative action, State liability, legal certainty, equality before the law, institutional balance (the separation of powers within the EU), effective judicial remedies, fair trial, the protection of legitimate expectations, prohibition of retroactivity, or proportionality – but explicitly derived and transferred them from the legal orders of the EU Member States, functioning as donor orders in this respect.[50]

While these different contexts and examples can only be considered a mere fraction of the entirety of the global process of rule of law transfers, they certainly are suitable to provide an impression of the variations in structure and direction of the transfer of the rule of law in the global plurality of legal orders – finding its recipient orders not only in the typical constellation of nation states, but also among the legal orders above and beyond them.

---

49 On the introduction of the Office of the Ombudsperson as a response to ECJ adjudication in *Kadi I* and *II* see P. Eden, 'United Nations Targeted Sanctions, Human Rights and the Office of the Ombudsperson', in M. Happold & P. Eden (eds), *Economic Sanctions and International Law* (2016), 135.

50 W. Schroeder, 'The European Union and the Rule of Law – State of Affairs and Ways of Strengthening', in Schroeder (ed.), *supra* note 45, 3, 6-9; S. Mangiameli, 'Article 2 [The Homogeneity Clause]', in H.-J. Blanke & S. Mangiameli (eds), *The Treaty on European Union (TEU)* (2013), 109, paras. 29-30.

D. A Legal Perspective on Rule of Law Transfers

I. The Multitude of (Extra-legal) Analytical Perspectives and Angles

Although legal transfers concern the dissemination of *legal* items between *legal* orders, the transfer as such is, at first sight, not a genuinely legal but rather an ontological process. Therefore, to legal transfers in general and to rule of law transfers in particular, a multitude of (often extra-legal) analytical perspectives has been applied.[51] Such perspectives predominantly focus on a better understanding of the variety of mechanisms underlying the process of rule of law transfers, including sociological, political science, international relations or ethnological perspectives.

To that end, the phenomenon of rule of law transfers is usually approached from a number of typical angles, including: the roles of different actors within the transfers of the rule of law (1.), the underlying motivations behind rule of law transfers (2.), the means and instruments of rule of law implementation (3.), the empirics of and conditions for success and failure of rule of law transfers (4.), or the legitimacy of transferring the rule of law (5.).[52]

1. Actors

The focal point of the actor-centered angle usually lies with the identification of the different actors and agents taking part in the process of transferring the rule of law, such as legislatures and other lawmakers, governments, administrative bodies, law enforcers, courts and judges, inter- and supranational institutions, multinational corporations, expert networks, political movements, civil societies, non-governmental organizations, lob-

51 For a general overview see Twining, 'Social Science and Diffusion of Law', 32 *Journal of Law and Society* (2005) 2, 203 [Twining, Social Science]; see also M. Siems, 'Malicious Legal Transplants', 38 *Legal Studies* (2018) 1, 1, 8-9.

52 *William Twining*, for example, identifies not less than twelve analytical angles to the issue of legal transfers: "Processes of diffusion can vary in respect of originating sources, scale, levels, pathways, objects of diffusion, changes in the objects, agents, degrees of formality, timing, relation to pre-existing law, degree of penetration, and consequences. Diffusion of law refers to a vast and complex range of phenomena, which can be studied from a variety of standpoints for a variety of purposes." Twining, 'Social Science', *supra* note 51, 203, 205, 206, 240.

byists, religious organizations and missionaries, refugees, educational institutions, scholarly elites, etc.[53]

The aim is to understand their particular roles and functions within and outside the involved donor and recipient orders, be it in an internal role as importers, exporters or appliers, but also when functioning as external facilitators or intermediaries[54] – *Günter Frankenberg* fittingly referring to them as "merchants of transfer"[55].

2. *Motivations*

This angle considers rule of law transfers with a particular interest in their underlying motivational patterns. It concerns not only the motivations existing within donor orders, be it the dissemination of particular legal cultures/narratives, geostrategic stability/security or the opening of new export markets, but also the motivations within recipient orders, such as desire for (economic) reform, development and modernization, membership in international organizations or simply prestige.

Various systematizations exist in this respect.[56] As one example – with a certain focus on recipient motivations – *Jonathan M. Miller*'s descriptive sociological typology may be provided, dividing the motivations for legal transfers into the four categories: "cost-saving" (saving time and costly experimentation), "externally-dictated" (reacting to external threats, promises or opportunities), "entrepreneurial" (prospects of material or political benefits for the individuals and/or groups engaged in the importing process), and "legitimacy-generating" (increase of legitimacy by implementation of a renowned foreign legal item).[57]

---

53 See Reitz, *supra* note 41, 429, 456-463; Twining, 'Social Science', *supra* note 51, 203, 236-238; J. Gillespie & P. Nicholson, 'Taking the Interpretation of Legal Transfers Seriously: The Challenge for Law and Development', in J. Gillespie & P. Nicholson, (eds), *Law and Development and the Global Discourses of Legal Transfers* (2012), 1, 9-10, 35-36.

54 See M. Seckelmann, 'Clotted History and Chemical Reactions – On the Possibility of Constitutional Transfer', in G. Frankenberg (ed.), *supra* note 20, 36, 54-55.

55 Frankenberg, 'Constitutions', *supra* note 22, 15, 25.

56 See Reitz, *supra* note 41, 448-451; Perju, *supra* note 18, 1317-1319.

57 Miller, *supra* note 23, 839.

3. Means and Instruments

Another angle emphasizes the relevance of the different means and instruments applied in rule of law implementation processes. Aiming at "a fuller appreciation of the empirical scope of external influence mechanisms deployed to affect domestic legal, institutional and normative reform", *Amichai Magen*, for example, refers to this aspect as the "spectrum of intervention", pointing out that

> "[a] non-exhaustive list of terms generated in an attempt to capture and explain external influence on domestic democratic development would include notions such as: demonstration effect, emulation, ordering-from-the-menu, diffusion, contagion, gravity, linkage, compliance, liberal community, learning, socialization, normative suasion, conditionality, and control."[58]

From there *Magen*'s contribution develops its own categorization of means and instruments, distinguishing between "coercive imposition and neo-trusteeship",[59] "punitive and positive external incentives",[60] "international democratic socialization",[61] and "demonstration and emulation".[62]

Others categorize by, for instance, "the imperial, the fashionable, the systemic and the tribal" means of transfer (*David A. Westbrook*),[63] "imposition,

58 Magen, *supra* note 44, 100-101.

59 "[...] the use of military force to directly overthrow an authoritarian regime and attempt to install a viable democratic regime in its place or, more commonly, attempt to build basic conditions of public safety and legality as part of a post-conflict state reconstruction effort." *Ibid.*, 101.

60 "External incentives fall into two broad categories: punitive or positive. Punitive measures, or sanctions, are non-military, coercive political, diplomatic and economic tools used to induce policy change in a targeted country." *Ibid.*, 103.

61 "[...] facilitate internalization of democratic norms, policies and institutions through the establishment and intensification of linkages between liberal international forums and state actors in transitional countries." *Ibid.*, 107.

62 "According to this rationale, state and societal actors in transitional states accept new rules, institutions and policy choices not as a result of coercion, external incentives or active social induction, but through emulation of external models or transnational cultural associations." *Ibid.*, 113.

63 D. A. Westbrook, 'Theorizing the Diffusion of Law in an Age of Globalization: Conceptual Difficulties, Unstable Imaginations, and the Effort to Think Gracefully Nonetheless', 56 *Annals of the Faculty of Law in Belgrade – Belgrade Law Review* (2008) 3, 159.

conditionality, socialization" (*Frank Schimmelfennig*),[64] or "persuasive authority" (*Patrick Glenn*).[65]

4. *Success Rates and Their Conditions*

A further typical angle does not put the *process* of rule of law transfers but rather their *results*, namely the success or (more often) the failure, in the center of its attention. The scholarly interest can essentially be separated into three subdivisions. First, an interest in what outcome of a legal transfer should actually be considered successful (and what a failure, or even malicious[66]), necessarily implying the development and application of certain theoretic criteria for the vague notion of the *success* of a rule of law transfer.[67] Second, an interest in the empirical assessment and evaluation of the success of rule of law transfers – which results not only in multiple case studies on various particular transfer processes[68] but is also closely related to the quite recent emergence of global rule of law indices trying to measure rule of law implementation in legal orders throughout the world.[69] And third, considering the two aforementioned aspects, an interest in which surroundings and conditions (cultural, geographic, ideological, institutional, organizational, etc.) have influence on rendering a transfer likely to be successful or unsuccessful – in particular, when it comes to the transfer of legal items from the sphere of public law, which usually feature a deep entrenchment in their respective societal and cultural surroundings.[70]

---

64 Schimmelfennig, *supra* note 44, 122-127.

65 H. P. Glenn, 'Persuasive Authority', 32 *McGill Law Journal* (1987) 2, 261.

66 See Siems, *supra* note 51, 1.

67 See J. Gillespie, 'Developing a Theoretical Framework for Evaluating Rule of Law Promotion in Developing Countries', in Zürn, Nollkaemper & Peerenboom (eds), *supra* note 30, 233, 234; D. Nelken, 'Towards a Sociology of Legal Adaptation', in D. Nelken & J. Feest (eds), *Adapting Legal Cultures* (2001), 7, 37-39, 46-50 [Nelken, Legal Adaptation].

68 See e.g. Carothers (ed.), *supra* note 41, 191-323; Gillespie & Nicholson (eds), *supra* note 53, 179-276; A. Magen & L. Morlino (eds), *International Actors, Democratization and the Rule of Law* (2009), 87-223.

69 See W. Merkel, 'Measuring the Quality of Rule of Law', in Zürn, Nollkaemper &. Peerenboom (eds), *supra* note 30, 21; Twining, 'Diffusion of Law', *supra* note 14, 30-34; see also all 11 articles of 3 *Hague Journal on the Rule of Law* (2011) 2.

70 See Reitz, *supra* note 41, 463-467; Gillespie, *supra* note 67, 234-248; Y. Dezalay & B. Garth, 'The Import and Export of Law and Legal Institutions: International

5. Legitimacy

Another angle is concerned with the legitimacy of rule of law transfers, in particular the legitimacy of donor orders' efforts to promote the rule of law abroad (not to be confused with the above-discussed aspect of (a recipient's) motivation of transferring the rule of law to generate legitimacy within the receiving legal order).[71] Again, three (rather normative and often critical) aspects of the scholarly discussion on legitimacy can be distinguished. First, the aspect whether the rule of law, at least in a formalist Western one-size-fits-all form, can actually be considered universally beneficial, meeting the needs of all kinds of communities (and therefore the question whether it always is, as such, a legitimate concept to promote and transfer).[72] Second, the aspect whether the various efforts of global rule of law promotion are always based on a sufficient knowledge of the cultural contexts and legal preconditions of the particular recipient order as well as a proper understanding of the general complexities of the implementation of legal items abroad.[73] Third, the issue whether the promotion of the rule of law, at least when aiming at post-colonialist, transitional and developing countries, is always truly intended to actually benefit the respective recipient order, or whether the often top-down imposition of rule of law transfers rather happens in the hegemonistic, imperialistic or even neo-colonialistic interest of capitalist donor orders (be it Western States, or such institutions like the EU, the *World Bank* or the UN, sometimes at the same time, not living up to the rule of law's demands themselves).[74]

Strategies in National Palace Wars', in Nelken & Feest (eds), *supra* note 67, 241; Nelken, 'Legal Adaptation', *supra* note 67, 39-46.

71 For an overview see J. A. Goldston, 'The Rule of Law at Home and Abroad', 1 *Hague Journal on the Rule of Law* (2009) 1, 38.

72 See F. Upham, 'Mythmaking in the Rule-of-Law Orthodoxy', in Carothers (ed.), *supra* note 41, 75.

73 See T. Carothers, 'The Rule of Law Revival', in Carothers (ed.), *supra* note 41, 15.

74 See R. E. Brooks, 'The New Imperialism: Violence, Norms, and the "Rule of Law"', 101 *Michigan Law Review* (2003) 7, 2275; R. Peerenboom, M. Zürn & A. Nollkaemper, 'Conclusion', in Zürn, Nollkaemper & Peerenboom (eds), *supra* note 30, 305, 310-311.

II. A Legal Perspective

The provided cross section of analytical perspectives (and their above-described application in the five different angles) illustrates a certain scholarly tendency to examine and emphasize the social, political or ethnological dimensions of rule of law transfers. With that, scholarship essentially seems to correspond to and reflect the practical challenges (and inefficiencies) that the field of rule of law promotion and implementation faced over the last couple of decades. Noteworthily, *David Marshall* – even if speaking of rule of law implementation in practice – asks:

> "And would the international rule of law movement not be better if it were run and staffed by anthropologists, sociologists, and linguistic and cultural experts? Is the rule of law about understanding and working with societies, or is it about understanding and building institutions around law and legal practice?"[75]

Without answering *Marshall*'s questions, it should not be doubted that a scholarly understanding of the social, political and ethnological mechanisms behind rule of law transfers is of high epistemic and practical relevance.

1. Departing From Common Scholarly Paths

There is, however, more to explore. The present volume, therefore, departs from above-described common scholarly paths and intends to assess and explain rule of law transfers as a *legal* phenomenon. Such a perspective – which has not yet received much scholarly attention – is based on the assumption that rule of law transfers do not only *consider* the law but, although being ontological processes, encompass a legal dimension *themselves*. In light of the aforesaid, the legal analysis of rule of law transfers is particularly concerned with understanding what positive legal norms impel and drive donor orders to promote the rule of law abroad. It strives to explore what legal instruments and mechanisms govern and organize the actual transfer processes. Furthermore, it asks what legal structures enable and facilitate the implementation of rule of law transfers within recipient orders.

---

75 D. Marshall, 'Introduction', in D. Marshall (ed.), *The International Rule of Law Movement – A Crisis of Legitimacy and the Way Forward* (2014), xiii, xvi.

2. Analytical Relevance of a Legal Perspective

Such an assessment of rule of law transfers from a legal perspective is not an end in itself, but holds a specific analytical relevance: It helps to clarify the underestimated role that legal norms, mechanisms and structures play with respect to rule of law transfers in the global plurality of legal orders. This actual analytical relevance can be well-illustrated when such perspective is applied to the five angles (actors, motivations, means and instruments, success and its conditions, legitimacy) discussed above:

With respect to the actor-centered angle, a legal perspective might provide epistemic benefits by understanding how the legally determined allocation of competences within a legal order can define and empower actors with respect to rule of law transfers.

A legal perspective might also find that the motivations of donor orders to foster the rule of law abroad lie not solely in political ventures or diplomatic agendas, but rather are the result of constitutional or high-ranking international treaty provisions that bindingly instruct the respective donor orders to do so.

Furthermore, a legal perspective might be able to illustrate that it is not only fashion or persuasive authority, but, for example, a particular legal design of (development) contracts (e.g. by implementation of condition precedent) that is the instrument to legally ensure rule of law implementation within a recipient order before being granted a promised benefit.

The analysis of rule of law transfers from the legal perspective might also demonstrate that the existence of particular laws and legal structures within recipient orders constitutes a decisive condition for high success rates of rule of law implementation.

Finally, the legal perspective might even contribute to solving legitimacy issues of rule of law transfers, since a context-specific doctrinal adjustment in substance and form of the usually transferred Western one-size-fits-all rule of law principle could potentially render the transfer to some extent more legitimate.

E. The Legal Perspectives in This Volume

This volume features seven distinct contributions, all of which apply the above-discussed legal perspective to the issue of rule of law transfers. And although, of course, not all legal aspects of such transfers can be provided for in the present volume, the contributors nevertheless approach the topic from rather diverse angles covering a wide range of legal fields. Each contribution, therefore, succeeds in highlighting the relevance of *the law* in rule of law transfers.

I. Constitutionalism and the Mechanics of Global Law Transfers

The contribution "Constitutionalism and the Mechanics of Global Law Transfers" by *Andreas L. Paulus* and *Johann Ruben Leiss* inquires into rule of law transfers from a global legal perspective.

Following the observation that the (German) proposal of an emerging international constitutional order seems to have lost momentum in recent years, *Paulus* and *Leiss* base their analysis on a theoretical approach that emphasizes a global legal reality which is characterized by a complex and rather non-hierarchical interplay between various (fragmented) international legal orders and suborders as well as national legal orders.

In this interplay, the authors identify three legal instruments of pivotal relevance with respect to global rule of law transfers: First, so-called *hinge provisions* as doorways between different legal orders, second, harmonious interpretation as a legal tool of integration, and, third, judicial dialogues as origins of transfer processes.

With an emphasis on hinge provisions (meaning positive legal provisions within a particular legal order that legally allow for or even stipulate the inclusion of norms of other legal regimes), *Paulus* and *Leiss* are able to show that this legal instrument can ensure the establishment of a common normative framework that is (albeit subject to certain conditions) applicable across systemic boundaries. Hinge provisions, therefore, enable the incorporation of rule of law principles emanating from international law into domestic law and from general international law into specialized international legal subsystems.

II. The Legal Dimensions of Rule of Law Promotion in EU Foreign Policy

In the second contribution *Till Patrik Holterhus* assesses "The Legal Dimensions of Rule of Law Promotion in EU Foreign Policy". With a particular focus on foreign trade and development policy, *Holterhus* finds that EU primary law (through Article 21 TEU) does not leave it to political discretion but legally obliges the EU to promote the rule of law in its foreign relations. He also shows that the rule of law concept that the EU applies when promoting it abroad is not a rudimentary but a sophisticated one, quite similar to the highly developed concept of the rule of law within the EU.

From there the author demonstrates that in order to fulfill its legal obligation to promote the rule of law abroad, the EU employs, as a key legal instrument, the mechanism of conditionality, putting trade preferences and development cooperation (either in autonomous measures or via international treaties) under the legal condition of domestic rule of law-coherency within the respective third States (*carrot-and-stick policy*). *Holterhus* concludes by pointing out that the EU's choice to fulfill its foreign policy obligations by combining its leading position in the trade and development nexus with legal means of rigid conditionality (as opposed to e.g. diplomatic persuasion) demonstrates a quite determined commitment to promoting the rule of law abroad and a rather uncompromising use of its capacity as a normative power.

III. Article 18 ECHR as a Legal Safeguard Against Rule of Law Backsliding

Floris Tan's contribution "The Dawn of Article 18 ECHR - A Safeguard Against European Rule of Law Backsliding?" takes a particular perspective on Article 18 ECHR and stresses its character as a legal instrument to safeguard the rule of law within the legal orders of the *Council of Europe*'s Member States. Based on the finding that governmental restrictions of individual rights under false pretenses present a clear danger to the principles of legality and the supremacy of law, the author observes that Article 18 ECHR (which stipulates that restrictions permitted to the rights and freedoms under the ECHR shall not be applied for any purpose other than those for which they have been prescribed) holds the potential to protect against such abuse of power by outlawing the restriction of rights for any *ulterior purpose* or *hidden agenda*. While *Tan* finds that the ECtHR's previous Article 18 ECHR case-law has not been very supportive in releasing this potential, he considers the ECtHR's recent Grand Chamber judgement in *Merabishvili v. Georgia* a turning point in this regard, since the judgement does not only severely widen Article 18 ECHR's operational scope of application, but also lowers the applicable standard of proof and no longer adheres to the one-sided allocation of the burden of proof. Article 18 ECHR, therefore, might, the author concludes, prospectively function as an early warning system for the European States who are at risk of becoming an illiberal democracy or even of reverting into totalitarianism.

IV. Promoting the Rule of Law Through the Law of Occupation

In the fourth contribution "Promoting the Rule of Law Through the Law of Occupation? An Uneasy Relationship", *Andreas Th. Müller* approaches the topic of rule of law transfers from the perspective of the law of occupation. Based on considering occupying powers as donor orders *vis-à-vis* the recipient orders of the local population and administration, *Müller* assesses the international humanitarian law of occupation as a potential driving force with respect to transferring the rule of law. The author finds, that the law of occupation stipulates not only constraints (negative obligations) on the occupying power but indeed also positive obligations to restore and ensure public order and safety. While *Müller* considers that one might address such positive obligations as a *duty of good governance* incumbent on the occupying power – which would typically also include the maintenance and, if necessary, the establishment of an adequate normative order, an adequate administrative apparatus, a functioning court system, effective law enforcement, etc. – he, however, emphasizes that interpreting the law of occupation as mandating for such a *mission civilisatrice* might also blur important lines of constraint and limitation in the sensitive situations of occupation.

V. The Law Behind Rule of Law Promotion in Fragile States

Astrid Wiik and *Frauke Lachenmann* contribute an article on "The Law Behind Rule of Law Promotion in Fragile States - The Case of Afghanistan". While, as the authors point out, the legitimacy and effectiveness of rule of law promotion (in particular within the overall context of international development assistance) have already been critically assessed, the aspect of the legality of rule of law promotion has not received similar attention. Based on that observation, *Wiik* and *Lachenmann* undertake to explore the relevant legal framework of post-conflict rule of law promotion in fragile states, using the extensive rule of law support provided to Afghanistan since 2001 as an example. Their assessment not only considers the international legal basis and mandate for rule of law promotion by the involved states, international development organizations, and NGOs, but also the legal rules that apply to the implementation activities on the ground, be it international legal standards, such as sovereignty, human rights or development laws, or national legal standards, such as domestic Afghan laws or the respective laws of the donors' order. The authors conclude that although detailed rules bind the monitoring and evaluation of rule of law activities in line with the existing international frameworks for development assistance, (too) few legal frameworks and principles guide the programming and implementation of rule of law promotion.

VI. The ICTY and its Rule of Law Promotion Efforts Through Rule 11bis

The sixth contribution "The Rule of Law á la ICTY - What the ICTY Deemed Just Good Enough and how it Supported the Countries in the Former Yugoslavia to Become Better" by *Kei Hannah Brodersen* is concerned with the ICTY's remarkable process of legal self-empowerment as a rule of law promoter in the countries within its jurisdiction. *Brodersen* shows that the ICTY – although established as an international criminal tribunal to conduct prosecutions and trials of international crimes committed in the Yugoslav Wars – slowly expanded its core mandate to also include actions of rule of law promotion by making use of a particular legal provision, namely Rule 11*bis* of its *Rules of Procedure and Evidence* (which allowed for a referral of cases from the ICTY to national courts under the condition that the respective courts were *adequately prepared*). The contribution illustrates that, based on the argument to help prepare national justice systems and in particular to achieve the necessary rule of law standard for being able to receive cases under Rule 11*bis*, the ICTY initiated a number of rule of law promotion measures. Although these initiatives were not based on a coherent and explicitly expressed definition of the rule of law, the author, based on comprehensive case law, discourse, and document analysis, nevertheless, puts together a mosaic of rule of law elements that the ICTY considered relevant in its promotion initiatives, and by that effectively manages to reconstruct the ICTY's (changing) conceptual rule of law approach.

VII. The Dynamics Between International Investment Law and the Rule of Law

Peter-Tobias Stoll approaches the topic of the law behind rule of law transfers with a particularly dynamic perspective on the relationship of "International Investment Law and the Rule of Law." *Stoll* begins his assessment with presenting international investment treaties as legal instruments that actually tend to foster and strengthen the rule of law in domestic legal orders as well as in the international sphere – by deterring unlawful and arbitrary governmental actions towards foreign investments (domestically) and by a certain legalization, judicialization and a strengthening of the individual internationally.

However, the author does not stop there, showing further that international investment law should not only be considered as donating but also as itself being informed, influenced and guided by an emerging international rule of law. From that *reverse perspective*, *Stoll* observes that the contemporary structures of international investment law have recently faced severe rule of law criticism – be it with respect to the legal uncertainty of the sometimes vague and broad terms used in international investment treaties or international investment law's manifold inconsistencies with other fields of international law (both issues contradicting a principle of international legality). Additionally, the relationship of the international legal field of investment law on the one side and (legally developed) domestic legal orders on the other often produces more cross-level legal conflicts than it solves. Although a certain adaptation of international investment law to the demands of an emerging international rule of law can lately be observed, *Stoll* still finds much room for potential rule of law transfers to international investment law in the future.

Constitutionalism and the Mechanics of Global Law Transfers

*Andreas L. Paulus** *and Johann Ruben Leiss*#

Table of Contents

Abstract

This article explores rule of law transfers from an international perspective. Based on the observation that the proposal of an emerging international constitutional order seems to have lost momentum this article emphasizes

---

* Prof. Dr. Andreas L. Paulus, Justice of the First Senate of the German Federal Constitutional Court and Professor of Public and International Law at the Georg-August-University Göttingen. The article reflects exclusively his personal views.

Dr. Johann Ruben Leiss, MLE, LL.M. (EUI), Assessor Juris, Research Fellow at the Faculty of Law at the University of Oslo.

a global legal reality that is characterized by a complex and rather nonhierarchical interplay between various (fragmented) international legal orders and suborders as well as national legal orders. This article discusses four legal mechanisms that are of pivotal relevance with respect to global rule of law transfers. These mechanisms include, first, so-called *hinge provisions* as doorways between different legal orders, second, harmonious interpretation as a legal tool of integration, third the sources of international law enabling transmission of norms and providing a framework for judicial interaction and, fourth, judicial dialogue as an informal means of rule of law transfer.

A. *Introduction*

The rule of law is a well-established concept of municipal legal systems.[1] Despite ongoing discussions about its content, it seems to be widely acknowledged that it refers to a core of essential features of legal systems, in particular a government of laws, the supremacy of the law, and equality before the law.[2] The government of laws requires that the exercise of public power may not be arbitrary but subject to law.[3] Law must be prospective,

1 See e.g. the *Rechtstaatsprinzip* (rule of law) in Germany (in particular Articles 20 (3), 101 and 103 of the *German Basic Law*). For a comprehensive discussion of the *Rechtstaatsprinzip*, see P. Kunig, *Das Rechtsstaatsprinzip: Überlegungen zu seiner Bedeutung für das Verfassungsrecht der Bundesrepublik Deutschland* (1986). For an early discussion of the rule of law in the UK, see A. V. Dicey, *Introduction to the Study of the Law of the Constitution*, 8th ed. (1915). On the evolution of the rule of law in national legal systems, see M. Krygier, 'Rule of Law,' in M. Rosenfeld & A. Sajó (eds), *The Oxford Handbook of Comparative Constitutional Law* (2012); the overview in S. Chesterman, 'An International Rule of Law?,' 56 *American Journal of Comparative Law* (2008) 2, 331, 333-340 [Chesterman, An International Rule of Law?]; and A. Watts, 'The International Rule of Law,' 36 *German Yearbook of International Law* (1993), 15, 17-18.

2 S. Chesterman, 'Rule of Law,' in R. Wolfrum (ed), *Max Planck Encyclopedia of Public International Law* (2007), para. 2 [Chesterman, Rule of Law], and Chesterman, 'An International Rule of Law?,' *supra* note 1, 342; Britannica Academic, Encyclopædia Britannica, 'Rule of Law,' available at https://www.britannica.com/topic/rule-of-law (last visited 13 December 2018).

3 Chesterman, 'Rule of Law,' *supra* note 2, para. 2, and Chesterman, 'An International Rule of Law?,' *supra* note 1, 342; Britannica Academic, *supra* note 2.

accessible, and clear.[4] In other words, those subjected to the law must be able to know the norms that they are supposed to follow in the future. The rule of law ensures the stabilization of normative expectations by requiring coherence and predictability.[5] It requires norms to be determinate in order to provide legal certainty. The supremacy of the law demands that all institutions and persons exercising public power are subordinated to the law.[6] Thus, the rule of law must be distinguished from the rule by law.[7] Law is more than simply an instrument to govern but also puts constraints on those exercising public power. The rule of law demands that "the creation of laws, their enforcement, and the relationships among legal rules are themselves legally regulated, so that no one – including the most highly placed official – is above the law".[8] The rule of law does not only subject all persons and institutions to the law but also provides mechanisms, in particular judicial review, to hold accountable those who exercise public power.[9] Equality before the law requires that laws must apply equally to all persons subjected to it.[10]

The substantive and institutional expansion of international law, the widening and deepening of international regulation and adjudication,[11] including its expansion into subject areas that were before solely a matter

4 Chesterman, 'Rule of Law', *supra* note 2, para. 2, and Chesterman, 'An International Rule of Law?', *supra* note 1, 342; J. Crawford, 'International Law and the Rule of Law', 24 *Adelaide Law Review* (2003) 1, 3, 4.

5 Cf. M. Kumm, 'International Law in National Courts: The International Rule of Law and the Limits of the Internationalist Model', 44 *Virgina Journal of International Law* (2003) 1, 19, 26.

6 Chesterman, 'Rule of Law', *supra* note 2, para. 2, and Chesterman, 'An International Rule of Law?', *supra* note 1, 342.

7 Chesterman, 'Rule of Law', *supra* note 1, para. 2, and Chesterman, 'An International Rule of Law?', *supra* note 1, 342.

8 Britannica Academic, *supra* note 2.

9 See e.g. K. J. Alter, *Establishing the Supremacy of European Law: The Making of an International Rule of Law in Europe* (2010); E.-U. Petersmann, 'How to Promote the International Rule of Law: Contributions by the World Trade Organization Appellate Review System', 1 *Journal of International Economic Law* (1998) 1, 25; Crawford, *supra* note 4, 4.

10 Chesterman, 'Rule of Law', *supra* note 2, para. 2; Britannica Academic, *supra* note 2.

11 On the substantive expansion of international law, see the Report of the Study Group of the International Law Commission, *Fragmentation of International Law: Difficulties Arising From the Diversification and Expansion of International Law*, UN Doc. A/CN.4/L.682, 13 April 2006 [ILC, Fragmentation Report]. On the expansion of international adjudication, see the special issue of the *New York University Journal of International Law & Politics*, Vol. 31 (1998). Publications that are more

of the *domaine réservé* of the nation State,[12] has posed the question of how the international rule of law can be upheld.[13] In particular, international sanctions against individuals by the *UN Security Council* (UNSC) have put concerns regarding the rule of law in a multilayer global legal order on the agenda.[14]

An approach that found particular support in German legal scholarship has proposed a constitutionalization of international law as a way of transferring the rule of law to the international level. By providing a clear normative hierarchy, granting supremacy to certain principles, and integrating all international legal subsystems into a unitary structure, constitutionalism aims at dealing with the expansion of international law by constitutional means.

The constitutionalist project, however, seems to have lost some of its momentum in recent years. Constitutionalism's suggestion of a unitary international normative system struggles to deal with some of international law's main successes, namely with the increasing internationalization of national law, the development of highly integrated supranational legal orders such as the *European Union*, and an increasing specialization of international subsystems. State organs increasingly apply international law in

recent include, e.g. G. Gaja, 'Relationship of the ICJ with Other International Courts and Tribunals', in A. Zimmermann et al. (eds), *The Statute of the International Court of Justice – A Commentary*, 2nd ed. (2012), 582-584 paras. 23-25 [Gaja, ICJ], and P.-M. Dupuy & J. E. Viñuales, 'The Challenge of "Proliferation": An Anatomy of the Debate', in C. P. R. Romano, K. J. Alter & Y. Shany (eds), *The Oxford Handbook of International Adjudication* (2014).

12 Cf. ILC, 'Fragmentation Report', *supra* note 11, 10, para. 7; Crawford, *supra* note 4, 7-8.

13 See e.g. Chesterman, 'An International Rule of Law?', *supra* note 1; A. Nollkaemper, *National Courts and the International Rule of Law* (2011) [Nollkaemper, National Courts]; Kumm, *supra* note 5; Watts, *supra* note 1; G. A. Christenson, 'World Civil Society and the International Rule of Law', 19 *Human Rights Quarterly* (1997) 4, 724; B. Zangl, 'Is There An Emerging International Rule of Law?', 13 *European Review* (2005) S1, 73; T. Nardin, 'Theorising the International Rule of Law', 34 *Review of International Studies* (2008) 3, 385; Crawford, *supra* note 4; J. Waldron, 'The Rule of International Law', 30 *Harvard Journal of International Law and Public Policy* (2006) 1, 15; B. Z. Tamanaha, *On the Rule of Law: History, Politics, Theory* (2004).

14 See e.g. S. Chesterman, *The UN Security Council and the Rule of Law: The Role fo the Security Council in Strengthening a Rule-based International System, Final Report and Recommendations from the Austrian Initiative, 2004-2008* (2008) [Chesterman, SC and Rule of Law].

domestic *fora*.[15] This growing intertwinement of national and international law has led to a paradoxical situation. On the one hand, international law is not exclusively an inter-State matter anymore (if it ever was). A constitutional hierarchy disconnected from domestic constitutional structures has difficulties to fulfill constitutionalist aspirations. On the other hand, national law has not become fully internationalized. National constitutions do not unconditionally give way to some sort of global constitution. Moreover, the proposed unity of international law has been increasingly challenged by the normative fragmentation and functional differentiation of international law. Thus, much of the constitutional discourse seems to have been replaced by a discourse on fragmentation.[16] While the fragmentation of international law does not necessarily exclude the implementation of certain elements of the rule of law, such as judicial review of the exercise of public power in restricted subject-areas,[17] it nevertheless implies a farewell to a broader rule of law vision of international law. It thus endangers rule of law transfers, referring to the dissemination and implementation of the rule of law across boundaries of international legal subsystems.

While we do not intent to revive a total constitutionalism as a utopian promise of an overarching global order, we do neither tune into fragmentation's requiem about the end of international law as common endeavor for the international implementation of the rule of law. While the different legal orders require analytical distinction, the plurality of the contemporary legal reality is characterized by a complex and dynamic interplay between various legal orders and sub-orders (including some private legal regimes). Instead of following a constitutional hierarchy, the law behind rule of law transfers and implementation is characterized by elements of mutual recognition of different legal orders – such as doorways for the application of norms of other legal systems, mutual respect, harmonious interpreta-

15 P. Allot, 'The Emerging Universal Legal System', in J. Nijman & A. Nollkaemper (eds), *New Perspectives on the Divide Between International Law and National Law* (2007); P. Allot, *Eunomia: New Order for a New World*, 2nd ed. (2001), 80-82.

16 On the fragmentation discourse, see e.g. M. Koskenniemi & P. Leino, 'Fragmentation of International Law? Postmodern Anxieties', 15 *Leiden Journal of International Law* (2002) 3, 553; B. Simma & D. Pulkowski, 'Of Planets and the Universe: Self-contained Regimes in International Law', 17 *European Journal of International Law* (2006) 3, 483; and A. Roberts, *Is International Law International?* (2017).

17 On the judicialization of specialized sub-regimes in international law as an aspect of an international rule of law, see Zangl, *supra* note 13.

tion, and informal means of dialogue – that enable integration and accommodation.

B. Rule of Law Transfers Between Constitutionalism and Fragmentation

I. The German Project: Rule of Law Transfers and International Constitutionalism

As a response to the expansion of international law and the disaggregation of the modern State,[18] an approach that found particular support in German legal scholarship has proposed the constitutionalization of international law as a means to implement the rule of law internationally.[19] A transfer of the concept of constitution from the domestic to the international level has been considered a way of administering the increasing exercise of public power on the international level by constitutional means.

Among the various constitutional approaches, we find a number of communalities. They are united in their emphasis on the rule of law in international relations by establishing a (hierarchical) structure, unity, and

---

18 Cf. A.-M. Slaughter, 'International Law in a World of Liberal States,' 6 *European Journal of International Law* (1995) 1, 503 [Slaughter, Int. Law and Liberal States].

19 Constitutionalism as an approach to international law can be traced back to the inter-war years, cf. A. Verdross, *Die Verfassung der Völkerrechtsgemeinschaft* (1926). For a comprehensive overview over constitutionalist approaches, see T. Kleinlein, *Konstitutionalisierung im Völkerrecht: Konstruktion und Elemente einer idealistischen Völkerrechtslehre* (2012) [Kleinlein, Konstitutionalisierung im Völkerrecht]. Contributions include A. Peters, 'The Merits of Global Constitutionalism,' 16 *Indiana Journal Global Legal Studies* (2009) 2, 397; A. Peters, 'Compensatory Constitutionalism: The Function and Potential of Fundamental International Norms and Structures,' 19 *Leiden Journal of International Law* (2006) 3, 579 [Peters, Compensatory Constitutionalism]; J. E. Alvarez, 'The Security Council's War on Terrorism: Problems and Policy Options,' in E. de Wet & A. Nollkaemper (eds), *Review of the Security Council by Member States* (2003); C. Tomuschat, 'Obligations Arising for States Without or Against Their Will,' 241 *Recueil des Cours* (1993), 195; B. Fassbender, *The United Nations Charter as the Constitution of the International Community* (2009); J. Klabbers, A. Peters & G. Ulfstein, *The Constitutionalization of International Law* (2009); J. L. Dunoff & J. P. Trachtman (eds), *Ruling the World: Constitutionalism, International Law, and Global Governance* (2009), 67. See also the lecture series of the Max-Planck Institute in Heidelberg on the future of international law scholarship in Germany in 67 *Zeitschrift für ausländisches öffentliches Recht und Völkerrecht* (2007), 583. See, furthermore, the references accompanying this section.

coherence of international law.[20] They are unified in their insistence on international law's legitimacy, in their support for coupling law and politics, and putting institutional and procedural restraints on those exercising public power internationally.[21] Another major concern among constitutionalists relates to the substantive dimension of international law (in particular human rights).[22] Most constitutionalists perceive international law as an order that is built upon some fundamental values[23] of the international community[24] that are *inter alia* reflected in the purposes and principles of the *Charter of the United Nations* (UN Charter)[25]. The normative substrate of such a "constitution of the international community" is to be found in the foundational principles that are enshrined in the UN Charter, in *jus cogens* and *erga omnes* obligations.[26] Accordingly, States as the relevant actors in international law are complemented by international organizations, actors of a global civil society, and international corporations in a single, constitutional framework.[27]

---

20 Cf. T. Kleinlein, 'Between Myths and Norms: Constructivist Constitutionalism and the Potential of Constitutional Principles in International Law', 81 *Nordic Journal of International Law* (2012) 2, 79 [Kleinlein, Constitutionalism].

21 Cf. J. Klabbers, 'Setting the Scene', in Klabbers, Peters & Ulfstein (eds), *supra* note 19, 11-14.

22 See e.g. G. Ulfstein, 'The Relationship Between Constitutionalism and Pluralism', 4 *Goettingen Journal of International Law* (2012) 2, 575.

23 See e.g. E. de Wet, 'The Emergence of International and Regional Value Systems as a Manifestation of the Emerging International Constitutional Order', 19 *Leiden Journal of International Law* (2006) 3, 611, 612-613; P.-M. Dupuy, 'Some Reflections on Contemporary International Law and the Appeal to Universal Values: A Response to Martti Koskenniemi', 16 *European Journal of International Law* (2005) 1, 131, 135; C. Tomuschat, 'International Law Ensuring the Survival of Mankind on the Eve of a New Century', 281 *Recueil des Cours* (1999), 9 ; D. Thürer, 'Modernes Völkerrecht: Ein System im Wandel und Wachstum – Gerechtigkeitsgedanke als Kraft der Veränderung?', 60 *Zeitschrift für ausländisches öffentliches Recht und Völkerrecht* (2000), 557, 598 ("ordre public").

24 On the so-called "international community school" of scholars, see B. Fassbender, 'The United Nations Charter as Constitution of the International Community', 36 *Columbia Journal of Transnational Law* (1998) 3, 529, 546-551. On the concept of "international community", see A. L. Paulus, *Die Internationale Gemeinschaft im Völkerrecht: Eine Untersuchung zur Entwicklung des Völkerrechts im Zeitalter der Globalisierung* (2001) [Paulus, Internationale Gemeinschaft].

25 *Charter of the United Nations*, 26 June 1945, 1 UNTS XVI.

26 Cf. Kleinlein, 'Constitutionalism', *supra* note 20, 89.

27 Cf. A. L. Paulus, 'International Community', in R. Wolfrum (ed), *Max Planck Encyclopedia of International Law* (2013) [Paulus, International Community], with further references.

However, constitutional discourse seems to be on the defensive in recent years.[28] In light of the dominant position of the nation State in international relations, autonomous constitutionalization of international law appears utopian.[29] Even though international law has become much more inclusive, an "international community" that includes other actors than States is still in its infancy.[30] The widespread disregard of the UN by many States and its inability to undergo necessary reforms due to the lack of basic consensus among its members challenge a qualification of the UN Charter as the all-embracing constitution. There is no real balance of power in the UN system, which would be an essential requirement for a system that adheres to the rule of law. In turn, except for the veto power of the permanent members, institutionalized restraint on the UNSC is almost nonexistent. Despite the multiplication of international judicial bodies and the growing application of international norms by domestic courts, judicial review mechanisms are still relatively underdeveloped. The development of many different powerful regimes also seems to preclude a *one-size fits all* approach of international constitutionalism. Fragmentation is fed by the increasing numbers of international treaty-regimes with their own dispute settlement procedures and mechanisms of implementation. They reflect remaining global dissent on important structural and value questions. The increasing differentiation of international law into specialized regimes, such as the international multilateral trade system, the international criminal legal system, and the highly integrated European legal order have led to the formation of different centers of gravity. Territoriality has been replaced by a differentiation of legal (sub-)system along functional lines instead of constitutional unification.[31]

As a consequence, a growing branch of international constitutionalism assumes a more integrated constitutionalization of both international law and domestic legal orders. Whereas few would suggest a radical monism, many of modern constitutionalists describe a unification of international

---

28 Cf. already G. Nolte, 'Zur Zukunft der Völkerrechtswissenschaft in Deutschland', 67 *Zeitschrift für ausländisches öffentliches Recht und Völkerrecht* (2007), 657.

29 Cf. A. L. Paulus, 'Zusammenspiel der Rechtsquellen aus völkerrechtlicher Perspektive', 46 *Berichte der Deutschen Gesellschaft für Internationales Recht* (2014), 13 [Paulus, Rechtsquellen].

30 See Paulus, 'Internationale Gemeinschaft', *supra* note 24.

31 Cf. A. Fischer-Lescano & G. Teubner, 'Regime-collisions: The Vain Search for Legal Unity in the Fragmentation of Global Law', 25 *Michigan Journal of International Law* (2003) 4, 999 [Fischer-Lescano & Teubner, Regime-collisions] and A. Fischer-Lescano & G. Teubner, *Regime-Kollisionen: Zur Fragmentierung des globalen Rechts* (2006) [Fischer-Lescano & Teubner, Regime-Kollisionen].

law and domestic law under the umbrella of a unified value system. The proposal of *the* "constitution of the international community" has been largely set aside by "complementary constitutionalism",[32] "constitutional principles",[33] and "constitutional networks".[34]

However, also proponents of an integrated constitutionalism of international and domestic law struggle in providing satisfactory answers to concerns of (democratic) legitimacy – regarding the justification of public authority[35] – resulting from the disaggregation of the functions of the State and their relocation to the international and supranational level. So far, only the State is able to provide democratic legitimacy to justify the exercise of public authority over individuals as well as the control of public authority. While our understanding of democratic legitimacy does not preclude a pluralist model of different democratic legal orders that complement each other and operate with different levels of (in)direct democratic legitimacy,[36] international and supranational orders remain deficient in this regard.

II. Fragmentation and Challenges to Law Transfers

Much of the constitutional discourse seems to have been replaced by a discourse on fragmentation.[37] As constitutionalism's antipode, fragmentation

---

32 Peters, 'Compensatory Constitutionalism', *supra* note 19, 579. See also C. Tomuschat, 'Der Verfassungsstaat im Geflecht der internationalen Beziehungen', in J. Frowein (ed), 36 *Veröffentlichungen der Vereinigung der Deutschen Staatsrechtslehrer* (1978), 52-53.

33 See e.g. S. Kadelbach & T. Kleinlein, 'International Law-A Constitution for Mankind? An Attempt at a Re-appraisal with an Analysis of Constitutional Principles', 50 *German Yearbook of International Law* (2007), 303, 342 (the principles discussed include respect for human rights and the environment, democracy, accountability and the rule of law). See also S. Kadelbach & T. Kleinlein, 'Überstaatliches Verfassungsrecht: Zur Konstitutionalisierung im Völkerrecht' (2006), 44 *Archiv des Völkerrechts* (2006) 3, 235.

34 Cf. e.g. A.-M. Slaughter, *A New World Order* (2004).

35 On *legitimacy* as a justification of public authority, see R. Wolfrum, 'Legitimacy in International Law', in R. Wolfrum (ed), *Max Planck Encyclopedia of Public International Law* (2011), para. 1.

36 Cf. J. Habermas, 'The Constitutionalization of International Law and the Legitimation Problems of a Constitution for World Society', 15 *Constellations* (2008) 4, 444, and J. Habermas, *Zur Verfassung Europas: Ein Essay*, 4th ed. (2012).

37 On the fragmentation discourse, see: Koskenniemi & Leino, *supra* note 16; Simma & Pulkowski, *supra* note 16; and Roberts, *supra* note 16.

embraces plurality and diversity.[38] The different legal orders, be they international or national, are considered as distinct legal systems with their own sources of legitimacy, institutions, and functional concerns. In other words, variety has become the new *avant-garde*.

Indeed, international law is subject to strong centrifugal forces, with heightened risks of normative fragmentation and a growing disparity in international law. Many international legal regimes have undergone a "functional differentiation" into various legal subsystems and seem to have developed into autonomous legal orders.[39] The lack of unity and clear structures in international law and the substantive fragmentation of international law cannot be seen as accidental phenomena. To a certain extent, they reflect the intention of States, who have decided to establish specialized legal regimes to solve special problems without foregoing sovereignty more generally.

Nevertheless, all international legal (sub)systems find their origin in general international law. In a formal sense, they are based in the sources of international law (Article 38 *Statute of the International Court of Justice*[40]) and derive their existence from States' consent. Thus, it would be premature to deny international law's systemic nature.

Despite the increasing receptiveness of national legal systems for international law, international law and domestic legal orders remain independent – at least in a formal sense.[41] International law does not determine or

---

38 See e.g. N. Krisch, 'The Pluralism of Global Administrative Law' (2006), 17 *European Journal of International Law* (2006) 1, 247; R. M. Cover, 'Uses of Jurisdictional Redundancy: Interest, Ideology, and Innovation', 22 *William and Mary Law Review* (1980) 4, 639; P. S. Berman, 'Global Legal Pluralism', 80 *Southern California Law Review* (2006) 6, 1155, 1155, 1164; N. Walker, 'The Idea of Constitutional Pluralism', 65 *Modern Law Review* (2002) 3, 317, 361. See also A. von Bogdandy, 'Pluralism, Direct Effect, and the Ultimate Say: On the Relationship Between International and Domestic Constitutional Law', 6 *International Journal of Constitutional Law* (2008) 3-4, 397, 398, who describes pluralism as a referring, descriptively and normatively, to the diversity within the legal sphere.

39 Fischer-Lescano & Teubner, 'Regime-collisions', *supra* note 31, and Fischer-Lescano & Teubner, 'Regime-Kollisionen', *supra* note 31. On *Regimetheorie*, see N. Luhmann, *Die Gesellschaft der Gesellschaft* (1997); N. Luhmann, *Das Recht der Gesellschaft* (1993).

40 *Statute of the International Court of Justice*, 26 June 1945, 33 UNTS 993 [ICJ Statute].

41 Nollkaemper, 'National Courts', *supra* note 13, 13; G. Gaja, 'Dualism – A Review', in J. Nijman & A. Nollkaemper (eds), *New Perspectives on the Divide between National and International Law* (2007), 52 [Gaja, Dualism].

describe legal validity in national law.[42] Thus, international law does not require direct effect in the domestic legal systems. Rather, the applicability of international law in domestic legal systems is contingent on national law.[43] The same holds true *vice versa*. The validity, applicability, and effect of domestic law in international law is contingent on the latter.

However, fragmentation fails to do justice to the various systemic elements that we can find in international law and in the relationship between national and international law.[44] It easily dismisses the agreement on many of the fundamental values underlying the international legal order that transgress international and domestic law. It is true that finding common principles risks falling prey to minimalism.[45] Nevertheless, we should not ignore the common ground that is shared by the various legal orders, in particular with regard to some fundamental norms, such as the prohibitions of the use of force, Genocide or torture.[46] The real divide is often not between different legal systems but between the rule of law and power politics.

Fragmentation that refers to a functional differentiation of international legal (sub)systems easily loses sight of the individual, on the one hand, and values, on the other hand, that have to be taken into account and balanced with each other.[47] Functional differentiation of *autopoietic* legal (sub)systems lacks legitimacy and does not offer a substitute for the democratic structures of the nation State. A return to legal fragmentation along territorial boundaries ignores the necessity to find common answers to global problems. While a fragmentation of international law does not necessarily exclude the implementation of certain elements of the rule of law interna-

---

42 Nollkaemper, 'National Courts', *supra* note 13, 68.

43 Nollkaemper, 'National Courts', *supra* note 13, 69; Gaja, 'Dualism', *supra* note 41, 52.

44 On tools dealing with the multiplication of international disputes settlement procedures, see e.g. L. Boisson de Charzournes, 'Plurality in the Fabric of International Courts and Tribunals: The Threads of a Managerial Approach', 28 *European Journal of International Law* (2017) 1, 13. On interpretative tools to deal with normative fragmentation, see e.g. ILC, 'Fragmentation Report', *supra* note 11.

45 A. L. Paulus, 'International Adjudication', in S. Besson & J. Tasioulas (eds), *The Philosophy of International Law* (2010), 209, 220 [Paulus, Adjudication].

46 Cf. Article 2 (4) UN Charter (Prohibition of the Use of Force); *Convention on the Prevention and Punishment of the Crime of Genocide*, 9 December 1948, 78 UNTS 277 (Prohibition of Genocide); and *Convention Against Torture and Other Cruel, Inhuman or Degrading Treatment or Punishment*, 10 December 1984, 1465 UNTS 85 (Prohibition of Torture).

47 Paulus, 'Adjudication', *supra* note 45, 215.

tionally, such as judicial review within different autonomous regimes,[48] it implies a farewell to a broader vision of the rule of law in international affairs. It waves normative coherence among different specialized fields of international law and prevents rule of law transfers across boundaries of international legal subsystems.

Approaches that try to reconcile constitutionalist concerns with a fragmented world order by proposing a plurality of constitutional sites[49] – or even "constitutional fragments"[50] within constitutional subsystems – seem to reflect, rather than to solve the crisis of the dichotomist conception of constitutionalism and fragmentation. International administrative law[51] has been proposed as a site for competition from which by way of induction common basic principles can be derived. This proposal appeals as a modest version of a pluralistic constitutionalism, but also struggles to overcome the underlying political tensions, which the fragmentation and constitutional dichotomy brought to the surface.

C. *Rule of Law Transfers in a Pluralist Order: Between Formal Structures and Mutual Respect*

A number of mechanisms offer a framework for the implementation of the rule of international law across legal (sub)systems and implement certain features of the rule of law. International law is characterized by a complex and dynamic interplay between various legal orders and sub-orders, including national legal systems.[52] It depends on a similar practice of mutual recognition of the different legal orders – such as doorways for the application of norms of other legal systems and mutual respect – that enable integration and accommodation.[53]

---

48 On an emerging rule of law through judicialization of specialized sub-regimes in international law, see Zangl, *supra* note 13.

49 Walker, *supra* note 38; M Avbelj & J Komárek, *Four Visions of Constitutional Pluralism* (2008).

50 G. Teubner, *Verfassungsfragmente – Gesellschaftlicher Konstitutionalismus in der Globalisierung* (2012).

51 See, for example, Krisch, *supra* note 38; B. Kingsbury, N. Krisch & R. B. Stewart, 'The Emergence of Global Administrative Law' 68 *Law and Contemporary Problems* (2005) 3, 15.

52 Cf. Paulus, 'Rechtsquellen,' *supra* note 29, 9. See in a similar line, Crawford, *supra* note 4, 10.

53 See further Paulus, 'Rechtsquellen,' *supra* note 29.

In the following, the article will highlight three mechanisms that play a pivotal role in the dissemination and implementation of an international rule of law. These mechanisms include so-called hinge provisions as doorways between different legal orders, harmonious interpretation as a tool for interpretative integration, and informal judicial dialogue. These mechanisms cannot compensate for the lack of a clear hierarchy and constitutional structure that would ensure unity in international law, whether within specialized international subsystems or in their application in national legal systems. They cannot fill the gaps left by the deficient judicial review mechanisms that could ensure accountability of those who exercise public power towards individuals directly or indirectly affected by international regulation and action. Nevertheless, these mechanisms may be able to mitigate a number of concerns arising from the expansion and fragmentation of international law. The overall structure, however, remains fragile. When the readiness for mutual respect breaks down, clashes are inevitable.

I. Hinge Provisions as Doorways between Legal Orders

So-called *hinge provisions* (*Scharniernormen*) constitute important mechanisms for the dissemination and implementation of the rule of international law.[54] These provisions establish doorways of legal orders for the inclusion of norms of other legal regimes. In doing so, hinge provisions ensure the establishment of a common normative framework that is (subject to certain conditions) applicable across systemic boundaries. These hinge provisions enable the incorporation of rule of law principles emanating from international law into domestic law and from general international law into specialized subsystems. The shared characteristic of these hinge provisions is that they recognize the applicability of general international law (Article 38 ICJ Statute) in their respective legal (sub)system as the residual rule in the absence of *lex specialis*.

Various constituent instruments of international courts and tribunals replicate or refer to Article 38 ICJ Statute.[55] For example, Article 21 of the

54 On this term, see P. M. Huber & A. L. Paulus, 'Cooperation of Constitutional Courts in Europe: The Openess of the German Constitution to International, European, and Comparative Constitutional Law', in M. Andenas & D. Fairgrieve (eds), *Courts and Comparative Law* (2015), 281.

55 Cf. A. Pellet, 'Article 38', in A. Zimmermann *et al.* (eds), *The Statute of the International Court of Justice – A Commentary*, 2nd ed. (2012), 745-747, paras. 49-54; Special Rapporteur Michael Wood, *Second Report on Identification of Customary Inter-*

Rome Statute[56] builds on the language of Article 38 and complements it.[57] Article 20 (1) of the *Protocol of the Court of Justice of the African Union* also takes up the wording of Article 38 and modifies it.[58] A number of instruments contain a general reference stating that judicial decisions shall be rendered in accordance with the "rules" or "principles" of "international law", thereby referring to Article 38 ICJ Statute.[59] Examples are Article 42 (1) of the ICSID Convention,[60] and Article 1131 (1) of the *North American Free Trade Agreement* (NAFTA).[61] Other instruments contain cross-references to Article 38, such as Articles 74 (1), 83 (1) and 311 of the *United Na-*

---

national Law, UN Doc A/CN.4/672, 22 May 2014, 5, para. 16 [ILC, Second Report on Custom]. See already the UN Secretariat, *Systematic Survey of Treaties for the Pacific Settlement of Disputes 1928-1948*, October 1948, 16-122 [Survey of Treaties], giving an extensive overview over applicable law provisions that make the sources of Article 38 ICJ Statute (or its predecessor Article 38 PCIJ Statute) applicable as the residual rule for international dispute settlement procedure in the absence of *lex specialis*.

56 *Rome Statute of the International Criminal Court*, 17 July 1998, 2187 UNTS 90.

57 Cf. W. A. Schabas, *An Introduction to the International Criminal Court*, 4th ed. (2011), 206-212, who argues that Article 38 ICJ Statute is applicable in the case of absence of special regulation in the *Rome Statute* (and *Rules of Procedure and Evidence*).

58 *Protocol of the Court of Justice of the African Union*, 1 July 2003, available at http://www.peaceau.org/uploads/protocol-court-of-justice-of-the-au-en.pdf, last visited 13 December 2018 (see also Article 20 (1)).

59 Cf. *Survey of Treaties*, *supra* note 55, 116-122.

60 *Convention for the Settlement of Investment Disputes between States and Nationals of Other States*, 18 March 1965, 575 UNTS 159 dealing with the applicable law. An explicit reference to Article 38 ICJ Statute was included in earlier drafts of Article 42, but eventually not taken up, cf. International Centre for Settlement of Investment Disputes, 'Draft Convention: Working Paper for the Legal Committee', 11 September 1964, in *History of the ICSID Convention – Documents Concerning the Origin and the Formulation of the Convention on the Settlement of Investment Disputes Between States and Nationals of Other States*, Vol II-1 (1968), Article 45, 610, 630 [History ICSID Convention]; see also the 'Memorandum From the General Counsel and Draft Report of the Executive Directors to Accompany the Convention', 19 January 1965, in *ibid.*, Vol II-2, 952, 962. The fact that no explicit reference was included, was not, however, perceived a substantial modification excluding an application of Article 38, cf. 'Modifications of Parts IV and V of the Draft Report of the Executive Directors to accompany the Convention', 9 March 1965, in *ibid.*, 1025, 1029, paras. 25-27. See further C. H. Schreuer, *The ICSID Convention: A Commentary*, 2nd ed. (2009), Article 42, 604-612, paras. 169-188, 613-630 paras. 192-244, and Paulus, 'Rechtsquellen', *supra* note 29, 17.

61 *North American Free Trade Agreement*, 17 December 1992, Canada, Mexico and United States of America, 32 ILM 289 [NAFTA]. See also *Methanex Corporation v. United States of America (Final Award on Jurisdiction and Merits)*, 3 August 2005,

tions Convention on the Law of the Sea (UNCLOS)[62] and Article 28 of the *General Act of Arbitration (Pacific Settlement of International Disputes)*.[63] Other instruments refer to parts of the language of Article 38, such as Article 3 of the *Understanding on Rules and Procedures Governing the Settlement of Disputes*.[64] By virtue of such hinge provisions, Article 38 ICJ Statute must be considered applicable as a general rule before courts and tribunals across different international legal subsystems, despite its wording and position in the Statute of the ICJ, which refers to "[t]he Court" and makes it applicable only before the ICJ.[65] Thus, "in substance, applicable law provisions

---

Part II Chapter B, 1, paras. 2-3 [Methanex v. USA], highlighting that the reference to "applicable rules of international law" in Article 1131 (1) NAFTA refers to Article 38 (1) ICJ Statute.

62 *United Nations Convention on the Law of the Sea*, 10 December 1982, 1833 UNTS 3.

63 *General Act of Arbitration (Pacific Settlement of International Disputes)*, 26 September 1928, 93 LNTS 343 refers to then Article 38 PCIJ Statute.

64 *Understanding on Rules and Procedures Governing the Settlement of Disputes, Annex 2 of the WTO Agreement*, 15 April 1994, 1869 UNTS 401. Most scholars support residual reliance on general international law in the WTO system. See, e.g.: L. Bartels, 'Applicable Law in WTO Dispute Settlement Proceedings', 35 *Journal of World Trade Law* (2001) 3, 499, 501-502, 504; D. Palmeter & P. C. Mavroidis, *Dispute Settlement in the World Trade Organization: Practice and Procedure*, 2th ed. (2012), 49-50; D. Palmeter & P. C. Mavroidis, 'The WTO Legal System: Sources of Law', 92 *American Journal of International Law* (1998) 3, 398, 398-399; J. Pauwelyn, 'The Role of Public International Law in the WTO: How Far Can We Go?', 95 *American Journal of International Law* (2001) 3, 535, 541-550 [Pauwelyn, Public International Law and WTO]; but see J. P. Trachtman, 'Institutional Linkage: Transcending 'Trade and...'', 96 *American Journal of International Law* (2002) 1, 77, 88, fn. 28 and G. Marceau, 'A Call for Coherence in International Law', 33 *Journal of World Trade* (1999) 5, 87, 109-115.

65 On the general relevance of Article 38 ICJ Statute before international courts and tribunals, see also: ILC, 'Second Report on Custom', *supra* note 55, 6, para. 16, fn. 15; Special Rapporteur Michael Wood, *First Report on Formation and Evidence of Customary International Law*, UN Doc A/CN.4/663, 17 May 2013, 14, para. 32 [ILC, First Report on Custom]; H. Mosler, 'General Principles of Law' in R. Bernhardt & R. L. Bindschedler (eds), *Encyclopedia of Public International Law*, Vol. 7 (1984), 89, 93; M. Virally, 'The Sources of International Law', in M. Sørensen (ed), *Manual of Public International Law* (1968), 116, 121-122; J. L. Brierly, *The Law of Nations: An Introduction to the International Law of Peace*, 6th ed. (1963), 56; R. Jennings & A. Watts, *Oppenheim's International Law*, Vol. 1, 9th ed. (1992), 24; ILC, *Survey of International Law in Relation to the Work of Codification of the International Law Commission: Preparatory work Within the Purview of Article 18, Paragraph 1, of the of the International Law Commission*, UN Doc A/CN.4/1/Rev 1, Extract from the Yearbook of the International Law Commission (1949), 22, para. 33 [ILC, Survey of International Law]; C. Brown, *A Common Law of International*

[...] do not depart from the general framework set up in Art. 38".[66] The constant practice of international courts and tribunals referring to this provision while relying on the ICJ's interpretation and modes of legal reasoning when determining rules of international law confirms the general applicability of Article 38 ICJ across international legal subsystems.[67] The application of Article 38 (1) ICJ Statute by arbitral tribunals serves as an illus-

---

Adjudication (2009), 36-37; I. Brownlie, *Principles of Public International Law*, 7th ed. (2008), 4-5; H. W. A. Thirlway, 'Unacknowledged Legislators: Some Preliminary Reflections on the Limits of Judicial Lawmaking', in R. Wolfrum & I. Gätzschmann (eds), *International Dispute Settlement: Room for Innovations?* (2012), 311, 313-314. See with regard to international arbitration: J. L. Simpson & H. Fox, *International Arbitration: Law and Practice* (1959), 130-131; see also Article 10 and the commentary of the *Model Rules on Arbitral Procedure with a General Commentary* (1958), Yearbook of the International Law Commission Vol. II(2), which can be found in *Report of the International Law Commission on the Work of its Tenth Session, 28 April – 4 July 1958*, UN Doc A/CN.4/117, UN Doc A/38/59, 84 and 87. Even Article 15 (1) of the *Rules for Uniform Domain Name Dispute Resolution Policy* as approved by the ICANN Board of Directors on 28 September 2013, available at www.icann.org/resources/pages/udrp-rules-2015-03-11-en (last visited 13 December 2018), as an example of an instrument of a modern form of transnational private/public judicial settlements procedure, is interpreted as relying on rules of general international law, to be applied by the ICANN review panel. Skeptical on a general application of Article 38 ICJ Statute to other courts: C. I. Fuentes, *Normative Plurality in International Law: A Theory of the Determination of Applicable Rules* (2016), 135-136.

66 M. Forteau, 'The Diversity of Applicable Law before international Tribunals as a Source of Forum Shopping and Fragmentation of International Law', in R. Wolfrum & I. Gätzschmann (eds), *supra* note 65, 417, 429. For an overview of the applicable law provisions in different international tribunals, see *Survey of Treaties*, *supra* note 55, 116-122. A number of instruments even include decisions *ex aequo et bono* (similarly to Article 38 (2) ICJ Statute) in their applicable law provisions.

67 See e.g. B. Cheng, *General Principles of Law as Applied by International Courts and Tribunals* (1953), 22; C. Tams & A. Tzanakopoulos, 'Barcelona Traction at 40: The ICJ as an Agent of Legal Development', 23 *Leiden Journal of International Law* (2010) 4, 781; J. d'Aspremont, 'If International Judges Say So, It Must Be True: Empiricism or Fetishism?', 4 *ESIL Reflections* (2015) 9 [d'Aspremont, International Judges]. See also J. d'Aspremont, 'International Lawyers and the International Court of Justice: Between Cult and Contempt', in J. Crawford *et. al.* (eds.), *The International Legal Order: Current Needs and Possible Responses – Essays in Honour of Djamchid Momtaz* (2017), 117, 122-123 [d'Aspremont, Lawyers and the ICJ], who argues that the ICJ fulfills the role of the "guardian of international lawyers' modes of legal reasoning". See also C. Tams, 'Meta-Custom and the Court: A Study in Judicial Law-Making', 14 *Law and Practice of International Courts and Tribunals* (2015) 1, 51-79. With a view to the interpretation of Article 38 (1) (b) ICJ Statute, see ILC, 'First Report on Custom', *supra* note 65, 28, para. 66; ILC, 'Second Report

trative example.[68] The applicability of Article 38 ICJ Statute, however, is not set in stone. If an instrument explicitly excludes the (residual) applicability of general international law, only the respective *lex specialis* applies.[69] With the exception of Article 103 UN Charter and *jus cogens*, international law remains dispositive and accepts the primacy of individual agreement.

Domestic legal systems also provide different kinds of hinge provisions which provide doorways for international law into their system.[70] For example, Articles 23, 24, 25, 59 (2) of the *German Basic Law* (the German Constitution, *Grundgesetz*)[71] constitute hinge provisions, which establish the "openness", or rather "friendliness", of the German legal order towards international and European law.[72] Articles 10 and 11 of the Italian Constitution provide additional examples of hinge provisions which open the Italian legal order to international and European law.[73] Without challeng-

---

on Custom', *supra* note 55, 6, para. 16, fn. 15. See already ILC, 'Survey of International Law', *supra* note 65, 22, para. 33.

68 See e.g. *Responsabilité de l'Allemagne à raison des dommages causés dans les colonies portugaises du sud de l'Afrique (sentence sur le principe de la responsabilité) (Portugal v. Germany)*, Award, 31 July 1928, 2 Reports of International Arbitral Awards (1949), 1011, 1016; *International Thunderbird Gaming Corporation v. Mexico*, Award, 26 January 2006, 31 para. 90; *Methanex v. USA*, *supra* note 61, Part II Chapter B, 1 paras. 2-3. See further Brown, *supra* note 65, 37, and ILC, 'Survey of International Law', *supra* note 65, 22 para. 33.

69 ILC, 'First Report on Custom', *supra* note 65, 14, para. 32; ILC, 'Second Report on Custom', *supra* note 55, 6, para. 16, fn. 15; Forteau, *supra* note 66, 421-423; '*Survey of Treaties*', *supra* note 55, 116-122.

70 Paulus, 'Rechtsquellen', *supra* note 29, 24-27.

71 An English translation can be found in the database of "Constitute: The World's Constitutions to Read, Search, and Compare", developed by the Comparative Constitutions Project at the University of Texas at Austin, available at https://www.constituteproject.org/constitution/German_Federal_Republic_2014?lang=en (last visited 13 December 2018).

72 On the "Friendliness" ("*Freundlichkeit*") and "openness" of the *German Basic Law*, see e.g. *Land Reform (Bodenreform) III*, Case No. 2 BvR 955/00, Order of the Second Senate of 26 October 2004, BVerfGE 112, 1, 25-26, para. 91-95. "Friendliness" expresses more distinctively the receptive approach of the *German Basic Law* to international and European law than the term "openness". The concept of "friendliness" finds its basis in the broader concept of "Open Statehood" ("*Offene Staatlichkeit*"), a label that was initially coined by K. Vogel, *Die Verfassungsentscheidung des Grundgesetzes für eine internationale Zusammenarbeit: ein Diskussionsbeitrag zu einer Frage der Staatstheorie sowie des geltenden deutschen Staatsrechts* (1964).

73 See e.g. Italian Constitutional Court, *Sentenza No 238/2014*, 22 October 2014, ECLI:IT:COST:2014:238, Conclusions in Point of Law, para. 3.1., available in Italian at https://www.cortecostituzionale.it/actionSchedaPronuncia.do?anno=2014&numero=238 (last visted 28 November 2018).

ing the formal division of international and domestic law, these hinge provisions make international law applicable in domestic legal systems as far as they incorporate international into domestic law.[74] International law is "agnostic" as to how (and how far) international law becomes applicable within the municipal legal system.[75] While a number of domestic legal orders allow for the automatic incorporation of international law,[76] others require its transformation (or rather explicit adaptation) into domestic legislation.[77] Others differentiate between the sources of international law. For instance, according to Article 25 of the *German Basic Law*, general international law, such as customary international law and general principles, are an integral part of federal law with direct effect on German citizens as far as they also address individuals.[78] In contrast, international treaties become part of German law only through legislative consent in the form of federal legislation according to Article 59 (2) of the *German Basic Law*.[79] From the international legal perspective, the only thing that counts is whether States fulfill their international obligations; how they do this remains their own business. This is even the case with regard to the *European Convention on Human Rights* (ECHR)[80] as a special international treaty that operates in a highly integrated European environment.[81]

---

74 Cf. Nollkaemper, *National Courts*, *supra* note 13, 70.

75 *Ibid.*

76 For examples of countries that provide for automatic incorporation *ibid.*, 73-77.

77 For examples of countries were international treaties require domestic legislations see *ibid.*, 77-81.

78 On customary international law in the German legal order, see A. L. Paulus, 'Customary Law Before the Federal Constitutional Court of Germany', in L. Lijnzaad & Council of Europe (eds), *The Judge and International Custom / Le juge et la coutume internationale* (2016) and A. L. Paulus, 'The Judge and International Custom', 12 *Law and Practice of International Courts and Tribunals* (2013) 2, 253.

79 On international treaty law in the German legal order, see A. L. Paulus, 'Germany', in D. Sloss & D. Jinks (eds), *The Role of Domestic Courts in Treaty Enforcement: A Comparative Study* (2009).

80 *Convention for the Protection of Human Rights and Fundamental Freedoms*, 4 November 1950, 213 UNTS 222.

81 See e.g. *Swedish Engine Drivers' Union v. Sweden*, ECtHR Application No. 5614/72, Judgment of 2 February 1976 [Swedish Engine Drivers' Union (ECtHR)].

II. Effects of Hierarchies Within International Law

The opening of legal orders through hinge provisions, however, is not unconditional and unlimited. The diversity of legal hierarchies is reflected in the permissibility of disengagement from *the other* legal order and in so-called *counter-limits* to their domestic application.[82]

On their own, clauses of supremacy or precedence, such as Article 103 UN Charter or Article 53 *Vienna Convention on the Law of Treaties* (VCLT) (*jus cogens*)[83] do not bring about but presuppose systemic unity in international law. They only lead to a certain superiority between international legal rules that have thereby not been detached from general international law. But these clauses do not apply in the relationship between domestic and international law, at least directly.[84] In spite of a general openness to international law, many (if not most) domestic legal systems have not given up their claim to normative sovereignty and thus final authority over the role of international law within the domestic legal system. Moreover, hinge provisions do not solve – at least directly – institutional conflicts between courts from different legal orders. Normative synchronization does not prevent divergent interpretation of international norms and conflicting judgments by different judicial bodies that are not part of one overarching hierarchical institutional structure.

Parties to international treaties may disengage from their international obligations through acts of revocation, if the treaty explicitly provides for it. Article 50 of the *Treaty on European Union* (TEU) serves as a well-known example in this regard explicitly allowing for exiting the EU.[85] As an alternative, States may invalidate, terminate, or suspend a treaty under the narrow conditions of Articles 46-53 VCLT. Under international law, simply in-

---

82 Paulus, 'Rechtsquellen', *supra* note 29, 30-37. See also A. L. Paulus & J.-H. Hinselmann, 'International Integration and Its Counter-Limits: A German Constitutional Perspective', forthcoming in C. Bradley (ed.), *Oxford Handbook on Foreign Relations Law* (2019). To our knowledge, the term "*contralimiti*" ("counter-limits") has been introduced by P. Barile, 'Ancora su diritto comunitario e diritto interno', in G. Ambrosini (ed), *Studi per il XX anniversario dell'Assemblea costituente*, Vol. VI (1969), 49 cited in accordance with G. Martinico, 'Is the European Convention Going to Be 'Supreme'? A Comparative-Constitutional Overview of ECHR and EU Law Before National Courts', 23 *European Journal of International Law* (2012) 2, 401, 419, fn. 103.

83 *Vienna Convention on the Law of Treaties*, 23 May 1969, 1155 UNTS 331.

84 Paulus, 'Rechtsquellen', *supra* note 29, 25.

85 *Consolidated Version of the Treaty of the European Union*, 26 October 2012, OJ C 326/13.

voking domestic reasons is generally not sufficient (Article 46 VCLT). If States override domestic legislation implementing treaty commitments, the international obligations remain untouched and the international responsibility of that State is triggered. Disengagement from international obligations deriving from the unwritten sources of international law (customary international law or general principles) is not less complicated. *Persistent objection* to new custom as one way of disengaging from customary international law is possible only under narrow conditions,[86] and is rarely successful in the long run.

III. Domestic Counterlimits to the Domestic Application of International Law

Moreover, domestic and international courts have developed a number of so-called counter-limits to the application of (general) international law in their respective legal (sub)systems, which enable disentanglement of different legal orders (even if only in the concrete case).[87]

1. Solange

Some counter-limits have a rather *outward-looking* character towards international (and European) law. They aim at fostering dialogue and accommodation, instead of outright disintegration. One example of such an outward-looking counter-limit is the so-called *Solange*-approach developed by the German Federal Constitutional Court (FCC; *Bundesverfassungsgericht*). Even though the FCC has developed this approach in the relationship between German constitutional law and EU law, it also finds application in the relationship with general international law and with other international courts and tribunals. The Court held that a supranational institution (in this context the EU) must ensure effective human rights protection equivalent to that under the domestic *German Basic Law* as a precondition for the opening of the German legal order. In *Solange II*, the FCC held that it would not exercise its jurisdiction and would abstain from reviewing EU secondary law against the *German Basic Law* "so long as" ("*solange*") the EU

86 On the persistent objector rule and its narrow scope, see Special Rapporteur Michael Wood, *Third Report on Identification of Customary International Law*, UN Doc A/CN.4/682, 27 March 2015, 59-67, paras. 85-95.

87 Paulus, 'Rechtsquellen', *supra* note 29, 7-37.

secured human rights protection that is equivalent to fundamental rights protection under German law.[88] The *Solange* approach aims at "equivalent protection" and harmonization rather than "identity" of human rights protection as the precondition for the reciprocal acceptance of different legal orders. It does not do so with a view to the individual case but it pursues systemic human rights protection in a multi-level system of law through "mutual respect" and engagement with foreign law.[89] Even though the *Solange* approach has successfully avoided a divergence between German fundamental rights protection and EU law, the potential for conflicts re-

88 *Re Wünsche Handelsgesellschaft (Solange II)*, Case No. 2 BvR 197/83, Order of the Second Senate of 22 October 1986, BVerfGE 73, 339, 387, para. 132 [Solange II (FCC)]. *The case Internationale Handelsgesellschaft mbH v. Einfuhr- und Vorratsstelle für Getreide und Futtermittel (Solange I)*, Case No. 2 BvL 52/71, Order of the Second Senate of 29 May 1974, BVerfGE 37, 271, 285, para. 56, marked the beginning of this approach. Given the then deficient human rights protection in the EU, the FCC held initially that it would exercise its jurisdiction over the application of EU law in German law "so long as" ("*solange*") the standard of fundamental rights protection under EU law is not "adequate" ("*ädequat*") compared to the fundamental rights protection under German law. See the further development of the *Solange II* jurisprudence in *Maastricht*, Case No. 2 BvR 2134, 2159/92, Judgment of the Second Senate of 12 October 1993, BVerfGE 89, 155 [Maastricht (FCC)]; *Lisbon (Lissabon)*, Case No. 2 BvE 2/08, Judgment of the Second Senate of 30 June 2009, BVerfGE 123, 267 [Lisbon (FCC)]; *Emission Allowance (Treibhausgas-Emissionsberechtigungen)*, Case No. 1 BvF 1/05, Order of the First Senate of 13 March 2007, BVerfGE 118, 79; *European Act on Warrants of Arrest (Europäisches Haftbefehlsgesetz)*, Case No. 2 BvR 2236/04, Judgment of the Second Senate of 18 July 2005, BVerfGE 113, 273; *Honeywell*, Case No. 2 BvR 2661/06, Order of the Second Senate of 6 July 2010, BVerfGE 126, 286 [Honeywell (FCC)]; *Data Retention (Vorratsdatenspeicherung)*, Case Nos. 1 BvR 256/08 and others, Judgment of the First Senate of 2 March 2010, BVerfGE 125, 260. The literature on the relationship between the FCC and the CJEU abounds. See e.g. T. Giegerich, 'Zwischen Europafreundlichkeit und Europaskepsis – Kritischer Überblick über die bundesverfassungsgerichtliche Rechtsprechung zur europäischen Integration', 19 *ZEuS Zeitschrift für Europarechtliche Studien* (2016) 1, 3; U. Kranenpohl, 'Kompetenzgerangel oder Interpretationsdiskurs? Intrajustizielle Kontrolle im Mehrebenensystem', 26 *Zeitschrift für Politikwissenschaft* (2016) 1, 149; M. D. Poli, 'Der Justizielle Pluralismus der Europäischen Verfassungsgemeinschaft: „Babylonische Gerichte“ oder „Gerichte für Babylon“?', 55 *Der Staat* (2016) 3, 373; C. Calliess, 'Die Rolle des Grundgesetzes und des Bundesverfassungsgerichts', in K. Böttger & M. Jopp (eds), *Handbuch zur Deutschen Europapolitik* (2016), 149; A. Voßkuhle, 'Multilevel cooperation of the European Constitutional Courts: Der Europäische Verfassungsgerichtsverbund', 6 *European Constitutional Law Review* (2010) 2, 175.

89 *Solange II (FCC)*, *supra* note 88; *Banana Market Regulation (Bananenmarktordnung)*, Case No. 2 BvL 1/97, Order of the Second Senate of 7 June 2000, BVerfGE 102, 147, 161-164, paras. 56-62.

mains.[90] The FCC does not grant an absolute precedence of EU law over national constitutional law rather, it requires that the constitutional limits of EU precedence (avoiding the more hierarchical term of "supremacy" as contained in Article 23 and Article 79 (3) *German Basic Law*) are respected.[91]

The *European Court of Human Rights* (ECtHR) applied an approach similar to the *Solange* jurisprudence in the *Bosphorus* case.[92] This case dealt with the responsibility of parties to the ECHR for legal measures imposed by the (then) *European Community*. The ECtHR made clear that Member States of an international organization (such as the EU) remain liable under the Convention for "all acts and omissions of its organs regardless of whether the act or omission in question was a consequence [...] of the necessity to comply with international legal obligations".[93] However, the ECtHR underlined that it would only review national measures implementing EU measures against the obligations arising from the ECHR if the organization did not offer human rights protection "at least equivalent to that for which the Convention provides".[94] Moreover, the Court applied a (rebuttable) presumption that a Member State complies with its obligations under the convention when fulfilling its obligations under EU law.[95] More recently, a Chamber of the ECtHR also applied an "equivalent protection test" when dealing with a possible conflict between obligations

90 Huber & Paulus, *supra* note 54, 286-287.

91 *Solange II (FCC)*, *supra* note 88, 375; *Lisbon (FCC)*, *supra* note 88, 346-369, paras. 225-272; *Honeywell (FCC)*, *supra* note 88, 292-295, paras. 55-61.

92 *Bosphorus Hava Yollari Turizm Ve Ticaret AS v. Ireland*, ECtHR Application No. 45036/98, Judgement of 30 June 2005 [Bosphorus (ECtHR)]. On the *Bosphorus* decision, see F. Schorkopf, 'The Judgment of the European Court of Human Rights in the Case Bosphorus Hava Yollari Turizm v Ireland', 6 *German Law Journal* (2005) 9, 1255; K. Kuhnert, 'Bosphorus – Double Standards in European Human Rights Protection?' (2006) 2 *Utrecht Law Review* (2006) 2, 177. See more recently the ECtHR Grand Chamber judgment in the case *Avotiņš v. Latvia*, ECtHR Application No. 17502/07, Judgment of 23 May 2016 [Avotiņš (ECtHR)] and the comment by S. Øby Johansen, 'EU Law and the ECHR: The Bosphorus Presumption is Still Alive and Kicking – The Case of Avotiņš v. Latvia' (2016), available at http://eulawanalysis.blogspot.com/2016/05/eu-law-and-echr-bosphorus-presumption.html (last visited13 December 2018).

93 *Bosphorus (ECtHR)*, *supra* note 92, para. 153.

94 *Ibid.*

95 *Ibid.*, 155-156.

arising from ECHR law and UN law.[96] The Grand Chamber, however, did not follow the Chamber's approach. Instead, it avoided the normative conflict by harmonizing interpretation.[97] Whether the *Solange-* or *Bosphorus*-style of reasoning becomes a blueprint for relationships between different legal (sub)orders remains to be seen.[98]

2. *Ultra vires*

The so-called *ultra vires* test developed by the FCC constitutes another outward-looking counter-limit that deals with possible conflicts over final claims of authority by providing a process of dialogue and accommodation, rather than confrontation.[99] The FCC held that the openness of the German legal order is limited to the powers that have been transferred to the EU level. Thus, EU law is only applicable in the German legal order to the extent that it finds a basis in the powers referred to the EU in accordance with the delegating act (Article 24 (1) and, explicitly, Article 23 of the *German Basic Law*) that emanates from the democratic will of the German legislator.[100] Acts of EU organs that are *ultra vires*, in other words which go beyond those transferred powers,[101] are not applicable in the

96 *Al-Dulimi and Montana Management Inc. v. Switzerland*, ECtHR Application No. 5809/08, Judgement of 26 November 2013, 55-58, paras. 111-121 [Al-Dulimi (ECtHR)].

97 *Al-Dulimi and Montana Management Inc. v. Switzerland* [GC], ECtHR Application No. 5809/08, Judgement of 21 June 2016, 65-67, paras. 134-140 [Al-Dulimi (Grand Chamber) (ECtHR)].

98 See e.g. the suggestion that the ICJ should apply a similar approach in P.-M. Dupuy, 'Competition Among International Tribunals and the Authority of the International Court of Justice', in U. Fastenrath *et al.* (eds), *From Bilateralism to Community Interest: Essays in Honour of Bruno Simma* (2011), 873 [Dupuy, International Tribunals].

99 On the *ultra vires* test as a counter-limit, see Paulus & Hinselmann, *supra* note 82, and Paulus, 'Rechtsquellen', *supra* note 29, 32-33, with further references.

100 *Maastricht (FCC)*, *supra* note 88, 187-188; *Lisbon (FCC)*, *supra* note 88, 346-369, paras. 225-272; *Honeywell (FCC)*, *supra* note 88, 303-302, paras. 54-57. On the purpose of the ultra vires control, see also *OMT (Judgment)*, Cases Nos. 2 BvR 2728/13 and others, Judgment of the Second Senate of 21 June 2016, BVerfGE 142, 123, Headnote 1 [OMT (Judgement) (FCC)].

101 *Maastricht (FCC)*, *supra* note 88, 187-188; *Lisbon (FCC)*, *supra* note 88, 352-355, paras. 240-241; *Honeywell (FCC)*, *supra* note 88, 302-303, paras. 54-57.

German legal order.[102] As a consequence, the FCC reserves a right of ultimate control of last resort of the European law principle of conferral (or enumerated powers) with regard to the powers transferred by the German legislator.[103] Importantly, however, the *ultra vires* test is less confrontational than it may seem at first glance. The FCC repeatedly emphasized that the constitutional principles of "open statehood", and more specifically the principle of "friendliness" to EU law, require an application of the *ultra vires* test in a "Union-friendly" manner. The FCC must request a preliminary reference under Article 267 TFEU from the CJEU before declaring an act *ultra vires* and nonbinding on German authorities.[104] Thus, the CJEU has the possibility to correct eventual transgressions of transferred competences itself while taking into consideration concerns of the FCC.[105] Moreover, only qualified transgressions may lead to an *ultra vires* finding by the FCC.[106] As the Court made clear:

> "Ultra vires review [...] is contingent on the act of the authority of the European Union being manifestly in breach of competences and the impugned act leading to a structurally significant shift to the detriment of the Member States in the structure of competences."[107]

Even though, conflicts cannot be categorically excluded as both the FCC and CJEU claim the competence to declare acts by EU organs *ultra vires*,[108] most potential conflicts between EU law and German constitutional law are likely to be prevented by the preliminary reference mechanism as long as both sides cooperate and aim at accommodation rather than confrontation. To date, the FCC has not found any acts by EU organs to be *ultra*

102 *Maastricht (FCC)*, *supra* note 88, 187-188; *Lisbon (FCC)*, *supra* note 88, 353-355, paras. 240-241; *Honeywell (FCC)*, *supra* note 88, 302-303, paras. 54-57. Nevertheless, the FCC constantly takes into account the CJEU's jurisprudence even beyond the scope of application of EU law, cf. Huber & Paulus, *supra* note 54, 298.

103 *Honeywell (FCC)*, *supra* note 88, 302, paras. 55.

104 *Lisbon (FCC)*, *supra* note 88, 353, para. 240, 397-398, para. 333; *Honeywell (FCC)*, *supra* note 88, 304, para. 60.

105 *Lisbon (FCC)*, *supra* note 88, 353, para. 240, 397-398, para. 333; *Honeywell (FCC)*, *supra* note 88, 304, para. 60.

106 *Honeywell (FCC)*, *supra* note 88, Headnote 1.

107 *Ibid.*

108 For the FCC, see *Eurocontrol I*, Cases Nos. 2 BvR 1107/77 and others, Order of the Second Senate of 23 June 1981, BVerfGE 58, 1, 30 and 31; *6th VAT Directive (6. Umsatzsteuerrichtlinie)*, Case No. 2 BvR 687/85, Order of the Second Senate of 8 April 1987, BVerfGE 75, 223, 235, 242; *Maastricht (FCC)*, *supra* note 88, 188; *Lisbon (FCC)*, supra note 88, 353-355, paras. 240-241; *Honeywell (FCC)*, *supra* note 88, 302-307, paras. 54-66.

vires.[109] The *ultra vires* control, however, does not seem to be easily transferrable to the relationship with other international legal orders (or to the relationship between different international legal orders) because it is based on an explicit dialogue of the two jurisdictions. It would require a formal mechanism comparable to the preliminary reference in Article 267 TFEU with a similar potential for accommodation and communication before irresolvable conflicts arise.

3. *Constitutional Identity*

The so-called "*identity control*" developed by the FCC is an example of a rather inward-looking counter-limit.[110] The Court held that the application of international law and EU law in the German legal order is subject to Germany's constitutional identity referring to the core values of the *German Basic Law* that are unmodifiable as enshrined in Articles 1-20, and 79 (3) *German Basic Law*.[111] In contrast to the *Solange* control and the *ultra vires* test, the *identity control* poses an absolute limit without leaving room for mutual accommodation.[112] Notably, however, until now the FCC has never applied it with a negative result.[113] But a violation of the *core* principles of the constitution by international norms is difficult to establish. So

---

109 So far, the FCC has referred preliminary requests in two cases. The first preliminary request was *OMT (Preliminary Reference)*, Case No. 2 BvR 2728/13, Order of the Second Senate of 14 January 2014, BVerfGE 134, 366 [OMT (Preliminary Reference) (FCC)]. The court accepted the response of the CJEU in *Gauweiler et al. v. Deutscher Bundestag*, Cases No. C-62/14 *et al.*, ECLI:EU:C:2015:400, Judgment of 16 June 2015 (though not without some critique), see *OMT (Judgment) (FCC)*, *supra* note 100, 222-223, para. 193. As a response to the second request of the FCC (cf. *Public Sector Purchase Program* (*EZB Ankauf*), Cases Nos. 2 BvR 859/15 and others, Order of the Second Senate of 10 October 2017 (FCC)), the CJEU rendered its judgment on 11 December 2018 (cf. Weiss *et al.*, Case No. C-493/17, ECLI:EU:C:2018:1000).

110 On the identity control as a counter-limit, see Paulus, 'Rechtsquellen,' *supra* note 29, 34-35.

111 *Lisbon (FCC)*, *supra* note 88, 353-355, paras. 240-241. See, comprehensive discussion in *Constitutional Identity (FCC)*, *supra* note 88.

112 The FCC considers the *identity control* to constitute an absolute limit, cf. *OMT (Preliminary Reference) (FCC)*, *supra* note 109, 368-387, para. 29.

113 However, see *Constitutional Identity (FCC)*, *supra* note 88.

far, reasonable interpretative divergence has not led to an *exit* from implementation, as best exemplified by the *OMT* case on *European Union*.[114]

Other national courts, however, have been less hesitant. For instance, the Italian Constitutional Court set up constitutional barriers towards international law in its 2014 *Sentenza 238/2014* decision.[115] It denied Germany's immunity for atrocities committed during World War II. In so doing, it took a considerably different approach than the ICJ in its *Immunities of the State* judgment.[116] The Court applied its *contralimiti* doctrine and held that the openness of the Italian legal order to international and supranational law (according to Articles 10 and 11 of the Constitution) finds its limits in fundamental principles and inviolable human rights enshrined in the Italian Constitution.[117] The Russian Constitutional Court also took a comparable approach in a recent decision putting itself in opposition to the ECtHR.[118] It underlined that the Russian legal order reserves barriers to international law.

In its famous *Kadi* judgment, the CJEU applied a similar rational itself, albeit with regard to the exercise of international executive rather than judicial powers.[119] When discussing a possible conflict between obligations emanating from UNSC resolutions and EU law, the Court granted supremacy to EU law from its internal perspective. It held that the EU has developed into an autonomous legal order with its own normative hierarchy.[120] It abstained from applying approaches that would have aimed at accommodation rather than confrontation, such as harmonious interpreta-

114 See the FCC in *OMT (Preliminary Reference)*, *supra* note 109 and the CJEU in *Gauweiler*, *supra* note 110.

115 *Sentenza No 238/2014*, *supra* note 73.

116 *Jurisdictional Immunities of the State (Germany v. Italy: Greece intervening)*, Judgement of 3 February 2012, ICJ Reports 2012, 99 [Jurisdictional Immunities].

117 *Sentenza No 238/2014*, *supra* note 73, Conclusions in Point of Law para. 3.4.

118 *OAO Neftyanaya Kompaniya Yukos v. Russia* [2017], 1-II/2017 (Russian Federation, Constitutional Court). See the critique of I. Marchuk & M. Aksenova, 'The Tale of Yukos and of the Russian Constitutional Court's Rebellion against the European Court of Human Rights' (2017), available at https://www.osservatorioaic.it/it/osservatorio/ultimi-contributi-pubblicati/iryna-marchuk/the-tale-of-yukos-and-of-the-russian-constitutional-court-s-rebellion-against-the-european-court-of-human-rights (last visited 13 December 2018).

119 *Yassin Abdullah Kadi and Al Barakaat International Foundation v. Council of the EU and European Commission*, Joined Cases Nos. C-402/05 P and C-415/05 P, ECLI:EU:C:2008:461, Judgment of 3 Septemeber 2008, [2008] ECR I-06351.

120 *Ibid.*, paras. 281-282, 286-288. See also *European Commission and Others v. Yassin Abdullah Kadi*, Joined Cases Nos. C-584/10 *et al.*, ECLI:EU:C:2013:518, Judgment of 18 July 2013.

tion or a kind of *Solange*-reservation. In our view, such an approach would have been an alternative, arguably even preferable solution.[121]

IV. The Sources of International Law as a Common Normative Framework

Article 38 ICJ Statute itself provides some sort of hinge provision and a framework for rule of law transfers as it allows for a reception of national law through customary international law, general principles, and judicial decisions. It seems to be commonly accepted that for the determination of rules of customary international law, in accordance with the so-called *two-elements* approach,[122] acts of the legislative, executive, and judicial branch may be taken into account for establishing the required practice and *opinio juris*.[123] Similarly, general principles may be drawn from manifestations of principles of national law from all branches of domestic government in accordance with the so-called *domestic* approach.[124] This is so despite the fact

121 Another alternative would have been the approach of the Court of First Instance of the EU in *Yassin Abdullah Kadi v. Council of the European Union and Commission of the European Communities*, Case No. T-315/01, ECLI:EU:T:2005:332, Judgment of 21 September 2005, [2005] ECR II-3649.

122 On the general support for the traditional *two-elements* approach by international judicial bodies (such as the WTO dispute settlement organs, IAtCHR, ECtHR, CJEU, ICTY, and ICTR), states, and scholarship, see the ILC, 'First Report on Custom', *supra* note 65, 20, paras. 50 and 52, 21-25, paras. 55-63, 28-37, paras. 66-82, 45-49, paras. 96-97, with further references.

123 See e.g. ILC, *Text of the Draft Conclusions on Identification of Custom*, UN Doc. A/73/10, 2018, Draft Conclusion 5 and Draft Conclusion 6 (2) [ILC, Draft Conclusions]; Jennings & Watts, *supra* note 65, 26; B. Simma & A. L. Paulus, 'The Responsibility of Individuals for Human Rights Abuses in Internal Conflicts: A Positivist View', 93 *American Journal of International Law* (1999) 2, 302, 306.

124 Cf. e.g. Pellet, *supra* note 55, 835, fn. 734 and 836, para. 260; W. Friedmann, 'The Uses of 'General Principles' in the Development of International Law', 57 *American Journal of International Law* (1963) 2, 279, 284 [Friedmann, General Principles]; J. Ellis, 'General Principles and Comparative Law', 22 *European Journal of International Law* (2011) 4, 949, 949-950; C. W. Jenks, *The Common Law of Mankind* (1958), 109-167 [Jenks, Comman Law of Mankind]; A. McNair, 'The General Principles of Law Recognized by Civilized Nations', 33 *British Yearbook of International Law* (1957), 1, 1-19; H. C. Gutteridge, 'The Meaning and Scope of Article 38(1)(c) of the Statute of the International Court of Justice', Discussion from 11 June 1952, printed in 38 *Transactions of the Grotius Society* (1952), 125. See further the references in J. G. Lammers, 'General Principles of Law Recognized by Civilized Nations', in F. Kalshoven, P. J. Kuyper & J. G. Lammers (eds), *Essays on the Development of the International Legal Order in Memory of Haro F Van*

that recourse to national law seems to be the exception rather than the rule, at least in the practice of the ICJ.[125] Since the *LaGrand* provisional measures decisions,[126] the *Immunity of the State*[127] and *Diallo* judgments,[128] however, the ICJ seems to have adopted a more inclusive approach towards domestic law that takes domestic constitutional law and Court decisions into account in the determination of international law and for the implementation of its decisions.

One aspect that has received remarkably little attention is that Article 38 ICJ Statute does not only provide a framework for the *substantive* dimension of international law but also for its *institutional*, judicial dimension.[129] Article 38 (1) ICJ Statute provides an important element in the institutional dimension of law transfers between domestic courts and international courts. Today, it has become generally acknowledged that national (and certain international) judicial decisions constitute formative elements of

---

Panhuys (1980), 53, 56-57. In the drafting committee of the PCIJ Statute, see *Procès-Verbaux of the Proceedings of the Advisory Committee of Jurists (16 June-24 July 1920) with Annexes* (1920), 335 (Lord *Phillimore*). See also Separate Opinion Judge *Simma, Case Concerning Oil Platforms (Islamic Republic of Iran v. United States of America)*, Judgment of 6 November 2003, ICJ Reports 2003, 161, 354-358, paras. 66-74.

125 With regard to custom, see S. Talmon, 'Determining Customary International Law: The ICJ's Methodology Between Induction, Deduction and Assertion', 26 *European Journal of International Law* (2015) 2, 417; A. Cassese, 'The International Court of Justice: It is High Time to Restyle the Respected Old Lady', in A. Cassese (ed), *Realizing Utopia: The Future of International Law* (2012), 239, 248, and A. Cassese, 'The Nicaragua and Tadić Tests Revisited in Light of the ICJ Judgment on Genocide in Bosnia', 18 *European Journal of International Law* (2007) 4, 649, 654-655. With regard to general principles, see Pellet, *supra* note 55, 839 para. 266.

126 *LaGrand Case (Germany v. United States of America)*, Provisional Measures, Order of 3 March 1999, ICJ Reports 1999, 9.

127 *Jurisdictional Immunities, supra* note 116.

128 *Case Concerning Ahmadou Sadio Diallo (Republic of Guinea v. Democratic Republic of the Congo)*, Preliminary Objections, Judgement of 24 May 2007, ICJ Reports 2007, 582, and *Case Concerning Ahmadou Sadio Diallo (Republic of Guinea v. Democratic Republic of the Congo)*, Compensation, Judgment of 19 June 2012, ICJ Reports 2012, 324.

129 M. Andenas & J. R. Leiss, 'The Systemic Relevance of 'Judicial Decisions' in International Law', 77 *Zeitschrift für ausländisches öffentliches Recht und Völkerrecht* (2017) 4, 907.

customary international law and general principles.[130] Furthermore, national and international judicial decisions constitute "subsidiary means" for the determination of the sources of international law as reflected in Article 38 (1) (a) to (c) ICJ Statute.[131] Article 38 ICJ Statute determines the judicial interaction and allocates authority between courts from different legal systems in the process of determination of international law. It offers a framework for authority and historical lineages of reasoning among different courts and so provides a communicative framework for the dissemination of the rule of law. Similar to Article 38 ICJ Statute's role as a blueprint for a common yet decentralized international legal order with limited means, it also provides guidance for the dialogue between courts be-

---

130 On national judicial decisions as elements of customary international law, see e.g. *Jurisdictional Immunities*, *supra* note 116, 122, para. 54, 127, para. 64, 129, para. 68, 131-134, paras. 71-75, 134, para. 76, 135, para. 78, 136, para. 83, 137, para. 85, 139, para. 90, 142, para. 96, 148, para. 118, and *Case Concerning the Arrest Warrant of 11 April 2000 (Democratic Republic of Congo v. Belgium)*, Judgment of 14 February 2002, ICJ Reports 2002, 3, 23-24, paras. 56-58; see also ILC, 'Draft Conclusions,' *supra* note 123, Draft Conclusion 5 and Draft Conclusion 6 (2), and ILC, *Identification of Customary International Law, The Role of Decisions of National Courts in the Case Law of International Courts and Tribunals of a Universal Character for the Purpose of the Determination of Customary International Law*, Memorandum by the Secretariat, UN Doc A/CN.4/691, 5, Observation 1 and 8, and 32, Observation 23 [ILC, Memorandum by the Secretariat on the Decisions of National Courts and Custom]; P. M. Moremen, *National Court Decisions as State Practice*, 1999-2000 Proceedings and Committee Reports of the American Branch of the International Law Association, 100, 119. In scholarship, see e.g. Brownlie, *supra* note 65, 6; Jennings & Watts, *supra* note 65, 26, 41; Pellet, *supra* note 55, 862 para. 321; M. N. Shaw, *International Law*, 5th ed. (2003), 78. See, however, the traditional view: L. Oppenheim, 'The Science of International Law: Its Task and Method,' 2 *American Journal of International Law* (1908) 2, 313, 336-341; K. Strupp, 'Regles générales du droit de la paix,' 47 *Recueil des Cours* (1934), 259, 313-315; D. Anzilotti, *Cours de Droit International*, Vol. 1 (1929), 74-75. On national judicial decisions as formative elements of general principles, see K. Doehring, 'The Participation of International and National Courts in the Law-Creating Process,' 17 *South African Yearbook of International Law*, 8; A. Nollkaemper, 'The Role of Domestic Courts in the Case Law of the International Court of Justice' 5 *Chinese Journal of International Law* (2006) 2, 301, 304 [Nollkaemper, Domestic Courts]; Nollkaemper, *National Courts*, *supra* note 13, 272. See also ILC, 'Memorandum by the Secretariat on the Decisions of National Courts and Custom,' *supra* note 131, 3-4 [4].

131 On judicial decisions as "subsidiary means," see Andenas & Leiss, *supra* note 129; A. Zammit Borda, 'A Formal Approach to Article 38 (1) (d) of the ICJ Statute From the Perspective of the International Criminal Courts and Tribunals,' 24 European Journal of International Law (2013) 2, 649.

longing to different legal systems.[132] It provides an instruction manual for the judicial interaction of courts and their mutual reception in the determination of the applicable international law. It is here where the role of domestic courts – in particular those with the highest jurisdiction – is of particular relevance.

V. *Harmonious Interpretation and Conflict Avoidance*

Harmonious interpretation is another mechanism for fostering normative coherence and thus the international rule of law across different legal systems. In case of (possible) normative conflict, it aims at giving effect to the norms of all legal systems involved to the greatest extent possible.[133] The *International Law Commission*'s Fragmentation Report suggests that the threat of fragmentation could be contained by recourse to interpretative devices as a means of countering the centrifugal forces of our multipolar world.[134] Consistent interpretation is considered one way to avoid possible conflicts between international norms, but also between domestic law and international law.[135] Most prominently, the principle of systemic integration reflected in Article 31 (3) (c) VCLT is considered a tool for avoiding normative conflicts and mitigating the substantive dimension of the fragmentation of international law.[136] Article 31 (3) (c) VCLT defines the con-

---

132 With regard to letter (d) of Article 38 (1) ICJ Statute, see Andenas & Leiss, *supra* note 129.

133 See Paulus, 'Rechtsquellen', *supra* note 29, 18. Other interpretative principles for conflict avoidance are *lex specialis* (cf. A. Lindroos, 'Addressing Norm Conflicts in a Fragmented Legal System: The Doctrine of *Lex Specialis*', 74 *Nordic Journal of International Law* (2005) 1, 27; ILC, 'Fragmentation Report', *supra* note 11, 30-115, paras. 46-222; Simma & Pulkowski, *supra* note 16, 485-490 and *lex posterior* (cf. ILC, 'Fragmentation Report', *supra* note 11, 115-166, paras. 223-323).

134 ILC, 'Fragmentation Report', *supra* note 11.

135 On consistent interpretation as a tool to give effect to international obligations in domestic law, see Nollkaemper, *National Courts*, *supra* note 13, 139-165; G. Betlem & A. Nollkaemper, 'Giving Effect to Public International Law and European Community Law Before Domestic Courts: A Comparative Analysis of the Practice of Consistent Interpretation', 14 *European Journal of International Law* (2003) 3, 569. See also A. Cassese, 'Modern Constitutions and International Law', 192 *Recueil des Cours* (1985), 331, 398.

136 See on this principle: C. McLachlan, 'The Principle of Systemic Integration and Article 31(3)(c) of the Vienna Convention', 54 *International and Comparative Law Quarterly* (2005) 2, 279; ILC, 'Fragmentation Report, *supra* note 11, 206-244, paras. 410-480.

text in the interpretation of treaties, providing that "[t]here shall be taken into account, together with the context [...] (c) any relevant rules of international law applicable in the relations between parties".[137] Accordingly, when interpreting international rules, the broader normative environment must be taken into account.[138] The provision aims at avoiding conflicting claims to final authority by preventing conflicts in the first place.[139] By taking into account norms of other legal (sub)systems, it ensures normative coherence and in the best case legal certainty – as a core element of the rule of law – for the addressees of norms. As the wording makes clear, Article 31 (3) (c) is not limited to "general international law" but covers "any relevant rules of international law applicable in the relations between the parties".[140] It is based on the insight that "treaties are themselves creatures of international law"[141] that derive their validity and character from general international law.[142] They do not operate in isolation but alongside rights and obligations derived from other international treaties, rules of customary international law and general principles.[143] Their nonhierarchical relationship "can only be approached through a process of reasoning that makes them appear as parts of some coherent and meaningful whole".[144]

As the principle of systemic integration's companion, the presumption of compatibility derives from the same rationale, namely that States do not intend to create conflicting legal norms.[145] As the ICJ put it in the *Right of Passage* case: "it is a rule of interpretation that a text emanating from a Gov-

---

137 Cf. ILC, 'Fragmentation Report', *supra* note 11, 208, para. 413.
138 Cf. *Ibid.*, 208, para. 413 and 209, para. 415.
139 On these principles in the broader context of the discussion on "normative hierarchy" in international law, see A. L. Paulus & J. R. Leiss, 'Article 103', in B. Simma *et al.* (eds), *The Charter of the United Nations: A Commentary*, Vol. 2, 3rd ed. (2012), 2116-2119, paras. 11-18.
140 Cf. ILC, 'Fragmentation Report', *supra* note 11, 212, para. 422.
141 McLachlan, *supra* note 136, 280.
142 Cf. ILC, 'Fragmentation Report', *supra* note 11, 208, para. 414.
143 McLachlan, *supra* note 136, 280.
144 Cf. ILC, 'Fragmentation Report', *supra* note 11, 208, para. 414.
145 On the presumption of compatibility, see the ICJ in the *Case Concerning Right of Passage Over Indian Territory (Portugal v. India) (Merits)*, Judgment of 12 April 1960, ICJ Reports 1960, 6, 142. See also the ECtHR in *Al-Jedda v. United Kingdom*, ECtHR Application No. 27021/08, Judgment of 7 July 2011, 60, para. 102 [Al-Jedda (ECtHR)], in *Nada v. Switzerland*, ECtHR Application No. 10593/08, Judgment of 12 September 2012, 48-49, paras. 170-172 [Nada (ECtHR)], and in *Al-Dulimi (Grand Chamber) (ECtHR)*, *supra* note 97, 66-67 paras. 138-140. See further: ILC, 'Fragmentation Report', *supra* note 11, 25 paras. 37; C. W. Jenks, 'The

ernment must, in principle, be interpreted as producing and as intended to produce effects in accordance with existing law and not in violation of it".[146] Thus, both principles require that normative conflicts be avoided by all available interpretative means.[147]

The ECtHR's Grand Chamber judgment in *Al-Dulimi* serves as an illustrative example.[148] The Court was confronted with possible conflicts between obligations emanating from the UN Charter, more specifically from UNSC resolutions, on the one hand, and obligations arising from the Convention, on the other hand. By applying Article 31 (3) (c) VCLT and the presumption of compatibility, the ECtHR concluded that a normative conflict did not exist.[149] Notably, however, eight out of seventeen judges disagreed with the majority opinion arguing that the latter's reasoning stretched harmonious interpretation too far.[150]

Conflict of Law-Making Treaties', 30 *British Yearbook of International Law* (1953), 401, 428-429 [Jenks, Law-Making Treaties]; J. Pauwelyn, *Conflict of Norms in Public International Law: How WTO Law Relates to Other Rules of International Law* (2003), 240-244 [Pauwelyn, Conflict of Norms]; Paulus & Leiß, *supra* note 139, 2118, para. 18.

146 *Case Concerning Right of Passage over Indian Territory (Portugal v. India) (Preliminary Objections)*, Judgment of 26 November 1957, ICJ Reports 1957, 125, 142.

147 See Jenks, 'Law-Making Treaties', *supra* note 145, 429; Pauwelyn, 'Conflict of Norms', *supra* note 145, 240-241 and 245-246; C. J. Borgen, 'Resolving Treaty Conflicts', 37 *George Washington International Law Review* (2005) 3, 573, 639.

148 *Al-Dulimi (Grand Chamber) (ECtHR)*, *supra* note 97, 66-71, paras. 138-149. See also *Al-Jedda (ECtHR)*, *supra* note 146, 60-63, paras. 102-109; *Nada (ECtHR)*, *supra* note 146, 48-49, paras. 170-172.

149 *Al-Dulimi (Grand Chamber) (ECtHR)*, *supra* note 97, 65-67, paras. 134-140. See also *Al-Jedda (ECtHR)*, *supra* note 145, 63, para. 102, and *Nada (ECtHR)*, *supra* note 145, 48-49, paras. 170-172. A similar approach was proposed by *Nigel Rodley* in his Concurring Opinion in *Sayadi and Vinck v. Belgium*, UNHRC Decision of 22 October 2008, UN Doc CCPR/C/94/D/1472/2006), 36, when discussing a possible conflict between obligations from UN Security Council resolutions and the *Optional Protocol to the International Covenant on Civil and Political Rights*, UNGA Res 2200A (XXI), 19 December 1966, 999 UNTS 302.

150 Vice-President *Nussberger* refers in her dissenting opinion to "fake harmonious interpretation", Dissenting Opinion of Judge *Nussberger, Al-Dulimi (Grand Chamber) (ECtHR)*, *supra* note 97, 140, 141. Judge *Pinto de Albuquerque*, joined by Judges *Hajiyev, Pejchal* and *Dedov*, recommended a *Bosphorus* approach, Concurring Opinion of Judge *Pinto de Albuquerque*, joined by Judges *Hajiyev, Pejchal* and *Dedov, ibid.*, 76-114. See also the concurring opinion of Judges *Keller* (Concurring Opinion of Judge *Keller, ibid.*, 123-125), *Kūris* (Partly Dissenting Opinion of Judge *Kūris, ibid.*, 133); and *Ziemele* (Partly Dissenting Opinion of Judge *Ziemele, ibid.*, 134-139).

As the disagreement between the majority's opinion and the numerous judges in their individual opinions demonstrates, conflict prevention by way of harmonious interpretation is not a magic weapon.[151] If norms stand in clear contradiction and do not leave any interpretative leeway that would allow interpreting the conflict away, the principle of systemic integration reaches its limits. Moreover, harmonious interpretation does not necessarily avoid conflicts between divergent interpretations of different actors, most importantly courts, in the interpretation and application of international law.

VI. *Informal Judicial Dialog*

Informal forms of judicial interaction, often discussed under the label of judicial dialog, constitute another device furthering the rule of law transfers in international law.[152] They include nonformal communicative processes of cooperation, interaction, and exchange,[153] collegiality among judges, and a common mind-set. The venues of this dialog among judges are international conferences, private gatherings, and meetings of the courts.[154] While generally informal judicial interaction is to be welcomed for a better mutual understanding and learning,[155] the turn to informal coordination and networks is not completely unproblematic,[156] given the of-

---

151 McLachlan, *supra* note 136, 318.

152 See e.g. A.-M. Slaughter, 'A Global Community of Courts', 44 *Harvard International Law Journal* (2003) 1, 191 [Slaughter, Global Community of Courts] and Boisson de Charzournes, *supra* note 44, who base significant parts of their analysis on informal elements of judicial interaction.

153 See on different forms of informal interaction: Slaughter, 'Global Community of Courts', *supra* note 152, 192-193; A.-M. Slaughter, 'Judicial Globalisation', 40 *Virginia Journal of International Law* (1999-2000) 4, 1103, 1120-1123 [Slaughter, Judicial Globalisation]; C. Baudenbacher, 'Judicial Globalization. New Developments or Old Wine in New Bottles', 38 *Texas Journal of International Law* (2003) 3, 505, 524-525.

154 Cf. Slaughter, 'Global Community of Courts', *supra* note 152, 192-193; Slaughter, 'Judicial Globalisation', *supra* note 153, 1120-1123.

155 See also T. Buergenthal, 'The Proliferation of Disputes, Dispute Settlement Procedures and Respect for the Rule of Law', 21 *ICSID Review – Foreign Investment Law Journal* (2006) 1, 126, 129, arguing that "[i]nformal contacts between the various courts should also be encouraged".

156 For some skepticism, see T. Streinz, 'Winners and Losers of the Plurality of International Courts and Tribunals: Afterword to Laurence Boisson de Chazournes' Foreword', 28 *European Journal of International Law* (2017) 4, 1251, 1251; Dupuy,

ten "competing loyalties, commitments, and obligations" of national courts *vis-à-vis* national and international law.[157] Due to their volatility, informal judicial networks cannot entirely compensate for the lack of formal structures. Their existence and functioning depends on numerous factors, in particular the persons involved and their commitment to a cooperative spirit among courts from different legal systems.

Moreover, it is important that informal judicial dialog be not entirely hidden from the public in order to dispel fears of nontransparent decisions-making. Transparency in international cooperation may help mitigating fears of an uncontrolled self-empowering global judiciary.

D. Conclusion

International (or even global) constitutionalism constitutes a utopian promise rather than an accurate reflection of the status of the integration of different legal orders into an overarching legal unity. As appealing as a clear constitutional setting may be, constitutionalism cannot simply do away *once and for all* with the tensions between different values and principles, which find the expression in the creation of specialized subsystems of international law. Thus, in order to strengthen the international rule of law it is required to deal with pluralism instead of fighting it. Finding the transitional elements between different normative orders rather than constructing another hierarchy can help us mitigating the challenges arising from the complex setting of international law. The practice of mutual recognition of the different legal orders through hinge provisions and harmonious interpretation that enable integration and accommodation are among the most important elements that are able to guarantee the implementation of the international rule of law. Only in applying these elements are we able to uphold the rule of law and avoid anarchy, which leads to nothing more than the *rule of the powerful*. However, given the often-deficient formal

---

'International Tribunals', *supra* note 98, 864; and W. Friedmann, *The Changing Structure of International Law* (1964), 146-147.

157 Nollkaemper, 'National Courts', *supra* note 13, 14. See also Y. Shany, 'Dédoublement Fonctionelle and the Mixed Loyalties of National and International Judges', in F. Fontanelli, G. Martinico & P. Carrozaa (eds), *Shaping Rule of Law Through Dialogue: International and Supranational Experiences* (2010), 36-37, and Y. Shany, 'Plurality as a Form of (Mis)management of International Dispute Settlement: Afterword to Laurence Boisson de Chazournes' Foreword', 28 *European Journal of International Law* (2017) 4, 1241, 1242, 1245.

structures in international law, the transfer and implementation of the international rule of law through mutual recognition requires a commitment of the actors involved, what *Raz* refers to as the "politics of the rule of law".[158]

As such, an international rule of law does not necessarily require a strong analogy with domestic conceptions of constitutions.[159] The international rule of law may differ from the standards that we are familiar with from national legal systems.[160] The rule of law in international law operates in a legal system where the subjects with plenary power remain States, in spite of the ever growing relevance of individual and human rights, whereas the rule of law in domestic legal systems is primarily concerned with the rights and obligations of individuals *vis-à-vis* each other and against the state. Nevertheless, the more international law also regulates the rights and duties of individuals,[161] and thus overlaps with domestic regulation, the more the international rule of law must work hand in hand with and conform to standards of the domestic rule of law. Thus, the need for coordination will continue to grow, even if the political winds are currently blowing into the face of the international rule of law. Respecting the pluralism of legal orders, and maintaining the authority of *the* rule of law, are more and more becoming two sides of the same coin. In this perspective, rule of law transfers are an important tool for keeping the rule of law alive.

---

158 J. Raz, 'The Politics of the Rule of Law', 3 *Ratio Juris* (1990) 3, 331, and J. Raz, 'The Politics of the Rule of Law', in J. Raz (ed), *Ethics in the Public Domain: Essays in the Morality of Law and Politics* (1995), 354. See also Crawford, *supra* note 4, 12.

159 H. Krieger & G. Nolte, 'The International Rule of Law – Rise or Decline? Points of Departure', KFG Working Paper Series No. 1, 2016/10.

160 Highlighting the difference between the rule of law in municipal law and in international law: Waldron, *supra* note 13; Watts, *supra* note 1, 16-17; Chesterman, 'An International Rule of Law?', *supra* note 1, 333.

161 Cf. Peters, 'Compensatory Constitutionalism', *supra* note 19.

The Legal Dimensions of Rule of Law Promotion in EU Foreign Policy – EU Treaty Imperatives and Rule of Law Conditionality in the Foreign Trade and Development Nexus

Till Patrik Holterhus[*]

Table of Contents

* Dr. Till Patrik Holterhus, MLE., LL.M. (Yale), Assistant Professor at the Institute for International Law and European Law at the Georg-August-University Göttingen and Professeur Invité at the Pantheon-Sorbonne University Paris (in 2018 and 2019).

Abstract

This article demonstrates that Articles 21 and 3 (5) of the *Treaty on European Union* (TEU) as well as Articles 205, 207 (1), 208 (1), 209 (2) of the *Treaty on the Functioning of the European Union* (TFEU), *legally* oblige the *European Union* (EU) to promote the rule of law in its foreign trade and development policy. Furthermore, it is shown that, in the context of such promotion, the EU applies not a rudimentary but a sophisticated concept of the rule of law – quite similar to the concept of the rule of law that has developed within the Union. To fulfill this legal obligation to promote the rule of law abroad, the EU employs, as a key instrument, the *legal* mechanism of conditionality, not only through autonomous instruments but also in its contractual international relationships (*carrot-and-stick policy*). The EU's foreign policy in the trade and development nexus, in particular when it comes to the promotion of the rule of law, can, therefore, be considered a process, to a large extent, determined and organized by the law.

A. *Introduction – A Legal Perspective*

The EU pursues a policy of promoting the rule of law. This applies not only within the EU – regarding its own Member States[1] and in the course of

1 See L. Pech & K. L. Scheppele, 'Illiberalism Within: Rule of Law Backsliding in the EU', in K. Armstrong (ed), *Cambridge Yearbook of European Legal Studies* (2017), 3; see also the contributions of L. W. Gormley, P. Wennerås, M. Broberg, L. Besselink, F. Amtenbrink, R. Repasi, O. Stefan, A. von Bogdandy, C. Antpöhler, M. Ioannidis & J. W. Müller, in A. Jakab & D. Kochenov (eds), *The Enforcement of EU Law and Values* (2017); see also C. Closa & D. Kochenov, 'Reinforcement of the Rule of Law Oversight in the European Union: Key Options', in W. Schroeder (ed), *Strengthening the Rule of Law in Europe* (2016), 173; [Schroeder (ed), Rule of Law in Europe], E. Crabit & N. Bel, 'The EU Rule of Law Framework', in *ibid.*, 197.

EU accession procedures[2] – but also with respect to legal orders beyond the EU's own (future) territory and jurisdiction.

For this policy of promoting the rule of law abroad, the EU employs a variety of instruments.[3] However, as the globally leading entity in development cooperation[4] and one of the world's largest trading powers,[5] the EU is particularly well-positioned to pursue the policy of *exporting values*, such as the rule of law, through the medium of its foreign trade and development policies.[6] A clear indication of such policy conception can be observed in the EU's recent 2017 *New European Consensus on Development* which states:

> "The EU and its Member States will promote the universal values of democracy, good governance, the rule of law and human rights for all, because they are preconditions for sustainable development and stabil-

---

2 F. Emmert & S. Petrovic, 'The Past, Present, and Future of EU Enlargement', 37 *Fordham International Law Journal* (2014) 5, 1349, 1349-1355; H. de Waele, *Legal Dynamics of EU External Relations* (2017), 157-162.

3 See extensively, though with a particular focus on human rights, V. Haász, J. Jaraczewski & K. Podstawa, 'The FRAME Toolbox for the EU Fundamental and Human Rights Policies', European Commission, GA No. 320000 (2017); see also Cremona, 'Values in EU Foreign Policy', in M. Evans & P. Koutrakos (eds), *Beyond the Established Legal Orders* (2011), 275, 292-307 [Cremona, Values in EU Foreign Policy]; A. Kumin, 'Global Activities and Current Initiatives in the Union to Strengthen the Rule of Law – A State of Play', in Schroeder (ed), 'Rule of Law in Europe', *supra* note 1, 207; L. Pech, 'Rule of Law as a Guiding Principle of the European Union's External Action', CLEER Working Papers (2012/3), 14-20 [Pech, Rule of Law].

4 European Commission, Press Release, 'EU Official Development Assistance Reaches Highest Level Ever', IP/18/3002 (10 April 2018), available at http://europa.eu/rapid/press-release_IP-18-3002_en.htm (last visited 13 December 2018); see also OECD, 'Development Aid Stable in 2017 With More Sent to Poorest Countries' (9 April 2018), available at http://www.oecd.org/development/financing-sustainable-development/development-finance-data/ODA-2017-detailed-summary.pdf (last visited 13 December 2018).

5 The EU-28 accounts for around 15 % of the world's trade in goods. In 2016 the EU-28 had the highest level of trade in goods (imports and exports) exceeding those of the US or China, see Eurostat, 'International Trade in Goods' (2017), 1, available at http://ec.europa.eu/eurostat/statistics-explained/pdfscache/1188.pdf (last visited 13 December 2018).

6 See J. Larik, 'Much More Than Tarde: The Common Commercial Policy in a Global Context', in M. Evans & P. Koutrakos (eds), *Beyond the Established Legal Orders* (2011), 13, 25-34 [Larik, Much More Than Tarde].

> ity, across the full range of partnerships and instruments in all situations and in all countries, including through development action."[7]

It is this rule of law promotion policy, in the so-called *foreign trade and development nexus*, that shall form the general backdrop of this article – with the foreign trade and development nexus in this context to be understood as the entirety of the EU's international action (uni-, bi- and multilateral) in the closely interlinked and mutually reinforcing fields of trade liberalization and development cooperation (after all, many of the EU's trade activities are not only conducted for the economic benefit of the Union but also for the development benefit of the respective partner States).[8]

In light of the specific topic of this volume, the article will approach the above-described general field of EU rule of law promotion in the foreign trade and development nexus from a particular analytical perspective – namely a *legal* perspective.[9] With this perspective, the article focuses not only on understanding which positive legal norms impel and drive the EU

---

7 European Commission, *Proposal for a New European Consensus on Development – Our World, our Dignity, our Future* (22 November 2016), (COM(2016)) 740 final/2, para. 49. The *New European Consensus on Development* is a non-legally binding joint statement of the *Council*, the *European Commission*, the *European Parliament* as well as the EU Member States, constituting a comprehensive common framework for European development cooperation, applying to the entirety of the EU's institutions and all EU Member States.

8 See Larik, 'Much More Than Tarde', *supra* note 6, 25-34; on development cooperation see generally P. Dann, *The Law of Development Cooperation: A Comparative Analysis of the World Bank, the EU and Germany* (2013).

9 For a related approach see e.g. J. Larik, 'Entrenching Global Governance: The EU's Constitutional Objectives Caught Between a Sanguine World View and a Daunting Reality', in B. van Vooren, S. Blockmans & J. Wouters (eds), *The EU's Role in Global Governance: The Legal Dimension* (2013), 7 [Larik, Entrenching Global Governance]. With this article's specific focus on the assessment of these *legal dimensions* of the EU's rule of law promotion, other issues, notwithstanding how related they may appear, shall not be discussed. In particular, such issues would not include the legitimacy (*legal imperialism*), overall effectiveness, or coherence of the EU's approach. See on these issues e.g. R. Brooks, 'The New Imperialism: Violence, Norms and the "Rule of Law"', 101 *Mich. L. Rev.* (2003) 7, 2275; A. Zimelis, 'Conditionality and the E-ACP Partnership: A Misguided Approach to Development?', 46 *Australian Journal of Political Science* (2011) 3, 389; R. Kleinfeld, *Advancing the Rule of Law Abroad: Next Generation Reform* (2012); A. Sepos, 'Imperial power Europe? The EU's relations with the ACP countries', 6 *Journal of Political Power* (2013) 2, 261; L. Pech, 'Promoting the Rule of Law Abroad: On the EU's Limited Contribution to the Shaping of an International Understanding of the Rule of Law', in D. Kochenov & F. Amtenbrink, *The European Union's Shaping of the International Legal Order* (2014), 108, 119-128 [Pech, Promoting the Rule of Law Abroad]; L. Bartels, 'The

to promote the rule of law abroad, but also on exploring what legal instruments and mechanisms employed by the EU govern and organize the actual promotion and transfer processes. Consequently, the assessment aims to emphasize the law's relevance in what often rather seems to consist of a sequence of decisions and aspirations in a predominantly socio-political sphere.[10]

With the aim of contributing to a better understanding of what might, therefore, be described as *the law behind rule of law transfers*, the article will proceed in two steps.

First, the article will deal with the EU's internal legal imperatives with respect to the promotion of the rule of law in the EU's foreign policy (B.). Within this part, it will be assessed why a certain detachment of foreign policies from legal determination and control, typically to be observed in western constitutional democracies, does not hold true for the EU (I.), to what extent the EU is actually legally obliged to promote the rule of law in foreign policy (II.), and, subsequently, what concept of the rule of law the EU applies when promoting it abroad (III.).

Based on these findings, the second part will then focus on a significant legal mean that the EU employs for external value promotion in its foreign trade and development policy, namely the mechanism of (rule of law) conditionality (C.). This conditionality will be analyzed in the context of two of its major fields of application in the trade and development nexus, namely the *Special Incentive Scheme of Preferences* (GSP+) (I.), and the *Cotonou Agreement*'s essential elements clause and noncompliance procedure (II.). For both, an examination of the mechanism's legal background and functionality, as well as two short case studies with respect to the mechanism's actual application, will be provided.

Application of Human Rights Conditionality in the EU's Bilateral Trade Agreements and other Trade Agreements with Third Countries' (2008), European Parliament, Policy Department External Policies; J.D. Saltnes, 'The EU's Human Rights Policy, Unpacking the literature on the EU's implementation of aid conditionality', ARENA Working Paper No. 2, (03/2013).

10 For a perspective rather emphasizing the political (science) and sociological dimension of rule of law promotion, see e.g. A. Magen & L. Morlino, 'Hybrid Regimes, the Rule of Law, and External Influence on Domestic Change', in A. Magen & L. Morlino (eds), *International Actors, Democratization and the Rule of Law* (2009), 1; L. Morlino & A. Magen, 'Methods of Influence, Layers of Impact, Cycles of Change', in A. Magen & L. Morlino (eds), *International Actors, Democratization and the Rule of Law* (2009), 26; or E. Baracani, 'EU Democratic Rule of Law Promotion', in A. Magen & L. Morlino (eds), *International Actors, Democratization and the Rule of Law* (2009), 53.

B. Legal Imperatives for Rule of Law Promotion in EU Foreign Policy

I. EU Foreign Policy as a Purely Political Sphere?

1. The Particularity of Foreign Policy

At first glance, an assertion of the EU's rule of law promotion in foreign policy as a process extensively influenced by *legal* imperatives appears to have a natural antagonist, best referred to as the "particularity of foreign policy"[11] – a phenomenon that denotes a certain detachment of the sphere of foreign policy from internal (in particular constitutional) legal determination and control, often to be observed in western constitutional democracies.[12]

Such exceptional status of foreign policy is usually reasoned with the particularly *political* nature of foreign policy – conceived as being highly complex and difficult to predict, in constant need of confidentiality, expert knowledge, compromise, political flexibility, and spontaneous decision-making. Only a certain detachment from legal constraints would, therefore, not hinder foreign policy's effectiveness in the context of largely power-driven international relations.[13]

Approaches of (a certain) particularity can be well-observed in, for example, France, the United Kingdom, the United States of America or Germany, referring to it with terms such as "*theorie de l'acte de gouvernement*", "*political question doctrine/crown prerogative*", "*acts of [S]tate doctrine*" or "*weiter Ermessensspielraum in Angelegenheiten des Auswärtigen*".[14]

11 See on this conceptual term ("Particularity of Foreign Affairs") D. Thym, 'Foreign Affairs', in A. von Bogdandy & J. Bast, *Principles of European Constitutional Law*, 2nd ed. (2009), 309, 309-311.

12 M. Krajewski, 'Foreign Policy and the European Constitution', 22 *Yearbook of European Law* (2003), 435, 438-442 with further references [Krajewski, Foreign Policy and the European Constitution]; see also Thym, *supra* note 11, 311-314.

13 See Thym, *supra* note 11, 314-316; see also T. M. Franck, *Political Questions/Judicial Answers* (1992), 45-60.

14 See Krajewski, 'Foreign Policy and the European Constitution', *supra* note 12, 440-441.

2. Legal Permeation of EU Foreign (Trade and Development) Policy

Regardless of the general question of whether the exceptional status of foreign policy is (still) a fitting approach in light of the increasing relevance and impacts of international relations within domestic legal spheres and the consequential need for legitimization,[15] such an exceptional status is, however, not an accurate description of the EU's constitutional structure when it comes to the trade and development nexus. Quite the contrary holds true: EU foreign trade and development policy is to be considered a field profoundly permeated by the law.

This legal permeation can be well-observed in two aspects.

The first aspect is, as will be shown below, the density of EU primary law that establishes substantive legal standards on the strategic orientation and direction of the EU's foreign (trade and development) policy.[16]

The second aspect is that, with respect to foreign (trade and development) policy,[17] the EU legal order assigns its judiciary rather extensive powers of review[18] – with the CJEU indeed making use of these powers, frequently subjecting acts within the field to quite a high level of scrutiny.

---

15 For a critical approach "in a post-national context" see Krajewski, 'Foreign Policy and the European Constitution', *supra* note 12, 441-443.

16 Thym, *supra* note 11, 326-330; Larik, 'Entrenching Global Governance', *supra* note 9, 7-12; C. Vedder, 'Linkage of the Common Commercial Policy to the General Objectives for the Union's External Action', in M. Bungenberg & C. Herrmann (eds), *European Yearbook of International Economic Law – Special Issue: Common Commercial Policy After Lisbon* (2013), 115; M. Cremona, 'Structural Principles and their Role in EU External Relations Law', in M. Cremona (ed), *Structural Principles in EU External Relations Law* (2018), 3 [Cremona, Structural Principles].

17 However, with the Common Foreign and Security Policy being, to a great extent, excluded from judicial review (Article 24 (1) TEU and Article 275 TFEU).

18 Thym, *supra* note 11, 326-330; P. Koutrakos, *EU International Relations Law* (2015), 229-235; M. Cremona, 'A Reticent Court? Policy Objectives and the Court of Justice', in M. Cremona & A. Thies (eds), *The European Court of Justice and External Relations Review* (2016), 15, 15-19, 29-31 [Cremona, A Reticent Court?].

This applies not only in terms of EU law's allocation of competences and procedural matters[19] but also in terms of substantive legal requirements.[20]

---

19 See e.g. *European Parliament v. Council* (EDF), Case No. C-316/91, Judgment of 2 March 1994, [1994] ECR I-00625, para. 29; *Parliament v. Council (Waste Shipment)*, Case No. C-187/93, Judgment of 28 June 1994, [1994] ECR I-2874, para. 17; *Parliament v. Council (Article 43 EEC)*, Case No. C-65/93, Judgment of 30 March 1995, [1995] ECR I-643, para. 23; *Parliament v. Council (Common Commercial Policy)*, Case No. C-360/93, Judgment of 7 March 1996, [1996] ECR I-1195, paras. 23-25; *Commission v. Council (Fishery Agreement)*, Case No. C-25/94, Judgment of 19 March 1996, [1996] ECR I-1496, para. 48; *Andersson and Wåkerås-Andersson*, Case No. C-321/97, Judgment of 15 June 1999, [1999] ECR I-03551, para. 26; *Commission v. Council (Accession to the Nuclear Safety Convention)*, Case No. C-29/99 Judgment of 10 December 2002, [2002] ECR I-11221, paras. 67-70; *Commission v. Council (Energy Star Agreement)*, Case No. C-281/01, Judgment of 12 December 2002, [2002] ECR I-12049, paras. 33-35; *Commission v. Council (Carriage of goods agreement)*, Case No. C-211/01, Judgment of 11 September 2003, [2003] ECR I-8913, para. 39; *Commission v. Council (Rotterdam Convention)*, Case No. C-94/03, Judgment of 10 January 2006, [2006] ECR I-1, paras. 50-51; *Parliament v. Council and Commission (PNR)*, Case No. C-317/04 and C-318/04, Judgment of 30 May 2006, [2006] ECR I-4721, para. 63 and 68.

20 See e.g. *Germany v. Council (Framework Agreement on Bananas)*, Case No. C-122/95, Judgment of 10 March 1998, [1998] ECR I-00973, paras. 62-64; *Yassin Abdullah Kadi and Al Barakaat International Foundation v. Council and Commission (Kadi I)*, Case No. C-402/05 P and C-415/05 P, Judgment of 3 September 2008, [2008] ECR I-06351, paras. 283-285, 326. Later confirmed by the joined cases *Faraj Hassan v. Council and Commission and Chafiq Ayadi v. Council*, Case No. C-399/06 P and C-403/06 P, Judgment of 3 December 2009, [2009] ECR I-11393, paras. 71-75; as well as *Commission and Others v. Yassin Abdullah Kadi (Kadi II)*, Cases No. C-584/10 P, C-593/10 P and C-595/10 P, Judgment of 18 July 2013, ECLI:EU:C:2013:518, paras. 66-67, 97; *Front Polisario v. Council*, Case No. T-512/12, Judgment of 10 December 2015, ECLI:EU:T:2015:953, paras. 227-233, later set aside by the follow-up case *Council v. Front Polisario*, Case No. C-104/16 P, Judgment of 21 December 2016, ECLI:EU:C:2016:973, paras. 92-99, 103-108; which in turn was confirmed through the recent case *Western Sahara Campaign UK v. Commissioners for Her Majesty's Revenue and Customs and Secretary of State for Environment, Food and Rural Affairs*, Case No. C-266/16, Judgment of 27 February 2018, ECLI:EU:C:2018:118, paras. 62-63. The reversal of the judgment was, however, not based on an incorrect legal assessment regarding the substantive consistency of the agreement with general principles of EU law, but rather on a faulty assessment of the agreement's territorial scope of application. See also *EEA I*, Opinion 1/91 of the Court of 14 December 1991, [1991] ECR I-06079, paras. 41-46; *European Common Aviation Area*, Opinion 1/00 of the Court of 18 April 2002, [2002] ECR I-03493, paras. 11-13; GATS, Opinion 1/08 of the Court of 30 November 2009, [2009] ECR I-11129, para. 108; *ECHR Accession*, Opinion 2/13 of the Court of 18 December 2014, ECLI:EU:C:2014:2454, paras. 168, 179-200, 258; *PNR*, Opinion 1/15 of the Court of 16 July 2017, ECLI:EU:C:2017:592, para. 67.

Accordingly, the law is anything but absent when it comes to the EU's (promotion of the rule of law in) foreign trade and development policy; as a matter of fact, the law widely determines and controls this policy, as will be elaborated further below.

II. The EU's Legal Obligation to Promote the Rule of Law Abroad

As indicated above, under EU primary law, the EU and its organs are not free to design its foreign policy and conduct its activities in the external sphere as they (politically) please. Instead, they have to comply with certain substantive requirements in EU primary law.[21] This includes an obligation to promote the rule of law abroad. With respect to the foreign trade and development policy, EU primary law establishes the relevant standards (on rule of law promotion) in Articles 21[22] and 3 (5) TEU as well as in Articles 205, 207 (1), 208 (1), 209 (2) TFEU.

---

21 The question as to what extent the EU might be obliged under international law to promote the rule of law in its foreign policy is not subject to this assessment; on this issue see Vedder, *supra* note 16, 140-141.

22 Article 21 TEU reads:
"(1) *The Union's action on the international scene shall be guided by the principles which have inspired its own creation, development and enlargement, and which it seeks to advance in the wider world*: democracy, *the rule of law*, the universality and indivisibility of human rights and fundamental freedoms, respect for human dignity, the principles of equality and solidarity, and respect for the principles of the United Nations Charter and international law.
The Union *shall seek to develop relations and build partnerships* with third countries, and international, regional or global organisations which share *the principles referred to in the first subparagraph*. It shall promote multilateral solutions to common problems, in particular in the framework of the United Nations.
(2) The Union *shall define and pursue common policies and actions, and shall work for a high degree of cooperation in all fields of international relations, in order to*:
[…]
(b) consolidate and support democracy, *the rule of law*, human rights and the principles of international law;
[…]
(3) The Union *shall respect the principles and pursue the objectives set out in paragraphs 1 and 2 in the development and implementation of the different areas of the Union's external action covered by this Title and by Part Five of the Treaty on the Functioning of the European Union, and of the external aspects of its other policies.*
[…]" (emphasis added).

1. Rule of Law Promotion in Article 21 TEU

Article 21 TEU stands in the center of this normative conglomerate, being the general and at the same time most detailed substantive provision. It applies to all fields of EU foreign policy as well as all forms and formats of the EU's external means (may it be diplomatic, autonomous/unilateral foreign policy instruments or bi-/multilateral treaty-making). Article 5 (3) TEU and Articles 205, 207 (1), 208 (1), 209 (2) TFEU in this regard do not substantially add to Article 21 TEU. However, they do (explicitly) repeat, refer back to, or incorporate its normative content and clarify its full applicability to the external dimensions of the common commercial policy (trade) and international development cooperation.

As an introductory provision to Title V of the TEU ("General Provisions on the Union's External Action"), Article 21 TEU establishes a framework of guiding principles and objectives concerning the EU's external action ("the Union's action on the international scene shall be guided by the principles which have inspired its own creation, development and enlargement"; Article 21 (1) TEU), thereby, as *Christoph Vedder* rightly notes, "externaliz[es] [the EU's] internal constitutional values".[23] These guiding principles and objectives comprise, among others, the rule of law, explicitly referred to in Article 21 (1), (2) TEU.

The reference to the rule of law in Article 21 TEU unfolds its relevance as a guiding principle in EU foreign policy in two dimensions. First, it constitutes the basic idea that the EU and its organs have to comply with the rule of law, not only when acting internally but also when acting externally. However, Article 21 TEU is not restricted to such a requirement to *respect* the rule of law when acting externally.[24] Actually, secondly, it also demands from the EU and its organs to *promote* the rule of law abroad, meaning to globally strengthen and support it beyond its own territory and jurisdiction ("which it seeks to advance in the wider world"; Article 21 (2) TEU).[25] This dimension, which is of specific relevance here, becomes even more evident when reading Article 21 TEU in conjunction with Article 3

23 Vedder, *supra* note 16, 120.

24 I. Vianello, 'The Rule of Law as a Relational Principle Structuring the Union's Action Towards its External Partners', in M. Cremona (ed), *Structural Principles in EU External Relations Law* (2018), 225.

25 Vedder, *supra* note 16, 115-119, 123, 127, 141; R. Geiger, D. E. Khan & M. Kotzur, *Commentary European Union Treaties* (2015), Art. 21, para. 9, 13; V. Kube, 'The European Union's External Human Rights Commitment: What is the Legal Value of Art. 21 TEU?', EUI Working Papers 2016/10, 26-29.

(5) TEU, which explicitly points out, that "[i]n its relations with the wider world, the Union shall uphold and promote its values and interests".

2. *The Legally Binding Character of Article 21 TEU*

Though not undisputed,[26] Article 21 TEU has to be considered as legally binding.[27]

This first and foremost follows from its explicit wording ("shall be guided", "shall seek", "shall pursue", "shall work for").[28]

a. ECJ Judgement *H v. Council and Commission*

Such literal interpretation of Article 21 TEU is also supported by the ECJ's (Grand Chamber) recent judgment in *H v. Council and Commission*.[29] The case did not directly concern the particular issue of Article 21 TEU as a legal guiding principle for the promotion of the rule of law abroad but instead dealt with the construction of CJEU jurisdiction in the field of Common Foreign and Security Policy (where such jurisdiction is principally excluded, Article 24 (1) TEU, Article 275 TFEU). However, in its findings, the ECJ reasoned the necessity of an effective judicial remedy even with respect to EU operational actions outside of the EU (in this case, the *European Union Police Mission in Bosnia and Herzegovina*), *inter alia*, with a reference to the rule of law demands of Article 21 TEU, and with that made Ar-

---

26 For a rather skeptical approach see e.g. S. Oeter, 'Art. 21', in H.-J. Blanke & S. Mangiameli (eds), *TEU Commentary* (2013), paras. 41-43.

27 Vedder, *supra* note 16, 137-138; Larik, 'Entrenching Global Governance', *supra* note 9, 10-12, 15-16; Cremona, 'Structural Principles', *supra* note 16, 12; M. Krajewski, 'The Reform of the Common Commercial Policy', in A. Biondi, P. Eeckhout & S. Ripley (eds), *EU-Law After Lisbon* (2012), 292, 296-298; J. Larik, *Foreign Policy Objectives in European Constitutional Law* (2016), 154-156 [Larik, Foreign Policy Objectives]; J. Larik, 'Shaping the International Order as an EU Objective', in Kochenov & Amtenbrink, *supra* note 9, 62, 78-86.

28 See European Commission, *English Style Guide – A handbook for authors and translators in the European Commission* (2016), 49, which states: "*Positive imperative*. To impose an obligation or a requirement, EU legislation uses *shall*." (emphasis added).

29 *H v. Council and Commission*, Case No. C-455/14 P, Judgment of 19 July 2016, ECLI:EU:C:2016:569.

ticle 21 TEU a normative standard against which EU external actions were legally measured. The judgment reads:

> "In that regard, it must be noted that, as is apparent from both Article 2 TEU, which is included in the common provisions of the EU Treaty, and Article 21 TEU, concerning the European Union's external action, to which Article 23 TEU, relating to the CFSP, refers, the European Union is founded, in particular, on the values of equality and the rule of law [...]. The very existence of effective judicial review designed to ensure compliance with provisions of EU law is inherent in the existence of the rule of law [...]."[30]

b. Opinion of Advocate General *Wathelet* in *Western Sahara Campaign UK*

An additional indicator of the legally binding character of Article 21 TEU is the quite explicit recent opinion of Advocate General *Wathelet* in *Western Sahara Campaign UK*.[31] The opinion – which concerned the *Fisheries Partnership Agreement between the European Community and the Kingdom of Morocco* and its Protocol setting out the fishing opportunities and financial contribution provided for in that agreement – explicitly states that Article 21 TEU forms a legal standard with respect to the EU's external actions. It reads:

> "Thus, the obligations imposed by an international agreement cannot have the effect of prejudicing the constitutional principles of the EU and FEU Treaties, such as Article 3 (5) TEU and Article 21 TEU, [...].[32] The Fisheries Partnership Agreement between the European Community and the Kingdom of Morocco and the Protocol between the European Union and the Kingdom of Morocco setting out the fishing opportunities and financial contribution provided for in that agreement are incompatible with Article 3(5) TEU, the first subparagraph of Arti-

30 *H v. Council and Commission*, Case No. C-455/14 P, Judgment of 19 July 2016, ECLI:EU:C:2016:569, para. 41.

31 Opinion of Advocate General *Wathelet*, *Western Sahara Campaign UK v. Commissioners for Her Majesty's Revenue and Customs and Secretary of State for Environment, Food and Rural Affairs*, Case No. C-266/16, Opinion of 10 January 2018, ECLI:EU:C:2018:1.

32 *Ibid*., para. 100.

cle 21 (1) TEU, Article 21 (2) (b) and (c) TEU and Articles 23 TEU and 205 TFEU […]."[33]

c. (Procedural) Consequences and Relativity

The direction to promote the rule of law in EU foreign policy laid down in Article 21 TEU, therefore, is not to be considered optional but establishes a legal obligation for the EU and its organs.

Accordingly, being part of the EU primary law, Article 21 TEU can also be made a standard of judicial review before the CJEU.[34] The actual possibility to measure an act of foreign policy against the requirements of Article 21 TEU could, for example, occur in the review of an envisaged international treaty in an Article 218 (11) TFEU procedure or in the context of reviewing the enactment of foreign policy-related EU secondary laws, e.g. in an Article 263 (1) TFEU annulment procedure over a Council decision on the signing of an international treaty.[35] Consequently, noncompliance with the requirement to promote the rule of law under Article 21 TEU could ultimately render an action illegal.

However, although of legally binding nature, certain aspects have to be pointed out that put the requirements of Article 21 TEU into perspective.[36] First, an obligation to promote the rule of law in foreign policy is necessarily a rather vague obligation, allowing for multiple paths of compliance.[37] Second, Article 21 TEU does not only mention the rule of law but also a number of other principles to be promoted in EU foreign policy (such as human rights, democracy, European security, international peace, environmentally sustainable development, or international economic liberalization, to name but a few). Although many of these principles are compatible and even mutually reinforcing, scenarios of incoherence or conflict

33 Opinion of Advocate General *Wathelet*, *Western Sahara Campaign UK v. Commissioners for Her Majesty's Revenue and Customs and Secretary of State for Environment, Food and Rural Affairs*, Case No. C-266/16, Opinion of 10 January 2018, ECLI:EU:C:2018:1, para. 286.

34 Kube, *supra* note 25, 26-29; Vianello, *supra* note 24, 228-230.

35 Vedder, *supra* note 16, 138; R. Geiger, D. E. Khan & M. Kotzur, *Commentary European Union Treaties* (2015), Art. 218, paras. 20-24; for an overview on the CJEU's jurisdiction with respect to EU foreign policy see P. Craig & G. de Burca, *EU Law: Text, Cases, and Materials* (2015), 369-375.

36 Larik, 'Much More Than Tarde,' *supra* note 6, 16-17.

37 Pech, 'Rule of Law,' *supra* note 3, 12; Oeter, *supra* note 26, para. 41; Cremona, 'Structural Principles,' *supra* note 16, 11-13.

seem possible. With Article 21 TEU not establishing a hierarchy among its principles, this, again, suggests that Article 21 TEU necessarily needs to allow for a certain flexibility with respect to its realization (as long as a certain consistency is ensured, Article 21 (3) TEU).[38] And third, when it comes to judicial review, the CJEU – though far from adopting an approach of a "particularity of foreign policy"[39] – grants the EU and its organs a certain margin of appreciation with respect to EU foreign policy decisions.[40]

Accordingly, for the assertion of an actual violation of the obligation to promote the rule of law abroad under Article 21 TEU, one would need to assume a rather severe disregard or neglect of the rule of law in an external context.

III. The EU's Rule of Law Concept With Respect to its External Promotion

With the recognition of the EU's legal obligation to promote the rule of law in its foreign policy, a question naturally arises as to which specific concept of the rule of law applies in this external regard.

1. Absence of an Explicit External EU Rule of Law Concept

Answering the above question is not easy since neither EU primary law nor CJEU adjudication provides for an explicit definition or conceptual description of the rule of law contained in Article 21 TEU.

However, with Article 21 (1) TEU stating that the EU's actions on the international scene shall be guided by principles "which have inspired [the EU's] own creation", much suggests that the concept of the rule of law to be promoted abroad corresponds to the one that already applies within the EU.[41] Respectively, in its recent (aforementioned) judgment of *H v. Council and Commission*, the ECJ has also implied this comparability of the two rule of law conceptions when, in the same sentence, the Court referred to

---

38 Kube, *supra* note 25, 11.

39 See *supra* B. I. 1.

40 On the discretion in the field of the EU's external economic relations see e.g. *Odigitria v. Council and Commission*, Case No. T-572/93, Judgment of 6 July 1995, [1995] ECR II-02025, para. 38; see also Vedder, *supra* note 16, 137; Cremona, 'A Reticent Court?', *supra* note 18, 25-31; Vianello, *supra* note 24, 232-235.

41 Speaking of "reflection" in this regard, Oeter, *supra* note 26, para. 27.

the EU's rule of law principle in internal and external dimensions without making any conceptual distinctions:

> "In that regard, it must be noted that, as is apparent from both Article 2 TEU, which is included in the common provisions of the EU Treaty, and Article 21 TEU, concerning the European Union's external action, [...], the European Union is founded, in particular, on the values of [...] the rule of law [...]."[42]

Accordingly, answering the question as to which specific concept of the rule of law has to be promoted by the EU in its external actions requires outlining the sophisticated concept of the rule of law that has developed *within* the EU legal order (2.).

Subsequently, this section shall assess whether EU foreign policy actually meets this (rather sophisticated) internal concept when promoting the rule of law abroad (3.).

2. *The (Internal) EU Rule of Law*

Generally, the concept of the rule of law can best be described as a set of principles organizing the relationship between a community and its governing institutions aiming at the subjection of power to law[43] – namely the principles of legality, the public monopoly of power, the supremacy of the law, the separation of powers, effective judicial remedies, and legitimacy.[44]

---

42 *H v. Council and Commission*, Case No. C-455/14 P, Judgment of 19 July 2016, ECLI:EU:C:2016:569, para. 41.

43 See M. Krygier, 'Rule of Law (and Rechtsstaat)', in J. R. Silkenat, J. E. Hickey Jr. & P. D. Barenboim (eds), *The Legal Doctrines of the Rule of Law and the Legal State (Rechtsstaat)* (2014) 45, 46; R. Grote, 'Rule of Law, Rechtsstaat and 'Etat de droit'', in C. Starck (ed), *Constitutionalism, Universalism and Democracy – A Comparative Analysis* (1999), 269, 270.

44 In its traditional form, the rule of law can be divided into six core principles. First, a community must be organized by general, clear, public and accessible, prospective, and predictive laws, being equally applied, instead of being ruled arbitrarily, in the sense of random individual decisions prone to unrestrained passion, bias, prejudice etc. (legality). Second, the right and power to enforce compliance with the law must lie with the public governing institutions and not with private actors (public monopoly of power). Third, the governing institutions themselves must be bound by the law (supremacy of the law). Fourth, the power of the governing institutions must be separated into independent branches, establishing checks and balances among them (separation of powers). Fifth, accessible, independent, effective, and fair mechanisms to settle legal disputes must exist, in particular al-

Mainly developed in the course of the struggle over the establishment of governmental powers in the Westphalian Nation-States of the 18th, 19th, and 20th centuries,[45] the rule of law, however, can, as a basic concept, be applied to any legal order that features public governance functions[46] – such as, for example, the EU.

As famously stated in the CJEU's early *Les Verts* decision, the EU legal order is a community based on the rule of law.[47] Among other principles (namely respect for human dignity, freedom, democracy, equality, and respect for human rights, including the rights of persons belonging to minorities), the rule of law also is explicitly mentioned as one of the EU's fundamental principles[48] in Article 2 TEU, forming part of the EU primary law. Accordingly, the subjection of governmental power to law, essentially

---

lowing the governed community to review the exercise of governmental power (effective judicial remedies). Sixth, the governing institutions, in particular with respect to the making, applying, enforcing, and interpreting of the law, must be legitimized by the governed community itself (legitimacy). See T. P. Holterhus, 'The History of the Rule of Law', in F. Lachenmann & R. Wolfrum (eds), 21 *Max Planck Yearbook of United Nations Law* (2018), 430, 432-433 with many further references.

However, beyond this quite widely accepted basis, much theoretical dispute over the rule of law's particular further content needs to be considered unsettled. Definitions range from purely formal to quite substantive approaches; formal definitions again being separated into thinner (demanding governance by general, clear, prospective, predictive, and equally applied laws) and thicker (additionally requiring the governing institutions to be bound and limited by the law as well as by a separation of powers and a certain level of participation of the governed community) versions. Substantive definitions again add features such as individual rights, dignity, justice, substantive equality, and other moral values or welfare. For an overview of the different definitions, see B. Z. Tamanaha, *On the Rule of Law: History, Politics, Theory* (2004), 91-113; Krygier, *supra* note 43, 51-54.

45 See extensively Holterhus, *supra* note 44; see also Tamanaha, *supra* note 44.

46 See R. McCorquodale, 'The Rule of Law Internationally', in C. A. Feinäugle (ed.), *The Rule of Law and its Application to the United Nations* (2016), 51, 55-59; S. Chesterman, 'An International Rule of Law?', 56 *The American Journal of Comparative Law* (2008) 2, 331, 350-360.

47 *"Les Verts" v. European Parliament*, Case No. 294/83, Judgment of 23 April 1986, [1986] ECR 1339, para. 23.

48 The fact that Article 2 TEU refers to them as "values" does not hinder their binding normative character (as principles), see on this issue S. Mangiameli, 'Article 2 [The Homogeneity Clause]', in H.-J. Blanke & S. Mangiameli (eds), *The Treaty on European Union (TEU)* (2013), para. 7; W. Schroeder, 'The European Union and the Rule of Law – State of Affairs and Ways of Strengthening', in Schroeder (ed), 'Rule of Law in Europe', *supra* note 1, 3, 14-15 [Schroeder, EU and Rule of Law]; D. Kochenov, 'The Acquis and Its Principles: The Enforcement of the 'Law' vs. the

to be accomplished by the above-named six core principles, constitutes a supreme legal imperative within the EU legal order ("the rule of law is the source of fully justiciable principles applicable within the EU legal system"[49]). Therefore, the rule of law as a principle legally binds and limits all EU organs and institutions with respect to their exercise of governmental powers, be it in administrative, judicial, or legislative matters.[50]

In need of an operationalization within the EU, the rule of law has experienced a broad and detailed concretization of its principles and sub-principles (*Werner Schroeder* fittingly speaks of a "conceptual puzzle"[51]). Such concretization is not only to be found in other EU primary law (e.g. in the numerous treaty provisions on the checks and balances among the EU's institutions or the judicial rights in the *EU Charter of Fundamental Rights*) but also in CJEU adjudication which extensively formed and developed rule of law aspects as general principles of EU law (being part of EU primary law as well[52]).[53]

Today, numerous such principles have been established within the EU legal order.[54] These include, *inter alia*, legality (of administrative action),[55]

Enforcement of 'Values' in the European Union', in A. Jakab & D. Kochenov (eds), *The Enforcement of EU Law and Values* (2017), 9, 9-12.

49 European Commission, *Annexes to the Communication of the Commission to the European Parliament and the Council – A New EU Framework to strengthen the Rule of Law* (11.3.2014), (COM(2014)) 158 final, 1.

50 See Schroeder, 'EU and Rule of Law', *supra* note 48, 14-15; Vianello, *supra* note 24, 231-232, on the binding character of principles in general see A. Jakab, 'Concept and Function of Principles', in M. Borowski (ed), *On the Nature of Legal Principles* (2009), 145, 152-158; see also generally A. von Bogdandy, 'Founding Principles of EU Law', 16 *European Law Journal* (2010) 2, 95.

51 Schroeder, 'EU and Rule of Law', *supra* note 48, 25.

52 On the hierarchical legal status of general principles of EU law see Craig & de Burca, *supra* note 35, 111-112.

53 T. von Danwitz, 'The Rule of Law in the Recent Jurisprudence of the ECJ', in Schroeder (ed), 'Rule of Law in Europe', *supra* note 1, 155.

54 See European Commission, *Annexes to the Communication of the Commission to the European Parliament and the Council – A New EU Framework to strengthen the Rule of Law* (11.3.2014), (COM(2014)) 158 final, 1; for an overview see also Schroeder (ed), 'Rule of Law in Europe', *supra* note 1, Part II; T. Konstadinides, *The Rule of Law in the European Union* (2017), 45-102.

55 *Nölle v. Council and Commission*, Case No. T-167/94, Judgment of 18 September 1995, [1995] ECR II-2589, para. 73; *New Europe Consulting and others v. Commission*, Case No. T-231/97, Judgment of 9 July 1999, [1999] ECR II-2403, para. 41.

the requirement of a legal basis for the exercise of governmental powers,[56] State liability,[57] legal certainty,[58] equality before the law,[59] institutional balance (being the separation of powers within the EU),[60] effective judicial remedies,[61] fair trial,[62] the protection of legitimate expectations,[63] prohibition of retroactivity,[64] and proportionality.[65]

As has been indicated above, it is this sophisticated internal rule of law conception of Article 2 TEU that, according to the wording of Article 21

56 *France v. Commission*, Case No. C-325/91, Judgment of 16 June 1993, [1993] ECR I-3283, para. 26; *France v. Commission*, Case No. T-240/04, Judgment of 17 September 2007, [2007] ECR II-4038, para. 31.

57 *Francovich and Others v. Italy*, Case No. C-6/90 and C-9/90, Judgment of 19 November 1991, [1991] ECR I-5357, para. 35; *Brasserie du pêcheur v. Factortame*, Case No. C-46/93 and C-48/93, Judgment of 5 March 1996, [1996] ECR I-1029, para. 31.

58 *Deutsche Milchkontor GmbH v. Germany*, Case No. 205-215/82, Judgment of 21 September 1983, [1983] ECR 2633, 2669, para. 30; *France v. Commission*, Case No. C-325/91, Judgment of 16 June 1993, [1993] ECR I-3283, para. 26; *BGL v. Germany*, Case No. C-78/01, Judgment of 23 September 2003, [2003] ECR I-9543, para. 71.

59 *Racke v. Hauptzollamt Mainz*, Case No. 283/83, Judgment of 13 November 1984, [1984] ECR 3791, 3800; *EARL de Kerlast v. Unicopa*, Case No. Case C-15/95, Judgment of 17 April 1997, [1997] ECR I-1961, para. 35.

60 *Parliament v. Council*, Case No. C-70/88, Judgment of 22 May 1990, [1990] ECR I-02041, paras. 21-26; *Parliament v. Council*, Case No. C-133/06, Judgment of 6 May 2008, [2008] ECR I-3189, para. 57.

61 *Johnston v. Chief Constable of the Royal Ulster Constabulary*, Case No. 222/84, Judgment of 15 May 1986, [1986] ECR 1651, paras. 13-21 and 58; *UNECTEF v. Heylens*, Case No. 222/86, Judgment of 15 October 1987, [1987] ECR 4097, para. 14.

62 *Baustahlgewebe v. Commission*, Case No. C-185/95 P, Judgment of 17 December 1998, [1998] ECR I-8417, para. 21; *Ordre des barreaux francophones et germanophone and Others*, Case No. C-305/05, Judgment of 26 June 2007, [2007] ECR I-5305, para. 29.

63 *Töpfer v. Commission*, Case No. 112/77, Judgment of 3 May 1978, [1978] ECR 1019, 1033, para. 19; *Deutsche Milchkontor GmbH v. Germany*, Case No. 205-215/82, Judgment of 21 September 1983, [1983] ECR 2633, 2667; *France and Ireland v. Commission*, Case No. C-296/93 and C-307/93, Judgment of 29 February 1996, [1996] ECR I-795, para. 59.

64 *Kirk*, Case No. 63/83, Judgment of 10 July 1984, [1984] ECR 2689, 2781, paras. 21-22; *Fedesa and Others*, Case No. C-331/88, Judgment of 13 November 1990, [1990] ECR I-4023, paras. 42-44.

65 *Testa*, Case No. 41/79, 121/79 and 769/79, Judgment of 19 June 1980, [1980] ECR 1979, 1997, para. 21; *Schräder v. Hauptzollamt Gronau*, Case No. 265/87, Judgment of 11 July 1989, [1989] ECR 2237, para. 21; *Pietsch v. Hauptzollamt Hamburg-Waltershof*, Case No. C-296/94, Judgment of 4 July 1996, [1996] ECR I-3409, para. 15.

(1) TEU and relevant case law, also needs to be understood as the concept of the rule of law the EU is obliged to promote abroad.

3. *The Rule of Law Conception in EU Foreign Policy Practice*

Accordingly, in its foreign policy, the EU does actively implement an external rule of law conception, which is not a reduced version but rather is comparable to the sophisticated conception applied internally.

This is demonstrated not only by EU organs' international treaty making practice but also by the EU's internal strategy documents with respect to the rule of law promotion in the trade and development nexus (see below a.-d.).[66]

a. In the Context of the *Cotonou Agreement*

A distinct example of the concept of the rule of law, which the EU applies when promoting it externally, can be found in the EU's most comprehensive international trade and development agreement, namely the Partnership Agreement between the EU and the 79 States of the African, Caribbean, and Pacific Group of States, more generally known as the ACP Group (the *Cotonou Agreement* – which shall also be considered with respect to the particular issue of rule of law conditionality in more detail below[67]).

The key provision in this regard is Article 9 *Cotonou Agreement*, in which the treaty parties agree to the reciprocal contractual obligation to implement and uphold rule of law-coherent domestic orders. Being an important legal tool in the EU's external rule of law promotion, Article 9 *Cotonou Agreement* (under the heading "Essential elements regarding human rights, democratic principles and the rule of law, and fundamental element regarding good governance") lists a number of rule of law principles such as: "transparent and accountable governance", an "organization of the state to ensure the legitimacy of its authority, the legality of its actions reflected in its constitutional, legislative and regulatory system, and the existence of participatory mechanisms" as well as "clear decision-making pro-

66 See on this similarity also Pech, 'Promoting the Rule of Law Abroad', *supra* note 9, 114-115.

67 See *supra* C. II.

cedures at the level of public authorities, transparent and accountable institutions, the primacy of law".[68]

It also points out that:

> "The structure of government and the prerogatives of the different powers shall be founded on rule of law, which shall entail in particular effective and accessible means of legal redress, an independent legal system guaranteeing equality before the law and an executive that is fully subject to the law."[69]

An even more explicit documentation of the EU's sophisticated concept of the rule of law with respect to its external promotion in the trade and development nexus can already be found in the EU Commission's early 1998 *pre-Cotonou Agreement communication*: "Democratisation, the rule of law, respect for human rights and good governance: the challenges of the partnership between the European Union and the ACP States".[70] The communication emphasizes elements such as the limitation of governmental power through the requirement of legality, a public monopoly of power, the separation of powers, effective judicial remedies, and governmental legitimacy:

> "The primacy of the law is a fundamental principle of any democratic system seeking to foster and promote rights, whether civil and political or economic, social and cultural. This entails means of recourse enabling individual citizens to defend their rights. The principle of placing limitations on the power of the State is best served by a representative government drawing its authority from the sovereignty of the people. The principle must shape the structure of the State and the prerogatives of the various powers. It implies, for example; a legislature respecting and giving full effect to human rights and fundamental freedoms; an independent judiciary; effective and accessible means of legal recourse; a legal system guaranteeing equality before the law; a prison system respecting the human person; a police force at the service of the

68 Article 9 (1), (2), (3) *Cotonou Agreement.*

69 Article 9 (2) *Cotonou Agreement.*

70 Commission of the European Communities, *Communication from the Commission to the Council and The European Parliament – Democratisation, the rule of law, respect for human rights and good governance: the challenges of the partnership between the European Union and the ACP States* (12.03.1998), (COM(1998)) 146 final.

law; an effective executive enforcing the law and capable of establishing the social and economic conditions necessary for life in society.[71] Legality means the existence of clear-cut rules that are applied to all citizens without discrimination. It is reflected in: an appropriate constitutional, legislative and regulatory system;[72] Effective application requires that the behavior and practices of the authorities, institutions and legal persons be consistent with the rule of law [...] It is against this background that the State's institutional set-up, transparent institutions and decision-making, institutional capacities and the existence of supervisory bodies acquire their full significance. This is a long-term process affecting both the structure of the State and its administration and the constitution of a democratic culture enabling the different social forces to interact and strengthen each other.[73] Effective application involves: [...] the separation of powers, which curbs the powers of the State and relates specifically to: the independence of the legislative and judicial powers from the executive power; the effective exercise of the three powers; [...] transparency and integrity of the institutions: [...] operational and independent control mechanisms; citizens' access to administrative services; regulations conducive to fighting corruption."[74]

b. In the *Action Plan on Human Rights and Democracy 2015-2019*

This level of sophistication in the EU's international treaty practice is confirmed by more recent EU statements in this regard (although the EU lately tends to discuss its concepts of external rule of law promotion under the captions of human rights, good governance, or sustainability). An insightful document with respect to the trade and development nexus is the Council's *Action Plan on Human Rights and Democracy 2015-2019*.[75] Within

---

71 Commission of the European Communities, *Communication from the Commission to the Council and The European Parliament – Democratisation, the rule of law, respect for human rights and good governance: the challenges of the partnership between the European Union and the ACP States* (12.03.1998), (COM(1998)) 146 final, 4-5.

72 *Ibid.*, 6.

73 *Ibid.*, 6.

74 *Ibid.*, 6-7.

75 Council of the European Union, *Council Conclusions on the Action Plan on Human Rights and Democracy 2015-2019*, (20.07.2015) Doc. 10897/15, Annex [Action

the annex category "Boosting Ownership of Local Actors; Delivering a comprehensive support to public institutions," the Action Plan lists specific goals of an external promotion of the rule of law, such as:

> "Monitor and promote at bilateral and multilateral level the compliance by partner countries of their international obligations in terms of access to justice and fair trial at all stages of the legal process; [...]; promote the independence of the judiciary; facilitate access to justice at local level (No. 4 b., Targeted support to justice systems)."[76]

or

> "Continue strengthening good governance and the rule of law through support to the separation of powers, independence and accountability of democratic institutions; promote the role of domestic actors in reform processes, including constitutional reforms, in order to better reflect the interests of various stakeholders (No. 5 a., Providing comprehensive support to public institutions)."[77]

c. In the 2017 *European Consensus on Development*

The same level of sophistication with respect to the rule of law conception can be found in the joint 2017 *European Consensus on Development*.[78] The Consensus again enumerates for the external sphere much of what is considered the EU's rule of law concept internally, putting a particular empha-

---

Plan]. The Action Plan is a political non-legally binding action plan adopted by the Council with respect to the EU's external relations. Stating, in para. I: "With this Action Plan, the Council reaffirms the European Union's commitment to promote and protect human rights and to support democracy worldwide".

76 Action Plan, *supra* note 75, Annex, No. 4 (Targeted support to justice systems).

77 *Ibid.*, Annex, No. 5 a. (Providing comprehensive support to public institutions).

78 Joint Statement by the Council and the Representatives of the Governments of the Member States Meeting within the Council, the European Parliament and the Commission, *The New European Consensus on Development – 'Our World, our Dignity, our Future'* (30.06.2017), 2017/C 210/01 [2017 European Consensus on Development]. The 2017 *European Consensus on Development* is a political, non-legally binding joint statement by the *Council*, the *European Parliament*, and the *European Commission* with the purpose, as per para. 6, "to provide the framework for a common approach to development policy that will be applied by the EU institutions and the Member States while fully respecting each other's distinct roles and competences" and to "guide the action of EU institutions and Member States in their cooperation with all developing countries".

sis on the existence of institutional checks and balances, governmental legitimacy, and the access to effective judicial remedies:

> "Good governance, democracy and the rule of law are vital for sustainable development. The rule of law is a prerequisite for the protection of all fundamental rights. Effective governance institutions and systems that are responsive to public needs deliver essential services and promote inclusive growth, while inclusive political processes ensure that citizens can hold public officials to account at all levels. The EU and its Member States will promote accountable and transparent institutions, [...]. They will promote independent and impartial courts, and support the provision of fair justice, including access to legal assistance. They will support capacity building for strong institutions and multi-level governance [...].[79]
> The EU and its Member States will foster efficient, transparent, independent, open and accountable justice systems and will promote access to justice for all – in particular the poor and persons in vulnerable situations."[80]

Interestingly, the Consensus also explicitly links its efforts of rule of law promotion to the above-discussed obligations under Article 21 TEU:

> "In line with the objectives set out in Article 21 (2) TEU, development policy also contributes, inter alia, to supporting democracy, the rule of law [...].[81]
> The EU and its Member States will promote the universal values of democracy, good governance, the rule of law and human rights for all, because they are preconditions for sustainable development and stability, across the full range of partnerships and instruments in all situations and in all countries, including through development action."[82]

79 2017 European Consensus on Development, *supra* note 78, para. 61.
80 *Ibid.*, para. 63.
81 *Ibid.*, para. 11.
82 *Ibid.*, para. 6.

d. In the *UN 2030 Agenda for Sustainable Development*

The 2017 *European Consensus on Development* also explicitly[83] incorporates and aims at framing the implementation of the *UN 2030 Agenda for Sustainable Development*,[84] which again, in Sustainable Development Goal 16, sets out a rule of law concept that is quite close to the EU's internal conception.[85]

> "Goal 16. Promote peaceful and inclusive societies for sustainable development, provide access to justice for all and build effective, accountable and inclusive institutions at all levels
> […]
> 16.3 Promote the rule of law at the national and international levels and ensure equal access to justice for all
> […]
> 16.5 Substantially reduce corruption and bribery in all their forms
> 16.6 Develop effective, accountable and transparent institutions at all levels
> 16.7 Ensure responsive, inclusive, participatory and representative decision-making at all levels
> […]
> 16.a Strengthen relevant national institutions, including through international cooperation, for building capacity at all levels, in particular in developing countries, to prevent violence and combat terrorism and crime
> 16.b Promote and enforce non-discriminatory laws and policies for sustainable development."

83 2017 European Consensus on Development, *supra* note 78, para. 5; see also chapters 1 and 5, "The EU's Response to the 2030 Agenda" and "The EU as a Force for the Implementation of the 2030 Agenda" respectively.

84 UN General Assembly, *Transforming our world: the 2030 Agenda for Sustainable Development*, A/RES/70/1, 21 October 2015.

85 On the rule of law as a Sustainable Development Goal in the 2030 Agenda see N. Arajärvi, 'The Rule of Law in the 2030 Agenda', 10 *Hague Journal on the Rule of Law* (2018) 1, 187, 205-209.

C. Legal Mechanism of Rule of Law Conditionality in EU Foreign Policy

As has been stated above, this article aims to emphasize the legal dimensions of the rule of law promotion in EU foreign policy.

So far, it has been established that EU foreign (trade and development) policy is not a particular and legally detached, but instead a widely legally determined field and that Article 21 TEU actually legally obliges the EU to promote the rule of law in its external actions. It has also been shown that the concept of the rule of law promoted abroad corresponds to the sophisticated rule of law concept applied within the EU.

However, it is not only the *if* but also the *how* of external rule of law promotion that holds a *legal* dimension (and is organized by *legal* means). This legal permeation is particularly well-illustrated by the EU's rule of law conditionality mechanism – a key legal instrument in this regard, especially when it comes to the promotion of the rule of law in the foreign trade and development nexus.[86] Rule of law conditionality in this context is to be understood as a mechanism that puts benefits granted by the EU in the international sphere (trade preferences, development cooperation, etc.) under the legal condition of a certain behavior or deliverable of a third State, namely the domestic implementation and upholding of a rule of law-coherent legal order (so-called *carrot-and-stick policy*).[87]

The EU employs the legal mechanism of conditionality to fulfill its external Article 21 TEU obligations quite extensively, not only via unilateral/autonomous instruments but also in its bilateral/contractual relationships.[88] Two manifestations of the EU's rule of law conditionality in the trade and development nexus are particularly well-suited to illustrate its legal functioning, namely the GSP+ (I.), and the *Cotonou Agreement*'s essen-

---

86 See Cremona, 'Values in EU Foreign Policy,' *supra* note 3, 292-307; Pech, 'Rule of Law,' *supra* note 3, 13-28; for an early assessment, though with a particular focus on human rights conditionality, see L. Bartels, *Human Rights Conditionality in the EU's International Agreements* (2005) [Bartels, Human Rights].

87 See (with a particular focus on human rights conditionality) Bartels, 'Human Rights,' *supra* note 86, 1-2.

88 With respect to contractual rule of law conditionality (see in detail *supra* at C. II. 1), the Treaties Office Database of the European External Action Service lists no less than 28 international agreements of the EU which make the domestic implementation and upholding of a rule of law-coherent legal order an essential element of the respective treaty (full text search in the 'Inventory of Agreements containing the Human Rights Clause,' SG.AFFGEN.3 Legal Affairs Division, available at http://ec.europa.eu/world/agreements/ClauseTreatiesPDFGeneratorAction.do?clauseID=26 (last visited 13 December 2018)).

tial elements clause and noncompliance procedure (II.). The GSP+ mechanism forms part of the autonomous instruments, while the *Cotonou Agreement*'s essential elements clause and noncompliance procedure form part of the contractual relationships.

I. GSP+

1. Unilateral Rule of Law Conditionality in the GSP+

Since 1971, the EU unilaterally grants trade preferences (easier access to the EU's common market, in particular through reduced tariffs) to developing countries under its so-called *generalized scheme of preferences* (GSP).[89]

This approach is currently based on the *GSP Regulation*[90] which explicitly aims to achieve "the objectives of the Union policy in the field of development cooperation, laid down in Article 208 of the TEU" (that refers back to Article 21 TEU).[91] The *GSP Regulation* also states that:

> "By providing preferential access to the Union market, the scheme should assist developing countries in their efforts to reduce poverty and promote good governance and sustainable development by helping them to generate additional revenue through international trade, which can then be reinvested for the benefit of their own development and, in addition, to diversify their economies."[92]

To this end, the preferential status is granted to all eligible developing countries, namely low-income or lower-middle income developing countries as listed in Annex I of the *GSP Regulation*.

However, apart from this general scheme, the *GSP Regulation* additionally establishes a special incentive scheme (the GSP+), offering extended trade benefits under certain conditions.

---

89 For a (historical) overview, with a particular focus on WTO law compatibility, of the EU's GSP+ scheme see P. Hilpold, 'The 'Politicisation' of the EU Development Policy', 9 *Trade Law & Development* (2017) 2, 89, 95-99; see also L. Bartels, 'The Trade and Development Policy of the European Union', in M. Cremona (ed), *Developments in EU External Relations Law* (2008), 128 [Bartels, The Trade and Development Policy].

90 Regulation (EU) No. 978/2012 of the European Parliament and Council of 25 October 2012 [GSP Regulation].

91 Recital 4 *GSP Regulation*.

92 Recital 7 *GSP Regulation*.

The most significant condition for admittance to the GSP+ is that the respective developing country has ratified (without reservations) and effectively implemented a list of 27 international conventions on core human and labor rights, environmental protection, and good governance, listed in Annex VIII of the Regulation. This condition also remains effective after admittance. If an admitted country seriously and systemically violates its obligations or terminates a convention, the GSP+ preferences are suspended or withdrawn.[93] The burden of proof with respect to the compliance with the GSP+ conditions rests with the beneficiary developing country.[94]

Although the 27 conventions listed in Annex VIII predominantly concern human rights, labor rights, or the protection of the environment, a rule of law dimension to the conditionality scheme does also exist. First, Annex VIII includes the *UN Convention Against Corruption* – with the absence of corruption being an essential sub-element of the rule of law principles of legality and the supremacy of the law. Second, Annex VIII demands the ratification of the *International Covenant on Civil and Political Rights*[95] (ICCPR) whose guarantees, although in the form of individual human rights, are closely interlinked and partly overlap with the rule of law – in particular with respect to Articles 14, 15, 25 and 26 ICCPR, establishing structural obligations regarding e.g. equality before the law, access to justice and effective judicial remedies, fair trial, the prohibition of retroactivity as well as certain basic aspects of democratic participation.

The unilateral GSP+ mechanism might therefore not be considered the EU's most significant rule of law conditionality instrument; it does, however, add to the EU's overall approach of rule of law promotion through legal means.

2. *Case Study – Sri Lanka (2009)*

The functionality of the instrument could be well-observed in the process of withdrawing Sri Lanka's GSP+ preferences in 2009. In the context of Sri Lanka's application for a renewal of its GSP+ eligibility (first granted in 2005), the EU in 2008 launched an independent expert's investigation with

93 Article 19 (1) (a) *GSP Regulation*.

94 Article 15 (2) *GSP Regulation*.

95 *International Covenant on Civil and Political Rights*, 16 December 1966, 999 UNTS 171, [ICCPR].

respect to the State of Sri Lanka's implementation of the GSP+ relevant conventions.[96]

Among the exposure of multiple other shortcomings, the investigation concluded that Sri Lanka lacked effective implementation of Article 14 ICCPR, in particular the guarantees of access to effective judicial remedies and a fair trial, both essential elements of the rule of law. Although Sri Lanka's Constitution *de jure* provided for judicial independence, the investigation concluded that, in fact, the judiciary showed critical shortcomings with respect to its independence, was subject to severe political interference (unjustified threats of impeachment, arbitrary dismissals, or transfers of judges), and also showed a remarkable inefficiency regarding the conviction of government officials.[97]

By applying the *GSP Regulation*'s standards to these deficiencies, the EU withdrew GSP+ preferences in October 2009[98] and in August 2010 Sri Lanka reverted to the general scheme GSP (not regaining its GSP+ status until 2017[99]).

The *Bertelsmann Transformation Index*,[100] which monitors and measures the development of governance factors such as democracy, market econo-

---

96 F. Hampson, L. Sevon & R. Wieruszewski, 'The Implementation of Certain Human Rights Conventions in Sri Lanka' (2009), Report for the European Commission.

97 *Ibid.*, 39-40, 101-104; see also C. Portela & J. Orbie, 'Sanctions under the EU Generalised System of Preferences and Foreign Policy: Coherence by Accident?', in M. Carbone & J. Orbie (eds), *The Trade-Development Nexus in the European Union: Differentiation, Coherence and Norms* (2016), 63, 69.

98 Implementing Regulation (EU) No 143/2010 of the Council, of 15 February 2010 temporarily withdrawing the special incentive arrangement for sustainable development and good governance provided for under Regulation (EC) No 732/2008 with respect to the Democratic Socialist Republic of Sri Lanka, 53 *Official Journal of the EU* L45 (20.02.2010); see also European Commission, Press Release, 'EU Temporarily Withdraws GSP+ Trade Benefits from Sri Lanka' (15 February 2010), available at http://trade.ec.europa.eu/doclib/docs/2010/february/tradoc_145799.pdf (last visited 13 December 2018).

99 Commission Delegated Regulation (EU) 2017/836 of 11 January 2017 amending Annex III to Regulation (EU) No 978/2012 of the European Parliament and of the Council applying a scheme of generalized tariff preferences, 60 *Official Journal of the EU* L125 (18.05.2017); see also European Commission, Press Release, 'EU Grants Sri Lanka Improved Access to its Market as Incentive for Reform', IP/17/1363 (17 May 2017), available at http://europa.eu/rapid/press-release_IP-17-1363_en.htm (last visited 13 December 2018).

100 Data available at https://www.bti-project.org/en/home/ (Transformation Atlas, Time Series, Sri Lanka 2006-2018, category: democracy, rule of Law) (last visited 13 December 2018).

my, and also the rule of law, provides some noteworthy data on Sri Lanka in this regard.

When inspecting the data (see next page), it turns out that the EU withdrew GSP+ benefits in 2009 at the beginning of a significant decline in the level of the rule of law in the Sri Lankan legal order. Then, after Sri Lanka achieved a significant recovery in the rule of law level in 2016, GSP+ benefits were re-granted in 2017. Although it appears difficult to prove a direct causality between Sri Lanka's desire for GSP+ benefits and the recovery of the Sri Lankan rule of law, the correlation of these developments is quite remarkable.

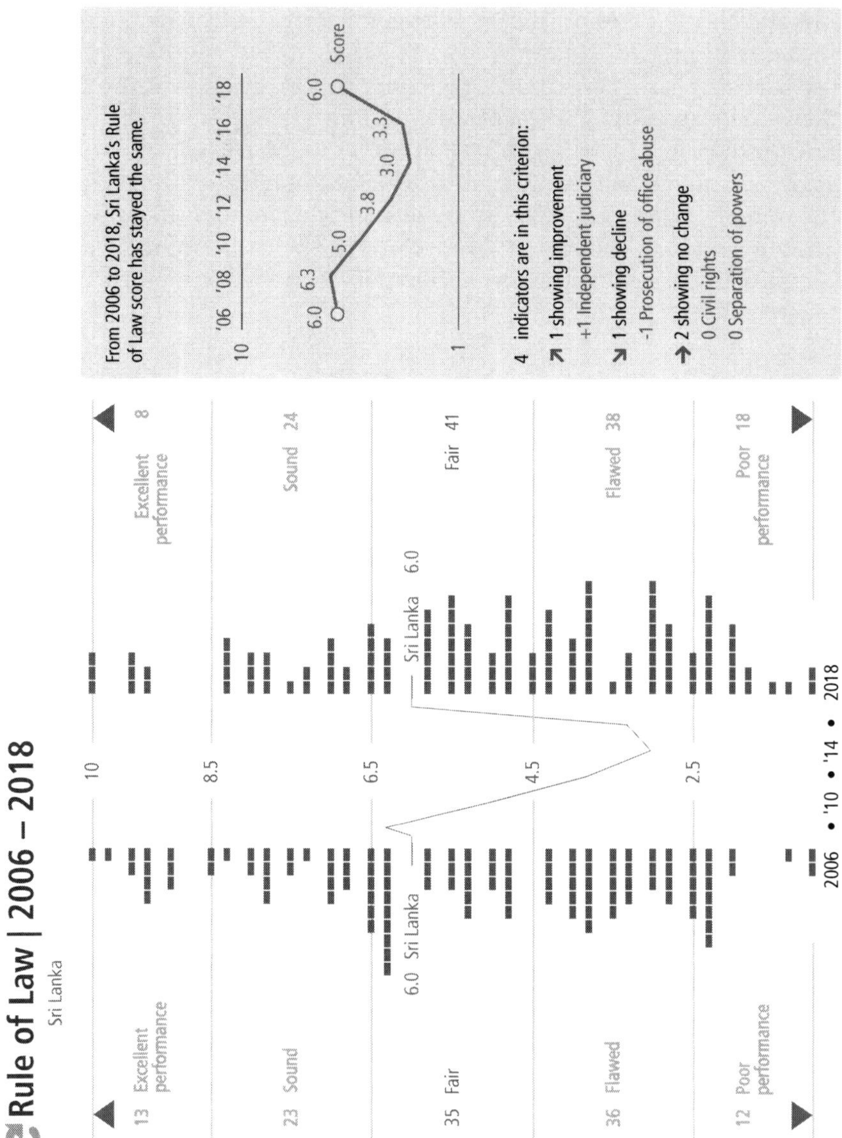
Rule of Law | 2006 – 2018
Sri Lanka
13 Excellent performance
23 Sound
35 Fair
36 Flawed
12 Poor performance
10
8.5
6.5
4.5
2.5
6.0 Sri Lanka
Sri Lanka 6.0
2006 • '10 • '14 • 2018
Excellent performance 8
Sound 24
Fair 41
Flawed 38
Poor performance 18
From 2006 to 2018, Sri Lanka's Rule of Law score has stayed the same.
'06 '08 '10 '12 '14 '16 '18
10
1
6.0 6.3 5.0 3.8 3.0 3.3 6.0
Score
4 indicators are in this criterion:
1 showing improvement
+1 Independent judiciary
1 showing decline
-1 Prosecution of office abuse
2 showing no change
0 Civil rights
0 Separation of powers

II. Cotonou Agreement

1. Contractual Rule of Law Conditionality in the Cotonou Agreement

When it comes to contractual relationships, the most relevant instrument of the EU's rule of law conditionality approach in the trade and development nexus can be found within the *Cotonou Agreement* of 2000.

The *Cotonou Agreement*, succeeding the *Lomé Convention* (*Lomé I – Lomé IV-bis*), is a comprehensive and overarching international framework agreement between the EU and its Member States on the one side and the 79 members of the African, Caribbean, and Pacific Group of States (ACP States) on the other. With the primary objective of reducing and eventually eradicating poverty in the ACP States (Article 1 *Cotonou Agreement*), the *Cotonou Agreement* legally organizes the supportive relationship between the EU and the ACP States with respect to development cooperation, political cooperation, and economic and trade cooperation.[101]

Support provided through means of development cooperation is usually granted in the form of financial and technical assistance under the Articles 59-78 *Cotonou Agreement*. With respect to the economic and trade cooperation, however, the *Cotonou Agreement* itself does not provide for substantive contractual trade liberalization as such, but only for a framework of objectives and principles. The specificities of the actual substantive reciprocal trade liberalization (market access, reduction of tariffs and nontariff trade barriers, etc.) are intended by the *Cotonou Agreement* to be arranged in ad-

101 Partnership Agreement between the Members of the African, Caribbean and Pacific Group of States of the one Part, and the European Community and its Member States of the other Part, signed in Cotonou on 23 June 2000 (OJ L317/3, 15.12.2000) as amended by the Agreement signed in Luxembourg on 25 June 2005 (OJ L209/27, 11.8.2005) and the Agreement signed in Ouagadougou on 22 June 2010 (OJ L287/3, 4.11.2010). For a comprehensive overview on the (historical development of the) *Cotonou Agreement* see C. Gammage, *North-South Regional Trade Agreements as Legal Regimes* (2017), 137-168; see also Bartels, 'The Trade and Development Policy,' *supra* note 89.

ditional so-called *Economic Partnership Agreements* (EPAs)[102] between the EU and different regional groups of the ACP States.[103]

To this day, a number of such regional EPA's have been concluded or are presently negotiated,[104] one of the most recent being the *Economic Partnership Agreement Between the European Union and its Member States, of the one Part, and the SADC EPA States, of the Other Part* (EU-SADC EPA)[105] of 2016 (currently in provisional application). With this EU-SADC EPA, the EU admits to an extensive scheme of reciprocal trade liberalization by agreeing to full market access and the elimination of almost all tariffs and quotas on goods imported from the *Southern African Development Community* (SADC).

a. Essential Elements Clause (Article 9 *Cotonou Agreement*)

The aforementioned rule of law conditionality mechanism of the *Cotonou Agreement* is enshrined in two central provisions, namely Articles 9 and 96 *Cotonou Agreement*.

102 With a clear development agenda, the EU had (under the *Lomé Conventions*) for over 25 years granted substantive trade preferences to the ACP States nonreciprocally. Due to the incompatibility of such nonreciprocal and discriminating trade preferences with WTO law, the *Cotonou Agreement*'s framework for economic and trade cooperation now (WTO waiver expired in 2007) only allows for trade liberalization to be arranged on a reciprocal basis. To take account of the differing demands of such reciprocal trade liberalization with the various ACP States, the *Cotonou Agreement* introduced the supplementary instrument of the regional EPAs (Article 36 *Cotonou Agreement*) see Hilpold, *supra* note 89, 99-106.

103 The ACP States have, based on Article 35 (2) *Cotonou Agreement*, formed seven regional groups to enter into EPAs: the *Economic Community of West African States* (ECOWAS); the *Economic and Monetary Community of Central Africa*; the *Southern African Development Community* (SADC); the *East African Community*; the *Eastern and Southern Africa* (ESA); the *Caribbean Community with the Dominican Republic* (CARIFORUM); the *Pacific Region*.

104 For an overview see European Commission, Overview of Economic Partnership Agreements [online], last updated March 2018, available at http://trade.ec.europa.eu/doclib/docs/2009/september/tradoc_144912.pdf (last visited 13 December 2018).

105 *Economic Partnership Agreement Between the European Union and its Member States, of the one Part, and the SADC EPA States, of the Other Part*, 16 September 2016, OJ L250, 3 [EU-SADC EPA]; for a comprehensive overview on the EU-SADC EPA see C. Gammage, *North-South Regional Trade Agreements as Legal Regimes* (2017), 231-267.

Although the Articles 9 and 96 *Cotonou Agreement* theoretically apply mutually, their obvious purpose – considering the dissimilar relationship of the EU and the ACP States, with the *Cotonou Agreement* essentially being an instrument of EU development cooperation – is to establish a (rule of law) monitoring mechanism to be predominantly used by the EU.

Article 9 *Cotonou Agreement* establishes the treaty parties' obligation to implement and uphold a rule of law-coherent domestic legal order as an "essential element" of the overall contractual relationship. Differing from the GSP+ mechanism, rule of law conditionality within the *Cotonou Agreement* therefore does not work as a unilateral (or autonomous) instrument but as part of a contractual relationship within an international treaty. Article 9 *Cotonou Agreement* ("Essential elements regarding human rights, democratic principles and the rule of law, and fundamental element regarding good governance") reads:

> "1. Cooperation shall be directed towards sustainable development centered on the human person [...].
> Respect for all human rights and fundamental freedoms, including respect for fundamental social rights, democracy based on the rule of law and transparent and accountable governance are an integral part of sustainable development.
> 2. The Parties refer to their international obligations and commitments concerning respect for human rights. [...]
> The Parties reaffirm that democratisation, development and the protection of fundamental freedoms and human rights are interrelated and mutually reinforcing. Democratic principles are universally recognised principles underpinning the organisation of the State to ensure the legitimacy of its authority, the legality of its actions reflected in its constitutional, legislative and regulatory system, and the existence of participatory mechanisms. [...]
> The structure of government and the prerogatives of the different powers shall be founded on rule of law, which shall entail in particular effective and accessible means of legal redress, an independent legal system guaranteeing equality before the law and an executive that is fully subject to the law.
> Respect for human rights, democratic principles and the rule of law, which underpin the ACP-EU Partnership, shall [...] constitute the essential elements of this Agreement.
> 3. In the context of a political and institutional environment that upholds human rights, democratic principles and the rule of law, good governance is the transparent and accountable management of human,

> natural, economic and financial resources for the purposes of equitable and sustainable development. It entails clear decision-making procedures at the level of public authorities, transparent and accountable institutions, the primacy of law in the management and distribution of resources and capacity building for elaborating and implementing measures aiming in particular at preventing and combating corruption.
> Good governance, which underpins the ACP-EU Partnership, shall [...] constitute a fundamental element of this Agreement. The Parties agree that serious cases of corruption, including acts of bribery leading to such corruption, as referred to in Article 97, constitute a violation of that element."

b. Suspension Procedure (Article 96 *Cotonou Agreement*)

The *Cotonou Agreement* does not stop at declaring the implementation and upholding of a rule of law-coherent domestic legal order a contractual obligation between the EU and the ACP States but additionally establishes a sophisticated legal procedure to be applied in cases of noncompliance. The procedure is enshrined in Article 96 *Cotonou Agreement* ("Essential elements: consultation procedure and appropriate measures as regards human rights, democratic principles and the rule of law"). It reads:

> "1. Within the meaning of this Article, the term 'Party' refers to the Community and the Member States of the European Union, of the one part, and each ACP State, of the other part.
> [...]
> 2. (a) If, despite the political dialogue on the essential elements [...], a Party considers that the other Party fails to fulfil an obligation stemming from respect for human rights, democratic principles and the rule of law referred to in Article 9 (2), it shall, except in cases of special urgency, supply the other Party and the Council of Ministers with the relevant information required for a thorough examination of the situation with a view to seeking a solution acceptable to the Parties. To this end, it shall invite the other Party to hold consultations that focus on the measures taken or to be taken by the Party concerned to remedy the situation in accordance with Annex VII.
> The consultations shall be conducted at the level and in the form considered most appropriate for finding a solution.
> [...]

> If the consultations do not lead to a solution acceptable to both Parties, if consultation is refused or in cases of special urgency, appropriate measures may be taken. These measures shall be revoked as soon as the reasons for taking them no longer prevail.
> (b) The term 'cases of special urgency' shall refer to exceptional cases of particularly serious and flagrant violation of one of the essential elements referred to in paragraph 2 of Article 9, that require an immediate reaction.
> [...]
> (c) The 'appropriate measures' referred to in this Article are measures taken in accordance with international law, and proportional to the violation. In the selection of these measures, priority must be given to those which least disrupt the application of this agreement.
> It is understood that suspension would be a measure of last resort."

Based on a careful reading, Article 96 *Cotonou Agreement* does not only provide for a consultation procedure if a party to the agreement is not fulfilling its rule of law obligations under Article 9 *Cotonou Agreement* (namely the obligation to implement and uphold a rule of law-coherent domestic legal order) but, more significantly, also explicitly allows for appropriate measures to be taken, in accordance with international law, if the consultations do not result in the cessation of the violations.

Appropriate measures in accordance with international law, meaning in accordance with Article 60 of the *Vienna Convention on the Law of Treaties*[106] (VCLT), comprise the suspension of the treaty or proportional parts of it (although considered a measure of last resort under Article 96 (2) (c) *Cotonou Agreement*).[107]

Such (partial) suspension under Article 96 (2) (a) and (c) *Cotonou Agreement* (in accordance with Article 60 VCLT) can theoretically concern all obligations agreed upon under the framework of the *Cotonou Agreement*.[108] It can, therefore, and often will (see the case study on Guinea-Bissau below) concern ongoing development programs already agreed upon under Articles 59-78 *Cotonou Agreement*.[109]

---

106 *Vienna Convention on the Law of Treaties*, 23 May 1969, 1155 UNTS 331 [VCLT].

107 Vedder, *supra* note 16, 135.

108 See T. Giegerich, 'Art. 60', in O. Doerr & K. Schmalenbach (eds), *The Vienna Convention on the Law of Treaties – A Commentary* (2018), 1095, para. 43.

109 Technically, pursuant to Article 17 of Annex IV (Implementation and Management Procedures) to the *Cotonou Agreement*, financial assistance, for instance, is granted through a financing agreement drawn up by the Commission and the ACP State (or the relevant organization or body at regional or intra-ACP level).

Somewhat more complex is the suspension of contractual trade preferences as an appropriate measure under Article 96 *Cotonou Agreement*, since these trade preferences, as has been discussed above, are not agreed upon directly within the *Cotonou Agreement*, but are granted via supplementary EPAs.[110] However, where the respective EPA explicitly incorporates the *Cotonou Agreement*'s essential elements clause, as, for example, the EU-SADC EPA does in its Article 2,[111] the suspension of trade preferences granted under the EPA is also feasible as an appropriate measure under Article 96 *Cotonou Agreement*.[112]

The noncompliance procedure under Article 96 *Cotonou Agreement* therefore offers the EU an effective legal instrument to conditionalize benefits in the trade and development nexus with the rule of law implementation in the respective ACP States. On account of, *inter alia*, *coup d'états*, flawed elections, or systematic rule of law violations, the Article 96 procedure has been invoked over 15 times since the conclusion of the *Cotonou Agreement* in 2000 – including procedures against Fiji (2000, 2007), Zimbabwe (2002), the Central African Republic (2003), Guinea-Bissau (2004, 2011), Togo (2004), Madagascar (2010), and Burundi (2015).[113]

These financing agreements then usually comprise a reference to the *Cotonou Agreement* treaty obligations and, again, explicitly specify that breaches of such obligations relating to respect of the rule of law may result in the suspension of the financing agreement. See, as an example, Article 23.1 of the 2012 'EDF Model Financial Agreement of the EU Commission' (Annex I General Conditions), available at https://ec.europa.eu/europeaid/sites/devco/files/general-conditions-financing-agreement-2012-edf_en.pdf (last visited 13 December 2018).

110 See on this issue in general Giegerich, *supra* note 108, para. 44 and with a particular focus on EPA's L. Beke et al., *The Integration of Human Rights in EU Development and Trade Policies*, FRAME, 2014, 63-64.

111 Article 2 (Principles) EU-SADC EPA reads:
"(1) This Agreement is based on the Fundamental Principles, as well as the Essential and Fundamental Elements, as set out in Articles 2 and 9, respectively, of the Cotonou Agreement. [...]
(2) This Agreement shall be implemented in a complementary and mutually reinforcing manner with respect to the Cotonou Agreement [...]."

112 The EU-SADC EPA does additionally stipulate its own dispute settlement mechanism with the possibility to adopt appropriate measures in case of noncompliance, Articles 75-87 EU-SADC EPA.

113 See European Council and Council of the European Union, 'Consultation Procedure (Article 96)', last updated February 2018, available at http://www.consilium.europa.eu/de/policies/cotonou-agreement/article-96-cotonou-agreement/ (last visited 13 December 2018).

2. Case Study – Guinea-Bissau (2011)

The application of Articles 9 and 96 *Cotonou Agreement*, with respect to the EU's rule of law conditionality approach, is well-illustrated by the procedures launched against Guinea-Bissau in 2011.[114]

In April 2010, military unrest took place in Guinea-Bissau, in the course of which the Guinea-Bissauan Prime Minister was arrested and eventually left the country while the coup's main instigators were appointed to high-ranking military positions. Furthermore, arbitrary detentions and illegal conduct of the acting security forces occurred and looting took place.[115] The significant interference with the Guinea-Bissauan constitutional order by this illegal military seizure of power gave rise to multiple rule of law concerns, in particular with respect to legality, the public monopoly of power, the supremacy of the law, and the separation of powers, as well as to the legitimacy of the governing institution.[116]

As a response, in January 2011, the EU launched consultations under Article 96 *Cotonou Agreement* with the Guinea-Bissauan authorities, considering the developments "a serious and evident breach of essential elements set out in Article 9 of the Cotonou Agreement".[117] However, the consultations, until their conclusion in July 2011, did not resolve the situation.

Consequently, the EU, as an "appropriate measure" under Article 96 *Cotonou Agreement*, suspended large parts of its ongoing budget support as well as other development cooperation within Guinea-Bissau and started to channel the remaining funding directly to the population through NGOs and international organizations. The suspension was scheduled to end in July 2012.[118]

However, due to the further deterioration of the rule of law in Guinea-Bissau, in particular with the 2012 overt military *coup d'état* during the na-

---

114 For an overview on the Guinea-Bissau procedures in particular see also European Council and Council of the European Union, 'Consultation Procedure (Article 96)', last updated February 2018, available at http://www.consilium.europa.eu/de/policies/cotonou-agreement/article-96-cotonou-agreement/ (last visited 13 December 2018).

115 For an extensive assessment see UNSC, *Report of the Secretary-General on developments in Guinea-Bissau and on the activities of the United Nations Integrated Peacebuilding Office in that country*, UN Doc S/2010/335, 24 June 2010.

116 Council of the European Union, Press Release, *Opening of Consultations With the ACP Side on Guinea-Bissau Under Article 96 of the Cotonou Agreement*, 8405/11 (29 March 2011).

117 *Ibid.*, 1.

118 Council Decision of 18 July 2011, OJ 2011 L 203.

tional election process, resulting in another displacement of the government and the illegal establishment of a so-called Transitional National Council by the military leadership and its supporters,[119] the suspension was extended.[120]

It was not until March 2015 that the suspension was finally lifted,[121] following a slowly emerging normalization of the situation, the basic restoration of Guinea-Bissau's constitutional order, and the free elections in 2014.[122]

D. Conclusion

It has been shown that Article 21 TEU (as well as Article 3 (5) TEU and Articles 205, 207 (1), 208 (1), 209 (2) TFEU) legally oblige the EU to pro-

---

119 UNSC, *Statement by the President of the Security Council*, UN Doc S/PRST/2012/15, 21 April 2012; for an extensive assessment see UNSC, *Report of the Secretary-General on developments in Guinea-Bissau and on the activities of the United Nations Integrated Peacebuilding Office in that country*, UN Doc S/2012/554, 17 July 2012.

120 Suspension was extended until 19 July 2013 by Council Decision 2012/387/EU of 16 July 2012, OJ 2012 L 187 and, subsequently, until 19 July 2014 by Council Decision 2013/385/EU of 15 July 2013, OJ 2013 L 194. Council Decision 2014/467/EU of 14 July 2014, OJ 2014 L 212 extended the validity of Council Decision 2011/492/EU of 18 July 2011, OJ 2011 L 203 by one year, until 19 July 2015, but suspended the application of the appropriate measures.

121 Council Decision (EU) 2015/541, OJ 2015 L 88; see Council of the European Union, Press Release, *EU to Resume Cooperation with Guinea-Bissau*, 11664/14 (14 July 2014) "The EU High Representative for Foreign Affairs and Security Policy, Catherine Ashton, and the EU Commissioner for Development, Andris Piebalgs, said: 'We are indeed very satisfied with this decision since it enables the EU to support the newly elected authorities on their path towards the reconstruction and stabilisation of the state by helping them rapidly to ensure vital state functions and provide basic social services to the population.' While today's decision suspends measures limiting EU cooperation with Guinea-Bissau, the EU expects that the Guinea-Bissauan authorities make every effort to fulfil their commitments to the EU as a matter of priority. These undertakings were made during consultations with the EU in 2011 and concern for instance the reform of the security sector, the renewal of the military hierarchy and the fight against impunity."; see also European Commission, Press Release, *A Fresh Start for Guinea-Bissau: EU to Resume Cooperation and Provide New Support*, IP/15/4663 (25 March 2015).

122 For an extensive assessment see UNSC, *Report of the Secretary-General on the restoration of constitutional order in Guinea-Bissau*, UN Doc S/2014/332, 12 May 2014.

mote the rule of law in its foreign trade and development policy. To fulfill this obligation, the EU employs, as a key instrument, the legal mechanism of rule of law conditionality, not only via unilateral/autonomous instruments but also in its bilateral/contractual relationships. The EU's foreign trade and development policy can, therefore, be considered as a process extensively determined and organized by means of law.

Four distinct conclusions can be drawn from these findings.

First, the functioning and development of the EU foreign trade and development policy, with respect to rule of law promotion, can neither be understood nor described without due consideration being afforded to, first and foremost, its legal grounding and permeation.

Second, the EU's hegemonial aspirations of *exporting* its values, are, in principle, not open to political debate. Instead, these aspirations derive from and are decided by a constitutional legal imperative of the EU treaties.

Third, the EU's choice to fulfill its foreign policy obligations by combining its leading position in the trade and development nexus with legal means of rigid conditionality (as opposed to e.g. diplomatic persuasion) demonstrates a quite firm commitment to promoting the rule of law abroad. With this combination, the EU can be seen as making a rather uncompromising use of its capacities as a normative power.

Fourth and final, the legal entrenchment of the above-described values and their promotion affords a certain predictability of the future direction of EU foreign policy – a welcome assurance in a currently quite unstable and unpredictable global international order.

The Dawn of Article 18 ECHR – A Safeguard Against European Rule of Law Backsliding?

Floris Tan[*]

Table of Contents

* Floris Tan, PhD candidate at the Grotius Centre for International Legal Studies, Leiden University. The research for this article was carried out as visiting researcher at the European Court of Human Rights, Strasbourg. The visit was sponsored by the Leiden University Fund / Kroese-Duijsters Fonds. I would like to thank Leonie Huijbers and the anonymous peer-reviewers for their thoughtful comments on an earlier draft.

Abstract

This article examines an underexplored avenue for the protection of the rule of law in Europe: Article 18 of the *European Convention on Human Rights*. This provision prohibits States from restricting the rights enshrined in the *European Convention* for any other purpose than provided for in the Convention. In this contribution, the author argues, based on a combination of textual, systematic and purposive interpretations of Article 18, that the provision is meant to safeguard against rule of law backsliding, in particular because governmental restrictions of human rights under false pretenses present a clear danger to the principles of legality and the supremacy of law. Such limitations of rights under the guise of legitimate purposes go against the assumption of good faith underlying the Convention, which presupposes that all States share a common goal of reinforcing human rights and the rule of law. Article 18 could therefore function as an early warning that European States are at risk of becoming an illiberal democracy or even of reverting to totalitarianism and the destruction of the rule of law. The article then goes on to assess the extent to which the European Court's case-law reflects and realizes this aim of rule of law protection, and finds that whereas the Court's earlier case-law left very little room for an effective application of Article 18, the November 2017 Grand Chamber judgment in *Merabishvili v. Georgia* has made large strides in effectuating the provision's *raison d'être*. As the article shows, however, even under this new interpretation, challenges remain.

A. Introduction

On the European level, the rule of law is safeguarded by multiple institutions on various levels. The primary organization engaged with the rule of law is the *Council of Europe* (CoE), obliging its members to "accept the principles of the rule of law".[1] Within this system, the *European Convention on Human Rights* (ECHR or Convention) and its Court enjoy most of the limelight, primarily due to the power of the Court to take binding judicial decisions.[2] Although the protection of human rights is often considered to be only one aspect of the rule of law, and the Convention does not contain

1 *Statute of the Council of Europe*, 5 May 1949, Article 3, 87 UNTS 103.

2 The Court itself has characterized the Convention as "a constitutional instrument of European public order", see among other authorities, *Al-Dulimi and Montana*

a right to be governed by the rule of law as such, the Court has nevertheless read certain rule of law requirements into the Convention. To this end, it held that "[o]ne reason why the signatory Governments decided to 'take the first steps for the collective enforcement of certain of the Rights stated in the Universal Declaration' was their profound belief in the rule of law".[3] This reasoning has led the Court to recognize the rule of law as "a concept inherent in all the Articles of the Convention",[4] and to employ it in the interpretation of various Convention rights.[5]

Beyond such interpretations, the Convention also contains a provision that could be considered specifically geared to the protection of the rule of law within the CoE. It concerns the rarely invoked – even more rarely found to be violated[6] – Article 18 of the Convention which provides that: "The restrictions permitted [to the rights and freedoms under the ECHR] shall not be applied for any purpose other than those for which they have been prescribed." At first glance this provision merely reiterates the obvious; when restricting rights, States must comply with the restriction clauses accompanying those rights. However, numerous judges, in separate opinions and invoking the *travaux préparatoires*, have expressed their belief that Article 18 was included in the Convention "as a defence against abusive limitations of Convention rights and thus to prevent the

---

Management Inc. v. Switzerland [GC], ECtHR Application No. 5809/08, Judgment of 21 June 2016, para. 145. Further on this subject, see E. A. Alkema, 'The European Convention as a Constitution and its Court as a Constitutional Court', in P. Mahoney *et al.* (eds.), *Protection des Droits de l'Homme: La Perspective Européenne/ Protecting Human Rights: The European Perspective. Mélanges à la Mémoire de/Studies in Memory of Rolv Ryssdal* (2000), 41, 41-63.

3 *Golder v. The United Kingdom*, ECtHR Application No. 4451/70, Judgment of 21 February 1975, para. 34.

4 *Mozer v. The Republic of Moldova and Russia* [GC], ECtHR Application No. 11138/10, Judgment of 23 February 2016, para. 134; *Baka v. Hungary* [GC], ECtHR Application No 20261/12, Judgment of 23 June 2016, para. 117 [Baka v. Hungary [GC]].

5 *Baka v. Hungary* [GC], *supra* note 4, for the right to access to court. See also *Brumărescu v. Romania* [GC], ECtHR Application No. 28342/95, Judgment of 28 October 1999, para. 61, pertaining to legal certainty and the finality of judicial decisions.

6 Also according to the Court itself, see *Khodorkovskiy and Lebedev v. Russia*, ECtHR Application No. 11082/06 and 13772/05, Judgment of 25 July 2013, para. 898 [Khodorkovskiy and Lebedev v. Russia].

resurgence of undemocratic regimes in Europe"[7] – indicating their view of Article 18 as a bulwark against dictatorial rule and as part of the arsenal of the militant democracy.[8] Such a view has also been defended in scholarly debate.[9]

The argument in essence provides that Article 18 protects against abuse of power (*détournement de pouvoir*) by outlawing the restriction of rights for any *ulterior purpose* – in other words, where rights are restricted in a way that serves a *hidden agenda*.[10] By way of example, several States have used their criminal justice systems and their powers of detention to take out political dissidents, detaining them under false pretenses – sometimes at tactical moments in order to frustrate their political ambitions.[11] Such limitations of rights under the guise of legitimate purposes go against the assumption of good faith underlying the Convention, which presupposes that all States share a common goal of reinforcing human rights and the rule of law. Article 18 could therefore function as an early warning system for European States who are at risk of becoming an illiberal democracy or even of reverting to totalitarianism and the destruction of the rule of law – a function that might prove crucial given the worrisome contemporary de-

7 Joint Partly Dissenting Opinion of Judges *Nicolaou*, *Keller* and *Dedov* to *Navalnyy and Ofitserov v. Russia*, ECtHR Application No. 46632/13 and 28671/14, Judgment of 23 February 2016, para. 2 [Navalnyy and Ofitserov v. Russia].

8 See also R. de Lange, 'Case Note: *Kasparov v. Russia*' (2017), 18 *European Human Rights Cases* 2017/31, para. 9. The author prefers the term *militant democracy* over the Court's terminology of a "democracy capable of defending itself" or "*démocratie apte à se défendre*" for the sake of brevity.

9 See H. Satzger, F. Zimmermann & M. Eibach, 'Does Art. 18 ECHR Grant Protection Against Politically Motivated Criminal Proceedings? Rethinking the Interpretation of Art. 18 ECHR Against the Background of New Jurisprudence of the European Court of Human Rights', 4 *European Criminal Law Review* (2014) 2, 91, 106 [Satzger, Zimmermann & Eibach, Art. 18 Part 1]; H. Satzger, F. Zimmermann & M. Eibach, 'Does Art. 18 ECHR Grant Protection Against Politically Motivated Criminal Proceedings? (Part 2) – Prerequisites, Questions of Evidence and Scope of Application', 4 *European Criminal Law Review* (2014) 3, 248 [Satzger, Zimmermann & Eibach, Art. 18 Part 2]; H. Keller & C. Heri, 'Selective Criminal Proceedings and Article 18 ECHR. The European Court of Human Rights' Untapped Potential to Protect Democracy', 37 *Human Rights Law Journal* (2016) 1, 1.

10 See e.g. *Rasul Jafarov v. Azerbaijan*, ECtHR Application No. 69981/14, Judgment of 17 March 2016, para. 153 [Rasul Jafarov v. Azerbaijan].

11 E.g. *Ilgar Mammadov v. Azerbaijan*, ECtHR Application No. 15172/13, Judgment of 22 May 2014 [Ilgar Mammadov v. Azerbaijan]. This appeared to be the case also in a number of Russian cases, although the Court ultimately did not decide this issue under Article 18. See e.g. *Kasparov v. Russia*, ECtHR Application No. 53659/07, Judgment of 11 October 2016 [Kasparov v. Russia].

velopments in a number of CoE Member States, such as Hungary, Poland, Russia and Turkey.

This potential of Article 18 has not materialized in the Court's case-law thus far.[12] Violations have proved extremely rare, and the burden of proof placed on applicants almost insurmountable. There has been clear dissonance within the Court on this issue, as is exemplified by the numerous separate opinions on this subject in recent years, with judges expressing their, at times, very outspoken and repeated discontent with the line in the Court's jurisprudence.[13] The landmark Grand Chamber judgment of 28 November 2017 in *Merabishvili v. Georgia* seems to take account of these critiques,[14] but as the issue pertaining to Article 18 was decided with a minimal majority of 9 versus 8 judges, and with the Article 18 case of *Navalnyy* pending before the Grand Chamber,[15] the discussion seems far from being put to bed.

Against this background, this contribution explores Article 18 in light of its purpose of protecting the rule of law and its function as an alarm against rule of law backsliding. In doing so, the article, firstly, sets out how restrictions of human rights under false pretenses present an early warning for a dismantling of the rule of law, and it argues that Article 18 was meant to serve as such a warning based on the *travaux préparatoires*, various separate opinions and legal scholarship (section B). Subsequently it critically assesses the Court's case-law under Article 18 from the perspective of rule of law protection, and maps out several problems preventing the realization of these broader rule of law aspirations (section C). These hindrances to Article 18's effective operation provide the framework for discussion of recent developments in the *Merabishvili* Grand Chamber judgment, analyzing how it potentially improves the workability of Article 18 (section D). Section E concludes.

---

12 See also Keller & Heri, *supra* note 9.

13 E.g. Concurring Opinion of Judge *Kūris* appended to *Tchankotadze v. Georgia*, ECtHR Application No. 15256/05, Judgment of 21 June 2016 [Tchankotadze v. Georgia].

14 *Merabishvili v. Georgia* [GC], ECtHR Application No. 72508/13, Judgment of 28 November 2017 [Merabishvili v. Georgia [GC]].

15 The Grand Chamber handed down its judgment in this case after this volume went to press, see *Navalnyy v. Russia*, ECtHR Application No. 29580/12 *et al.*, Judgment of 15 November 2018. For a first reaction, see F. Tan, ,'The European Court's Role as Warden of Democracy and the Rule of Law: Navalnyy v Russia' (2018), available at http://echrblog.blogspot.com/2018/11/guest-blog-on-grand-chamber-judgment-in.html (last visited 16 December 2018).

B. The Rationale of Article 18 ECHR: Protecting the Rule of Law

The aim of the present argument is to analyze the case-law of the Court under Article 18 in light of its role in the protection of the rule of law in the CoE. Before turning to the in-depth case-law analysis, the article therefore begins here by constructing the link between the rule of law and, briefly, the European Convention as a whole, and Article 18 specifically. A first step in doing so is fleshing out the notion of *rule of law* a little bit further as any meaningful connection between it and Article 18 is contingent on a proper understanding of the rule of law as such.

I. The Notion of the Rule of Law

What is the *rule of law*? Many answers are possible, and it goes well beyond the confines of this article to address or even scratch the surface of the full extent of the discussion. Rather, the point is to address certain commonalities in legal scholarship; the *bare fundamentals* of the rule of law, so to speak.[16]

A core commonality appears to be that the concept entails not merely that governments rule *by* law, in the sense that they espouse their orders through legislation, but that there exists a rule *of* law.[17] This entails that State authorities are bound to respect the law, and that their actions must be based in law – also referred to as the principle of legality.[18] This, however, is not all. Legal theorists studying the rule of law usually conceive of the concept in procedural terms,[19] meaning the law must meet a number of formal criteria to be rule of law-compliant. This covers concepts such as those proposed by *Lon Fuller*: generality, publicity, prospectivity, intelligi-

---

16 This discussion is not strictly speaking limited to the rule of law as it was conceived in common law systems, but borrows also from the French *État de droit*, and the German and Dutch *Rechtsstaat*. Such a *European* rule of law conception corresponds with the Preambular consideration that CoE States have a "common heritage" when it comes to the rule of law (*Convention for the Protection of Human Rights and Fundamental Freedoms*, 4 November 1950, Preamble, para. 5, ETS 5 [ECHR]).

17 E.g. M. Krygier, 'Rule of Law', in M. Rosenfeld & A. Sajó (eds.), *The Oxford Handbook of Comparative Constitutional Law* (2012), 233, 234.

18 C. A. J. M. Kortmann, *Constitutioneel recht*, 7th ed. (2016), edited by P. P. T. Bovend'Eert *et al.*, 51-52.

19 J. Waldron, 'The Rule of Law and the Importance of Procedure', in J. E. Fleming (ed.), *Getting to the Rule of Law* (2011), 4.

bility, consistency, practicability, stability, and congruence.[20] What these formal requirements have in common is that they provide for *legal certainty*. Or, put negatively, they ensure legislation is not arbitrary. Combined with the principle of legality, if every exercise of State power must be based in legislation and legislation may not be arbitrary, this provides a strong safeguard against the arbitrary exercise of power as such.

The constraint of State power by law, meeting certain formal criteria, is a fundamental tenet of societies governed by the rule of law, and in this respect the restraint of arbitrary exercise of power is not just a means, but an end in itself.[21] The article will argue below that it is precisely this core rule of law value of non-arbitrariness and governance constrained by law, that is at issue in cases concerning Article 18 of the ECHR.

II. The Specter of Totalitarianism and Rule of Law Protection in the ECHR

The European Convention on Human Rights and the rule of law are closely interlinked. Beyond the Preambular reference to the rule of law, the Court has in its case-law repeatedly referenced the importance of the rule of law – most prominently in its assessments of the quality of national legislation and judicial safeguards, tying in with the procedural conception of the rule of law.[22] Further, when reading the Convention's preparatory works it becomes abundantly clear that the experiences of the Second World War had impressed on the drafters the paramount importance of a Europe governed by the rule of law and democracy. The drafters tellingly considered

> "[d]emocracies do not become Nazi countries in one day. Evil progresses cunningly, with a minority operating, as it were, to remove the levers of control… It is necessary to intervene before it is too late. A

---

20 L. L. Fuller, *The Morality of Law* (1969), as summarized by J. Waldron, 'The Rule of Law and the Importance of Procedure', in J. E. Fleming (ed.), *Getting to the Rule of Law* (2011), 5-6.

21 Krygier, *supra* note 17, 241-242; more extensively, see C. Brettschneider, 'Of the Rule of Law: Nonarbitrary Treatment and the Limits of Procedure', in J. E. Fleming (ed.), *Getting to the Rule of Law* (2011), 52.

22 D. Kosař & K. Šipulová, 'The Strasbourg Court Meets Abusive Constitutionalism: Baka v. Hungary and the Rule of Law', 10 *Hague Journal on the Rule of Law* (2018) 1, 83, 104. On the function of Article 6 ECHR as a safeguard for the rule of law through protection of judicial independence, see R. A. Lawson, 'Protecting the Independence of the Judiciary: Possibilities and Limits of the European Convention on Human Rights', *Journal of the Brazilian Institute of Human Rights* (forthcoming).

> conscience must exist somewhere which will sound the alarm to the minds of a nation, menaced by this progressive corruption, to war[n] them of the peril and to show them that they are progressing down a long road which leads far, sometimes even to Buchenwald or Dachau."[23]

When reading this powerful statement, the reader cannot help but feel the strong imprint that totalitarian rule had left upon the drafters, and their commitment to install a *conscience to sound the alarm* when totalitarianism threatened to emerge and overthrow the rule of law. Moreover, the drafters were keenly aware that this threat comes from within, contemplating as they did that "what we must fear today is not the seizure of power by totalitarianism by means of violence, but rather that totalitarianism will attempt to put itself in power by pseudo-legitimate means".[24] In light of such fears, the drafters not only envisioned a Court[25] to represent the conscience of Europe, but also attempted to limit any risk of the Convention being used by anti-democratic and totalitarian forces to overthrow the rule of law, and install a repressive government. To this effect, they included two specific provisions in the Convention.

Articles 17 and 18 respectively aim to ensure, first, that individuals and groups cannot invoke the Convention with the aim of overthrowing democracy and destroying fundamental rights, and second, that State authorities cannot themselves act in contravention with the rule of law by restricting human rights for ulterior purposes. The first aim is embodied by Article 17,[26] which militates against any abusive reliance on ECHR rights

23 French representative *Pierre-Henri Teitgen* in a speech for the Consultative Assembly in 1949, in Council of Europe, *Collected Edition of the 'Travaux Préparatoires' of the ECHR, Vol. I.* (1975), 266, 292 [TP of the ECHR, Vol. I]. See also E. Bates, *The Evolution of the European Convention on Human Rights. From its Inception to the Creation of a Permanent Court of Human Rights* (2010), 44; and A. C. Buyse, 'Contested Contours. The Limits of the Freedom of Expression from an Abuse of Rights Perspective – Articles 10 and 17 ECHR', in E. Brems & J.H. Gerards, *Shaping Rights in the ECHR. The Role of the European Court of Human Rights in Determining the Scope of Human Rights* (2009), 183.

24 L. Benvenuti, in Council of Europe, *Collected Edition of the 'Travaux Préparatoires' of the ECHR, Vol. II.* (1975), 136.

25 And before it, the *European Commission of Human Rights*.

26 As the focus of this contribution is Article 18, it provides only a very cursory and incomplete overview of Article 17. For a comprehensive and in-depth analysis, see P. E. de Morree, *Rights and Wrongs Under the ECHR. The Prohibition of Abuse of Rights in Article 17 of the European Convention on Human Rights* (2016).

with the aim of destroying the rights enshrined in the Convention.[27] Thus, Article 17 provides a line of defense where groups or individuals attempt to invoke rights such as the freedom of expression and association in order to set up extremist parties propagating Nazism,[28] communism,[29] or other extremist ideologies that cannot coexist with the rights enshrined in the ECHR,[30] or propose a racist regime that allows such rights only for certain groups and not others.[31] Democratic European States therefore do not need to stand idly by where such groups rise to prominence – if they choose to forbid and criminally prosecute such parties and their adherents, they can successfully invoke Article 17 to deflect claims of a violation of the freedom of expression or association. Article 17 in this respect is therefore part of the toolbox of the militant democracy.[32] The second aim is embodied by Article 18, which is discussed in more detail in the next section.

---

27 In the words of the Court, "It cannot be ruled out that a person or group of persons will rely on the rights enshrined in the Convention or its Protocols in order to attempt to derive therefrom the right to conduct what amounts in practice to activities intended to destroy the rights or freedoms set forth in the Convention; any such destruction would put an end to democracy", *Ždanoka v. Latvia* [GC], ECtHR Application No. 58278/00, Judgment of 16 March 2006, para. 99. See also *Perinçek v. Switzerland* [GC], ECtHR Application No. 27510/08, Judgment of 15 October 2015, para. 113.

28 E.g. *W.P. and Others v. Poland* (dec.), ECtHR Application No. 42264/98, Decision of 2 September 2004.

29 European Commission of Human Rights, *German Communist Party v. Germany* (1957), Application No. 250/57, *Documents and Decisions* (1959), 222-225.

30 E.g. *Belkacem v. Belgium* (dec.), ECtHR Application No. 34367/14, Decision of 27 June 2017, para. 27-37, concerning the leader of *Sharia4Belgium* who propagated the enactment of Sharia law in Belgium.

31 E.g. European Commission of Human Rights, *Glimmerveen and Hagenbeek v. The Netherlands* (dec.) (1979), Application No. 8348/78 and 8406/78, DR 18, 187.

32 The article leaves aside the possibility for Article 17 to be invoked against the State, which is rarely assessed on the merits. For an example pertaining to the right to derogate from the Convention, see *The Greek Case – Denmark, Norway, Sweden and the Netherlands v. Greece (Part I)*, Application No. 3321/67 *et al.*, Commission Report of 5 November 1969, para. 222-225. In this case a number of States brought a case against Greece, who under the *Colonels Regime* had derogated from the Convention. In the end, the Commission did not find it necessary to rule on the Article 17 issue, as it had already concluded that the material conditions for a lawful derogation had not been met. Further on Article 17 and militant democracies, see De Morree, *supra* note 26.

III. Article 18 and the Rule of Law

Article 18, contrary to the primary function of Article 17, protects against abuse *by the State* – therefore giving expression to the reality that it is often State authorities themselves who pose the biggest risk to democracy and the rule of law.[33] That Article 18 has a major role to play in safeguarding the rule of law is not self-evident from a cursory reading of the provision, and I will therefore use the remainder of this section to flesh out further the linkages between the two, drawing on the *travaux préparatoires* as well as arguments in separate opinions and legal scholarship. Broadly speaking, the arguments rely on a combination of a textual, systematic and purposive interpretation of Article 18.[34]

Article 18 provides that "the restrictions permitted under this Convention to the said rights shall not be applied for any purpose other than those for which they have been prescribed". This somewhat awkwardly phrased provision has led a largely dormant life, and it was not until 2004 that it was found to be violated for the first time.[35] This very modest role in the Convention system has everything to do with the text of the provision, that appears to do no more than reiterate what is already clear from the limitation clauses accompanying many ECHR provisions:[36] in order for a restriction of a right to be justifiable, it must pursue a legitimate aim. Most rights already provide that restrictions can only be justified when pursuing certain legitimate purposes, such as national security, public safety, to prevent disorder and crime, or the protection of the rights and freedoms of others.[37] Article 18 has on this basis often been interpreted to be no more than a *limitation on limitations*,[38] lacking autonomous meaning and fulfilling a

33 For an excellent elaboration, see Keller & Heri, *supra* note 9, 2-3.

34 These are accepted principles of treaty interpretation both in public international law, and under the ECHR. See Articles 31-32 *Vienna Convention on the Law of Treaties*, and e.g. *Golder v. UK*, *supra* note 3, para. 29.

35 *Gusinskiy v. Russia*, ECtHR Application No. 70276/01, Judgment of 19 May 2004 [Gusinskiy v. Russia]. For a Commission finding of a violation in 1993, later overturned by the Court, see *Quinn v. France*, ECtHR Application No. 18580/91, Judgment of 22 March 1995.

36 Compare W. A. Schabas, *The European Convention on Human Rights: A Commentary* (2015), 623.

37 See e.g. § 2 of Articles 8, 9, 10, 11 ECHR, as well as Article 4 § 3 of Protocol No. 2 ECHR.

38 E.g. P. Santolaya, 'Limiting Restrictions on Rights. Art. 18 ECHR (A Generic Limit on Limits According to Purpose)', in P. Santolaya & J. G. Roca (eds.), *Europe of Rights: A Compendium on the European Convention on Human Rights* (2012), 527.

merely *auxiliary* function.[39] Nevertheless, as *Bill Schabas* rightly notes in his Commentary, Article 18 ECHR is a unique provision, that has no counterpart in other human rights treaties.[40] To illustrate, whereas the *Universal Declaration of Human Rights*[41] and the *EU Charter of Fundamental Rights*,[42] contain provisions limiting restrictions to certain aims, these have to be distinguished from the ECHR system because they are *general limitation clauses*. The Universal Declaration and the EU Charter do not set out limitations per right, but contain just one clause that allows for the limitation of the entire catalogue of rights. In lieu of specific limitation clauses, a provision restricting the aims in pursuance of which rights may be limited serves an obvious purpose: preventing the arbitrary interference with, and hollowing-out of, rights. The inclusion of such a clause in the ECHR, already providing as it does for specific limitation clauses that prescribe an exhaustive list of aims, on the contrary, would be devoid of any meaning if interpreted in this way. Granted, this in itself cannot provide the basis for a wholly autonomous meaning for Article 18, but it is, at the very least, a first indication that it was included for some other purpose.

In construing the object and purpose of Article 18 within the Convention system, most judges (in separate opinions to judgments) and scholars have relied on the *travaux préparatoires* of Article 18. They indeed provide a useful tool to discern what the drafters had in mind for the provision.[43] *Keller* and *Heri* write that the drafters meant for the Court "to prune undemocratic buds from the legal systems of Member States before these can bloom and bear the fruit that represents a larger problem".[44] This finding is supported by the drafters' consideration that the purpose of restricting the

39 Satzger, Zimmermann & Eibach, 'Art 18. Part 1', *supra* note 9, 105-109.

40 Schabas, *supra* note 36, 623.

41 Article 29 (2) of the UDHR provides: "In the exercise of his rights and freedoms, everyone shall be subject only to such limitations as are determined by law solely for the purpose of securing due recognition and respect for the rights and freedoms of others and of meeting the just requirements of morality, public order and the general welfare in a democratic society."

42 Article 52 (1) of the EU Charter provides: "Any limitation on the exercise of the rights and freedoms recognised by this Charter must be provided for by law and respect the essence of those rights and freedoms. Subject to the principle of proportionality, limitations may be made only if they are necessary and genuinely meet objectives of general interest recognised by the Union or the need to protect the rights and freedoms of others."

43 Though some authors find the *travaux* pertaining to Article 18 generally unhelpful, see C. Ovey & R. C. A. White, *Jacobs & White: The European Convention on Human Rights* (2006), 437 and Santolaya, *supra* note 38, 527.

44 Keller & Heri, *supra* note 9, 3.

aims that can justify limiting rights, is "to ensure that no State shall in fact aim at suppressing the guaranteed freedoms, by means of minor measures which, while made with the pretext of organising the exercise of these freedoms on its territory, or of safeguarding the letter of the law, have the opposite effect".[45] The drafters, in other words, feared that States would at some point attempt to limit human rights merely to bolster their own position of power at the expense of the political opposition.[46] Further, they were wary of States doing so under a guise of lawfulness, under the *pretext* of some legitimate aim – in other words that States would limit rights under false pretenses, serving ulterior purposes or hidden agendas. Ultimately, Article 18 was included to counter such tendencies.

When States limit human rights under false pretenses, this violates the rule of law. They must conform to the law and act within the confines of the law, and do so in good faith. When they not only contravene the law, but do so deliberately and they in fact attempt to camouflage this – arguing that a restriction of a right pursues a legitimate purpose, when in fact the State pursued another, hidden aim – this exacerbates the mere violation of the law, and strikes at the heart of the rule of law. After all, the State authorities in this situation maliciously attempt to circumvent the principle of legality and the restrictions the law places on their actions, thereby engaging in a classic form of abuse of power.[47] This is the more so because any effective control of State power is rendered obsolete where the real motivation and purpose behind repressive action is kept secret. In short, this entails a clear disregard of core tenets of the rule of law, legal certainty and non-arbitrariness.

Where States start using the law merely as camouflage for the raw exercise and abuse of power, and thereby prevent individuals from mounting any meaningful legal defense, the rule of law is in clear danger. Article 18 of the ECHR is geared toward situations where States limit rights for ulterior, hidden purposes, and therefore provides a warning signal *par excellence* of rule of law backsliding. It is the hallmark of totalitarianism to misuse the State apparatus and criminal justice system to suppress the opposi-

---

45 French representative *Pierre-Henri Teitgen* in a speech to the Consultative Assembly on 7 September 1949, in *TP of the ECHR, Vol. I, supra* note 23, 276.

46 *Ibid.*

47 See G. Palombella, 'The Abuse of Rights and the Rule of Law', in A. Sajó (ed.), *Abuse: The Dark Side of Fundamental Rights* (2006), 6, explaining the concept of abuse as follows: "The 'abuse' perspective highlights the unlawfulness of infringing an interest on the part of the holder of a right or a power who acts *in apparent compliance with a legal rule*."

tion, civil society and other voices of dissent. When finding a violation of Article 18, the Court therefore truly acts as the conscience of Europe, sounding the alarm the drafters envisioned in 1949.[48] At least, in theory – practice shows that the Court's case-law showcases a number of obstacles to fulfilling this function.

C. *The Defective Application of Article 18 in the Court's Case-Law*

I. *Introduction*

Thus far – or at least until very recently – Article 18's potential as an early warning system for threats to the rule of law has not been realized. This section explains why that has been the case, structuring the discussion of relevant case-law around shortcomings in relation to the effective protection of the rule of law, rather than presenting a chronological case-by-case oversight.[49] The discussion in this light focuses successively on the very limited scope of application of Article 18 (C. II.), and issues pertaining to the burden and standard of proof (C. III.). Together, these issues have limited the application of Article 18 to such an extent, that the Court's function as warden for the rule of law has been rendered largely illusory. The following section, section D., then goes on to address recent developments marked by the landmark Grand Chamber judgment in *Merabishvili v. Georgia*, as this has to an extent changed the outlook.

II. *An Extremely Narrow Scope of Application*

Article 18 pertains to the restrictions of other Convention rights, meaning it can only be applied in conjunction with other Articles of the Conven-

---

48 See also Satzger, Zimmermann & Eibach, 'Art. 18 Part 1', *supra* note 9, 112.

49 This has been done before, see *ibid.*, and Keller & Heri, *supra* note 9; for an extensive historical overview of the case-law, see *Merabishvili v. Georgia* [GC], *supra* note 14, para. 265-281. For a comprehensive discussion of the case-law, see also Directorate of the Jurisconsult & F. Tan, 'Guide on Article 18 of the European Convention on Human Rights, Strasbourg: European Court of Human Rights' (2018), available at https://www.echr.coe.int/Documents/Guide_Art_18_ENG.pdf (last visited 12 December 2018).

tion and has an accessory nature.[50] It is, however, autonomous in the sense that it can be violated even though the right in conjunction with which it was invoked, was not violated separately.[51] Further, a claim under Article 18 is compatible *ratione materiae* with the Convention only where it is invoked in conjunction with a *qualified* right, i.e. a right that is subject to restrictions.[52] As the subject-matter of Article 18 is a situation where State authorities pursued ulterior purposes under the guise of an aim prescribed by the Convention, ill-treatment in contravention with Article 3 for example falls outside the scope of Article 18, as interferences with that right can never be justified, no matter the aim pursued.[53]

So far so good. A closer look at the case-law, however, reveals that the scope of application of Article 18 is limited in two primary ways that prevent it from being an effective tool for the protection of the rule of law. The first addressed here is the Court's practice of declaring it "unnecessary to examine" an Article 18 claim in a variety of situations. This has effectively limited the application of Article 18, to the point where Judge Keller has argued that it is deprived of any scope of application whatsoever.[54] The second issue addressed is that the Court has thus far found violations of Article 18 in conjunction with the right to liberty only – effectively limiting its supervision to situations of abusive pre-trial detention. As the article will argue below, this insufficiently reflects the often broader context of a fully politically motivated criminal prosecution.

The Court's examination of complaints, or lack thereof, under Article 18 of the Convention has thus far been unpredictable. Early cases, up until as recently as 2004, were hardly ever examined on the merits and were most often dismissed for being unsubstantiated.[55] Although the case-law shifted when in 2004 the Court for the first time found a violation of Arti-

50 For the first time, see European Commission of Human Rights, *Kamma v. the Netherlands* (1974), Application No. 4771/71, DR 1, 4; see further e.g. *Gusinskiy v. Russia*, *supra* note 35, para. 73.

51 See *supra* note 50, and for the first application of this in practice, see *Merabishvili v. Georgia* [GC], *supra* note 14.

52 *Merabishvili v Georgia* [GC], *supra* note 14, para. 287.

53 European Commission of Human Rights, *Timurtaş v. Turkey*, Application No. 23531/94, DR 31, para. 329.

54 Writing both on the bench and academically. See the Partly Dissenting Opinion of Judge *Keller* appended to *Kasparov v. Russia*, *supra* note 11 and Keller & Heri, *supra* note 9, 9.

55 See the Court's exposé of its case-law in *Merabishvili v. Georgia* [GC], *supra* note 14, para. 265-269.

cle 18 in the *Gusinskiy* judgment,[56] the Court's willingness to assess Article 18 complaints on the merits has remained haphazard and inconsistent. First, in a number of cases the Court has found it unnecessary to examine the Article 18 complaint despite ostensibly falling within its purview. By way of example, a number of predominantly Russian cases have featured opposition leaders who have been detained for relatively short periods of time, which prevented them from attending opposition manifestations and protests. In these cases, despite finding in its examination under Article 11 that "the applicant's arrest and administrative detention had [had] the effect of preventing and discouraging him and others from participating in protest rallies and actively engaging in opposition politics", the Court nevertheless held it was not necessary to examine the (same) issue under Article 18.[57] This, moreover, is just an example of a broader practice.[58] Second, the Court's practice shows a similar approach in cases where it found no violation of other Convention rights, declaring that as those rights had not been violated, Article 18 was not violated either.[59] When taking these two practices together, no scope of application for Article 18 effectively remains: when the right in conjunction with which it was invoked was not violated, neither is Article 18; when the right in conjunction with which it was invoked was violated, there is no separate issue under Article 18, even if the case pertains to ulterior purposes. This practice undercuts Article 18's autonomous meaning and importance for the protection of the rule of law. Numerous judges have acknowledged this problem, with Judge *Kūris* even writing an 8,500 word dissent to outline the various ways the Court has avoided examining Article 18 on the merits.[60]

56 *Gusinskiy v. Russia*, *supra* note 35.

57 *Nemtsov v. Russia*, ECtHR Application No. 1774/11, Judgment of 31 July 2014, para. 129; *Navalnyy and Yashin v. Russia*, ECtHR Application No. 76204/11, Judgment of 4 December 2014, para. 116 [Navalnyy and Yashin v. Russia]; *Frumkin v. Russia*, ECtHR Application No. 74568/12, Judgment of 5 January 2016, para. 172; *Yaroslav Belousov v. Russia*, ECtHR Application Nos. 2653/13 and 60980/14, Judgment of 4 October 2016, para. 188; *Kasparov and Others v. Russia (No. 2)*, ECtHR Application No. 51988/07, Judgment of 13 December 2016, para. 55 [Kasparov and Others (No. 2)].

58 E.g. *Bozano v. France*, ECtHR Application No. 9990/82, Judgment of 18 December 1986, para. 61. See also the case-law references in *Merabishvili v. Georgia* [GC], *supra* note 14, para. 296.

59 E.g. *Engel and Others v. the Netherlands*, ECtHR Application No. 5100/71 *et al.*, Judgment of 8 June 1976, para. 104; *Handyside v. the United Kingdom*, ECtHR Application No. 5493/72, Judgment of 7 December 1976, para. 52.

60 Concurring Opinion of Judge *Kūris* appended to *Tchankotadze v. Georgia*, *supra* note 13.

When despite the issue outlined above an application *is* examined on the merits, another obstacle arises in cases where applicants allege their prosecution as a whole has been politically motivated, in contravention with the rule of law. Thus far, the Court has found violations of Article 18 only in conjunction with the right to liberty,[61] and save for one or two exceptions[62] all cases where the Court has scrutinized a complaint of misuse of power have similarly related to Article 5. Although pre-trial detention on trumped up charges is certainly an extreme misapplication of power that strikes at the heart of the rule of law, especially when also coinciding with certain important events such as political manifestations or even elections, a finding to that effect nevertheless fails to address the potential political motivation of the criminal proceedings as a whole. That would require applying Article 18 in conjunction with the right to a fair trial enshrined in Article 6, but the Court's case-law has thus far not left much scope for such a complaint. The reasons for this are twofold.

Firstly, the Court has not yet made up its mind when it comes to the question whether Article 6 is subject to restrictions and lends itself to be applied in conjunction with Article 18.[63] The Court recently acknowledged its case-law on this issue has been inconsistent and that the question therefore remains open.[64] This is a significant finding, as on two earlier occasions the Court had declared complaints under Article 18 in conjunction with Article 6 incompatible *ratione materiae* with the Convention – reasoning that as Article 6 is not subject to restrictions, it cannot be restricted for

61 *Gusinskiy v. Russia*, *supra* note 35, para. 78; *Cebotari v. Moldova*, ECtHR Application No. 35615/06, Judgment of 13 November 2007, para. 53; *Lutsenko v. Ukraine*, ECtHR Application No. 6492/11, Judgment of 3 July 2012, para. 110 [Lutsenko v. Ukraine]; *Tymoshenko v. Ukraine*, ECtHR Application No. 49872/11, 30 April 2013, para. 301 [Tymoshenko v. Ukraine]; *Ilgar Mammadov v. Azerbaijan*, *supra* note 11, para. 144; *Rasul Jafarov v. Azerbaijan*, *supra* note 10, para. 163; *Merabishvili v. Georgia* [GC], *supra* note 14, para. 354; *Mammadli v. Azerbaijan*, ECtHR Application No 47145/14, Judgment of 19 April 2018, para. 105.

62 *OAO Neftyanaya Kompaniya Yukos v. Russia*, ECtHR Application No. 14902/04, Judgment of 20 September 2011, para. 663-666 [OAO Neftyanaya Kompaniya Yukos v. Russia]. *Khodorkovskiy and Lebedev v. Russia*, *supra* note 6, likely also falls in this category, though the Court in that case oddly did not specify in conjunction with which provision(s) it applied Article 18.

63 Similarly, see F. Tan, 'Case Note: *Ilgar Mammadov (No. 2)*' (2018), 19 *European Human Rights Cases* 2018/28, 74-79.

64 *Ilgar Mammadov v. Azerbaijan (No. 2)*, ECtHR Application No. 919/15, Judgment of 16 November 2017, para. 261 [Ilgar Mammadov v. Azerbaijan (No. 2)].

ulterior purposes.[65] In both these cases three judges dissented on this point, and in the recent case of *Ilgar Mammadov (No. 2) v. Azerbaijan* the Court unanimously held the questions remains open – with a majority of four judges expressing their preference of referring the case to the Grand Chamber to remedy the inconsistencies in the case-law, but opting not to as the applicant in this case was still in detention, and the case therefore did not allow for a delay of justice of at least a year.[66]

Secondly, where applicants' complaints as to the political motivation of the criminal proceedings lodged against them have not been declared inadmissible, they have met with an insurmountable burden of proof, rendering it practically impossible to prove their case. This is addressed further in the following section.

III. An Insurmountable Burden and Standard of Proof

Applicants have struggled to prove their allegations of a violation of Article 18. As the Court made clear on many occasions, it applied in this context "a very exacting standard of proof" and "[a]s a consequence, there are only few cases where a breach of that Convention provision has been found".[67] The Court's treatment of Article 18 as a provision *sui generis* has made it difficult to rely on it successfully, which has to do with a number of peculiarities. Primary factors have been the one-sided division of the burden of proof, and the "very exacting standard of proof" the Court has until recently used in Article 18 cases.[68] Another less-explored issue pertains to the distinction in the standards applied by the Court depending on whether the case before it concerned a general allegation of political motivation of the criminal prosecution as a whole – in a sense almost amounting to an *in abstracto* accusation of bad faith on the part of the State – and those cases showcasing certain *distinguishable features*, which permitted zooming in on

---

65 *Navalnyy and Ofitserov v. Russia*, *supra* note 7, para. 129-130; *Navalnyy v. Russia*, ECtHR Application No. 101/15, Judgment of 17 October 2017, para. 88 [Navalnyy v. Russia October 2017].

66 Joint Concurring Opinion of Judges *Nußberger*, *Tsotsoria*, *O'Leary* and *Mits*, *Ilgar Mammadov v. Azerbaijan (No. 2)*, *supra* note 64.

67 Amongst others *Khodorkovskiy v. Russia*, ECtHR Application No. 5829/04, Judgment of 31 May 2011, 66, para. 256 [Khodorkovskiy v. Russia]; *Tymoshenko v. Ukraine*, *supra* note 61, 66, para. 295; *Tchankotadze v. Georgia*, *supra* note 13, para. 113.

68 See the literature cited *supra* note 9.

one specific episode in pre-trial detention indicating a misuse of power by the authorities. These issues are addressed below.

1. *The Burden of Proof*

A primary reason many applicants have failed to satisfy the Court that their prosecution, detention or restriction of rights had been ordered for ulterior purposes, has been the Court's insistence that it is for the applicant to show convincingly that the real aim of the authorities was not the same as that proclaimed.[69] Indeed, in what it later referred to as a "foundational statement", the Court held in *Khodorkovskiy* that

> "[...] the whole structure of the Convention rests on the general assumption that public authorities in the member States act in good faith. Indeed, any public policy or an individual measure may have a 'hidden agenda', and the presumption of good faith is rebuttable. However, an applicant alleging that his rights and freedoms were limited for an improper reason must convincingly show that the real aim of the authorities was not the same as that proclaimed (or as can be reasonably inferred from the context). A mere suspicion that the authorities used their powers for some other purpose than those defined in the Convention is not sufficient to prove that Article 18 was breached."[70]

The presumption of good faith on the part of the authorities, therefore, put the burden of proof firmly and irreversibly upon the applicant. In *Khodorkovskiy and Lebedev v. Russia* the Court firmly rejected the applicants' claim that the burden ought to shift where they made out a *prima facie* case or *arguable claim* of a violation of Article 18.[71] This meant that

---

69 *Khodorkovskiy v. Russia*, *supra* note 67, para. 255; *Lutsenko v. Ukraine*, *supra* note 61, para. 106; *Tymoshenko v. Ukraine*, *supra* note 61, para. 294; *Khodorkovskiy and Lebedev v. Russia*, *supra* note 6, para. 899; *Ilgar Mammadov v. Azerbaijan*, *supra* note 11, para. 137; *Rasul Jafarov v. Azerbaijan*, *supra* note 10, para. 153; *Tchankotadze v. Georgia*, *supra* note 13, para. 113.

70 *Khodorkovskiy v. Russia*, *supra* note 67, para. 255.

71 *Khodorkovskiy and Lebedev v. Russia*, *supra* note 6, para. 903. The Court considered "that even where the appearances speak in favour of the applicant's claim of improper motives, the burden of proof must remain with him or her. It confirms its position in *Khodorkovskiy v. Russia* that the applicant alleging bad faith of the authorities must 'convincingly show' that their actions were driven by improper motives. Thus, the standard of proof in such cases is high".

although the applicants had submitted various views by international NGOs on the targeted destruction of their oil company by the Russian State, and cited foreign courts who had declined to extradite individuals to Russia in this case for fear of politically motivated proceedings, Russia was not required to bring forth any evidence or arguments to debunk the applicants' claims. After all, the assumption of good faith, similar to a presumption of innocence, was on its side.

Successfully addressing politically motivated proceedings has thus been rendered increasingly difficult. It should be borne in mind that the allegation is that the *purpose* pursued by the authorities in detaining or prosecuting individuals was not the one officially proclaimed, that there was a *hidden* agenda, an ulterior and covert aim – in other words that the authorities had acted in bad faith. This is not unlike the concept of intent or *mens rea* in criminal law, it being for the applicant to show the purpose pursued by the authorities, which is incredibly difficult to attain if the authorities are in no way held to refute allegations by the applicant.[72] Although there is a case to be made for the heavy burden placed on applicants given the exceptional severity of finding that a State has acted in bad faith,[73] requiring applicants to provide all the evidence of the subjective aims of State authorities has prevented Article 18 from fulfilling its potential as a warning for rule of law backsliding. Practice has shown the nigh impossibility for applicants to prove their case,[74] which is exacerbated further by the evidentiary requirements set by the Court, to which the article turns below.

2. *The Standard and Means of Proof*

In addition to the requirement that applicants prove their allegation in full, the Court also emphasized the (very) high standard of proof in cases concerning Article 18,[75] and consistently applied a "very exacting standard

72 See also Satzger, Zimmermann & Eibach, 'Art. 18 Part 2', *supra* note 9, 253.

73 *Ibid.*, 253; see also C. Foster, *Science and the Precautionary Principle in International Courts and Tribunals. Expert Evidence, Burden of Proof and Finality* (2011), 189-190, noting that "there is a presumption that all states are committed to the good of the community and all act consistently with the applicable norms ('presumption of compliance' as it is known)".

74 Before the Grand Chamber judgment in *Merabishvili v. Georgia* [GC], *supra* note 14, the Court had only found a total of six violations of Article 18.

75 *Khodorkovskiy and Lebedev v. Russia*, *supra* note 6, para. 903; *Khodorkovskiy v. Russia*, *supra* note 67, para. 260.

of proof".[76] This high standard of proof meant that for an applicant to rebut the presumption of good faith, he had to "convincingly show" that the real aim of the authorities was not the same as that proclaimed (or as can be reasonably inferred from the context). In this regard, a "mere suspicion" the authorities acted in bad faith and pursued improper motives was not sufficient, "no matter how arguable that suspicion may be".[77] The Court in this context reasoned that as the prosecution of anyone in a high political position will necessarily have far-reaching political consequences, from which political opponents and others might directly or indirectly benefit, this could always lead to suspicions that the prosecution was politically motivated. As the Court held, however, "high political status does not grant immunity".[78]

Adding further to the burden on the applicant, the Court applied special evidentiary standards in Article 18 cases. It found for instance that domestic court findings in extradition procedures to the effect that prosecutions were politically motivated, were insufficient in light of the very high standard of proof applied by the Court.[79] Further, in a number of cases the Court even required "incontrovertible and direct proof" of the ulterior purpose.[80] As State authorities limiting individuals' rights under false pretenses and in pursuit of a hidden agenda do not normally leave such evidence lying around, and since the applicant in obtaining such evidence is completely reliant on the authorities, this has effectively presented a bar to applicants successfully pleading a case before the Court.[81] In other cases

76 *Khodorkovskiy and Lebedev v. Russia*, *supra* note 6, para. 899 and para. 256; see further *Lutsenko v. Ukraine*, *supra* note 61, para. 107; *Dochnal v. Poland*, ECtHR Application No. 31622/07, Judgment of 18 September 2012, para. 112 [Dochnal v. Poland]; *Tymoshenko v. Ukraine*, *supra* note 61, para. 295; *Ilgar Mammadov v. Azerbaijan*, *supra* note 11, para. 138; *Rasul Jafarov v. Azerbaijan*, *supra* note 10, para. 154; *Tchankotadze v. Georgia*, *supra* note 13, para. 113.

77 *Tchankotadze v. Georgia*, *supra* note 13, para. 114.

78 *Khodorkovskiy v. Russia*, *supra* note 67, para. 258.

79 *Ibid.*, 67, para. 260; referenced with approval in *Khodorkovskiy and Lebedev v. Russia*, *supra* note 6, para. 900.

80 *Khodorkovskiy v. Russia*, *supra* note 67, para. 260; *Dochnal v. Poland*, *supra* note 76, para. 116; *Nastase v. Romania*, ECtHR Application No. 80563/12, Decision of 18 November 2014, para. 109 [Nastase v. Romania]; *OAO Neftyanaya Kompaniya Yukos v. Russia*, *supra* note 62, para. 663; *Bîrsan v. Romania*, ECtHR Application No. 79917/13, Decision of 2 February 2016, para. 73.

81 See also Keller & Heri, *supra* note 9, 8-9; P. Leach, 'Georgia: Strasbourg's Scrutiny of the Misuse of Power' (5 December 2017), available at www.opendemocracy.net/od-russia/philip-leach/georgia-strasbourgs-scrutiny-of-the-misuse-of-power (last visited 12 December 2018), who describes this as the "smoking gun".

the Court was more willing to assess circumstantial evidence,[82] but the Court never explained on what basis it decided whether direct evidence was required, or whether circumstantial evidence sufficed. Judging from the large number of separate opinions addressing this issue, it may have been a matter of which judges were on the bench in a specific case.[83] These separate opinions address the difficulties for applicants to find direct evidence of the purposes pursued by the authorities, and tellingly, in no case where the Court applied this high evidentiary requirement did it find a violation. This again shows the difficulties in bringing successful claims of bad faith rule of law meddling before the Court.

3. *What Must Be Proven*

A final point that has prevented applicants' hopes of proving a breach of Article 18 from materializing, was the lack of clarity regarding *what* it was they needed to prove. In other words, what does it mean where Article 18 prohibits restrictions being applied "for any other purpose than that for which it has been prescribed"? The above discussion illustrates that the

---

82 Such as in the case of *Rasul Jafarov v. Azerbaijan*, where the finding of a violation could even be said to have been based solely on contextual factors: the Court found that the applicant's arrest and detention were part of a larger campaign to "crack down on human rights defenders in Azerbaijan", basing itself on (1) "the increasingly harsh and restrictive legislative regulation of NGO activity and funding"; (2) the narrative of high-ranking officials and pro-government media to the effect that NGOs and their leaders (including the applicant) were foreign agents and traitors; and (3) the fact that several notable human rights activists, who had also cooperated with international organisations protecting human rights, had been similarly arrested. *Rasul Jafarov v. Azerbaijan*, *supra* note 10, para. 158-163.

83 See the Joint Concurring Opinion of Judges *Jungwiert, Nußberger* and *Potocki*, appended to *Tymoshenko v. Ukraine*, *supra* note 61; Partly Dissenting Opinion of Judge *Tsotsoria*, appended to *Georgia v. Russia (I)* [GC], ECtHR Application No. 13255/07, Judgment of 3 July 2014; Concurring Opinion of Judge *Pinto de Albuquerque*, appended to *Navalnyy and Yashin v. Russia*, *supra* note 57; Joint Partly Dissenting Opinion of Judges *Nicolaou, Keller* and *Dedov*, appended to *Navalnyy and Ofitserov v. Russia*, *supra* note 7; Joint Concurring Opinion of Judges *Sajó, Tsotsoria* and *Pinto de Albuquerque* and Concurring Opinion by Judge *Kūris*, appended to *Tchankotadze v. Georgia*, *supra* note 13; Partly Dissenting Opinion of Judge *Keller*, appended to *Kasparov v. Russia*, *supra* note 11; Partly Dissenting Opinion of Judge *Keller*, appended to *Kasparov and Others (No. 2)*, *supra* note 57; and Joint Partly Dissenting Opinion of Judges *Lopez Guerra, Keller* and *Pastor Vilanova*, appended to *Navalnyy v. Russia February 2017*, *supra* note 15.

Court in essence required proof of *bad faith* on the part of the authorities, in other words, applicants had to 1) rebut the assumption of good faith on the part of the authorities, and 2) prove that the authorities had moreover been driven by improper motives, showing their bad faith. The Court, however, employed two different formulations of what bad faith entails.

First, the overarching standard entailed "that the real aim of the authorities was not the same as that proclaimed (or as can be reasonably inferred from the context)".[84] In other words, the applicants had to show that despite the authorities' reliance on legitimate grounds for restricting their rights, they in reality acted for ulterior purposes and sought to advance a hidden agenda. The Azeri cases *Ilgar Mammadov* and *Rasul Jafarov* best illustrate how this pans out for cases relating to a deprivation of liberty. In these cases, an opposition politician and a human rights-defender, respectively, had been remanded in pre-trial detention on charges for which the Court could discern no reasonable suspicion, which led to violations of Article 5.[85] Examining the complaints under Article 18, the Court then found that whereas the finding that there had been no reasonable suspicion undermined the assumption of good faith on the part of the authorities, this was not sufficient for finding a violation of Article 18.[86] This required further evidence, showing that the authorities had moreover been driven by improper motives, and in these cases such proof of bad faith indeed flowed from various contextual factors.[87] Although extremely exacting, there have therefore been cases where applicants were able to meet the standards as set by the Court.

In a number of other cases, however, the Court on top of its high standard of proof raised the bar for applicants yet further. In these cases, the Court did not only require them to "convincingly show that the real aim of the authorities was not the same as that proclaimed (or as can be reasonably inferred from the context)", but they had to moreover prove "that the

84 *Lutsenko v. Ukraine*, *supra* note 61, para. 106; *Tymoshenko v. Ukraine*, *supra* note 61, para. 294; *Khodorkovskiy and Lebedev v. Russia*, *supra* note 6, para. 899; *Ilgar Mammadov v. Azerbaijan*, *supra* note 11, para. 137; *Rasul Jafarov v. Azerbaijan*, *supra* note 10, para. 153. In the cases pertaining to full political motivation, the Court also refers to this standard, but afterwards formulates the much more demanding standard discussed immediately below.

85 *Ilgar Mammadov v. Azerbaijan*, *supra* note 11, para. 100; *Rasul Jafarov v. Azerbaijan*, *supra* note 10, para. 130-133.

86 *Ilgar Mammadov v. Azerbaijan*, *supra* note 11, para. 141, and *Rasul Jafarov v. Azerbaijan*, *supra* note 10, para. 157.

87 *Ilgar Mammadov v. Azerbaijan*, *supra* note 11, para. 142-144 and *Rasul Jafarov v. Azerbaijan*, *supra* note 10, 158-163.

whole legal machinery of the respondent State […] was *ab initio* misused, that from the beginning to the end the authorities were acting with bad faith and in blatant disregard of the Convention".[88] No applicant has succeeded in meeting this standard, leading a number of judges to qualify it as "prohibitively high".[89] Aside from critiques on the standard as such, a clear explanation of when the Court applies which standard has proved elusive.

The author holds the opinion, an explanation is perhaps best derived from what was at stake in the case at hand. In cases where applicants alleged in general terms that they had become the victims of political persecution, without furnishing this claim with case-specific evidence, the Court has applied the practically unattainable standard that, from the beginning to the end, the authorities must be shown to have been acting with bad faith and in blatant disregard of the Convention.[90] In cases, however, pertaining to a specific measure or where a specific episode was at stake – either because the applicant had formulated a more narrow complaint or because the Court could itself distinguish this episode from the case as a whole – the somewhat less stringent standard has been employed.[91]

By way of illustration, in the Ukrainian cases *Lutsenko* and *Tymoshenko*, although the applicants alleged that the criminal proceedings against them as a whole had been politically motivated, the Court observed "distinguishable features" or "specific features" of the case, allowing it "to look into the matter separately from the more general context of politically motivated prosecution of the opposition leader".[92] In both cases it found that the pretrial detention had been ordered for reasons not permitted by Article 5, basing itself on the written reasoning accompanying the detention orders – from which it was clear that the authorities' aim had been to punish the applicants for their communications with the media and perceived con-

88 *Khodorkovskiy v. Russia*, *supra* note 67, para. 255, 260 [spelling error corrected]; *Khodorkovskiy and Lebedev v. Russia*, *supra* note 6, para. 905; *Dochnal v. Poland*, *supra* note 76, para. 115 (in a slightly modified way); *Nastase v. Romania*, *supra* note 80, para. 109; *Tchankotadze v. Georgia*, *supra* note 13, para. 114.

89 Joint Concurring Opinion of Judges *Sajó*, *Tsotsoria* and *Pinto de Albuquerque*, appended to *Tchankotadze v. Georgia*, *supra* note 13, para. 7.

90 See the case law cited *supra* note 88.

91 Coming to a similar conclusion, see Satzger, Zimmermann & Eibach, 'Art. 18 Part 2', *supra* note 9, 249-252. They have the impression that the Court distinguishes between "first and second degree violations".

92 *Lutsenko v. Ukraine*, *supra* note 61, para. 108; *Tymoshenko v. Ukraine*, *supra* note 61, para. 298.

temptuous behavior.[93] By limiting the case in this way to the arrest of the applicants, the Court was able to steer clear of the question of whether these were instances of political persecution full stop, which of course was the more sensitive as well as simply more complicated issue. Understandable as that may be and as was discussed above, by rendering it practically impossible to prove allegations of political persecution, the Court has limited Article 18's utility in safeguarding the rule of law. Judges *Jungwiert*, *Nußberger* and *Potocki* noted this in their Joint Concurring Opinion to the case of *Tymoshenko*, setting out "that the reasoning of the majority does not address the applicant's main complaint, which concerns the link between human rights violations and democracy, namely that her detention has been used by the authorities to exclude her from political life and to prevent her standing in the parliamentary elections".[94] Despite the extreme seriousness of the findings in these cases, therefore, they still do not address the real heart of the issue.

IV. Résumé

Section B. I. concluded that Article 18 addresses a particularly malicious situation of rule of law circumvention by State authorities, because it is aimed at addressing situations where the State restricts individual rights under false pretenses. Assessing the case-law discussed above in light of the drafters' ambition of creating a resounding alarm where totalitarian tendencies threaten the rule of law, leads to a somewhat ambiguous outlook. On the one hand, the scope of the provision has been drawn too narrowly, and the threshold for proving a violation has been too high. This has led to a very limited role for Article 18, and it had up until the *Merabishvili* case only been found to be violated a total of six times.[95] On the other hand, this rarity has added to the special stigma associated with a violation,[96] and from this perspective, a finding of a violation of Article 18 in conjunction

93 *Lutsenko v. Ukraine*, *supra* note 61, para. 109 and *Tymoshenko v. Ukraine*, *supra* note 61, para. 299-300.

94 Joint Concurring Opinion of Judges *Jungwiert*, *Nußberger* and *Potocki*, appended to *Tymoshenko v. Ukraine*, *supra* note 61.

95 See the case-law cited *supra* note 61.

96 Compare Leach, *supra* note 81, where he argues that an Article 18 violation ought to be taken very seriously as it is a very rare occurrence. See also Satzger, Zimmermann & Eibach, 'Art. 18 Part 2', *supra* note 9, 253, where they argue that the "special weight" of Article 18 convictions could be diluted when arrived at too easily.

with another Convention provision has surely had added value as compared to the mere violation of a substantive right alone, *enhancing* the finding. Article 18 violations have in this respect constituted qualified violations, carrying a special stigma and conveying a strong message, which can be associated with the sounding of the alarm envisioned by the drafters.

Nevertheless, the practical hurdles in the case-law have downgraded Article 18 to a largely idle provision, as either the Court has not addressed complaints at all, or set the threshold for proving a violation so high that a finding of a violation has been largely impossible.[97] Moreover, it is precisely the most pertinent cases, where criminal proceedings as a whole were politically motivated, that Article 18 is either not applied, or the evidentiary standard is raised even further. This means that the provision must, on balance, be seen as largely ineffective in protecting the rule of law.

The following section assesses whether this outlook changed when the *Merabishvili* Grand Chamber judgment was handed down in November 2017.

D. A New Dawn for Article 18? Merabishvili v. Georgia and Beyond

Against the background of the unsatisfactory and inconsistent line in the case-law, many judges have appended separate opinions to Article 18 cases to express their discontent, and the few scholarly contributions on the topic have been equally critical. It was therefore not a question of if, but when a case would come before the Grand Chamber. In the end it was the case of former Georgian Minister for the Interior and Prime-Minster *Merabishvili*, which was referred to the Grand Chamber after a Chamber had unanimously found a violation of Article 18 in conjunction with Article 5 in 2016.[98] The Grand Chamber, taking note of the criticisms of the previous case-law, formulated a fresh take on Article 18 and in a closely contended decision held that Georgia had violated Article 18, by nine votes to eight.[99] In the present section, this new judgment is put to the test: does it manage to better realize the rule of law protection and the alarm function Article 18 was designed for?

---

97 Compare Keller & Heri, *supra* note 9, 9, arguing that the Azeri cases have showcased a potential lowering of the threshold.

98 *Merabishvili v. Georgia*, ECtHR Application No. 72508/13, Judgment of 14 June 2016 [Merabishvili v. Georgia].

99 *Merabishvili v. Georgia* [GC], *supra* note 14.

By way of brief introduction: *Merabishvili* was not a low-profile case. It pertained to a former Head of Government who alleged that he had become the victim of a political prosecution, and the case was moreover linked with some other highly sensitive issues in Georgian politics. Mr. *Merabishvili* was arrested for numerous offenses, amongst which abuse of power, shortly after leaving office due to losing the elections in 2012. He was held in pre-trial detention for almost seven months, when one day he was removed from his cell in the dead of night, and questioned by two high-ranked officials on the death of a former Prime-Minister and crimes allegedly committed by the former President.[100] He was moreover offered to have the charges against him dropped should he cooperate, but was threatened with worsening prison conditions should he decline. He chose the latter, and in Strasbourg he alleged that the incident showed that the authorities' purpose in remanding him in pre-trial detention had not been the allegations against him, but rather had served ulterior, hidden motives, namely to remove him from the political scene and to gather information in unrelated cases. The potential rule of law implications then, were clear; the stage was set, but the case-law up until 2017 left recourse to Article 18 dubious at best. How did the Grand Chamber proceed?

I. Two Steps Forward…

As has been argued extensively above, an effective interpretation of Article 18 requires a widening of its scope, and even more so a clear delineation of its autonomous function as a rule of law safeguard. The Grand Chamber takes up the gauntlet in this respect. By setting out more clearly the purpose of Article 18 and emphasizing its application even if other rights have not been violated, it sets out the margins for Article 18's operation. Moreover, it seems to do away with the "not necessary to examine"-approach by finding that ulterior purpose claims must be addressed when they are a "fundamental aspect" of a case,[101] which will presumably be so at least in cases of politically motivated rights restrictions.[102]

---

100 See *Merabishvili v. Georgia* [GC], *supra* note 14, para. 333-350 for the Court's considerations as to the applicant's removal from his cell. All facts in the case were contested by the State, but the Court found the applicant's statements to be proven.

101 *Ibid.*, para. 291.

102 Nevertheless, only the future will tell how the Court interprets the "fundamental aspect"-criterion. It has formulated the same criterion in Article 14 (non-discrim-

In setting out the role of Article 18 within the Convention system, the Court finds the added value of the provision in its *detournement de pouvoir*-function, explicitly forbidding States from misusing their power to restrict rights.[103] This entails a move-away from the focus on *bad faith* on the part of the authorities as such, and a stronger emphasis on the question of whether the authorities have pursued any ulterior purposes – purposes that do not provide a lawful basis for restricting rights, and that were not the ones officially cited. The Court however recognizes that often State authorities pursue more than one purpose, and that when States pursue both legitimate and illegitimate (ulterior) purposes, Article 18 may be violated even if substantive rights are not. By thus carving out a distinct territory for Article 18, the author would expect it to be applied more often, and thereby to become a more feasible avenue for redress when States suppress individual rights in pursuance of a hidden agenda. Whether this also goes for wholly politically motivated criminal proceedings (as opposed to e.g. restrictions of liberty) remains to be seen, as *Merabishvili* did not address the question of whether Article 18 can be applied in conjunction with the right to a fair trial under Article 6. This issue therefore remains, for now, undecided.

When it comes to issues of proof, the Grand Chamber – noting the earlier inconsistencies – firmly moves away from previous case-law. It significantly lowers the applicable standard of proof and no longer adheres to the one-sided allocation of the burden of proof, thereby greatly increasing the practicability of Article 18 and applicants' chances of actually convincing the Court that a violation has taken place. The Court held that there is no reason to apply any special approach to proof as compared to other Convention provisions,[104] meaning all issues regarding burden of proof,[105] standard of proof,[106] and types of evidence[107] are normalized and therefore no longer raise issues particular to Article 18.

Undoubtedly it will remain challenging for applicants to sufficiently furnish claims of improperly motivated restrictions of their rights, as the knowledge of what has driven the authorities remains within the exclusive

ination) cases, but application has proved unpredictable. Explaining the complex applicability of Article 14 ECHR, see J.H. Gerards, '*Commentaar op art. 14 EVRM*', Sdu Commentaar EVRM, C.1.2 (online, last revised on 15 June 2015).

103 *Ibid.*, para. 283 and 306. It does so with reference to the *travaux préparatoires*.

104 *Merabishvili v. Georgia* [GC], *supra* note 14, para. 310.

105 *Ibid.*, para. 311.

106 *Ibid.*, para. 314.

107 *Ibid.*, para. 316-317.

purview of the authorities themselves, but at least the overly restrictive demands have been downscaled.[108] Furthermore, because the Court emphasizes the importance of the authorities' response to allegations and also references the relevance of circumstantial evidence such as reports from NGOs and international observers to shed light on the facts, it appears large steps have been made to remedy the evidentiary problems outlined above.[109] This is not to say of course that all criticisms are hereby stifled, as the Court's adoption of a standard of "beyond reasonable doubt", despite its long pedigree,[110] is itself not free from controversy.[111] As this point is a more general critique of the Court's approach to evidence as such, it shall be left it aside.

II. …And One Step Back?

In *Merabishvili*, the Grand Chamber clearly takes two leaps forward. In clearing up the scope of application and downscaling the evidentiary requirements, the practicability of Article 18 is sure to increase. The most ferocious critiques on the old case-law had moreover been targeted at precisely those two issues. Then why was the Grand Chamber so deeply divided in handing down its judgment?

As was mentioned above, the focus in what must be proven under Article 18 shifts in *Merabishvili* from bad faith to a more objective assessment of ulterior purpose. This shift entails two important changes. First, the Court accounts for the eventuality where authorities pursued multiple aims when restricting rights, and where they for example detained an individual on a reasonable suspicion of having committed an offense, but simultaneously served a covert purpose – such as preventing him from attending a political manifestation or, as was the case in *Merabishvili*, to ob-

108 See also C. Heri, 'Merabishvili, Mammadov and Targeted Criminal Proceedings: Recent Developments under Article 18 ECHR' (15 December 2017), available at https://strasbourgobservers.com/2017/12/15/merabishvili-mammadov-and-targeted-criminal-proceedings-recent-developments-under-article-18-echr/ (last visited 12 December 2018).

109 Further on this, see J. Mačkić, 'Case Note: *Merabishvili v. Georgia*' (2018), 19 *European Human Rights Cases* 2018/41, 109-121.

110 See *Ireland v. The United Kingdom*, ECtHR Application No. 5310/71, Judgment of 18 January 1978, para. 161.

111 G. Bonello, 'Evidentiary Rules of the ECHR in Proceedings Relating to Articles 2, 3 and 14 – A Critique', 2 *Inter-American and European Human Rights Journal* (2009) 1-2, 66.

tain information into unrelated investigations.[112] Second, the Court no longer applies a separate standard for allegations of political persecution, thereby departing from its previous requirement that the authorities misused the entirety of their legal machinery from beginning to end in blatant disregard of the Convention. The Grand Chamber aims to simplify the case-law by formulating a two-step approach: the examination must first focus on whether it can be proven that the authorities pursued an ulterior purpose, and second, if there was also a legitimate aim, whether the ulterior purpose was predominant.[113] This approach certainly clarifies what is required, but it also raises new issues, and indeed the four concurring judges and the eight dissenting judges all focused their critiques on this point. Early responses to the judgment similarly target this aspect of the case.[114]

Zooming in on the new predominant purpose-test, what is clear is that whenever authorities have pursued both legitimate and illegitimate aims, Article 18 is only violated where the illegitimate aim was predominant. Further, where a restriction is of a continuing nature such as in the case of detention, if at any moment in time an ulterior purpose was predominant, this violates Article 18.[115] Most enlightening regarding what the new approach entails, is the Court's consideration that

> "[t]here is a considerable difference between cases in which the prescribed purpose was the one that truly actuated the authorities, though they also wanted to gain some other advantage, and cases in which the prescribed purpose, while present, was in reality simply a cover enabling the authorities to attain an extraneous purpose, which was the overriding focus of their efforts."[116]

112 *Merabishvili v. Georgia* [GC], *supra* note 14, para. 333-353.

113 *Ibid.*, para. 309.

114 See Leach, *supra* note 81; B. Çalı, 'Merabishvili v. Georgia: Has the Mountain Given Birth to a Mouse?' (3 December 2017), available at http://verfassungsblog.de/merabishvili-v-georgia-has-the-mountain-given-birth-to-a-mouse/ (last visited 12 December 2018); Heri, *supra* note 108. See also F. Tan, 'Case Note: *Merabishvili v. Georgia*' (2018), 19 *European Human Rights Cases* 2018/41, 109-121.

115 *Merabishvili v. Georgia* [GC], *supra* note 14, para. 308 and para. 351.

116 *Ibid.*, para. 303.

This approach to Article 18 has attracted fundamental criticisms from the four concurring judges,[117] as well as academic commentators.[118] They argue that because a restriction will only fall foul of Article 18 if it served a predominantly illegitimate purpose, the Convention thereby provides legitimacy to States limiting human rights for ulterior purposes, so long as those purposes were not predominant. In the words of *Başak Çalı*, "the plurality of purposes presumption turns bad faith into a banal state of affairs. It normalises its occurrence so long as it is not a predominant reason for restricting rights".[119] This was not the majority's intention, and in fact the Grand Chamber no longer sees Article 18 as pertaining only to cases of "bad faith"; its aim seems to have been precisely to normalize and objectify the provision by moving away from bad faith and towards a more neutral assessment of purposes.[120] From the perspective of the protection of the rule of law, the concern is therefore not so much that *bad faith* cases will fall outside of the new approach, but rather that the objectivization brings situations under Article 18's scope that do *not* pertain to core bad faith cases, and therefore have less bearing on the rule of law. This may dilute the finding of a violation of Article 18, as it will be more mundane and not every violation will be equally serious. Of course, the concurring judges' concerns cannot be discounted, and a normalization of bad faith human rights restrictions is a bleak outlook, but it would appear to the author that the risk is greater that the normalization of Article 18 makes violations of the provision lose their edge, as an extremely serious, qualified breach that signifies a complete disregard for the rule of law. This would put the added value of the provision at risk.

More practical problems also arise under the predominant purpose-test. First, it will be very difficult for applicants to prove that the ulterior purpose pursued by the authorities, was predominant.[121] Second, the test for determining predominance is vague and difficult to apply, as is illustrated by the eight dissenters who were in fact in favor of introducing the test but disagreed with the application to the facts of the case. The test as formulat-

117 Joint Concurring Opinion of Judges *Yudkivska*, *Tsotsoria* and *Vehabović*, appended to *Merabishvili v. Georgia* [GC], *supra* note 14, para. 1; Concurring Opinion of Judge *Serghides*, appended to *Merabishvili v. Georgia* [GC], *supra* note 14, para. 3; Joint Concurring Opinion of Judges *Sajó*, *Tsotsoria* and *Pinto de Albuquerque*, appended to *Tchankotadze v. Georgia*, *supra* note 13, para 1.

118 Çalı, *supra* note 114; Heri, *supra* note 108.

119 Çalı, *supra* note 114.

120 More extensively, see Tan, *supra* note 114.

121 Çalı, *supra* note 114; Heri, *supra* note 108.

ed by the Court, though ambiguous, does provide opportunities for rule of law protection. Which purpose was predominant in the Grand Chamber's view depends on all the circumstances of the case, in addition to which "the Court will have regard to the nature and degree of reprehensibility of the alleged ulterior purpose, and bear in mind that the Convention was designed to maintain and promote the ideals and values of a democratic society governed by the rule of law".[122] That is a rather indeterminate criterion and appears to take onboard the concurring judges' criticisms that wherever there was a political aim to a prosecution, this ought to constitute directly a violation of Article 18. After all, against the background of maintaining democracy and the rule of law, the purpose of getting rid of political dissidents seems to be on top of the list of reprehensibility. Problematic in this approach, however, is that how reprehensible the ulterior purpose was seems to have little or nothing to do with what purpose was *predominant* – in other words what purpose drove the authorities to take action. Whereas the criterion, therefore, provides very little practical guidance, it does appear to provide room to find Article 18 violations more easily in cases where the rule of law is under threat.

III. Résumé

Reflecting on the *Merabishvili* case, it is a clear landmark case that has significantly developed the case-law on Article 18. We are left with one question though. How did Mr. *Merabishvili* fare in Strasbourg? The Grand Chamber considered his account of the facts sufficiently proven, and nine judges were equally convinced that the predominant aim of Mr. *Merabishvili*'s detention following his removal from his cell had shifted to garnering information for other proceedings. The Grand Chamber was not satisfied, however, that the authorities' aim in arresting the applicant had been predominantly to remove him from the political scene. Meanwhile, at the time of writing, Mr. *Merabishvili* remains in jail, and Georgian authorities claim the European Court confirmed he is not a political prisoner.[123]

---

122 *Merabishvili v. Georgia* [GC], *supra* note 14, para. 307.

123 G. Gabekhadze, 'President Says Ex-Interior Minister's Rights Were Violated in Prison' The Messenger Online (10 May 2018), available at http://www.messenger.com.ge/issues/4137_may_10_2018/4137_margvelashvili.html (last visited 12 December 2018).

State reactions to Article 18 violations have more broadly speaking been ambivalent. As a clear positive example, the case of former Prime-Minister *Tymoshenko* springs to mind. In this case, the Court found that Article 18 had been violated in conjunction with Article 5 because *Tymoshenko*'s detention had been ordered to punish her for perceived contemptuous behavior rather than for the purpose of the trial against her.[124] In a separate case, *Tymoshenko* complained that beyond her pre-trial detention, her criminal proceedings as a whole had been politically motivated. After the Court had decided the first case, Ukraine decided to settle the second, admitting it had violated Article 18 in conjunction with Articles 6, 8 and 10.[125] In addition to, and in line with this admission, Ukraine further gave notice to the Committee of Ministers that *Tymoshenko* had been released from prison following a parliamentary resolution.[126] The combination of a judicial decision finding a violation of Article 18 and the political supervision by the Committee of Ministers therefore led to the favorable result of Ukraine both admitting to having had political motives in prosecuting *Tymoshenko*, and releasing her from prison.

On the other side of the spectrum, there is the case of *Ilgar Mammadov v. Azerbaijan*. In this case, opposition politician *Mammadov* had been detained in order to silence him and punish him for spreading information revealing that the cause for Azerbaijani riots had been concealed by the authorities – leading the Court to find a violation of Article 18 in conjunction with Article 5. Despite this ruling in 2014, *Mammadov* has yet to be released. The Committee of Ministers has continuously kept this case on its agenda,[127] calling for his release but to no avail. The Committee has now for the first time in history initiated infringement proceedings, requesting the Court to decide whether Azerbaijan has given effect to its judgment.[128] Meanwhile, two weeks before the Committee's decision, the

124 *Tymoshenko v. Ukraine*, *supra* note 61.

125 *Tymoshenko v. Ukraine (No. 2)*, ECtHR Application No. 65656/12, Decision of 16 December 2014 [*Tymoshenko v. Ukraine (No. 2)*].

126 See the database of the Department for the Execution of Judgments of the ECHR, HUDOC-EXEC, available at https://hudoc.exec.coe.int/eng#{%22EXECDocumentTypeCollection%22:[%22CEC%22]} (last visted 17 December 2018), *Tymoshenko v. Ukraine*, ECtHR Application No. 49872/11.

127 See L. R. Glas, 'The Committee of Ministers Goes Nuclear: Infringement Proceedings Against Azerbaijan in the Case of Ilgar Mammadov' (20 December 2017), available at https://strasbourgobservers.com/2017/12/20/the-committee-of-ministers-goes-nuclear-infringement-proceedings-against-azerbaijan-in-the-case-of-ilgar-mammadov/ (last visited 12 December 2018).

128 Interim Resolution of 7 December 2017, CM/ResDH(2017)429.

Court decided in *Ilgar Mammadov (No. 2)* that Azerbaijan had not only violated Article 18 in conjunction with Article 5, but had also manifestly failed to provide *Mammadov* with a fair trial.[129] Despite the dialog first at the Court, then at the Committee of Ministers with further Court proceedings having been brought, and the discussion now flowing back to the Court, there appears to be no clear solution to the *Ilgar Mammadov v. Azerbaijan*-saga. This goes to show that even with Article 18's alarm sounding, and immense political pressure, the CoE system for rule of law and human rights protection remains dependent on the good will of States, and their willingness to comply with binding Court judgments. That, however, is of course precisely what is at stake in States who no longer strictly adhere to the rule of law. Whereas a finding of a breach of Article 18 may, therefore, be a clear sounding of the alarm for the rule of law, the real litmus test may be in how a State executes that judgment.

E. Conclusion

Human rights restrictions under false pretenses present a clear danger to the rule of law, and Article 18 presents a powerful tool to address such backslides. The *European Court of Human Rights* has struggled to get a grip on such pernicious practices, but has shown a willingness to develop its case-law to better deal with such situations and offer applicants a real chance of addressing these issues. The Grand Chamber case of *Merabishvili* presents a turning point in this regard, offering some realistic chance for victims of politically motivated repression to bring their claims to Strasbourg, and even if applicants remain in a difficult position to successfully complain of an Article 18 violation given the authorities' sole knowledge of their intentions and the difficulty of finding evidence indicating such intentions, dialog will at least increase as States can no longer remain passive. Further, the Court's finding to the effect that it will address complaints of authorities being driven by ulterior purposes whenever that complaint constitutes a fundamental aspect of the case, at least in theory ensures that it will no longer declare serious cases unnecessary to examine. Test case and the next trial for the Court in this context will be the Grand Chamber case of *Alexei Navalny*,[130] the Russian opposition leader who is

129 *Ilgar Mammadov v. Azerbaijan (No. 2)*, *supra* note 64.

130 *Navalnyy v. Russia February 2017*, *supra* note 15. A Grand Chamber hearing was held in January 2018.

regularly arrested when he attempts to take part in political manifestations, but whose Article 18 complaints the Court has consistently refused to address.[131]

Despite the developments in *Merabishvili*, the case-law under Article 18 remains complex and challenges endure. In particular, the Court will need to somehow strike a balance between an interpretation that renders Article 18 a realistic avenue for proceedings where the rule of law is at stake, while at the same time safeguarding its exceptional status as a *qualified violation*. After all, it may no longer connote the same clear and unequivocal ruling of bad faith – that "the foundation of trust that normally exists between all signatory States is shattered".[132] A further threat looming is that States acting in bad faith may get away with their malicious rights restrictions because it cannot be proved that their ulterior purpose was *predominant*. Because all information regarding the authorities' purposes is necessarily within the exclusive knowledge of the State, the Court will need to be sufficiently vigilant in requiring it to furnish the necessary evidence, or to draw adverse inferences from the State's unwillingness to do so. All in all, the Court needs to walk a fine line if Article 18 is to function as the alarm bell that the drafters envisioned, whilst safeguarding the legitimacy of its decisions.

131 See *Navalnyy and Yashin v. Russia*, *supra* note 57; *Navalnyy and Ofitserov v. Russia*, *supra* note 7; *Navalnyy v. Russia February 2017*, *supra* note 15; *Navalnyy v. Russia Ocotber 2017*, *supra* note 65.

132 Satzger, Zimmermann & Eibach, 'Art. 18 Part 2', *supra* note 9, 249.

Promoting the Rule of Law Through the Law of Occupation? An Uneasy Relationship

Andreas Th. Müller[*]

Table of Contents

Abstract

A core objective of the law of occupation has traditionally been that the occupying power should heed rule of law standards in the administration of the occupied territory. Less clear is whether it should also seek to inculcate rule of law standards into the local government. To be sure, the pertinent rules of the law of occupation provide for far-reaching competences of the occupying power. However, given the predominately negative, security-focused and conservationist nature of the occupier's powers, its involvement in the *rule of law transfer business* should not be overrated. While it is true that two major post-1945 developments, i.e. international human rights law and the involvement of the *UN Security Council* (UNSC), have contributed toward broadening, recalibrating, and dynamizing the applicable legal standards in situations of occupation, it is nonetheless crucial to resist

* Prof. Dr. Andreas Th. Müller, LL.M. (Yale), Full Professor at the Department of European Law and Public International Law at the University of Innsbruck.

the temptation to concede, in the name of promoting the rule of law, too much legislative leeway to the occupying power. Thus, the question whether, and to what extent, the law of occupation mandates the occupying power to engage in promoting the rule of law in the occupied territory, calls for a differentiated, and cautious, answer.

A. Introduction

When *Ernst Fraenkel* published his "Military Occupation and the Rule of Law" in 1944,[1] World War II was still raging in Europe and beyond. By studying the post-World War I occupation of the Rhineland from 1918 through 1923, he sought to contribute to "[…] understanding the problems that will confront a future occupation regime".[2] He felt that the traditional law of occupation was not equipped to deal with the challenges of the imminent post-World War II occupation of Germany.

Interestingly, the lens through which *Fraenkel* chose to look at occupation was the concept of the rule of law, "[…] one of the basic elements of western civilization".[3] Against this background, he asked "[…] whether a principle that is applicable to national governments, exercising their powers by virtue of national laws, is not also applicable to the regimes of foreign governments that exercise their powers by virtue of international law".[4]

This question is directed, on the one hand, to the occupying power in the sense that it should itself heed rule of law standards in the administration of the occupied territory (e.g. maintaining the local court system, providing for effective law enforcement or respecting fundamental fair trial and due process guarantees). This has traditionally been one of the core objectives of the international law of occupation.[5] Less clear is whether the occupying power, on its part, should seek to inculcate rule of law standards into the local government. That such *mission civilisatrice* is within the remit of the powers, or even obligations, of the occupying power is subject to considerable doubt.

---

1 E. Fraenkel, *Military Occupation and the Rule of Law. Occupation Government in the Rhineland, 1918-1923* (1944).

2 *Ibid.*, ix.

3 *Ibid.*, x.

4 *Ibid.*, x.

5 See, e.g., Y. Dinstein, *The International Law of Belligerent Occupation* (2009), 132-145.

To be sure, Article 43 of the *Hague Regulations* (HR)[6] and Article 64 of the *Fourth Geneva Convention* (IV GC)[7] provide for far-reaching competences of the occupying power[8] that may also include promoting the rule of law in the occupied territory. Yet, given the predominantly negative, security-focused and conservationist nature of the occupier's powers (B.), its involvement in the *rule of law transfer business* should not be overrated, at least as far as the law of occupation in the strict sense, i.e. as an element of international humanitarian law, is concerned.

It has become common, however, to underscore the relevance of two major post-1945 developments[9] – international human rights law (C.) and action by the UNSC (D.) in situations of occupation or similar situations – with a view of arguing in favor of broadening, recalibrating, and dynamizing the applicable legal standards under the label of a law of occupation in the wider sense. This has the potential of greatly increasing the occupying power's rights and obligations to act as a rule of law transferor *vis-à-vis* the local population and administration. There are indeed sound reasons to follow such an approach, but, as will be shown, also significant risks and pitfalls and therefore limits to such undertaking.

Thus, the overall question underlying the present contribution, namely whether, and to what extent, the law of occupation mandates the occupying power to engage in promoting the rule of law in the occupied territory, calls for a differentiated and cautious answer (E.).

B. *Is the Promotion of the Rule of Law Outside the Remit of the Law of Occupation?*

As has already been mentioned, promotion of the rule of law does not sit easily with the traditional setup of the law of occupation. This can be explained by the generally negative approach of the law of occupation (I.), its

6 *Convention (IV) Respecting the Laws and Customs of War on Land and its annex: Regulations concerning the Laws and Customs of War on Land*, 18 October 1907, Art. 43, available at https://ihl-databases.icrc.org/ihl/WebART/195-200053?OpenDocument (last visited 13 December 2018).

7 *Convention (IV) Relative to the Protection of Civilian Persons in Time of War*, 12 August 1949, Art. 64, 75 UNTS 287.

8 For a more detailed analysis of these provisions see B. II.

9 See, e.g., A. Roberts, 'Transformative Military Occupation: Applying the Laws of War and Human Rights', 100 *American Journal of International Law* (2006) 3, 580, 589 [Roberts, Transformative Military Occupation]; E. Benvenisti, *The International Law of Occupation*, 2nd ed. (2012), 9, 12-15.

focus on the security of the occupying power (II.) as well as its conservationist character (III.). When delving into these aspects in the following, it will also become manifest, however, that rule of law promotion is not in itself alien to the law of occupation.

I. Negative Approach

The traditional law of occupation is chiefly concerned with stipulating prohibitions *vis-à-vis* the occupying power, e.g. the prohibition to force the inhabitants of the occupied territory to furnish information about the army of the other belligerent or about its means of defense (Article 44 HR), to compel those inhabitants to swear allegiance to the occupying power (Article 45 HR), to confiscate private property (Article 46 HR), to resort to pillage (Article 47 HR) or collective punishment (Article 50 HR), or to seize, destroy or willfully damage the property of institutions dedicated to religion, charity, and education as well as of works of art and science (Article 56 HR).[10] This negative approach reflects the renunciation of the old doctrine that acquiring effective control over a territory was considered a sufficient legal basis to assert a right of conquest and obtain full sovereign rights over it, and its replacement by the doctrine of *occupatio bellica* characterized as "[...] a temporary state of fact arising when an invader achieves military control of a territory and administers it on a provisional basis, but has no legal entitlement to exercise the rights of the absent sovereign".[11]

Also, the *Fourth Geneva Convention*, while endorsing the concept of a comparably more active occupying power,[12] still focuses on prohibitions. Accordingly, the occupying power shall not, for instance, deprive protected

10 See also corresponding prohibitions in *Actes de la Conférence réunie à Bruxelles, du 27 juillet au 27 août 1874, pour régler les lois et coutumes de la guerre*, 27th August 1874, Art. 3, 36-39, 4 *Nouveau recueil général de traités* (1879-1880), 219 [Brussels Declaration].

11 N. Bhuta, 'The Antinomies of Transformative Occupation', 16 *European Journal of International Law* (2005) 4, 721, 725; for a historical account of the development see *ibid.*, 724-733.

12 As to the drafting history see, e.g., Roberts, 'Transformative Military Occupation', *supra* note 9, 587-588; see in particular the analysis of the relationship between Article 43 HR and Article 64 IV GC in M. Sassòli, 'Legislation and Maintenance of Public Order and Civil Life by Occupying Powers', 16 *European Journal of International Law* (2005) 4, 661, 669-670; Benvenisti, *supra* note 9, 95-102; Y. Arai-Takahashi, 'Law-Making and Judicial Guarantees in Occupied Territories' in

persons in the occupied territory of the benefits of the Convention (Article 47 IV GC), prevent other nationals from leaving the occupied territory (Article 48 IV GC), deport or transfer protected persons to the territory of the occupying power or its own civilian population into the occupied territory (Article 49 IV GC), compel protected persons to serve in its armed forces (Article 51 IV GC), create unemployment (Article 52 IV GC), destroy real or personal property belonging individually or collectively to private persons, public authorities or social or cooperative institutions (Article 53 IV GC), alter the status of public officials or judges in the occupied territory (Article 54 IV GC), apply retroactive or disproportionate laws to the occupied population (Articles 65, 67 IV GC) or impose the death penalty against the occupied population except in cases of espionage, serious acts of sabotage or killings, with the further proviso that these acts were punishable by death before the occupation began and that juveniles may never be subjected to capital punishment (Article 68 IV GC).

This *status negativus*,[13] however, is not without limits: Firstly, many of the aforementioned prohibitions are qualified inasmuch as they accept restrictions in case these are "[...] rendered absolutely necessary by military operations" (Article 53 IV GC), due to "imperative military reason" (Article 49 IV GC), "imperative reasons of security" (Articles 62, 78 IV GC) or the like. Secondly, provisions such as Articles 50 and 55 to 59 IV GC require positive action on the part of the occupying power with respect to children, the food and medical supply of the occupied population, medical and hospital establishments and services, public health and hygiene in the occupied territory as well as in regard to relief schemes and consignments in favor of the population under occupation.[14]

II. Relative Focus on the Security Interests of the Occupying Power

As already indicated, the security interests of the occupying power pose a limit to (many of) its negative obligations under the law of occupation. In addition, according to other provisions, the occupying power may use its prerogatives "[...] for the needs of the army or of the administration of the

A. Clapham, P. Gaeta & M. Sassòli (eds), *The 1949 Geneva Conventions. A Commentary* (2015), 1421, 1422-1423.

13 See G. Jellinek, *System der Subjektiven Öffentlichen Rechte*, 2nd ed. (1905), 87.

14 See in a similar vein *Protocol Additional to the Geneva Conventions of 12 August 1949, and relating to the Protection of Victims of International Armed Conflicts*, 8 June 1977, Art. 69-71, 1125 UNTS 3, 35-36.

territory in question" (Article 49 HR) or "[…] for the needs of the army of occupation" (Article 52 HR). Hence, the law of occupation accepts positive intervention on the part of the occupying power mostly when its own military or security interests are at stake.[15]

Yet the law of occupation also takes into account the interests of the local population. When the aforementioned Article 49 HR allows for the levying of money contributions in the occupied territory "[…] for the needs […] of the administration of the territory in question", the existence of such administration is also to the benefit of the population under occupation. Furthermore, Articles 50 and 55 to 59 IV GC, as referred to above, call for the occupying power's action with respect to food and medical services. Moreover, Article 49 IV GC authorizes the occupying power to undertake total or partial occupation of an area "[…] if the security of the population […] so demand[s]".

The two most interesting, and therefore most discussed, provisions are Article 43 HR and Article 64 IV GC. According to the former, "[t]he authority of the legitimate power having in fact passed into the hands of the occupant, the latter shall take all the measures in his power to restore and ensure, as far as possible, public order and safety, while respecting, unless absolutely prevented, the laws in force in the country".

To start with, this provision is of negative character insofar as it generally obliges the occupying power not to change the laws in the occupied territory but for a rather strictly crafted exception clause ("unless absolutely prevented"). If this requisite is met, however, the occupying power has the positive obligation to "restore and ensure", as the English text puts it, "public order and safety". When considering the (solely authentic[16]) French version of Article 43 HR,[17] the provision still manifests the characteristic security focus of the law of occupation, but it also makes clear that the occupying power, beyond its responsibility for "*l'ordre public*", has a broader mandate to restore and ensure "*la vie publique*" i.e. public or civil life in a broader sense.[18] Thus, occupation law's security focus has always been relative, not absolute in nature.

15 See notably Sassòli, *supra* note 12, 673-674.

16 See D. Schindler & J. Toman, *The Laws of Armed Conflict*, 4th ed. (2004), 56.

17 Speaking of "*l'ordre et la vie publics*".

18 See Sassòli, *supra* note 12, 663-664, also referring to *Baron Lambermont*, the Belgian representative at the negotiations for the 1874 *Brussels Declaration*, who considered this phrase to encompass "*des fonctions sociales, des transactions ordinaires, qui constituent la vie de tous les jours*". See *Grahame v. Director of Public Prosecutions, British Zone of Control, Control Commission Court of Appeal*, Case No. 103, 26 July

This becomes even clearer when analyzing Article 64 IV GC which was adopted half a century after Article 43 HR, with a view of, to a certain extent at least, widening the scope for changes in the existing local legislation[19]:

> "The penal laws of the occupied territory shall remain in force, with the exception that they may be repealed or suspended by the Occupying Power in cases where they constitute a threat to its security or an obstacle to the application of the present Convention. Subject to the latter consideration and to the necessity for ensuring the effective administration of justice, the tribunals of the occupied territory shall continue to function in respect of all offences covered by the said laws.
>
> The Occupying Power may, however, subject the population of the occupied territory to provisions which are essential to enable the Occupying Power to fulfil its obligations under the present Convention, to maintain the orderly government of the territory, and to ensure the security of the Occupying Power, of the members and property of the occupying forces or administration, and likewise of the establishments and lines of communication used by them."

The main duty of the occupying power, under the first paragraph, remains negative, i.e. to respect the penal laws of the occupied territory. Yet, such laws may be repealed or suspended, not only if "absolutely prevented", but in more generous terms.[20] By not only offering the security of the occupying power as a justification to act, but also the proper "application of the present Convention", the operational range of the occupying power is considerably widened, since it can in principle draw on every interest recognized in the Convention to justify its pushing back of the existing local penal legislation.

This is confirmed by the analysis of the second paragraph of the provision, which deals with the legislation in the occupied territory in general and is phrased in positive terms. The three grounds for creating new law for the occupied population, which are offered by it to the occupying power, are, on equal footing, the (already familiar) security interests of the oc-

1947, 14 *Annual Digest and Reports of Public International Law Cases* (1947), 228, 232: "'*l'ordre et la vie publics*' [is] a phrase which refers to the whole social, commercial and economic life of the community". See in a similar vein Arai-Takahashi, *supra* note 12, 1425-1426; Benvenisti, *supra* note 9, 78-79.

19 See in particular the analysis of the two provisions in *supra* note 12.

20 See notably Benvenisti, *supra* note 9, 95-96, with further references.

cupying power, the fulfillment of the occupying power's obligations under the *Fourth Geneva Convention*, and the maintenance of the orderly government of the occupied territory.

When assessing this rather broad authorization, it becomes obvious that rule of law issues are not beyond the remit of the law of occupation.[21] This already holds true for Article 43 HR, where it may be argued that the concept of "civil life" can be drawn upon to justify (moderate) rule of law transfer, e.g. by abolishing discriminatory laws.[22] More boldly put, "[i]n modern understanding, 'public order and safety' means a guarantee of the rule of law […]".[23]

This idea applies with even more force to Article 64 IV GC. Fulfilling its duties under the Convention means that the occupying power must take care of a whole range of rule of law-related issues, including negative duties such as not to alter the status of public officials or judges in the occupied territories (Article 54 IV GC), but also positive responsibilities such as ensuring the existence of a functioning (penal) court system which applies nonretroactive and proportionate laws (Articles 66, 67 IV GC) or respecting fundamental fair trial and due process guarantees (Articles 71 to 73 IV GC).[24] Moreover, this is reinforced by the express inclusion of the occupying power's responsibility for the "orderly government" of the occupied territory into the Convention. While these provisions primarily address the administration set up by the occupying power, it is not a far-fetched thought to also apply such rule of law standards to the existing local courts. After all, Article 64 (1) IV GC states that the courts existing in the occupied territory shall continue to function in respect of the pertinent pe-

21 See also UK War Office, *The Law of War on Land, Being Part III of the Manual of Military Law* (1958), 145 according to which an occupying power may repeal or suspend laws if in the occupied territory there is no "adequate legal system in conformity with generally recognised principles of law"; see, in a similar vein, UK Ministry of Defence, *The Manual of the Law of Armed Conflict* (2004), 284: "The occupying power should make no more changes to the law than are absolutely necessary, particularly where the occupied territory has an already adequate legal system".

22 As to this example see Arai-Takahashi, *supra* note 12, 1426.

23 M. Bothe, 'The Administration of Occupied Territory', in A. Clapham, P. Gaeta & M. Sassòli (eds), *The 1949 Geneva Conventions. A Commentary* (2015), 1455, 1469.

24 See in this regard also common Article 3 (1) (d) of the *Geneva Conventions*; Articles 99-108 and 130 last sentence of the *Third Geneva Convention*; Article 75, paragraphs 3-8 of the *First Additional Protocol*; as well as Article 8 (2) (a) (vi) of the *Rome Statute of the International Criminal Court*, 17 July 1998, 2187 UNTS 3; see also Arai-Takahashi, *supra* note 12, 1433-1434, 1438-1450 in this regard.

nal law provisions "[s]ubject [...] to the necessity for ensuring the effective administration of justice".

Hence, in spite of the law on occupation's relative focus on its own security, the occupying power also has responsibilities in terms of promoting the rule of law, authorizing, and even obliging it, if need be, to subject the population of the occupied territory to new legal provisions, i.e. to legislate in favor of the rule of law although the existing law in the occupied territory points in another direction. One might even find it useful to address these obligations "in modern parlance" as a "duty of good governance"[25] incumbent on the occupying power. This would typically include the maintenance and, if necessary, the establishment of an adequate normative order, an adequate administrative apparatus, a functioning court system, effective law enforcement, etc.[26]

Thus, the promotion of the rule of law complements the safeguarding of the occupying power's legitimate security interests as an additional objective of the law of occupation – if one does not want to make the further argument, merging the two objectives as it were, that promoting the rule of law in the occupied territory is in itself a major contribution to the occupying power's security since it will typically raise the legitimacy and stability of the occupier's administration in the eyes of the population under occupation.

III. Conservationist Character

A third characteristic of the law of occupation is its conservationist character.[27] As the occupying power is not the territorial sovereign, but only enjoys temporally limited powers over the occupied territory, this body of law seeks to preserve the legal position of the ousted sovereign as well as its

25 Bothe, *supra* note 23, 1467; see also Arai-Takahashi, *supra* note 12, 1462-1463.

26 See Bothe, *supra* note 23, 1467.

27 See Roberts, 'Transformative Military Occupation', *supra* note 9, 580, referring to the "conservationist principle"; see also Sassòli, *supra* note 12, 668 ("the conservative approach of [international humanitarian law] towards belligerent occupation"); Bhuta, *supra* note 11, 726: "[...] the fundamental principle of occupation law accepted by mid-to-late 19th-century publicists was that an occupant could not alter the political order of territory"; Bothe, *supra* note 23, 1460 ("[...] continuity of the pre-existing legal system (conservationist principle, *principe de stabilité juridique*)").

nationals who are now under foreign occupation.[28] Against this background, the law of occupation is reticent, even hostile *vis-à-vis* any attempt on the part of the occupying power to alter the legal status of the occupied territory or population beyond the necessary minimum.[29]

Article 47 IV GC is emblematic of this approach: "Protected persons who are in occupied territory shall not be deprived, in any case or in any manner whatsoever, of the benefits of the present Convention by any change introduced, as the result of the occupation of a territory, into the institutions or government of the said territory, nor by any agreement concluded between the authorities of the occupied territories and the Occupying Power, nor by any annexation by the latter of the whole or part of the occupied territory." In addition, the aforementioned Articles 43 HR and 64 IV GC also testify to the law on occupation's interest in conserving, as far as possible, the *status quo* in the occupied territory.

Three developments qualifying this analysis deserve to be highlighted. To start with, in particular in the post-World War II law of occupation, there has been a notable shift from the interests of the ousted sovereign to those of the population under occupation, not the least under the influence of the principle of the self-determination of peoples.[30] Hence, in the triangle of interests[31] between the occupying power, the ousted sovereign, and the occupied population, which the law of occupation has always sought to manage, the interests of the latter have been accorded increasing relevance over the last couple of decades.[32] Inasmuch as the needs of the local population so require, the occupying power is justified, and even

---

28 Benvenisti, *supra* note 9, 69-70; see also Roberts, 'Transformative Military Occupation,' *supra* note 9, 585: "temporary trusteeship". As regards the occupier's role as a (mere) *de facto* administrator of the occupied territory see notably J. S. Pictet (ed), *Commentary on the Geneva Convention (IV) relative to the Protection of Civilian Persons in Time of War* (1958), 273.

29 See Roberts, 'Transformative Military Occupation,' *supra* note 9, 582: "The assumption that, the occupant's role being temporary, any alteration of the existing order in the occupied territory should be minimal lies at the heart of the provisions on military occupation in the laws of war".

30 See Article 1 (2) of the *Charter of the United Nations*, 26 June 1945, 1 UNTS XVI; common Article 1 of the *International Covenant on Economic, Social and Cultural Rights*, 16 December 1966, 993 UNTS 3, 5, and of the *International Covenant on Civil and Political Rights*, 16 December 1966, 999 UNTS 171, 173.

31 See Dinstein, *supra* note 5, 1; Benvenisti, *supra* note 9, 69.

32 See the *dictum* from Judge Hardy Dillard's Separate Opinion in *Western Sahara*, Advisory Opinion, 16 October 1975, ICJ Reports 1975, 12, 116, 122: "It is for the people to determine the destiny of the territory and not the territory the destiny of the people." See further O. Ben-Naftali, '"A la recherche du temps perdu": Re-

obliged, to pursue a more activist approach, even though this might interfere with the ousted government's interest in the maintenance of the *status quo* and run counter to the traditional ideal of an occupation characterized by the "[...] minimal necessary interaction [...]"[33] between the occupying power and the population under occupation. As the "lodestar guiding the law of belligerent occupation [...] is the principle that the civilian population of an occupied territory must benefit from maximal safeguards feasible in the circumstances",[34] the ICRC Commentary to the *Fourth Geneva Convention* already noted that "[c]ertain changes might conceivably be necessary and even an improvement [...] [Article 47 IV GC] is of an essentially humanitarian character; its object is to safeguard human beings and not to protect the political institutions and government machinery of the State as such."[35]

The second issue is the experience of the Allied occupations immediately after World War II, notably that of Germany. The Allies were eager to avoid the impression that their military and administrative presence was legally based on, and therefore limited by, the framework set by the *Hague Regulations*. Various justifications were relied upon in this regard: that, due to major security issues and the very nature of the Nazi regime, the Allied powers were "absolutely prevented" from maintaining the existing system of government,[36] that Germany's political and military institutions had completely disintegrated by May 1945, and that, for lack of any government-in-exile or any kind of resistance on behalf of Germany, there was a situation of *debellatio*[37] or that, by virtue of Germany's unconditional surrender, the Allies vested themselves with the powers of the German govern-

---

thinking Article 6 of the Fourth Geneva Convention in the Light of the Legal Consequences of a Wall in the Occupied Palestinian Territory Advisory Opinion', 38 *Israel Law Review* (2005) 1-2, 211, 221: "Although previously owed to the ousted political sovereign, the contemporary concept of self-determination, which vests [...] sovereignty in the people themselves [...] decree[s] that such trust is owed to the occupied population".

33 Benvenisti, *supra* note 9, 70.

34 Dinstein, *supra* note 5, 286.

35 Pictet, *supra* note 28, 274; see also Arai-Takahashi, *supra* note 12, 1428.

36 Roberts, 'Transformative Military Occupation', *supra* note 9, 587, fn. 22.

37 See A. Roberts, 'What is a Military Occupation?', 55 *British Yearbook of International Law* (1984) 1, 249, 268-269 [Roberts, What is a Military Occupation?]; Benvenisti, *supra* note 9, 162; Sassòli, *supra* note 12, 672.

ment and erected an occupation régime *sui generis* on this basis.[38] Thus, the restrictions entailed by the traditional law of occupation should be avoided and a fundamental reshuffle of the German political, economic, social, and legal system should become possible. There was consensus among the Allies that only such complete turnover of the structures existing in Germany would permit a truly new start, notably a comprehensive and ambitious *rule of law program*.[39] It is crucial to have this precedent in mind not merely as a matter of historical curiosity, but because the current debate on human rights-informed occupation policies[40] considerably draws, explicitly or implicitly, on Germany's (and, for that matter, Japan's) post-World War II occupation.

Third, occupation's conservationist character is further challenged by the phenomenon of long-standing occupations, such as the already half-century old Israeli occupation of the Occupied Palestinian Territory (OPT), but also the decades-long Moroccan and Turkish military presences in Western Sahara and Northern Cyprus. The traditional law of occupation was modeled on rather short-term occupations of several months or years, but not for protracted occupations that give rise to additional challenges, notably in view of the developing needs of the population under occupation.[41] As has been stated by the Israeli Supreme Court already at the beginning of the occupation of the OPT, "[l]ife does not stand still, and no

38 Also the text of the *Berlin Declaration* of 5 June 1945, 68 UNTS 189, 190, according to which the Allies announced that they had assumed "[...] supreme authority with respect to Germany, including all the powers possessed by the German Government, the High Command and any State, municipal, or local government or authority", can be read in this regard.

39 See Proclamation No. 1 by the Supreme Commander of the Allied Forces, General *Dwight D. Eisenhower*, dating from September 1944, announcing that "[w]e shall overthrow the Nazi rule, dissolve the Nazi Party and abolish the cruel, oppressive and discriminatory laws and institutions which the Party has created", as well as Law No. 1 on the *Abrogation of Nazi Law*, Law and Orders of Military Government Complete Collection up to June 30th 1945, 3 which sought "to eliminate from German law and administration within the occupied territory the policies and doctrines of the National Socialist Party, and to restore to the German people the rule of justice and equality before the law [...]".

40 See C.

41 See, for instance, the controversy regarding the introduction, in 1975, of a value added tax in the OPT (analogous to that in Israel) which was justified as an equalizing device, i.e. to augment the free flow of goods and services between Israel and the OPT; Supreme Court of Israel, *Abu Aita et al. v. Commander of Judea and Samaria et al.*, HCJ 69/81, Judgment of 5 April 1975, 37(2) PD 197; see the discussion in Dinstein, *supra* note 5, 128.

administration, whether an occupation administration or another, can fulfil its duties with respect to the population if it refrains from legislating and from adapting the legal situation to the exigencies of modern times."[42] According to such reasoning, limiting oneself to simply preserving the *status quo* cannot be considered a viable option in situations of long-standing occupation. In this regard, it has, for instance, been submitted that the exceptions to Article 43 HR should be interpreted more extensively the longer an occupation regime lasts.[43]

It is generally agreed that these developments have a dynamizing effect on the contemporary interpretation of the law of occupation. As has been stated, "[r]ecent practice [...] seems to suggest that there are reasons to shift the emphasis from maintaining the status quo to [...] especially the duty of good governance".[44] Going beyond gradual approaches, the aforementioned developments have motivated some scholars to conceive of novel approaches to the law of occupation. One of the most prominent concepts in the present debate is that of *transformative* occupation,[45] posing the question whether "[w]ithin the existing framework of international law, [it is] legitimate for an occupying power, in the name of creating the conditions for a more democratic and peaceful state, to introduce fundamental changes in the constitutional, social, economic, and legal order within an occupied territory".[46]

It is fairly obvious that such a dynamic and activist take on the law of occupation can hardly be based on the provisions of the *Hague Regulations* and the *Fourth Geneva Convention*, as discussed above. At the same time, the said academics would claim that theirs is not only a project *de lege fer-*

42 Supreme Court of Israel, *The Christian Society for the Sacred Places v. Minister of Defence*, HCJ 337/71, 26(1) PD 574, 582.

43 See R. Kolb, *Ius in bello. Le droit international humanitaire des conflits armés* (2002), 186; Arai-Takahashi, *supra* note 12, 1425; Bothe, *supra* note 23, 1462-1463, 1467.

44 Bothe, *supra* note 23, 1462.

45 As regards the term see Roberts, 'Transformative Military Occupation', *supra* note 9, 580; Bhuta, *supra* note 11, 721; A. Carcano, *The Transformation of Occupied Territory in International Law* (2015); see also D. Scheffer, 'Beyond Occupation Law', 97 *American Journal of International Law* (2003) 4, 842, 847, fn. 18 (and *passim*): "transformational".

46 Roberts, 'Transformative Military Occupation', *supra* note 9, 580; see also Scheffer, *supra* note 45, 849, pleading for an expanded scope of permissible action if the occupied population requires "[...] revolutionary changes in its economy (including a leap into robust capitalism), rigorous implementation of international human rights standards, a new constitution and judiciary, and a new political structure (most likely consistent with principles of democracy) [...]".

enda, but reflects actual legal transformations in international law. In this regard, they commonly refer to the impact of international human rights (C.) as well as of the UNSC's involvement in situations of occupation and post-conflict administrations (D.) on the international law of occupation. Against this background, it may be asked how these two phenomena can be reconciled with the account of the international law of occupation in the strict sense given above and to what extent they have contributed their share to promoting rule of law transfers in situations beyond the traditional law of occupation.

C. The Impact of International Human Rights Law

Much ink has been spilled on the question of the relationship of international humanitarian law and international human rights law.[47] Already *Fraenkel* envisaged the application of "an international bill of rights [...] to an occupation regime, at least after the purely military phase of the occupation has ended".[48] As early as 1968, the *UN General Assembly* adopted a resolution on "respect for human rights in armed conflicts".[49] Subsequently, in 1970, the General Assembly defined, as a "basic principle" to be applied for the protection of the civilian population, that "[f]undamental human rights, as accepted in international law and laid down in international instruments, continue to apply fully in situations of armed conflict".[50] Irrespective of whether one considers the *lex specialis* approach championed by

47 See, for instance, L. Doswald-Beck & S. Vité, 'International Humanitarian Law and Human Rights Law', 33 *International Review of the Red Cross* (1993) 293, 94; T. Meron, 'The Humanization of Humanitarian Law', 94 *American Journal of International Law* (2000) 2, 239; R. Provost, *International Human Rights and Humanitarian Law* (2002); H. Krieger, 'A Conflict of Norms: The Relationship Between Humanitarian Law and Human Rights Law in the ICRC Customary Law Study', 11 *Journal of Conflict and Security Law* (2006) 2, 265; D. Droege, 'The Interplay Between International Humanitarian Law and International Human Rights Law in Situations of Armed Conflict', 40 *Israel Law Review* (2007) 2, 310; A. Orakhelashvili, 'The Interaction Between Human Rights and Humanitarian Law: Fragmentation, Conflict, Parallelism or Convergence?', 19 *European Journal of International Law* (2008) 1, 161; Roberts, 'Transformative Military Occupation', *supra* note 9, 590-595, with further references.

48 Fraenkel, *supra* note 1, 205.

49 GA Res. 2444 (XXIII), UN Doc A/RES/2444, 19 December 1968.

50 GA Res. 2675 (XXV), UN Doc A/RES/2675, 9 December 1970.

the ICJ[51] as an appropriate description of this intricate relationship, there can be no doubt today that international human rights law is in principle also applicable and relevant in situations of armed conflict, including in situations of occupation.[52]

In particular, the ICJ has not only held that the *International Covenant on Civil and Political Rights* does not cease to apply in times of war, except by operation of the derogation clause in its Article 4,[53] but has explicitly stated that this covers situations of occupation and encompasses other international human rights instruments, such as the *International Covenant on Economic, Social and Cultural Rights* and the *Convention on the Rights of the Child* (including its *Optional Protocol on the Involvement of Children in Armed Conflict*) as well as the *African Charter on Human and Peoples' Rights*, i.e. the *Banjul Charter*.[54]

In addition, it has become common to highlight the relevance of international human rights law in terms of legal interpretation. This means that the law of occupation should be read in the light of, and in conformity with, international human rights law. Such a call for the harmonious interpretation of the two bodies of law can be based on Article 31 (3) (c) of the *Vienna Convention on the Law of Treaties* according to which, when interpreting an international treaty (such as the *Hague Regulations* or the *Fourth Geneva Convention*), "any relevant rules of international law applicable in the relations between the parties" shall be taken into account. The rele-

51 See *Legality of the Threat or Use of Nuclear Weapons*, Advisory Opinion, ICJ Reports 1996, 226, 240, para. 25; *Legal Consequences of the Construction of a Wall in the Occupied Palestinian Territory*, Advisory Opinion, ICJ Reports 2004, 136, 178, para. 106 [ICJ, Wall Opinion]; *Armed Activities on the Territory of the Congo (Democratic Republic of the Congo v. Uganda)*, Judgment, ICJ Reports 2005, 168, 242, 243, para. 216.

52 See also the pertinent statements of international human rights courts and bodies; *Loizidou v. Turkey*, ECtHR Application No. 15.318/89, Judgment (Preliminary Objections) of 23 March 1995, para. 62; *Ilaşcu and others v. Moldova and Russia*, ECtHR Application No. 48.787/99, Judgment of 8 July 2004, para. 312; *Salas and others v. United States*, IACHR Case No. 10.573, Report No. 31/93, para. 6. See, however, Benvenisti, *supra* note 9, 14-15, who refers to the US and Israel as persistent objectors in this regard.

53 See the references *supra* note 51.

54 ICJ, 'Wall Opinion', *supra* note 51, 180, 181, paras. 111-113; *Armed Activities on the Territory of the Congo (Democratic Republic of the Congo v. Uganda)*, Judgment, ICJ Reports 2005, 168, 243, 244, para. 217.

vance of this principle of "systemic integration"[55] for the proper construction of international humanitarian law becomes particularly obvious when considering Article 72 of the 1977 *First Additional Protocol* according to which its provisions shall be "additional [...] to other applicable rules of international law relating to the protection of fundamental human rights during international armed conflict".

In addition, there is consensus among all international human rights courts and treaty bodies that international human rights treaties, by virtue of their *telos* of not only protecting, but promoting human rights,[56] should be considered "living instruments"[57] and should therefore be subject to dynamic or evolutive interpretation.[58]

It is quite obvious that, when combining the two approaches, the conservationist character of the law of occupation tends to be complemented, and superseded, by the dynamizing force of human rights interpretation.[59] Thus, the potential for human rights to promote the rule of law[60] may help a great deal in opening up the rather reluctant attitude of traditional occupation law *vis-à-vis* rule of law transfers on the part of the occupying power.[61]

---

55 See, e.g., O. Dörr, 'Article 31: General Rule of Interpretation', in: O. Dörr & K. Schmalenbach (eds), *Vienna Convention on the Law of Treaties*, 2nd ed. (2018), 604; C. McLachlan, 'The Principle of Systemic Integration and Article 31(3)(c) of the Vienna Convention', 54 *The International and Comparative Law Quarterly* (2005) 2, 279.

56 See, e.g., Preamble of the *Convention for the Protection of Human Rights and Fundamental Freedoms*, 4 November 1950, 213 UNTS 221, 222: "[...] maintenance and further realization of Human Rights and Fundamental Freedoms".

57 *Tyrer v. United Kingdom*, ECtHR Application No. 5856/72, Judgment of 25 April 1978, para. 31; *The Right to Information on Consular Assistance in the Framework of the Guarantees of the Due Process of Law*, Advisory Opinion, 1 October 1999, IACtHR No. 16, OC-16/99, para. 114.

58 See E. Bjorge, *Domestic Application of the ECHR. Courts as Faithful Trustees* (2015), 131-133, with further references.

59 See in particular the analysis in Roberts, 'Transformative Military Occupation', *supra* note 9, 595-601; Benvenisti, *supra* note 9, 74-76; Arai-Takahashi, *supra* note 12, 1426-1427.

60 See, e.g. Articles 6-11 of the *Universal Declaration of Human Rights*, G.A. Res. 217 A(III), UN Doc. A/RES/3/217 A, 10 December 1948; Articles 14-16 of the *International Covenant on Civil and Political Rights*, 16 December 1966, 999 UNTS 171 [ICCPR]. It is worth noting in this context that Article 75 of the First Additional Protocol on "fundamental guarantees" is directly derived from the ICCPR; Roberts, 'Transformative Military Occupation', *supra* note 9, 591.

61 See Benvenisti, *supra* note 9, 102-103.

In particular, the *Human Rights Committee* has stated:

> "Safeguards related to derogation, as embodied in article 4 of the Covenant, are based on the principles of legality and the rule of law inherent in the Covenant as a whole. As certain elements of the right to a fair trial are explicitly guaranteed under international humanitarian law during armed conflict, the Committee finds no justification for derogation from these guarantees during other emergency situations. The Committee is of the opinion that the principles of legality and the rule of law require that fundamental requirements of fair trial must be respected during a state of emergency."[62]

In addition, the *European Court of Human Rights* has activated the rule of law-promoting potential of Article 6 ECHR when requiring Turkey, as the occupying power in Northern Cyprus, to try civilians accused of acts characterized as military offences before courts warranting the necessary guarantees of independence and impartiality.[63] While such a call can relatively easily be reconciled with the law of occupation, in other cases the human rights-induced activity may well go beyond what would traditionally be demanded, and accepted, by the law of occupation, e.g. in instances where "Convention rights would clearly be incompatible with the laws of the territory occupied".[64]

This result is corroborated by the fact that, whereas the traditional law of occupation is primarily negative in character, it has become common to conceive of international human rights law not only as a source of negative obligations (duty to respect), but of a whole series of positive obligations (duty to protect and to fulfill).[65] Hence, the States, under whose jurisdic-

---

62 Human Rights Committee, *CCPR General Comment No. 29: Article 4: Derogations during a State of Emergency*, CCPR/C/21/Rev. 1/Add.11, 31 August 2001, para. 16. This notably includes the right of access to a court of law in case of criminal proceedings, the right to be presumed innocent as well as the right to *habeas corpus*.

63 *Cyprus v. Turkey*, ECtHR Application No. 25781/94, Judgment of 10 May 2001, paras. 358-359.

64 UK House of Lords, *Al-Skeini and others v. Secretary of State for Defense*, [2007] UKHL 26, para. 129, where Lord Brown acknowledges that the occupant's obligation to respect Article 43 HR might be in conflict with its obligations under the ECHR and offers the example of the existence of Sharia law in the occupied territory.

65 See in this regard, for instance, W. Kälin & J. Künzli, *The Law of International Human Rights Protection* (2009), 96-98.

tion[66] territories and persons fall (and this notably includes occupying powers[67]), are positively obliged to create and maintain a certain rule of law standard in the occupied territory, irrespective of whether the previous government took care of such human rights obligations.[68] Hence, an otherwise careful and sober analysis of the occupant's prerogatives concludes that the occupying power

> "[...] has an obligation to abolish legislation and institutions which contravene international human rights standards. [...] Today, an occupying power has a strong argument that it is 'absolutely prevented' from applying local legislation contrary to international law. Human rights [...] often require the state to take positive (including legislative) action. Thus, one may even go so far as to allow the occupying power to adopt new, additional laws that are genuinely necessary to protect international human rights law."[69]

Going even further than that, some scholars would distill from the body of international human rights law – in a somewhat constitutionalist perspective – the insight that all (including international) law exists *hominum*

---

66 See Article 1 of the *Convention for the Protection of Human Rights and Fundamental Freedoms*, 4 November 1950, 213 UNTS 221 as well as Article 1 of the *International Covenant on Civil and Political Rights*, 16 December 1966, 999 UNTS 171; in regard to the latter see ICJ, 'Wall Opinion', *supra* note 51, 178, paras. 108-111.

67 See e.g., in regard to the UK occupation of Iraq, *Al-Skeini and others v. United Kingdom*, ECtHR Application No. 55721/07, Judgment of 7 July 2011, paras. 138-140, 143-150.

68 In view of the fact that the major part of the aforementioned international human rights guarantees is customary in nature, such obligations even exist widely independently of whether the territory in question falls in the territorial scope of application of international human rights treaties.

69 Sassòli, *supra* note 12, 676; however, he adds in *ibid.*, 677: "As long as local legislation falls within [the] latitude [left by international human rights law to the State on how to implement it], an occupying power may certainly not replace it"; see further Pictet, *supra* note 28, 336 noting that occupying authorities may not change local legislation "merely to make it accord with their own legal conceptions". In a similar vein, see Bothe, *supra* note 23, 1462: "The duty to maintain the pre-existing law of the territory could not require the Occupying Power to violate human rights."; *ibid.*, 1469: "In modern understanding, 'public order and safety' means a guarantee of the rule of law, and therefore of human rights." See also (arguably more carefully) Benvenisti, *supra* note 9, 75: "the occupant's authority to rule as well as to modify the law is now subjected to human rights obligations, which arguably mandate the obligation to maintain basic demands of a system based on the rule of law."

causa, i.e. for the sake of human beings.[70] When applying such a hermeneutic approach to the law of occupation,[71] the interests and well-being of the population under occupation become an even more urgent responsibility of the occupying power, justifying and demanding sweeping interventions into the law existing in the occupied territory. Against this background, the characteristic traits of the traditional law of occupation, as identified above, tend to lose any restraining effect on the authority of the occupying power, as long as its action appears necessary to promote the local population's well-being.

The far-reaching impact of international human rights law on the law of occupation has been addressed by a broad range of scholars, opting for varying degrees and intensities of such impact.[72] Some have even sought to reflect this reality by coining neologisms such as "humanitarian occupation"[73] or the "humanization of humanitarian law".[74] That international human rights law (including the pertinent case-law of international human rights courts and bodies[75]) has had a substantial effect on the law of occupation cannot be denied. Thus, the significant rule of law-promoting potential of international human rights informs the law of occupation in the strict sense and adds to the (if somewhat limited) rule of law transfer

70 See Hermogenianus, *Iuris epitomae*, Liber I, Dig. 1.5.2: "*hominum causa omne jus constitutum est*". See, in this respect, *Prosecutor v. Duško Tadić*, ICTY Appeals Chamber, Decision on the Defence Motion for Interlocutory Appeal on Jurisdiction, IT-94-1-AR72, 2 October 1995, para. 97: "A State-sovereignty-oriented approach has been gradually supplanted by a human-being-oriented approach. Gradually the maxim of Roman law *hominum causa omne jus constitutum est* (all law is created for the benefit of human beings) has gained a firm foothold in the international community as well [...] [I]nternational law, while of course safeguarding the legitimate interests of States, must gradually turn to the protection of human beings".

71 As has been done for the concept of sovereignty; see notably A. Peters, 'Humanity as the A and Ω of Sovereignty', 20 *European Journal of International Law* (2009) 3, 513 as well as the commentary in A. T. Müller, 'Sovereignty 2010: The Necessity of Circling the Square', 4 *Vienna Journal on International Constitutional Law* (2010) 4, 624, 635-640.

72 See the references in Benvenisti, *supra* note 9, 13, 74-76, 102-104; Dinstein, *supra* note 5, 69-88.

73 G. H. Fox, *Humanitarian Occupation* (2008).

74 Meron, *supra* note 47.

75 See in this regard notably Benvenisti, *supra* note 9, 74; see further the references *supra* notes 52, 62-63, 67.

potential of the latter, as identified above.[76] This notably holds true in case of long-standing occupations.[77]

At the same time, one should resist the temptation of taking the dynamism and transformative power of international human rights law too far, lest the wisdom underlying the restraining of the powers of the occupying power be lost. To be sure, already under *normal* circumstances, the State is not only the prime guarantor of human rights, but also the greatest threat to these very same human rights. This truth applies with even greater force when a population is confronted with an occupying power which will virtually always be guided by interests that are alien to the occupied territory and population. The ideal of the benevolent and humanitarian occupier can easily prove a dangerous illusion. Not only remote instances of occupation, but more recent and persisting situations of occupation (e.g. Crimea, Iraq, Northern Cyprus, the OPT, the Western Sahara) provide abundant, and painful, proof for it. This should serve as a powerful reminder for the soundness of the traditionally cautious approach with respect to the construction of the occupier's prerogatives, also in the light of international human rights law.

D. *The Impact of the Involvement of the Security Council*

In the relevant debate, quite a few commentators have shared these concerns and notably referred to the 2003 occupation of Iraq by the United States and the United Kingdom as a recent case in point.[78] Yet this brings to the fore a further actor relevant for the present discussion, not hitherto mentioned: the UNSC. Drawing on its powers under Chapter VII of the UN Charter, the UNSC sought to create a legal framework for the occupation of Iraq,[79] calling upon "all concerned to comply fully with their obli-

76 See B. III.

77 Roberts, 'Transformative Military Occupation', *supra* note 9, 600, states in this regard that "because of the broad subject matter coverage, [human rights instruments] may be cited particularly often in occupation that continue for a long time, even into something approximating peacetime, and that present problems different from those addressed by the laws of war". See B. III.

78 See e.g. D. Thürer & M. MacLaren, '"*Ius post bellum*" in Iraq: A Challenge to the Applicability and Relevance of International Humanitarian Law?', in K. Dicke et al (eds), *Weltinnenrecht: Liber Amicorum Jost Delbrück* (2005), 753.

79 See SC Res. 1483, UN Doc S/RES/1483 (2003), 22 May 2003; SC Res. 1490, UN Doc S/RES/1490 (2003), 3 July 2003; SC Res. 1500, UN Doc S/RES/1500 (2003),

gations under international law including in particular the Geneva Conventions of 1949 and the Hague Regulations of 1907".[80]

It is remarkable that the UNSC also called for the appointment of a UN Special Representative whose responsibilities would include efforts to restore and establish national and local institutions for representative governance, encouraging international efforts to contribute to basic civilian administration functions, and promoting the protection of human rights, as well as encouraging international efforts to rebuild the capacity of the Iraqi civilian force and to promote legal and judicial reform.[81] In this regard, the UNSC entrusted the Special Representative, in support of, and collaboration with, *the Authority* (i.e. the *Coalition Provisional Authority* as the occupation government set up by the US and the UK) with a rule of law-promoting mandate.[82] It has been rightly noted that "the purposes of the occupation as outlined in Resolution 1483 went beyond the confines of the Hague Regulations and the Fourth Geneva Convention. Yet the resolution did not explain the relation between the transformative purposes of this occupation and the more conservative purposes of the existing body of law on occupations."[83]

Having in mind that the UN Member States confer on the UNSC, pursuant to Article 24 of the UN Charter, primary responsibility for the main-

14 August 2003; SC Res. 1511, UN Doc S/RES/1511 (2003), 16 October 2003; SC Res. 1546, UN Doc S/RES/1546 (2004), 8 June 2004.

80 SC Res. 1483, UN Doc S/RES/1483 (2003), 22 May 2003, para. 5.

81 See *ibid.*, para. 8, lit. c, f, g, h.

82 See also SC Res. 1511, UN Doc S/RES/1511 (2003), 16 October 2003, pream. para. 10 ("[a]ffirming the importance of the rule of law, national reconciliation, respect for human rights including the rights of women, fundamental freedoms, and democracy including free and fair elections") as well as op. para. 7, lit. b sub-lit. iii ("promote the protection of human rights, national reconciliation, and judicial and legal reform in order to strengthen the rule of law in Iraq").

83 Roberts, 'Transformative Military Occupation', *supra* note 9, 613. See in this regard also Scheffer, *supra* note 45, 845: SC Res. 1483 "rested uncomfortably within occupation law" and the latter "was never designed for such transforming exercises", *ibid.*, 849. Calling for a restrictive reading G. H. Fox, 'The Occupation of Iraq', 36 *Georgetown Journal of International Law* (2005) 2, 195; Sassòli, *supra* note 12, 679-682; as well as Bhuta, *supra* note 11, 735 seeing "persuasive reasons to construe Resolution 1483 and 1500 as not entitling the US and UK to derogate from the preservationist core of occupation law", but nonetheless conceding that the resolutions "are sufficiently ambiguous to permit a colourable claim of legitimation – if not legalization – of the idea that the occupying power is authorized, in the interests of the population, to exceed its order-preserving functions and embark on a project of state-building".

tenance of international peace and security and that the UNSC, in carrying out its duties under this responsibility, acts on their behalf, the risk of bias and one-sidedness referred to before might not exist in regard to the UNSC. After all, it is not dominated by the interests of a single great power, but its decisions reflect a certain consensus at least of its permanent members so that one might expect the UNSC to take decisions reflecting the common interest of the international community.[84]

Whilst this is certainly a controversial assumption, notably in regard to the Iraqi occupation, another question is whether the UNSC can at least be considered a neutral arbitrator of interests when it comes to so-called *post-conflict administrations*[85], i.e. UN-run administrations of territories such as in the cases of Cambodia,[86] Kosovo,[87] and East Timor.[88] These cases are of interest in the context of the present discussion, since they all involve quite ambitious rule of law-promoting mandates.[89]

The question is, however, how these instances of territorial administrations by the UN relate to the law of occupation. In this respect, the prevailing opinion appears to be that they do not constitute situations of occupation and do not therefore trigger the applicability of the international law

---

84 See, however, Sassòli, *supra* note 12, 693, criticizing that the reliance on the Security Council is "not satisfactory from a humanitarian point of view and [...] also raises concerns from the point of view of the rule of international law because of the selective and short-term political approach of the Council".

85 See in this regard, e.g., S. Chesterman, *You, the People: The United Nations, Transitional Administration and State-Building* (2004); R. Wolfrum, 'International Administration in Post-Conflict Situations by the United Nations and Other International Actors', in A. von Bogdandy & R. Wolfrum (eds), 9 *Max Planck Yearbook of United Nations Law* (2005), 649; R. Wilde, *International Territorial Administration* (2008).

86 See SC Res. 745, UN Doc S/RES/745 (1992), 28 February 1992, para. 2, establishing the *UN Transitional Administration in Cambodia* – UNTAC.

87 SC Res. 1244, UN Doc S/RES/1244 (1999), 10 June 1999, para. 10, establishing the *UN Interim Administration Mission in Kosovo* – UNMIK.

88 SC Res. 1272, UN Doc S/RES/1272 (1999), 25 October 1999, para. 1, establishing the *UN Transitional Administration in East Timor* – UNTAET.

89 See SC Res. 1244, UN Doc S/RES/1244 (1999), 10 June 1999, para. 11, lit. b, c, d and in particular lit. i ("maintaining civil law and order") and j ("protecting and promoting human rights"); Special Representative of the Secretary-General, Regulation No. 1999/1 on the Authority of the Interim Administration in Kosovo, UNMIK/REG/1999/1, 25 July 1999, Sect. 1 (1); SC Res. 1272, UN Doc S/RES/1272 (1999), 25 October 1999, para.2, lit. b, e; Special Representative of the Secretary-General, Regulation No. 1999/1 on the Authority of the Transitional Administration in East Timor, UNTAET/REG/1999/1, 27 November 1999, Sect. 1 (1).

of occupation.[90] It has certainly been correctly observed that, as opposed to *Security Council Resolution 1483*,[91] the pertinent resolutions and regulations do not contain any reference to obligations under international humanitarian law in general or the law of occupation in particular; at the same time, they place emphasis on human rights law.[92] Furthermore, the *United Nations Organization*, which is as such not a Party to the *Geneva Conventions*, has never accepted that it is formally bound by the obligations arising from these Conventions. It has rather committed itself to respect the fundamental principles and rules of international human rights and humanitarian law,[93] without, however, expressly endorsing one single rule of the international law of occupation.[94] In addition, there is an ongoing debate as to whether, and to what extent, UN action (be it in the context of territorial administrations or peace-keeping/-making operations) is subject to obligations arising from customary law inasmuch as it also binds international

90 See E. de Wet, 'The Direct Administration of Territories by the United Nations and its Member States in the Post Cold War Era: Legal Bases and Implications for National Law', 8 *Max Planck Yearbook of United Nations Law* (2004), 291, 292; Roberts, 'Transformative Military Occupation', *supra* note 9, 612. See, however, G. T. Harris, 'The Era of Multilateral Occupation', 24 *Berkeley Journal of International Law* (2006) 1, 1; Roberts, 'What is a Military Occupation?', *supra* note 37, 289; S. R. Ratner, 'Foreign Occupation and International Territorial Administration: The Challenges of Convergence', 16 *European Journal of International Law* (2005) 4, 695, 696: "Over the last decade, a new set of occupiers has increasingly administered territory – international organizations." See also Sassòli, *supra* note 12, 688, fn. 157, at least when the UN (or, for that matter, a regional organization) enjoys effective control over a territory without the volition of the sovereign of that territory. Hence, in Sassòli's view *ibid.*, 689 the law of occupation is not applicable to the international administrations in Kosovo and East Timor since the States concerned consented to the presence of foreign troops and administrators.

91 See *supra* note 80.

92 See SC Res. 1244, UN Doc S/RES/1244 (1999), 10 June 1999, para. 11, lit. j; Special Representative of the Secretary-General, Regulation No. 1999/1 on the Authority of the Interim Administration in Kosovo, UNMIK/REG/1999/1, 25 July 1999, Sect. 2; Special Representative of the Secretary-General, Regulation No. 1999/1 on the Authority of the Transitional Administration in East Timor, UNTAET/REG/1999/1, 27 November 1999, Sect. 2; see also Roberts, 'Transformative Military Occupation', *supra* note 9, 595.

93 Secretary General's Bulletin, *Observance by United Nations Forces of International Humanitarian Law*, UN Doc. ST/SGB/1999/13, 6 August 1999.

94 See Sassòli, *supra* note 12, 687.

organizations.[95] This would then also include the core guarantees under the *Hague Regulations* and the *Fourth Geneva Convention*.[96]

The legal discourse is, moreover, enriched by Article 103 UN Charter, according to which the Charter prevails in the event of a conflict between obligations arising under itself and obligations arising under any other international agreement. Insofar as UNSC resolutions – at least those adopted under Chapter VII that give rise to legal obligations, taking into account that the Member States agree, pursuant to Article 25 UN Charter, to accept and carry out such resolutions – also profit from the primacy privilege enshrined in Article 103 UN Charter,[97] it can be argued that the UNSC even has the authority to modify, amend, or suspend the rules of the international law of occupation.[98] Accordingly, it is a plausible contention that the involvement of the UNSC "can assist in setting or legitimizing certain transformative policies during an occupation",[99] notably when it

---

95 See *Interpretation of the Agreement of 25 March 1991 between the WHO and Egypt*, Advisory Opinion, ICJ Reports 1980, 73, para 37: "International organizations are subjects of international law and, as such, are bound by any obligations incumbent upon them under general rules of international law [...]", i.e. customary international law and general principles of law; see M. Nowak & K. Januszewski, 'Non-State Actors and Human Rights', in M. Noortmann, A. Reinisch & C. Ryngaert (eds), *Non-State Actors in International Law* (2015), 113, 157. See also the discussion in G. Verdirame, *The UN and Human Rights. Who Guards the Guardians?* (2011), 55-89, concluding that "much – probably most – human rights law binds the UN and other international organisations already through custom", *ibid.*, 89.

96 As regards the customary character of Article 43 HR see International Military Tribunal in Nuremberg, *Trial of the Major War Criminals*, 41 *American Journal of International Law* (1947) 1, 172, 248-249; ICJ, 'Wall Opinion', *supra* note 51, 172, paras. 89, 124.

97 *Questions of Interpretation and Application of the 1971 Montreal Convention arising from the Aerial Incident at Lockerbie (Libya v. United Kingdom)*, Order of 14 April 1992, ICJ Reports 1992, 3, 15, para. 39.

98 See, e.g., Fox, *supra* note 83, 296: such a mandate "would have superseded the conservationist principle by invoking a superior international obligation and could have provided an opportunity to make clear that a consensus within the United Nations supported reform in Iraq"; see also Roberts, 'Transformative Military Occupation', *supra* note 9, 622: "[i]n the light of the powers vested in the Council, its capacity [to vary the application of even quite fundamental rules of international law] is hard to deny – especially in a case where what is at issue is reconciling divergent principles of international law on a specific and limited matter relating to the maintenance of peace and security". See in a similar vein Arai-Takahashi, *supra* note 12, 1427.

99 Roberts, 'Transformative Military Occupation', *supra* note 9, 580.

comes to rule of law-transfers by occupying and quasi-occupying powers. As has been aptly stated,

> "[...] the UN Security Council may mandate conditions in which the population of the occupied territory can freely determine its future life under the rule of law and enjoy the respect of human rights. It may consider that this necessitates the establishment of new local and national institutions and legal, judicial and economic reform. According to the principles of the rule of law – which are essential to any peace-building effort – all this implies the need to adopt legislation which may go further than what can be justified under the exceptions to the principle of Article 43 [...]."[100]

This position is particularly convincing in the case of post-conflict UN territorial administrations, not only because the UN can claim the role of a neutral administrator rather than an occupying State,[101] but also because the hitherto existing experience of such administrations nourishes the hope that they remain temporally limited and actually contribute toward preparing the independence and self-government of the people under international administration.

One should be more careful, however, when it comes to instances of traditional occupation, i.e. with State involvement. This already becomes manifest in the aforementioned case of the occupation of Iraq. It applies with even more force to the Turkish occupation of Northern Cyprus, the Moroccan occupation of Western Sahara, the Russian occupation of Crimea, or the Israeli occupation of the OPT, to only name some major cases of contemporary occupation. Particularly in the latter case, the heavy involvement of the UNSC[102] had the function of affirming the full applicability of the international law of occupation rather than modifying it.

Hence, in the event of UNSC action allegedly entailing a modification of the international law of occupation, interpretative restraint is required. In the light of the peculiarities of the interpretation of UNSC resolu-

---

100 Sassòli, *supra* note 12, 680.

101 See Ratner, *supra* note 90, 702, referring to "distinctive paradigms of governance" and opposing the *status quo* approach of the law of occupation to the transformative approach of international territorial administration; see also Scheffer, *supra* note 45, 859; Fox, *supra* note 83, 262-269.

102 See only SC Res. 242, UN Doc S/RES/242 (1967), 22 November 1967; SC Res. 476, UN Doc S/RES/476 (1980), 30 June 1980; SC Res. 478, UN Doc S/RES/478 (1980), 20 August 1980; SC Res. 2334, UN Doc S/RES/2334 (2016), 23 December 2016.

tions,[103] their legal effects must be established on a case-by-case basis, considering all relevant circumstances. For lack of any express or otherwise sufficiently clear indication to the contrary, there cannot be any presumption that the UNSC, in discharging its peace-maintaining and peace-restoring duties under Chapter VII, seeks to amend the existing international law of occupation. Put differently, such resolutions should as far as possible be construed in harmony with the law of occupation.[104] In particular, "[a] simple encouragement of international efforts to promote legal and judicial reform by an occupying power is certainly too vague to justify an occupying power to legislate beyond what [international humanitarian law] permits."[105]

E. Concluding Remarks

While in 1944, when *Fraenkel*'s book was published, understandable concern existed that the rule of law "which is basic in American political philosophy [but] alien to German ideals and traditions"[106] might constitute a bad legal transplant, today the references to the concept of the rule of law in the international legal order abound. From the preamble of the 1948 *Universal Declaration of Human Rights* and the 1970 *Friendly Relations Declaration*, which referred to "the paramount importance of the Charter of the United Nations in the promotion of the rule of law among nations",[107] to the 1993 *Vienna Declaration and Programme of Action*[108] and the Outcome Document of the 2005 *World Summit*,[109] the UN has time and again, and with increasing intensity and visibility, drawn upon the rule of law as a paramount principle of the international community.

---

103 *Accordance with International Law of the Unilateral Declaration of Independence in Respect of Kosovo*, Advisory Opinion, ICJ Reports 2010, 403, paras. 94, 117.

104 See Sassòli, *supra* note 12, 690.

105 *Ibid.*, 681.

106 F. G. Munson, 'Review of Ernest Fraenkel: Military Occupation and the Rule of Law', 239 *Annals of the American Academy of Political and Social Science* (1945) 1, 192, 193; see in a similar vein R. S. T. Chorley, 'Review of Ernst Fraenkel: Military Occupation and the Rule of Law', 8 *Modern Law Review* (1945) 3, 119, 121.

107 GA Res. 2625 (XXV), UN Doc A/RES/2625, 24 October 1970, pream. para. 4 and also Fraenkel, *supra* note 1, 225-226.

108 *Vienna Declaration and Programme of Action*, UN Doc A/CONF.157/23, 25 June 1993.

109 GA Res. 60/1, UN Doc A/RES/60/1, 24 October 2005.

Against this background, it should not come as a surprise that the rule of law has also found, and consolidated, its place in the international law governing situations of occupation. As has been shown in a diachronic perspective, the law of occupation in the strict sense, which already comprises certain rule of law elements, has been widened and enriched by the impact of international human rights law and the actions of the UNSC in situations of occupation, thus substantially increasing the rule of law-promoting potential of the law of occupation in the wider sense. From a synchronic perspective, this signifies that all these elements have to be applied together as forming part of the contemporary *corpus* of the international law governing situations of occupation.

Hence, it can be rightly said that "[h]uman rights and the rule of law (indispensable elements in any peace-building effort) demand that the maintenance of public order be based on law".[110] Whereas such a statement may be primarily aimed at the structure and performance of the administration set up by the occupying power, we have seen that the law of occupation can also function as a driving force concerning rule of law-transfers *vis-à-vis* the local administration.

At the same time, and to deliberately end on a cautious note, it is crucial to resist the temptation to concede, in the name of promoting the rule of law, too much legislative leeway to the occupying power. Treating "the occupant as the bringer of progress […] can lead to a dangerous mix of crusading, self-righteousness, and self-delusion".[111] Indeed, "experience suggests that even overtly transformative occupants would be wise to recognize the strength and continuing validity of the law on occupation in general, and the conservationist principle in particular".[112]

Restraint is therefore advised when assessing the good measure of prerogatives of the occupying power. In spite of seductive promises of *transformative* and *humanitarian* occupation or the like, also the rule of law is not the panacea allowing us to conceive of a *modern* occupation law that would strip off the risks inherent to a political and military power governing a foreign population. These risks do not necessarily diminish over time, but the appetite of a power in control of another territory and population can also well grow. This *caveat* should remain on the international lawyer's mind notably when dealing with long-standing occupations and the dan-

110 Sassòli, *supra* note 12, 663.
111 Roberts, 'Transformative Military Occupation', *supra* note 9, 601.
112 *Ibid.*, 620.

gers regarding not only formal, but also *de facto* and creeping annexation.[113]

In that sense, the rule of law eventually remains a means to temper the perils involved in the existence of situations of occupation, knowing that it may all too easily be employed for purposes alien to the noble aspirations underlying the idea of the rule of law. As *Fraenkel* both soberly and wisely concluded his study:

> "The rule of law in a democratic state is based on the consent of the citizens. In an occupied territory, public power is enforced upon the residents regardless of their inner feelings. Therefore the concept of 'rule of law' has different meanings in a government based on democratic consent and a government based on military force. It was the failure to recognize this fundamental fact that constituted the greatest weakness of the Rhineland Agreement."[114]

113 See notably ICJ, 'Wall Opinion', *supra* note 51, 184, para. 121 in this regard.
114 Fraenkel, *supra* note 1, 227.

The Law Behind Rule of Law Promotion in Fragile States – The Case of Afghanistan

Astrid Wiik[*] and Frauke Lachenmann[#]

Table of Contents

* Dr. Astrid Wiik, Research Fellow (Habilitandin) at Heidelberg University Faculty of Law and a Senior Research Fellow at the Max Planck Foundation for International Peace and the Rule of Law.

\# Dr. Frauke Lachenmann, Senior Research Fellow at the Max Planck Foundation for International Peace and the Rule of Law.

Abstract

Rule of law promotion has become a go-to-tool in the complex process of stabilizing and rebuilding (post-)conflict States. The process is driven by a heterogeneous group of national, foreign, and international actors who define and prescribe rule of law norms and standards, who program, finance, implement, and eventually monitor rule of law reforms. While the legitimacy and effectiveness of rule of law promotion has undergone scrutiny, particularly within the overall context of international development assistance, an aspect that has so far received little attention is the legality of rule of law promotion. This concerns both the mandate of the various actors and the execution of rule of law activities on the ground.

Since 2001, the international community has intensely supported the rule of law in Afghanistan rendering it a veritable testing ground for rule of law promotion. The article explores the legal framework for actors in rule of law promotion in Afghanistan from 2001 up to the present day, with a focus on the German Government, its development cooperation agencies, and private nongovernmental organizations (NGOs).

The article shows that while detailed rules bind the monitoring and evaluation of rule of law activities in line with the existing international frameworks for development assistance, few laws and principles guide the programming and implementation of rule of law promotion. The existing standards are generally too abstract to guide specific rule of law promotion activities. Further concretization and harmonization is necessary in the interest of the sustainability of rule of law promotion in Afghanistan – and elsewhere.

A. Introduction

Over the last decade, rule of law promotion has become a go-to-tool in the complex process of stabilizing and (re-)building (post-)conflict States. Rule of law promotion in this context is driven by a heterogeneous group of national and international actors who define and prescribe rule of law norms and standards, who program, finance, implement, and eventually monitor rule of law promotion activities. While the legitimacy and sustainability of rule of law promotion has undergone scrutiny, an aspect that has so far received little attention is its *legality*. This concerns both the mandate of the various actors and the execution of specific rule of law activities.

Since 2001, the international community has strongly supported the rule of law in Afghanistan. Following 30 years of war and unrest, the Afghan State institutions were largely destroyed, "making the country a test case for law-based nation building".[1] Germany is one of the central contributors in this process: Between 2009–2017, Germany alone disbursed €1.24 billion on good governance in Afghanistan, out of a total €3.5 billion investment in the country, making Germany the second largest donor in Afghanistan.[2]

This article explores the legal framework for key actors in rule of law promotion in Afghanistan, with a focus on the German Government, its development cooperation agencies, and private nongovernmental organizations (NGOs). It argues that a set of detailed rules exist that derives from the framework binding official development assistance (ODA) and also applies to rule of law promotion in Afghanistan. However, these rules are not designed to guide specific rule of law promotion activities. Further rule development and concretization is necessary in the interest of the legitimacy and sustainability of rule of law promotion in Afghanistan and elsewhere.

B. *Rule of Law Promotion in Afghanistan*

I. *Terminology*

It is impossible to give a complete overview of the rule of law actors and their activities in Afghanistan. In 2008, the US representative to the UN estimated that "more than 30 national embassies and bilateral development agencies, several UN agencies, four development banks and [International Financial Institutions], and about 2,000 nongovernmental organizations

1 International Development Law Organization, 'Afghanistan' (2015), available at http://www.idlo.int/where-we-work/asia/afghanistan (last visited 12 December 2018); E. Gaston & E. Jensen, 'Rule of Law and Statebuilding in Afghanistan: Testing Theory with Practice', in S. Smith & C. Cookman (eds), *State Strengthening in Afghanistan: Lessons Learned, 2001–14*, Peaceworks (2016) 116, 69, 70.

2 BMZ, 'German Cooperation with Afghanistan 2009–2017' (2017), available at http://www.germancooperation-afghanistan.de/sites/default/files/Datasheet 2017EN.pdf (last visited 12 December 2018).

and contractors are involved in rebuilding [in Afghanistan]"[3] – not to mention foreign militaries which have been involved in rule of law promotion individually and as part of the international military coalition engaged in Afghanistan. The mapping of the field of rule of law actors and rule of law promotion activities is contingent on the concept of rule of law and what is included under the term rule of law promotion. Yet, no rule of law concept was agreed on between the Afghan Government and the various international actors. In fact, not even the German Government operates with a uniform understanding of what is the rule of law although attempts are currently being undertaken in this respect.[4]

What is the rule of law? Scholars have long distinguished between *thick* and *thin* concepts of rule of law.[5] The *thin*, formalistic model requires that government officials and citizens are bound by and act consistent with the law. The law as such must be public, general, clear, certain, known in advance, and applied to everyone in the same manner. This minimal view of rule of law has the advantage of being amenable to a broad range of systems and societies. More substantive or *thicker* definitions of rule of law, on the other hand, include references to fundamental rights, democracy, and/or criteria of justice or right, imbuing rule of law with ethical overtones.

As early as 2004, the *UN Secretary-General*, recognizing that the UN members were struggling with conceptual disagreements, sought to "articulate a common language of justice"[6] for the UN. His Report to the *UN Security Council* (UNSC) on *The Rule of Law and Transitional Justice in Conflict and Post-Conflict Societies* defined rule of law as

> "a concept at the very heart of the [United Nation's] mission. It refers to a principle of governance in which all persons, institutions and entities, public and private, including the State itself, are accountable to laws that are publicly promulgated, equally enforced and independent-

---

3 Cited by M. Tondini, 'Justice Sector Reform in Afghanistan: From a 'Lead Nation' Approach to a 'Mixed Ownership' Regime?', 15 *Transition Studies Review* (2009) 4, 660, 668 [Tondini, Justice Sector Reform in Afghanistan].

4 German Federal Government, *Krisen verhindern, Konflikte bewältigen, Frieden fördern, Leitlinien der Bundesregierung* (2017), 40. In addition, rule of law activities may be carried out together with other activities, or under broader concepts such as good governance, rendering any attempt at categorization imprecise.

5 Compare the seminal work by B. Tamanaha, *On the Rule of Law: History, Politics, Theory* (2004).

6 UN Secretary-General, *The Rule of Law and Transitional Justice in Conflict and Post-Conflict Societies*, UN Doc S/2004/616 (2004), 23 August 2004, 4.

ly adjudicated, and which are consistent with international human rights norms and standards. It requires, as well, measures to ensure adherence to the principles of supremacy of law, equality before the law, accountability to the law, fairness in the application of the law, separation of powers, participation in decision-making, legal certainty, avoidance of arbitrariness and procedural and legal transparency."[7]

This comprehensive, *thick* approach became a blueprint for a number of later UN documents dealing with rule of law such as the 2008 *Guidance Note of the Secretary-General on the UN Approach to Rule of Law Assistance* and the 2011 DPKO/OHCHR *UN Rule of Law Indicators Implementation Guide and Project Tools*. In 2016, the *Venice Commission* of the *Council of Europe* followed suit, warning against a purely formalistic understanding of rule of law and claiming that

> "despite differences of opinion, consensus exists on the core elements of the Rule of Law as well as on those of the *Rechtsstaat* and of the *État de droit*, which are not only formal but also substantive or material (*materieller Rechtsstaatsbegriff*). These core elements are: (1) Legality, including a transparent, accountable and democratic process for enacting law; (2) Legal certainty; (3) Prohibition of arbitrariness; (4) Access to justice before independent and impartial courts, including judicial review of administrative acts; (5) Respect for human rights; and (6) Non-discrimination and equality before the law."[8]

It is doubtful whether the *Venice Commission*'s optimism concerning a rule of law consensus is warranted: Recent experiences such as the controversial negotiations regarding Sustainable Development Goal No. 16 have shown that far from all UN members, not even all members of the *Council of Europe*, subscribe to a substantial, human rights-infused and democracy-oriented definition of rule of law, which is bound to lead to discrepancies in their assistance approaches.[9]

Rachel Kleinfeld Belton has noted yet another discrepancy that influences rule of law promotion. She points out that definitions of rule of law com-

7 UN Secretary-General, *The Rule of Law and Transitional Justice in Conflict and Post-Conflict Societies*, UN Doc S/2004/616 (2004), 23 August 2004, para. 6.

8 Venice Commission, *Rule of Law Checklist*, CDL-AD(2016)007, 18 March 2016, para. 18.

9 On the negotiation history of SDG 16, see A. Wiik & F. Lachenmann, 'Rule of Law and the Sustainable Development Goals', in F. Lachenmann, T. J. Röder & R. Wolfrum (eds), 18 *Max Planck Yearbook of United Nations Law* (2014), 286, 304.

monly fall into two categories: (1) those that emphasize the ends that the rule of law is intended to serve within society (e.g. law and order, predictability of judgments), and (2) those that highlight the institutional attributes believed necessary to activate the rule of law (such as comprehensive laws, efficient courts, trained lawyers and judges). For practical and historical reasons, *Kleinfeld* claims, legal scholars and philosophers have favored the first type of definition; whereas practitioners of rule of law development programs, struggling with the conditions on the ground, tend to use the second type of definition.[10] It follows that international donors and practitioners are not necessarily on the same page as far as their understanding of the goals of the rule of law, and the means towards its achievement, are concerned.

II. Rule of Law Actors

At the international level, there are two key groups of rule of law providers in Afghanistan: the UN with its specialized development agencies, and multilateral development banks. The EU can be added as an international actor *sui generis*.[11] The *UN Assistance Mission in Afghanistan* (UNAMA) was established by the UNSC in 2002, upon request by the Afghan Government. Headed by the *Special Representative of the UN Secretary-General for Afghanistan*, it is designed as a political assistance mission and ensures a coherent development approach by the international community. In addition to UNAMA, a UN Country Team for Afghanistan bundles the activities of the specialized UN agencies, funds and programs, the *World Bank*, the *International Monetary Fund*, and other affiliated members.[12]

Foreign States make up the largest donor group. They carry out their rule of law activities through different agencies, organizations, and con-

---

10 R. Kleinfeld Belton, 'Competing Definitions of the Rule of Law: Implications for Practitioners', *Carnegie Papers Rule of Law Series* (2005) 55, 16.

11 P. Dann & M. Riegner, 'Globales Entwicklungsverwaltungsrecht', in P. Dann, S. Kadelbach & M. Kaltenborn (eds), *Entwicklung und Recht* (2014), 723, 728.

12 These are: *Asian Development Bank*, *Food and Agriculture Organization*, *International Fund for Agricultural Development*, *International Labour Organization*, *International Monetary Fund*, *International Organization for Migration*, *Office for the Coordination of Humanitarian Affairs*, *Office of the High Commissioner for Human Rights*, *UN Human Settlements Programme*, UNAIDS, UNAMA, UNCTAD, UNDP, *UN Department of Safety and Security*, UNEP, UNESCO, UNFPA, UNHCR, UNICEF, UNIDO, UNMAS, UNODC, UNOPS, UNW, *World Bank*, *World Food Programme*, WHO.

tracting international governmental and nongovernmental organizations. As regards Germany, three federal ministries have competences in civilian rule of law promotion to Afghanistan:[13] the *Federal Ministry for Economic Cooperation and Development* (BMZ), the *Federal Foreign Office* (AA) and the *Federal Ministry of the Interior*. BMZ implements its rule of law activities predominantly through the *German Society for Development Cooperation* (GIZ) and the *KfW Development Bank* and focuses on long-term development measures, while the AA works with a number of different organizations and focuses on crisis stabilization and prevention. The *Ministry of the Interior* has relied on public officials – mostly police officers – to carry out specific rule of law activities.

The German Government programs, finances, and implements its activities directly[14] or jointly with other donors, German State institutions, such as political foundations, with Afghan line ministries, government organizations, international organizations such as UNDP, domestic or international NGOs, and subnational governance bodies, such as community development councils and Provincial Councils.[15] The German Government cooperates with a total of 83 German, international and Afghan NGOs to implement the projects it funds.[16] This multi-agency approach is typical for rule of law promotion by States, owed to the different areas of competence.[17]

13 The *Ministry of Defense* has also carried out rule of law assistance directly through the armed forces, see German Federal Government, *Fortschrittsbericht Afghanistan 2014*, (2014), 53 [German Federal Government, Fortschrittsbericht Afghanistan 2014]; German Federal Government, *Deutsches Engagement im Bereich der Sicherheitssektorreform*, BT-Drucks, 18/11458 (3 July 2017), 7.

14 Predominantly with regard to capacity-building of police forces. See German Federal Government, 'Fortschrittsbericht Afghanistan 2014', *supra* note 13, 23-25.

15 BMZ, 'Neue entwicklungspolitische Strategie für die Zusammenarbeit mit Afghanistan im Zeitraum 2014–2017', BMZ-Strategiepapier 3/2014, 15 [BMZ, Strategie Afghanistan].

16 A list is available at http://www.germancooperation-afghanistan.de/en/page/ngo-partners (last visited 12 December 2018).

17 See, for instance, the list of tasks of various US agencies – and their multiple programs – listed in United States Department of State and the Broadcasting Board of Governors, Office of Inspector General, 'Report of Inspection, Rule-of-Law Programs in Afghanistan (2008)', Report Number ISP-I-08–09, 8, available at https://oig.State.gov/system/files/106946.pdf (last visited 12 December 2018).

III. Rule of Law Promotion Activities

The German Government has broadened its rule of law-related engagement in Afghanistan over the years.[18] Initially, it focused on security sector reform, particularly police reform, which remains a priority. However, it has since 2003 expanded to other areas, including justice sector and administration reform. Since 2012, the BMZ's Afghanistan strategy lists good governance, of which the rule of law is declared a sub-component, as one of its five strategic sectors.[19] BMZ-funded rule of law activities and programs pursue as an overall objective the establishment of stable and responsive State institutions.[20]

Important rule of law-projects carried out by GIZ for the BMZ include: the project *Promotion of the Rule of Law in Afghanistan* (since 2003), which provides capacity trainings for the judicial and quasi-judicial sector, mentoring for judicial employees and mediators, and legal awareness-raising campaigns for civil society in relation to the judicial sector;[21] another project organizes study meetings and trainings for mullahs on women's rights to obtain their support in improving the situation of women;[22] the *Open Policy Advisory Fund* (OPAF) (2010–2016) supports the Afghan Government in addressing corruption, transparency and administration reform with the aim of increasing respect for the rule of law by State institutions; the *Governance Forum for Afghanistan* (Gov4Afg) (since 2015), which aims at establishing a good-governance-focused knowledge management system to be used for political and legislative decision-making;[23] the *Regional Capacity Development Fund* (RCDF) and its follow-up program *Promotion of Good Governance in Afghanistan* (RCD), which funds a variety of projects containing rule of law objectives at the national and subnational govern-

---

18 A. Suhrke, 'Exogenous State-Building: The Contradictions of the International Project in Afghanistan', in W. Mason (ed.), *The Rule of Law in Afghanistan* (2011), 225, 238. For a standardized set of rule of law activities, see UN Secretary-General, *UN Approach to Rule of Law Assistance, Guidance Note of the UN Secretary-General*, April 2008 [UN Secretary-General, Rule of Law Assistance].

19 GIZ, *State-Building in a Fragile Environment – Strengthening Afghan Institutions Through the Work of Returning and Integrated Experts* (2016), 30 [GIZ, State-Building in a Fragile Environment].

20 *Ibid.*, 31.

21 GIZ, *Good Governance in Afghanistan* (2017), 10-11 [GIZ, Good Governance].

22 *Ibid.*, 12-13.

23 GIZ, *The Promotion of Good Governance in Afghanistan – RCD* (2016), 28 [GIZ, Promotion of Good Governance].

ment level in Kabul and six northern Afghan provinces.[24] Activities include up to 14 monthly capacity trainings for public officials on specific administrative issues, such as budgeting, but also on specific relevant legal topics such as the public procurement law, as well as projects intending to increase public participation and dialog between government agencies and citizens.[25]

In addition, the AA supports a number of rule of law projects. These include projects addressing security, good governance, especially public administration reform, higher education, and cultural preservation.[26] One central rule of law project is the *Special Programme for Supporting the Development of Afghan Ministries and Administrative Systems at National and Sub-National Level* (since 2010), which is implemented by GIZ and the *Centre for International Migration* (CIM), and through which approximately 70 so-called Integrated and Returning Experts have been placed in key positions in central government "with a great deal of influence"[27], mostly in the areas of good governance and security, to support and mentor Afghan public officials and fill gaps in the local labor market.[28] Tasks of experts at the independent *Joint Anti-Corruption Monitoring and Evaluation Committee* (MEC) include, for instance, the drafting of anti-corruption legislation and capacity building within their team.[29] Other AA-funded programs include capacity trainings for the Afghan police and the judicial sector, transitional justice initiatives, and administrative reform projects, such as a project on strengthening administrative law in Afghanistan.[30] Carried out by the *Max Planck Foundation for International Peace and the Rule of Law*, this project included the training of around 1,200 public officials in administrative law, as well as provision of legislative drafting support to the Afghan *Ministry of Justice* (MoJ), the *Independent Administration Reform Civil Service Commission* (IARCSC), and the Afghan *Supreme Court* (SC) in respect of an administrative procedures law and an administrative court procedure law.

The target audience of the above projects is as wide as the various activities. Two central groups emerge: public officials, notably employees in the public administration at the national and subnational level as well as

24 GIZ, 'State-Building in a Fragile Environment', *supra* note 19, 31-32.
25 GIZ, 'Promotion of Good Governance', *supra* note 23, 12; GIZ, 'Good Governance', *supra* note 21, 19-26.
26 GIZ, 'State-Building in a Fragile Environment', *supra* note 19, 30.
27 *Ibid.*, 45.
28 *Ibid.*, 41.
29 *Ibid.*, 80.
30 *Ibid.*, 31.

judges and prosecutors, on the one hand; and civil society in general as those who shall both benefit and hold public officials to account, on the other hand.

IV. Challenges and Shortcomings in Rule of Law Promotion

No recent empirical study on German-funded rule of law projects in Afghanistan exists, and it would go beyond the scope of this paper to close this gap. However, reports provided by the AA, BMZ, and GIZ indicate some challenges, and reports exist about shortfalls in similar projects by other donors. Some of them are here summarized to illustrate potential pitfalls of rule of law promotion activities.

One area where difficulties – and the need for clear legal frameworks to guide rule of law promotion projects – are apparent is the embedding by donors of foreign and domestic nationals as experts and mentors in line ministries and other State institutions. They are a preferred means to foster long-term capacity building in the face of limited local capacities, lack of (legal) expertise, and corruption in partner institutions. In addition to the AA, the EU, the German *Ministry of Interior*, GIZ, USAID, and US contractors all have embedded advisors in justice and security institutions, usually at high authority levels – some even with direct access to the President.[31] In 2010, the Afghan *Ministry of Finance* estimated that around 7,000 Afghan consultants worked in government institutions.[32]

There have been reports that these advisors have taken over key tasks, such as preparing national development strategies and drafting entire laws.[33] The *Afghanistan National Development Strategy* is said to have been almost fully prepared by foreign actors, including the *World Bank*, foreign

31 See M. Hartmann, 'Casualties of Myopia,' in Mason (ed.), *supra* note 18, 172, 188; BMZ, 'Strategie Afghanistan,' *supra* note 15, 19.

32 F. de Weijer, 'A Capable State in Afghanistan,' Harvard CID Working Papers No. 2013/059, 5.

33 Tondini, 'Justice Sector Reform in Afghanistan,' *supra* note 3, 664-665. Here, *Tondini* also mentions the 2004 *Interim Criminal Procedure Code*, the 2005 *Juvenile Code*, and the 2005 *Law on Prisons and Detention Centers* as being drafted with main inputs from the Italian Justice Project Office and that there was a push to "perform justice reform by influencing the political will of local authorities"; de Weijer, *supra* note 32, 11. She mentions the *National Education Support Programme* at the *Ministry of Higher Education*.

embassies, and UNAMA.[34] Infamously, an Italian legal scholar was entrusted with drafting an interim criminal procedure code but failed to consult Afghan officials on the issue. Resenting their exclusion, the Afghan officials asked the President to refuse approving the draft. In support of their legal expert, the Italian Government threatened the withdrawal of funding for related projects unless the draft was approved.[35] The reasons for this development are complex. Partly, they are a consequence of lacking local capacities, partly they are due to donor politics and project strategies such as overly short project cycles focused on concrete results that leave little room for the building up of capacities within the government agencies.[36]

A related recurring problem is that donor support often fails to take into account the Afghan local context, that laws are drafted based on, possibly, conflicting donor perspectives (supply-, not demand-driven), and that local laws, legal traditions and the context within which measures are to operate are not sufficiently researched.[37] GIZ has acknowledged shortcomings in needs-based projects planning concerning the program RCDF, which it has sought to avoid in the follow-up program RCD by creating a detailed bottom-up communication process for approval of specific projects.[38] The Germany-funded expert placement project is lauded by Afghan partners for its strong involvement of the target institution in the expert selection process.[39] Similarly, the GIZ-run Gov4Afg project was set up in 2015 to mitigate earlier planning and implementation shortcomings with regard to management and collection of local knowledge and priority setting. Further, projects increasingly are designed to include civil society input at both the planning and implementation stage.[40] However, still, foreign influence on legislative drafting and administration processes often result in legal and management reforms that are too complex and insufficiently tailored to the specific context to be effectively operationalized by local actors. Technical capacity-building trainings are often not able to close this gap.[41]

---

34 S. M. Shah, 'Afghanistan National Development Strategy (ANDS) Formulation Process: Influencing Factors and Challenges', AREU 2009; de Weijer, *supra* note 32, 5-7; Tondini, 'Justice Sector Reform in Afghanistan', *supra* note 3, 669.

35 de Weijer, *supra* note 32, 17.

36 *Ibid.*, 16.

37 *Ibid.*, 26.

38 GIZ, 'Promotion of Good Governance', *supra* note 23, 9, 12.

39 GIZ, 'State-Building in a Fragile Environment', *supra* note 19, 65.

40 GIZ, 'Promotion of Good Governance', *supra* note 23, 28-29.

41 de Weijer, *supra* note 32, 24.

Finally, questions have been raised with regard to the legality of informal justice programs framed within legal pluralist approaches. Conceptualized by foreign donors, they aim at engaging existing local customary and Islamic legal structures or religious leaders, which are considered to be more legitimate than State authority outside of urban centers. *Gaston* and *Jensen* point to the frictions of this approach with human rights, particularly women's and minorities' rights.[42] Ideas to establish mechanisms of State recognition of informal justice dispute settlement potentially violate the Afghan Constitution as well as Afghanistan's international human rights obligations. They might be also problematic under Western donors' international and domestic legal frameworks as well as policy strategies for Afghanistan, which often focus on human rights promotion. These problems are more pronounced in informal justice programming but also apply to some degree in state-institution building:

> "There is no shortcut to justice. In the short term, this can put Western state-building practitioners in the uncomfortable position of supporting institutions or individuals that are still neglecting minority rights, increasing inequality, or committing or condoning rights abuses – critiques that could be lodged against both community-based *and* formal institutions. This is evident by the dilemma faced in continuing to work with an Afghan Government that punishes women from running away from abusive situations, sentences alleged blasphemers to death, or routinely tortures security detainees to coerce confessions."[43]

Are donors and implementing organizations legally free to plan and carry out such activities despite possibly violating their own or Afghanistan's domestic and international legal obligations? In the following, the article will consider the legal framework applicable to rule of law actors, looking at the rules addressing the *if* and *how* of their rule of law-related work.

C. Legal Basis and Mandate for Rule of Law Promotion by International Organizations and States

A web of international legal sources regulates the engagement of the international community in Afghanistan, including for rule of law promotion. International organizations and States derive their rule of law promotion

42 Gaston & Jensen, *supra* note 1, 74-75.

43 *Ibid.*, 76.

mandates largely from two sources: First, States and international organizations have concluded multilateral framework agreements with the Afghan Government on the general post-conflict order of the nation and the State-building process. These agreements have been flanked and elaborated by bi- and multilateral agreements on specific areas of cooperation between the Afghan Government and foreign and international donors. Secondly, a number of UNSC Resolutions mandates the UN's presence in the country.

The following section traces the legal evolution and key legal characteristics of the approach to rule of law promotion in Afghanistan, as reflected in the bi- and multilateral agreements and UNSC Resolutions.

I. Donor-Driven v. Local Owner- and Leadership

1. Light Footprint and Lead Nations (2001–2006)

The rule of law formed a part of the earliest state-building effort in post-2001 Afghanistan. The outcome document of the UN-administered talks between the various Afghan factions and facilitating foreign representatives, the so-called *Bonn Agreement* (*Agreement on Provisional Arrangements in Afghanistan Pending the Re-establishment of Permanent Government Institutions*) of 5 December 2001 envisaged a number of rule of law-based reforms in the process of power transition to the Afghan people. These included a process for the drafting and passing of a new constitution and the reconstruction of the defunct justice system and public administration.

These measures were needed. Three decades of civil unrest and war had destroyed Afghanistan's infrastructure, including the pre-war legal infrastructure as represented in a body of State, customary, and Islamic laws and a central State that had been built in urban areas during several periods of modernization in the 20th century. The rule of law-based institutions, particularly the judiciary with its complex unification of State and Islamic laws and practices, were in a desolate state.[44]

The mandates for rule of law promotion have been embedded in the overall framework of civilian and military assistance to Afghanistan. For roughly the first five years after the fall of the Taliban regime, the reconstruction process can be denoted by two legal characteristics: a limitation of the UN to a coordinating role and strong control of foreign donor nations over the process irrespective of pledges to Afghan ownership.

---

44 Gaston & Jensen, *supra* note 1, 70.

In accordance with emerging international development law at the time, it was agreed that the international community's involvement in Afghanistan should be limited to military, technical and financial assistance. Sovereignty and responsibility for reconstruction was to rest in the hands of the Afghan people, represented by an Interim Authority until elections had been held.[45]

The *Bonn Agreement* was endorsed by *UNSC Resolution 1383*, issued on 6 December 2001[46], which also issued a plea for reconstruction assistance to donors and envisaged only a coordinating role for the UN. This *light footprint* approach deviated from previous mission models, used in East Timor, Kosovo and Bosnia Herzegovina, where the UN had assumed civilian executive powers.[47] The Resolution further contained a "strong commitment to the sovereignty, independence, territorial integrity and national unity of Afghanistan"[48], a pledge that would be reiterated in many later Resolutions.

UNSC Resolution 1401 (2002)[49] established the UNAMA, with the mandate and structure of the mission laid out in a report of the *UN Secretary-General*, and furnished the Special Representative of the *UN Secretary-General* with authority over the planning and conduct of all UN activities in Afghanistan. The initial mandate was established for one year, and has since been renewed and reviewed annually, with structural changes to the mandate when considered necessary.[50]

In his Report outlining UNAMA's mandate, the *UN Secretary-General* warned UNAMA against meddling with Afghanistan's affairs to an undue degree – a mistake of earlier missions:

> "98 (c) UNAMA should undertake close coordination and consultation with the Afghan Interim Authority and other Afghan actors to ensure that Afghan priorities lead the mission's assistance efforts;

---

45 Hartmann, *supra* note 31, 180.

46 SC Res. 1383, UN Doc S/RES/1383 (2001), 6 December 2001.

47 This approach was controversial, see F. Vendrell, 'The International Community's Failures in Afghanistan', in Mason (ed.), *supra* note 18, 53, 54-55; L. Miller & R. Perito, 'Establishing the Rule of Law in Afghanistan', in United States Institute for Peace (USIP), *Special Report* (2004) 117, 4. See also E. de Brabandere, *Post-Conflict Administrations in International Law* (2009), 3.

48 SC Res. 1383, *supra* note 46, 1.

49 SC Res. 1401, UN Doc S/RES/1401 (2002), 28 March 2002.

50 For previous renewals see SC Res. 1662 (2006), 1746 (2007), 1806 (2008), 1868 (2009), 1917 (2010), 1974 (2011), 2041 (2012), 2096 (2013), 2145 (2014), 2210 (2015), 2274 (2016).

(d) UNAMA should aim to bolster Afghan capacity (both official and non-governmental), relying on as limited an international presence and on as many Afghan staff as possible, and using common support services where possible, thereby leaving a *light expatriate 'footprint'*."[51]

The role – and mandates – of foreign donor nations was developed at subsequent international conferences between the international community and the Afghan Interim Authority in Tokyo, Geneva and Kabul in 2002. International organizations and 60 governments pledged 4.5 billion US dollars in foreign aid to the reconstruction effort for the period 2002–2006.[52] However, rather than channeling the foreign aid trough reconstruction funds – the favored Afghan approach and a state-of-the-art means to ensure national ownership over national reconstruction policy and spending – a strong donor-driven process was established.[53]

Bilateral agreements between donors and Afghanistan characterized the process, a model that already then was considered difficult with regard to aid coordination and needs-based programming. To ensure donor coordination, five countries assumed the role of *lead nations* over specific sectors in the *security and rule of law* portion of the interim government's reform agenda. The role of lead nation entailed the provision of financial assistance, the coordination of foreign commitments, and oversight of activities in the particular area assigned – thereby arguably undermining the local ownership narrative justifying the light footprint approach.[54] UNSC Resolutions between 2002 and 2006 mostly reiterated the coordination and assistance mandate and the objectives laid out in the *Bonn Agreement*.

51 Emphasis added by the authors.

52 M. Tondini, *Statebuilding and Justice Reform: Post-Conflict Reconstruction in Afghanistan* (2010), 46 [Tondini, Statebuilding and Justice Reform].

53 Given the limited infrastructure, a typical budget support funding mechanism by the *World Bank* was not an option in view of the strict criteria governments must fulfill, see World Bank, *Principles for Development Policy Financing, Operational Procedure 8.60*, 13 July 2017, OPS5.02-POL.105; BMZ, *Leitlinien für die bilaterale Finanzielle und Technische Zusammenarbeit mit Kooperationspartnern der deutschen Entwicklungszusammenarbeit*, BMZ Konzepte 165 (2008), 12-14 [BMZ, Leitlinien]. Several trust funds managed by international organizations were set up. The multi-donor trust fund of the *World Bank*, the *Afghanistan Reconstruction Trust Fund* (ARTF), is the largest. See 'The Afghanistan Reconstruction Trust Fund', available at http://www.artf.af/ (last visited 12 December 2018).

54 Tondini, 'Statebuilding and Justice Reform', *supra* note 52, 46; N. Stockton, 'Strategic Coordination in Afghanistan', *Afghanistan Research and Evaluation Unit Issues Paper Series* (2002), 25.

Despite the pledges in the *Bonn Agreement*, rule of law reform received limited attention in this period, with the largest share of aid routed into military and police reforms. Rule of law-related activities focused on the priorities listed in the *Bonn Agreement*. Drawing from liberal Western State systems, donors designed *top-down, state-centric* programs focused on rebuilding State institutions, modernizing the State legal system, and expanding their reach and capacities beyond urban centers.

2. *Towards Local Ownership* (2005–2009)

With the Bonn process coming to an end with the election of a President and a Parliament, 2005/2006 became a turning point for assistance efforts in Afghanistan. This also had effects on the mandates for rule of law promotion. The new Afghan Government started to formulate their own rule of law reform goals and sought to have more input in the process, as evidenced in the 2005 document *Justice for All: A Comprehensive Needs Analysis for Justice in Afghanistan*[55]. The paper aimed to provide an analysis of what needed to be done over the next 12 years to build and maintain a minimally functional justice system in Afghanistan. It formulated a clear Afghan ownership vision in terms of decision-making and the content of judicial rule of law reforms, while reducing the role of donors to one of assistance:

> "The Government must lead on justice reform. [...] To the extent possible, decisions about justice reform should be made by the Government and implemented through the normal processes of Government.
> [...]
> Justice reform must be appropriate to Afghanistan. In its policy, it must reflect Afghan political circumstances, social and legal traditions and aspirations for the future."[56]

The paper displayed the Afghan Government's dilemma: the State was dependent on donor money and technical expertise, yet the donors' influence on policy decisions was increasingly perceived as encroaching on Afghan self-determination and pushing for rule of law reforms that were incompatible with local traditions. At the same time, the international

55 Government of the Islamic Republic of Afghanistan, Ministry of Justice, 'Justice for All: A Comprehensive Needs Analyse for Justice in Afghanistan' (2005), available at https://www.cmi.no/pdf/?file=/afghanistan/doc/Justice%20for%20all%20MOJ%20Afgh.pdf (last visited 19 December 2018).

56 *Ibid.*, 4.

community, faced with limited progress, insurgencies and an increase in the narcotics trade, realized that a change in approach was needed.

Accordingly, the international assistance agreement *Afghanistan Compact of the International Conference on Afghanistan* (London, 2006) terminated the lead-nations approach, sought to strengthen local ownership, and formulated specific rule of law reform goals concerning passing and publication of constitutionally required legislation, the judiciary, and the penal system with specific benchmarks.[57] The benchmarks mirrored reform plans laid out in the shortly before prepared ANDS by the Afghan Government, a (nominally) Afghan needs-based political framework for international cooperation. *UNSC Resolution 1659* of 15 February 2006 endorsed the Afghanistan Compact and called on the Afghan Government and the international community to implement it in full.[58] It also welcomed the Afghan Government's interim ANDS. The UNSC stressed the "inalienable right of the people of Afghanistan freely to determine their own future".[59]

After the *Afghanistan Compact*, rule of law became an integral element of the Afghanistan documents. The *Rome Conference on Justice and Rule of Law in Afghanistan* (Rome, 2007), endorsed by *UNSC Resolution 1746* of 23 March 2007, recognized "that without justice and the rule of law no sustainable security, stabilization, economic development and human rights can be achieved".[60] The Conference also fully endorsed a stronger locally owned processed. It endorsed the *Afghanistan Compact* but also the Government's paper *Justice for All* and the ANDS. Rule of law reform was to be implemented through a *National Justice Programme* to be funded in significant part through the multi-donor trust fund ARTF. The document also envisaged an Afghan-led monitoring and evaluation system for the justice sector.

The goals of the *Afghanistan Compact* were at the focus of all further Resolutions, with the UNSC increasingly urging the observance of its benchmarks and timelines (e.g. *Resolution 1868* of 23 March 2009[61]) and the implementation of the *National Justice Programme* "in view of accelerating the establishment of a fair and transparent justice system, eliminating impuni-

57 *Afghanistan Compact*, Annex I 'Benchmarks and Timelines', 1 February 2006.

58 SC Res. 1659, UN Doc S/RES/1659 (2006), 15 February 2006.

59 *Ibid.*, 1.

60 *Chairs' Conclusions*, Rome Conference on Justice and Rule of Law in Afghanistan, 3 July 2007.

61 SC Res. 1868, UN Doc S/RES/1868 (2009), 23 March 2009.

ty and contributing to the affirmation of the rule of law throughout the country" (*Resolution 1917* of 20 March 2010[62]).

At subsequent international conferences in London (2010) and Kabul (2010), stakeholders acknowledged shortcomings of the previous multi-donor-driven approach. Both the *London* and *Kabul Conference Communiqué* further streamlined the engagement of the international community, whilst moving towards greater ownership of the Afghan Government through agreement of specific areas of engagement with clear benchmarks. The *Kabul Communiqué* is remarkable in several ways: it for the first time addressed the issue of international legitimacy of the aid to Afghanistan by linking it to the UNSC Resolutions mandating UNAMA and the general stabilization process, but also democratic legitimacy of the steps undertaken by the Afghan Government such as noting that "it is also crucial that the Government, in pursuing its reforms, continue to consult with the people through their representative bodies, civil society, and other mechanisms".[63] The *Kabul Communiqué* also spelt out the importance of Afghan leadership and ownership and especially its "unique and irreplaceable knowledge of its own culture and people"[64] for the success of the aid efforts, whilst stating that the contribution of the international community should consist of lending of "resources and technical knowledge to the implementation of Afghan-defined programs".[65] Subsequent agreements have confirmed this approach. For instance, the 2011 *Bonn International Afghanistan Conference*, celebrating the tenth anniversary of the *Bonn Agreement* and at the same time ringing in the "Transition to Transformation Decade of 2015–2024"[66] after the completion of the ISAF mission in 2014, affirmed that:

> "This Transformation Decade will see the emergence of a new paradigm of partnership between Afghanistan and the International

---

62 SC Res. 1917, UN Doc S/RES/1917 (2010), 22 March 2010.

63 Kabul Conference Communiqué, 'A Renewed Commitment by the Afghan Government to the Afghan People. A Renewed Commitment by the International Community to Afghanistan' (2010), 3, para. 9, available at https://www.unodc.org/documents/afghanistan/Kabul_Conference/FINAL_Kabul_Conference_Communique.pdf (last visited 12 December 2018).

64 *Ibid.*, 2, para. 7.

65 *Ibid.*

66 International Afghanistan Conference, 'Afghanistan and the International Community: From Transition to the Transformation Decade. Conference Conclusions' (5 December 2011), available at https://peacemaker.un.org/sites/peacemaker.un.org/files/AF_111205_BonnConference.pdf (last visited 12 December 2018).

Community, whereby a sovereign Afghanistan engages with the International Community to secure its own future and continues to be a positive factor for peace and stability in the region."[67]

3. Mutual Accountability and Afghan Leadership (Since 2012)

Finally, through the *Tokyo Declaration*, entitled *Partnership for Self-Reliance in Afghanistan: From Transition to Transformation*[68] (Tokyo, 2012), the Afghan Government and the international community have aimed to transform their mutual commitments into a binding framework focused on the priorities of the Afghan Government as contained in its strategy papers. Afghanistan and the international community have established the *Tokyo Mutual Accountability Framework* (TMAF). It is the first time that mutual accountability was addressed in the multilateral negotiations on Afghanistan, in line with recent reforms of development law.

As regards the rule of law specifically, donors not only agreed on which areas to focus their rule of law promotion efforts, such as access to justice, enforcement of the constitution and fundamental laws, equality of women, and anti-corruption, but they also agreed to modify their mode of implementation of projects, that is, to "move from service delivery to building capacity and providing support". In exchange, the Afghan Government itself "promised to reinvigorate key development priorities such as anti-corruption and rule of law, honour its obligations to international human and gender rights mechanisms, and to continue the fight against drug cultivation".

This move of international actors from direct service delivery to support and capacity building for Afghan institutions, enabling the Government of Afghanistan to exercise its sovereign authority in all its functions, was also envisaged by *UNSC Resolution 2096* of 19 March 2013[69], as well as *UNSC Resolution 2145* of 17 March 2014[70]. While the end of assistance efforts in

---

67 International Afghanistan Conference, 'Afghanistan and the International Community: From Transition to the Transformation Decade. Conference Conclusions' (5 December 2011), available at https://peacemaker.un.org/sites/peacemaker.un.org/files/AF_111205_BonnConference.pdf (last visited 12 December 2018), 6, para. 30.

68 *The Tokyo Declaration: Partnership for Self-Reliance in Afghanistan: From Transition to Transformation*, UN Doc A/66/867–S/2012/532, 12 July 2012.

69 SC Res. 2096, UN Doc S/RES/2096 (2013), 19 March 2013.

70 SC Res. 2145, UN Doc S/RES/2145 (2014), 17 March 2014.

Afghanistan has hardly been reached, the stance of the UNSC today is that aid has evolved into partnership and Afghanistan is, at least nominally, standing on its own feet as far as governance is concerned.

Mutual accountability and conditionality were further pursued in 2015 with the *Self-Reliance through Mutual Accountability Framework*[71] (SMAF) which consolidates the TMAF and the Afghan Government's policy paper for the London 2014 Conference *Realizing Self-Reliance: Commitments to Reforms and Renewed Partnerships*.[72] It establishes ten *principles of mutual accountability*, including a commitment by the international community to support the development priorities identified by the Afghan Government in exchange for the "government's delivery of the mutually agreed commitments", an aim to include the "[l]essons learned from aid effectiveness" by all sides, and a reiteration of the importance of governance building.[73] Rule of law related indicators – developed to measure concrete progress – foresee the development and implementation of a *Justice Sector Reform* plan, laws to implement administration reform, and developments in the legal and policy framework for empowering women. These indicators are concretized into short term deliverables for 2016 in the SMAF. Notably, the donor community for the first time also committed to a set of deliverables concerning improving the partnership and aid effectiveness.

This push for rule of law promotion and the detailing of the mandate is in line with the renewed emphasis given to rule of law activities, particularly the justice sector which remains a key rule of law concern.[74] There seems to be unanimity that the rule of law is indispensable to transfer legitimacy onto the power holders. Funding in rule of law assistance has surged.[75] Rule of law assistance has continued with respect to classic forms of state-focused institution and capacity building.[76] In addition, rule of law activities were widened to include civil society, subnational governance,

71 Islamic Republic of Afghanistan, 'Self-Reliance through Mutual Accountability Framework' (2015), available at http://ez-afghanistan.de/sites/default/files/SMAF-MAIN_with_annex_3_%20sep_2015.pdf (last visited 12 December 2015) [SMAF].

72 T. Ruder, 'Lessons and Opportunities From the Tokyo Mutual Accountability Framework', *United States Institute of Peace Special Report* (2015) 378, 2, 4, 17.

73 SMAF, *supra* note 71, 1.

74 Islamic Republic of Afghanistan, *Afghanistan National Peace and Development Framework 2017 to 2021* (2016) 40.

75 Between 2009–2010 alone, USAID's rule of law budget doubled to 75 million US dollars. Rule of law assistance is also a main policy strategy for the EU, see Council of the European Union, *3288th Council Meeting Foreign Affairs*, Press Release 5425/14, 20 January 2014, 12-13.

76 E.g. BMZ, 'Strategie Afghanistan', *supra* note 15, 3, 4, 21.

and administration reform outside of Kabul.[77] Especially informal, often community-based justice systems, became the focus of rule of law activities in an effort to establish a *bottom-up* rule of law-based system accepted by society at large.[78]

4. A Paradigm Change?

In its most recent Resolution 2344 of 17 March 2017[79] extending the UNAMA mission, the UNSC again emphasized Afghan leadership and ownership over security, governance, and development. However, the Resolution signals and prepares a paradigm change to the current rule of law- and state-building approach. This is due to the deterioration of the security situation since 2015, the advent of parliamentary and presidential elections in 2018 and 2019, and the need for an inclusive and Afghan-led peace process to halt the widening insurgency. To this end, the UNSC has ordered a strategic review of the UNAMA mandate by the *UN Secretary-General* including its tasks, priorities, and resources to determine its efficiency and effectiveness.

The Resolution contains some substantive pointers for the UNAMA in regard of its rule of law activities. It states that UNAMA is to lead the

> "international civilian efforts aimed at reinforcing the role of Afghan institutions to perform their responsibilities, *with an increased focus on capacity building in key areas identified by the Afghan Government*, with a view, in all UN programmes and activities, to *move towards a national implementation model with a clear action-oriented strategy for mutually agreed condition-based transition* to Afghan leadership and ownership".[80]

The Resolution further stresses the need to accelerate

> "the establishment of a fair and transparent justice system, eliminating impunity and strengthening the rule of law throughout the country, anti-corruption measures, and progress in the reconstruction and re-

---

77 E.g. USAID's *Afghan Civic Engagement Program and Initiative to Strengthen Local Administrations*; GIZ's *Förderung der Rechtsstaatlichkeit, Regionale Kapazitätsentwicklungsfonds* (RCDF), *Stabilisierungsprogramm Nordafghanistan* (SPNA).

78 So-called second-generation rule of law concepts. See Gaston & Jensen, *supra* note 1, 73.

79 SC Res. 2344, UN Doc S/RES/2344 (2017), 17 March 2017.

80 *Ibid*., 4, para. 9 (emphasis added).

> form of the prison sector in Afghanistan, in order to improve the respect of the rule of law and human rights therein, [...] and calls for full respect for relevant international law including humanitarian law and human rights law".[81]

In his strategic review of the UNAMA, presented in autumn 2017, the *UN Secretary-General* endorses a significant strategic and policy remodelling of the UNAMA for its operations until 2020 which entails structural changes, based on interviews with Afghan and international stakeholders.[82] The review has an impact on rule of law activities. It is significantly informed by the UN's ongoing general redesigning of peace operations and development approach,[83] as well as the described fragile political and economic situation, and the difficult security situation. The *UN Secretary-General* advises to move from state- and institution-building towards focusing on sustainable peace and self-reliance of Afghanistan. Three strategic priorities are formulated: primacy of peace; strategic coordination of assistance through UNAMA to ensure, on the one hand, alignment with the Afghan Government's development priories as set out in the *Afghanistan National Peace and Development Framework* and, on the other hand, reflection of the *2030 Agenda for Sustainable Development*; and human rights.

Rule of law activities are relegated to a supporting role of the peace process. Possible rule of law activities listed are constitutional reform, transitional justice, and reconciliation.[84] To this end, the separate *Rule of Law Unit* is to be abolished. It remains to be seen to what extent the UNSC endorses these suggestions, but they could signal a significant shift of UN-bound resources away from the current broad rule of law promotion mandate.

To conclude, the UNSC Resolutions and the multilateral agreements have shaped the reconstruction process and imply a request by the Afghan

---

81 SC Res. 2344, UN Doc S/RES/2344 (2017), 17 March 2017, 8, para. 28.

82 UN Secretary-General, *Special Report on the Strategic Review of the UNAMA*, UN Doc. A/72/312–S/2017/696, 10 August 2017 [UN Secretary-General, Strategic Review of UNAMA].

83 *Report of the High-level Independent Panel on Peace Operations*, UN Doc A/70/95–S/2015/446, 17 June 2015 and UN Secretary-General, *The Future of United Nations Peace Operations*, UN Doc A/70/357–S/2015/682, 2 September 2015, requesting a unity of effort across the UN family; UN Secretary-General, *Repositioning the United Nations Development System to Deliver on the 2030 Agenda: Our Promise for Dignity, Prosperity and Peace on a Healthy Planet*, UN Doc A/72/684–E/2018/7, 21 December 2017.

84 *Ibid.*, para. 35.

Government for support from the international community. The request, and the overall relationship, has changed over the years, from dependence and delivery towards Afghan ownership and mutual commitments. Despite their abstract nature, the agreements thus convey a number of principles that guide the activities of rule of law actors, namely ownership, mutual accountability, cooperation, and aid effectiveness. However, despite all the efforts to strengthen ownership and coherence, the key instrument remains bilateral assistance.

II. Bilateral Agreements

While the multilateral agreements of the international conferences set the tone regarding the engagement of the international community, many States, international organizations, and also NGOs have concretized their relationship with Afghanistan through bilateral agreements.[85] The structure of these bilateral agreements is twofold: general, long-term framework agreements address the general scope and structure of cooperation, mutual commitments, and the legal position of staff in the country assisted.[86] Subsequently, supplementary, (often) legally nonbinding agreements on specific development measures are concluded. These concrete arrangements, at least as far as Germany is concerned, are not made public.[87] For this reason, this article can only review the current framework agreements between Afghanistan and Germany.

In 2012, the German and Afghan Governments entered into an *Agreement on Bilateral Cooperation*.[88] Drafted to complement the *EU–Afghanistan Partnership Agreement*, the agreement addresses cooperation with regard to a wide range of areas excluding military cooperation, which is to be addressed separately. Article 3 of the agreement covers "development, civilian reconstruction, cooperation on education". Short-term assistance is agreed

85 E.g. the UN special agencies have concluded "core agreements" with Afghan line ministries on their cooperation, see UN Secretary-General, *Special Report on the Strategic Review of the UN Assistance Mission in Afghanistan*, UN Doc A/72/312-S/2017/696, 10 August 2017, para. 38 [UN Secretary-General, UN Mission in Afghanistan].

86 J. Neumann, *Die Förderung der Rule of Law in der Entwicklungszusammenarbeit* (2013), 191.

87 BMZ, 'Leitlinien', *supra* note 53, 23, para. 35.

88 *Agreement between the Government of the Federal Republic of Germany and the Government of the Islamic Republic of Afghanistan Concerning Bilateral Cooperation*, 16 May 2012, Germany and Afghanistan, 2921 UNTS, I-50874.

among others in the building of the justice sector. An *Afghan-German Government Committee* is created by Article 7 to decide on a consensual basis on goals, priorities, and measures. Article 8 regulates "foundations for cooperation"; but like the rest of the agreement, they are highly abstract and do not contain any concrete guidelines on how the cooperation is to be carried out.

On 18 February 2017, the Afghan Government, the EU, and its Member States signed the *Cooperation Agreement on Partnership and Development* (CAPD) to formalize their cooperation.[89] The CAPD is remarkable for a number of reasons: First, it is a mixed agreement, meaning that it addresses areas that fall under exclusive EU competence and areas within the Member States' – thus, also Germany's – competence. Pending the process of Member State ratifications, it is provisionally applicable with regard to the areas falling under EU competence, including development cooperation. Second, the scope of the agreement is very broad (and yet more detailed than any of the comparable bilateral agreements). It covers cooperation in political dialog, security, economic and political issues, and specific sectors such as migration, natural resources, education, energy, transport, and home and justice affairs.

In addition to specific goals and rules, the agreement sets out general principles to guide cooperation, as well as specific principles for certain areas of cooperation.

Two of the general rules are notable. First, Article 1 (3) gives preference to a certain type of (rule of law promotion) programs by stipulating that "capacity building shall be given particular attention in order to support the development of Afghan institutions and ensure that Afghanistan can benefit fully from the opportunities offered [...] under this Agreement". Second, Article 2 in unprecedented detail establishes principles for cooperation, notably: a commitment to the values of the UN Charter; a recognition of Afghan people's ownership and leadership; "[r]espect for democrat-

89 *Cooperation Agreement on Partnership and Development Between the European Union and its Member States, of the One Part, and the Islamic Republic of Afghanistan, of the Other Part*, 16 November 2016, 12966/16 [CAPD]. The CAPD complements the EU's Strategy on Afghanistan. The Multiannual Indicative Programme for Afghanistan is valid for the period 2014–2020, available at https://eeas.europa.eu/sites/eeas/files/multi-annual-indicative-programme-2014-2020_en_0.pdf (last visited 12 December 2018). It identifies key priorities for development, such as application of the rule of law and State accountability through democratization, but also expresses the intention to ensure a stronger alignment with the ANPDF. In addition to this agreement, the EU and Afghanistan in 2016 entered into a *State Building Contract*.

ic principles and human rights [...] and for the principle of the rule of law underpins the internal and international policies of the Parties and constitutes an essential element of this Agreement"; a "commitment to cooperating further towards the full achievement of internationally agreed development goals, including the Millennium Development Goals, as adopted by Afghanistan"; "attachment to the principles of good governance, including the independence of parliaments and the judiciary and the fight against corruption at all levels"; and, finally, an agreement that their cooperation under the CAPD "will be in accordance with their respective legislation, rules and regulations".

As regards specific rules, reference is often made to existing international treaty law and standards as basis for cooperation, and programming is often mainstreamed to a certain substantive standard. This article will look at two specific, rule of law-related issues: development cooperation (Article 12) and Cooperation in matters of justice and home affairs (Title V) specifically on rule of law, legal cooperation, and policing (Article 24).

Development cooperation is subjected to a rigorous set of objectives and rules. Substantively, the *Millennium Development Goals* (MDGs), poverty eradication, sustainable development, and integration into the world economy are regarded as key objectives. Cooperation is to take into account Afghanistan's development strategies and international agreements since 2010 including the TMAF and the SMAF. Noteworthy is the agreement in Article 12 (7) that some themes

> "will be systematically mainstreamed in all areas of development cooperation, [namely] human rights, gender issues, democracy, good governance, environmental sustainability, climate change, health, institutional development and capacity building, anti-corruption measures, counter-narcotics and aid effectiveness".[90]

The parties also subscribe to the *Paris Declaration on Aid Effectiveness*, the *Accra Agenda for Action*, and the *Busan Outcome Document*, and Article 12 (5) notes that:

> "The Parties agree to promote cooperation activities in accordance with their respective regulations, procedures and resources and in full respect for international rules and norms. They agree that their development cooperation will be consistent with the requirements of their common commitment to aid effectiveness, implemented in a manner

90 CAPD, *supra* note 89, Article 12 (7).

> that respects Afghan ownership, aligned with Afghanistan's national priorities, and conducive to tangible and sustainable development outcomes for the people of Afghanistan and to the long-term economic sustainability of the country, as agreed in the context of international conferences on Afghanistan."[91]

Article 24 on the rule of law, legal cooperation, and policing pursues a classic, thin rule of law concept. The defined cooperation goal "on matters of justice and home affairs" is "the consolidation of the rule of law, the strengthening of institutions at all levels in the areas of law enforcement and administration of justice, including the penitentiary system". Paragraphs 3 and 4 specify the cooperation by agreeing on further reforms, including of the judiciary and the justice system. Novel is the agreement in paragraph 2 that "[t]he parties shall exchange information on legal systems and legislation. They shall pay particular attention to the rights of women and other vulnerable groups and the protection and implementation of those rights". Formulated as an obligation, this provision might be viewed as to impose a kind of due diligence on the parties to familiarize themselves with relevant legal contexts when cooperating in this sector.

The substantive framework is complemented by an institutional framework in Title VIII, built towards close coordination and mutual accountability. Article 49 establishes a Joint Committee to oversee the functioning and implementation of the agreement. This Joint Committee is furnished with powers to request information, including from other bodies established under other agreements between the parties and – in a laudable effort towards the rule of law – it is to adopt rules of procedure. Noteworthy is also the establishment of detailed rules on cooperation to prevent, address, and investigate fraud within the assistance in Article 51. Article 53 clarifies that the Member States may continue to engage in bilateral cooperation with Afghanistan, thus repeating the basic principle of parallel competence expressed in Article 4 (4) TFEU.[92]

In short, bilateral agreements between the Afghan Government and individual or several donors serve an important concretizing function as long as donors avoid committing to specific cooperation in the broad framework agreements. Like the CAPD, these agreements can fulfill important normative functions. The CAPD particularly is noteworthy for its level of

---

91 CAPD, *supra* note 89, Article 12 (5).

92 For a general overview of European Development Law, see L. Müller, 'Europäisches Entwicklungsrecht', in Dann, Kadelbach & Kaltenborn (eds), *supra* note 11, 677.

detailed rules for the cooperation partnership, as well as its conscious integration of existing international frameworks, such as the TMAF and the SMAF, the MDGs, and the rules on aid effectiveness.

D. Legal Basis and Mandate for the Rule of Law Promotion by Non-State Actors

This section focuses on the legal mandate for NGOs in Afghanistan, using German NGOs, especially the GIZ and Germany-based NGOs without State ownership, as an example. The GIZ is the German Government's development aid organization. It is organized as a limited liability company under German law, with the German Government as its sole shareholder. Its key task is technical assistance (meaning nonfinancial assistance given by experts).

The legal mandate for the implementation of rule of law assistance projects usually derives from two sources: a contractual agreement or grant approval (possibly, in the form of an administrative decision) between the non-State actor and the donor. Second, the NGOs conclude a contract or a nonbinding memorandum of understanding with Afghan partner institutions.

Where the German Government is the donor, the process has been somewhat formalized in the *Guidelines for Bilateral Financial and Technical Assistance with Cooperation Partners of German Development Cooperation* (*BMZ Leitlinien*), which are internally binding administrative regulations (*Verwaltungsvorschriften*) issued by the BMZ, the AA, the *Federal Ministry of Finance*, and the *Federal Ministry for Economic Affairs and Energy* and directed at the German Government, German implementing organizations, primarily GIZ and the *KfW Banking Group*, and other involved entities.[93]

The *BMZ Leitlinien* foresee that as far as BMZ funds are concerned, technical assistance predominantly is to be carried out through GIZ.[94]

The *BMZ Leitlinien* regulate the process. In addition, BMZ and GIZ have concluded a framework treaty. These framework agreements, based

93 BMZ, 'Leitlinien', *supra* note 53, 7 and 15, para. 16. Together with earmarking in the national budget, the BMZ Guidelines and the guidelines of other ministries, form the substantive policy framework for development (including rule of law) support. See T. Groß, 'Deutsches Entwicklungsverwaltungsrecht', in Dann, Kadelbach & Kaltenborn (eds), *supra* note 11, 659.

94 Groß, *supra* note 93, 661. Since 2010, the BMZ has implemented development projects through two main implementation organizations: the GIZ for technical assistance and the *KfW Banking Group* for financial assistance.

on the information available, bind GIZ to the German Government's overall development strategy, but they do not contain any specific rules on the substantive implementation of a measure.[95] Based on the *BMZ Leitlinien*, GIZ implements the concrete project on the basis of a contract with an Afghan partner institution, usually the competent line ministry. The contract usually sets out goals and indicators to assess achievement of the goals, the respective parties' contributions, the timeline, organizational, and technical modalities and also consequences for breach of contract.[96] The *BMZ Leitlinien* do not seem to consider the influence of public international law to the validity and enforcement of the contract as demonstrated by the fact that they are silent on what would be the consequences of breach of human rights standards, rule of law, or corruption. This is not surprising given the absence of such standards in the legal framework (including the government's agreement on development and the framework agreements which are often referenced).[97] GIZ is allowed to subcontract certain tasks (*Direktleistungen*) if appropriate and economically useful, including to international organizations.[98]

The AA recently published additional *Guidelines for Project Funding*.[99] The guidelines provide details on the scope of activities that can be supported, as well as the legal, administrative, and financial and accountability framework for implementing organizations. The focus, however, is on financial accountability. The *Guidelines* do not establish substantive criteria for programming of tasks or criteria to be observed by the NGO. Upon conclusion of a project, the NGO needs to report to the AA as a funding agency, providing details on the achievements *vis-à-vis* the defined goals and indicators. But only the necessity and adequacy of the work carried out need to be elaborated – an indication for emphasis on cost effectiveness as required by § 7 of the *Federal Budget Code*.[100] Recipients must report to the AA if the intended use or any other relevant circumstances for the

95 For an in-depth analysis of this legal relationship, see P. Dann, *Entwicklungsverwaltungsrecht* (2012).

96 BMZ, 'Leitlinien', *supra* note 53, 23, para. 36.

97 Neumann, *supra* note 86, 194.

98 BMZ, 'Leitlinien', *supra* note 53, 16, para. 19.

99 German Foreign Office, *Förderkonzept des AA von Projekten zur Unterstützung von internationalen Maßnahmen auf den Gebieten der Krisenprävention, Konfliktbewältigung, Stabilisierung und Friedensförderung durch das AA (Referat S 03) in Afghanistan*, 1 July 2017.

100 German Federal Office of Administration, *Allgemeine Nebenbestimmungen für Zuwendungen zur Projektförderung*, as of 4 November 2016, para. 6.2 [BVA, ANBest-P]. For a detailed analysis of the evaluation process, see Groß, *supra* note

grant of the donation change, or if it becomes apparent that the goal will not be achieved with the grant. This could be a means to address significant shortcomings or project violations by a partner institution in Afghanistan.[101]

The *BMZ Leitlinien* contain few, rather vague substantive pointers, but none that are directly applicable to NGOs other than the state-owned implementing organizations. These rules will be addressed below.

Thus, where the German Government acts as the donor, the mandate for rule of law activities by German organizations are derived from the bilateral agreements concluded by Germany with Afghanistan (or its respective other partner country) mediated through a contract or administrative decision between the disbursing ministry and the implementing organization, and the specifics of the concrete measure are elaborated on a contractual basis between the non-State actor and the donor recipient. The latter might engage private international law questions in case of conflict.

In addition, private actors are bound by national law limitations arising out of their domestic law as well as Afghan law – to the extent rule of law activities are carried out on the ground. As will be shown below, apart from the Afghan Constitution, the laws do not establish significant limitations.

E. *Rules Guiding the Programming and Implementation of Rule of Law Assistance*

As shown above, foreign experts participate actively in rule of law promotion. What are the limits to the legal contents conveyed by foreign experts in the implementation of rule of law activities?

The implementation of rule of law promotion measures finds its boundaries, first, in the above-mentioned UNSC Resolutions and the consent given by Afghanistan in multi- and bilateral agreements and policy accords. Yet there are other principles and standards that become relevant for an assessment of the activities of the different actors.

93, 674. Other project evaluations also consider sustainability, see BMZ, 'Leitlinien', *supra* note 53, para. 44.

101 BVA, 'ANBest-P', *supra* note 101, para. 5.

I. International Legal Standards

International legal standards limiting the rule of law activities can derive from treaty law, customary international law, UNSC Resolutions, and from nonbinding but persuasive international instruments.

The *UN Secretary-General* in the 2008 *Guidance Note on UN Approach to Rule of Law Assistance* outlines guiding principles for the rule of law activities of the UN in all its operations. The *Guidance Note* lists the following guiding principles:

> "1. Base assistance on international norms and standards
> 2. Take account of the political context
> 3. Base assistance on the unique country context
> 4. Advance human rights and gender justice
> 5. Ensure national ownership
> 6. Support national reform constituencies
> 7. Ensure a coherent and comprehensive strategic approach
> 8. Engage in effective coordination and partnerships."[102]

The *Guidance Note* translates to "base assistance on international norms and standards" as the normative basis for the UN's rule of law work. This is derived primarily from the UN Charter, but also from "international human rights law, international humanitarian law, international criminal law and international refugee law",[103] as well as UN treaties, declarations, guidelines, and principles. The following considers the extent to which these sources, as well as the principles established in the normative framework for the reconstruction of Afghanistan, mandate the programming and content of rule of law assistance.

1. Accordance with the UN Charter Principles

The extent of involvement of the international community with Afghanistan's governance rebuilding is unprecedented. How does this fit in with the UN Charter principles? Article 2 (7) of the UN Charter says:

> "Nothing contained in the present Charter shall authorize the UN to intervene in matters which are essentially within the domestic jurisdiction of any State or shall require the Members to submit such matters

102 UN Secretary-General, 'Rule of Law Assistance', *supra* note 18, 1.
103 *Ibid.*, 2.

> to settlement under the present Charter; but this principle shall not prejudice the application of enforcement measures under Chapter VII."

One might ask what meaning (if any) the domestic jurisdiction clause has today, in an age of globalization and ever-increasing interdependence between States. In practice, however States and the UN regularly emphasize the continued existence and importance of the principle of sovereignty[104], even though it is agreed that sovereignty cannot mean complete independence in internal matters. According to the 1970 *Friendly Relations Declaration*,[105] "all States enjoy the rights that are inherent in full sovereignty," and "each State has the right freely to choose and to develop its political, social, economic and cultural systems". The 2001 *Bonn Agreement* on Afghanistan itself started by

> "*Reaffirming* the independence, national sovereignty and territorial integrity of Afghanistan,
> *Acknowledging* the right of the people of Afghanistan to freely determine their own political future in accordance with the principles of Islam, democracy, pluralism and social justice".[106]

According to its text, Article 2 (7) of the UN Charter protects only against acts of the UN and not against acts of other States. While it has sometimes been applied to States as well, it seems more accurate to say that the extent of protection against acts of the UN and acts of individual States was not meant to be identical, and that Article 2 (7) is thus *lex specialis* to the general principle of nonintervention enshrined in Article 2 (1), (4) of the UN Charter.[107]

Article 2 (7) applies to all organs of the UN and all their activities; this does not, however, include legally separate specialized or related agencies.[108]

---

104 See e.g. SC Res. 2032, UN Doc S/RES/2032 (2011), 22 December 2011; SC Res. 1271, UN Doc S/RES/1271 (1999), 22 October 1999; SC Res. 1101, UN Doc S/RES/1101 (1997), 28 March 1997; GA Res. 65/222, UN Doc A/RES/65/222, 21 December 2010; GA Res. 65/203, UN Doc A/RES/65/203, 21 December 2010; UNHRC, UN Doc A/HRC/RES/18/6, 13 October 2011.

105 GA Res. 2625 (XXV), UN Doc A/RES/25/2625, 24 October 1970.

106 UNSC, *Agreement on Provisional Arrangements in Afghanistan Pending the Re-Establishment of Permanent Government Institutions*, UN Doc S/2001/1154, 5 December 2001, Preamble [UNSC, Provisional Arrangements in Afghanistan].

107 See G. Nolte, 'Article 2 (7)', in B. Simma *et al.* (eds), *The Charter of the UN: A Commentary*, Vol. I, 3rd ed. (2012), 284.

108 *Ibid.*, 285.

The debate concerning the meaning of Article 2 (7) has not abated although its focus has shifted. The interpretation of the term "to intervene" has broadened over time; the *Friendly Relations Declaration* stated that intervention comprises not only armed intervention, but also "all other forms of interference or attempted threats against the personality of the State or against its political, cultural and economic elements".[109] At the same time, the sphere of *domestic jurisdiction* has constantly been reduced as more and more areas that used to be regulated by internal law are coming under the remit of international law. As the PCIJ in the *Case of Nationality Decrees in Tunis and Morocco* famously argued: "The question whether a certain matter is or is not solely within the jurisdiction of a State is an essentially relative question: it depends on the development of international relations."[110]

In the words of *Hans Kelsen*, the idea that there are "matters which, by their very nature, are solely within the domestic jurisdiction of a State, is erroneous. There is no matter that cannot be regulated by a rule of customary or contractual international law; and if a matter is regulated by a rule of international law it is no longer 'solely within the domestic jurisdiction' of the State concerned."[111] So while respect for sovereignty and domestic jurisdiction is still regularly expressed in Resolutions by the *UN General Assembly* and other UN organs, the precise meaning and significance of these concepts is increasingly unclear.

It also comes to mind that rule of law assistance, seen as political interference, might violate the principle of nonintervention enshrined in Article 2 (1), (4) of the UN Charter:

> "The Organization and its Members, in pursuit of the Purposes stated in Article 1, shall act in accordance with the following Principles.
> (1) The Organization is based on the principle of the sovereign equality of all its Members. [...]
> (4) All Members shall refrain in their international relations from the threat or use of force against the territorial integrity or political inde-

---

109 While the Declaration only concerns relations between States and not between the UN and its member States, it is regarded as giving 'expression to a consensus about an enlarged concept of intervention under general international law', G. Nolte, 'Article 2 (7)', in B. Simma *et al.* (eds), *The Charter of the UN: A Commentary*, Vol. I, 3rd ed. (2012), 288.

110 Nationality Decrees Issued in Tunis and Morocco on November 8th 1921, PCIJ Series B, No. 4 (1923), 24.

111 H. Kelsen, *The Law of the UN: A Critical Analysis of Its Fundamental Problems* (1950), 771.

> pendence of any State, or in any other manner inconsistent with the Purposes of the UN."

Today it is agreed that the principle of nonintervention in the internal affairs of States is not limited to the prohibition of the threat or use of force, but also signifies that a State should not otherwise intervene in a dictatorial way in the internal affairs of other States.[112] The ICJ in the *Nicaragua Case* referred to an "element of coercion, which defines, and indeed forms the very essence of, prohibited intervention".[113] According to *Oppenheim*, "the interference must be forcible or dictatorial, or otherwise coercive, in effect depriving the State intervened against of control over the matter in question. Interference pure and simple is not intervention."[114] Also, intervention (even military intervention) with the proper consent of the government of a State is not precluded.[115]

Afghanistan has long been in a State of rebuilding, aggravated by inner turmoil and the threat of terrorism. Its economic and military dependence on the international community, and the influence this has given foreign actors over Afghanistan for many decades, cannot be denied. There is a fine line between political influence and coercion where economic conditions between international partners are as unequal as in the case of Afghanistan. Yet insofar as activities are based on agreements with the Afghan Government and UNSC Resolutions, these override the applicability of the general principle of nonintervention.

2. *Human Rights Law*

In how far is a State like Germany bound to observe international human rights standards when, for example, assisting in the drafting of Afghan legislation?

In dualist countries such as Germany, international agreements are transformed into domestic law through a legislative act. The question,

112 The provision is also applied to the UN, compare A. Randelzhofer and O. Dörr, 'Article 2 (4)', in B. Simma *et al.* (eds), *supra* note 107, 213.

113 *Military and Paramilitary Activities in and Against Nicaragua (Nicaragua v. United States of America)*, Judgment, ICJ Reports 1986, 14, 108, para. 205.

114 L. Oppenheim, *Oppenheim's International Law*, Vol. I: Introduction and Part 1, 9th ed. (1992), 432.

115 M. Wood, 'Non-Intervention (Non-Interference in Domestic Affairs)', in *Encyclopedia Princetoniensis: The Princeton Encyclopedia of Self-Determination*, available at https://pesd.princeton.edu/?q=node/258 (last visited 12 December 2018).

then, is the extent of extraterritorial applicability of domestic law, especially constitutional rights and constraints on the exercise of executive powers, and the obligations that Germany has versus the citizens of foreign countries in the context of development aid.[116] The answer depends, in part, on the scope of the international agreement in question. For example, Article 2 (1) of the *International Covenant on Civil and Political Rights*[117] (ICCPR) provides that:

> "Each State Party to the present Covenant undertakes to respect and to ensure to all individuals within its territory and subject to its jurisdiction the rights recognized in the present Covenant, without distinction of any kind, such as race, colour, sex, language, religion, political or other opinion, national or social origin, property, birth or other status."

The wording allows for extraterritorial application within the jurisdiction of Germany. This would not seem to apply to countries receiving development aid.

Article 2 of the *International Covenant on Economic, Social and Cultural Rights*[118] (ICESCR), on the other hand, would seem to allow more leeway for extraterritorial application:

> "1. Each State Party to the present Covenant undertakes to take steps, individually and through international assistance and co-operation, especially economic and technical, to the maximum of its available resources, with a view to achieving progressively the full realization of the rights recognized in the present Covenant by all appropriate means, including particularly the adoption of legislative measures.
> 2. The States Parties to the present Covenant undertake to guarantee that the rights enunciated in the present Covenant will be exercised without discrimination of any kind as to race, colour, sex, language, religion, political or other opinion, national or social origin, property, birth or other status.
> 3. Developing countries, with due regard to human rights and their national economy, may determine to what extent they would guarantee

116 This issue is comprehensively discussed in Dann, *supra* note 95, 238-259. Concerning the extraterritorial application of basic rights enshrined in the German Constitution, see below II. 2.

117 *International Covenant on Civil and Political Rights*, 19 December 1966, 999 UNTS 171.

118 *International Covenant on Economic, Social and Cultural Rights*, 16 December 1966, 991 UNTS 3.

the economic rights recognized in the present Covenant to non-nationals."

The scope of obligations deriving from Article 2 ICESCR has been debated. Some have argued that the *travaux préparatoires* of the ICESCR do not imply that the drafters intended to create extraterritorial obligations for the parties. Others contend that the Covenant emphasizes international assistance and co-operation, which may entail obligations beyond the domestic realm.[119] Regarding the limits of the international dimension of the ICESCR, the *Committee on Economic, Social and Cultural Rights* (CESCR) in its *Concluding Observations of 1998 on Israel* confirmed that the ICESCR "applies to all areas where Israel maintains geographical, functional or personal jurisdiction" and that "the State's obligations under the Covenant apply to all territories and populations under its effective control".[120] The Committee's interpretation of the extraterritorial application of the ICESCR is thus concurrent with the ICCPR; both depend on effective control of the populace. The international donors, however, do not possess effective control over the Afghan people. Therefore, we cannot assume the extraterritorial applicability of the Covenants.

Dann sidesteps this problem by arguing that a donor country may become complicit in the human rights violations of a recipient country towards its citizens if both countries are party to an international treaty and the donor is aware of the rights violation. According to Article 16 of the 2001 *Draft Articles on State Responsibility*[121],

> "[a] State which aids or assists another State in the commission of an internationally wrongful act by the latter is internationally responsible for doing so if: (a) that State does so with knowledge of the circumstances of the internationally wrongful act; and (b) the act would be internationally wrongful if committed by that State."

Such a constellation is possible since Afghanistan is party to most of the major human rights treaties, including the *Covenants*. Considering the far-reaching influence that donor countries have on Afghan affairs, and the active role they play in the regulation of the relationship between citizens

---

119 *International Covenant on Economic, Social and Cultural Rights*, 16 December 1966, 991 UNTS 3, 239-240.

120 CESCR, *Concluding Observations: Israel*, UN Doc E/C.12/1/Add.27, 4 December 1998, 6, 8.

121 ILC, *Draft Articles on Responsibility of States for Internationally Wrongful Acts* (2001), Vol. II Part 2, 26.

and State, it seems adequate to assume a correspondent responsibility. Making the donor country *complicit* in the recipient's human rights violations allows us to leave open the issue of extraterritoriality: Rather than imposing the donor country's international obligations on the recipient, we only look at the recipient's own obligations, thus safeguarding its sovereignty.

3. *Development of Law Standards*

Standards derived from development law feature prominently in the network of legal bases described above as well as the Afghan national development strategies. These standards originate largely from the OECD's frameworks for ODA and from the *World Bank*.[122] Two concepts have been adopted over the years of assistance.[123] First, the aid effectiveness principles as laid down in the *Paris Declaration on Aid Effectiveness*[124] and its implementation and successor regimes, a soft law standard drafted by the *OECD Development Assistance Committee* to which a large number of States, international organizations, and civil society organizations have subscribed,[125] and which have been expressly adopted in the international agreements since 2007.[126] And, second, the principle of conditionality.

122 Dann & Riegner, *supra* note 11, 723.

123 *Tondini* notes that there was a real-time implementation of novel IFI policies to Afghan state-building. See Tondini, 'Justice Sector Reform in Afghanistan', *supra* note 3, 663. See for instance the reference in the shared principles of the *Rome Communiqué* (2007).

124 OECD, Paris Declaration on Aid Effectiveness (2005), available at http://www.oecd.org/dac/effectiveness/34428351.pdf (last visited 12 December 2018).

125 For a discussion of the legal nature of the *Paris Declaration*, see P. Dann & L. Vierck, 'Paris Declaration on Aid Effectiveness/Accra Agenda for Action (2008)', in R. Wolfrum (ed.), *Max Planck Encyclopedia of Public International Law* (2011), paras. 14-16, available at http://opil.ouplaw.com/view/10.1093/law:epil/9780199231690/law-9780199231690-e2097 (last visited 12 December 2018).

126 For example, TMAF Section 14 where international community commits "to taking concrete steps to improve aid delivery consistent with partnership and global aid effectiveness principles, and adhering to the Afghan Government's Aid Management Policy upon completion and endorsement by the JCMB by December 2012".

a. Aid Effectiveness

The *Paris Declaration on Aid Effectiveness* and its successor agreements stipulate five principles to increase aid effectiveness, known as partnership commitments: ownership, alignment, harmonization, managing for results, and mutual accountability; and they include indicators to measure progress in achieving the principles. All principles are prominent in the above-mentioned documents on state-building and rule of law promotion in Afghanistan.[127] However, their outcome-oriented focus on economically measurable results[128] – as embedded in the principle of *managing for results* – distracts from the goal of ensuring a sustainable and legally sound outcome. Especially as regards rule of law promotion, which needs to accommodate the larger socio-legal context, quantitative evaluation tools risk undermining the holistic and long-term approaches necessary to foster lasting reconstruction. The focus on measuring also risks turning the implementation of rule of law promotion into a black box.

The ownership principle in regard of OAD standards requires that "[p]artner countries exercise effective leadership over their development policies and strategies and coordinate development actions."[129] This principle will be addressed jointly with considerations on local ownership below.

Closely connected is the principle of alignment, which requires donors to "base their overall support on the partner countries' national development strategies, institutions and support."[130] This principle has lately been taken more seriously by donors in rule of law assistance and other programming, although donors have not committed to it in a legally binding

127 For harmonization, see the commitment by donors in the SMAF. In addition to the request to increase on-budget aid and align donor strategies to NPPs, indicators to measure progress towards increased aid effectiveness include that donors "ensure timely, accurate and complete aid information" and "work towards a single mechanism for provision of Technical Assistance [...] to the government", to "complement Development Framework Agreements [...] for improving harmonization and aid predictability" and to "complete Financing Agreements [...] with the government for all off-budget projects, in line with the agreed Aid Management Policy as well as to carrying out annual portfolio performance reviews". Regarding mutual accountability, the SMAF aims at a unified approach to performance evaluation, namely that a "[t]ransparent, citizen-based monitoring of development and governance benchmarks provides accountability to the Afghan people, and reinforces the reciprocal commitments of donors and the government to improved development performance."

128 Remeasuring of results, see Dann & Riegner, *supra* note 11, 746.

129 *Paris Declaration on Aid Effectiveness*, *supra* note 124, 3.

130 *Ibid.*

manner, likely because they still seek to match aid assistance to their own priorities. Donor policies and programs are increasingly aligned with the ANPDF and the priorities set out in the *National Priority Plans*, and the presentation of development strategies at international donor conferences since the 2006 presentation of the *Afghanistan Compact* has served to give prominence to the Afghan Government's development strategies.[131] The SMAF, in a notable deviation from the TMAF, contains an explicit commitment to support the development priorities identified by the Afghan Government. For the first time, donors submitted to binding commitments, in the Annex to the SMAF – mostly regarding performance review and information exchange, but they also agreed that a joint working group was to produce a roadmap for sector-wide approaches.[132] Shortcomings continue in particular with regard to the Afghan Government's wish that foreign aid be disbursed as financial aid into the national budget or as on-budget support. The latter has become a key tool for conditionality, as discussed below.

Full alignment to government priorities is also problematic from a conceptual perspective. In Afghanistan, the government has an institutional interest in state-building and power centralization which both directly benefit it. International pressure was necessary to extend development assistance to neglected issues, including rule of law promotion in provincial areas.

b. Conditionality

Conditionality is the second tenet of development standards in the current legal framework for Afghan reconstruction. Used by the *World Bank* since the 1970s and core component of the EU's development approach, it describes

> "the practice of international organizations and States of making aid and cooperation agreements with recipient States conditional upon

131 See for example Germany's commitment to align development cooperation to Afghan national development priorities, BMZ, 'Strategie Afghanistan', *supra* note 15, 15.

132 These include joint performance reviews of their projects if they achieve or exceed 60 per cent on-budget target, and to provide all aid information, including spending, both on and off budget in Afghanistan, to be recorded in the Development Assistance Database.

the observance of various requirements, such as financial stability, good governance, respect for human rights, democracy, peace and security. Diverse consequences are also attached to the disrespect of the condition by the recipient State."[133]

The TMAF and SMAF framework tie international aid to the achievement of concrete reforms.[134] The tangible goals Afghanistan has committed to include rule of law reforms in the justice sector, including overall measures to combat corruption. They are not formulated as conditional, but the conditionality is clearly implied.[135] Foreign governments, including Germany, state to expressly condition aid to specific achievements by the donor recipient, most notably related to gender equality and the overall situation of women and children.[136] The German Government has noted its successful efforts to include human rights-based hard deliverables (i.e. measurable targets) in the TMAF.[137] In Afghanistan, the donors' willingness to increase on-budget support for Afghanistan through the ARTF or other development funds comes with conditions. Germany, in response to limited success in implementation of the deliverables agreed within the TMAF, in 2013, paid only 20 of the pledged 40 million Euros into the ARTF.[138]

Conditionality is not unproblematic with regard to the principle of sovereignty – including as expressed in the concept of local ownership.

4. *Local Ownership*

Few terms have been used throughout the above legal documents as often as local ownership. The concept is referred to both in the state-building

133 C. Pinelli, 'Conditionality', in R. Wolfrum (ed.), *Max Planck Encyclopedia of Public International Law* (2013), para. 1, available at http://opil.ouplaw.com/abstract/10.1093/law:epil/9780199231690/law-9780199231690-e1383?rskey=GmY0vX&result=1&prd=EPIL (last visited 12 December 2018). See also L. Bartels, *Human Rights Conditionality in the EU's International Agreements* (2005).

134 See also BMZ, 'Strategie Afghanistan', *supra* note 15, 13.

135 Ruder, *supra* note 72, 3.

136 BMZ, 'Strategie Afghanistan', *supra* note 15, 27 ("Die Bundesregierung hält an der Überzeugung fest, dass eine maßvolle Konditionalisierung der in Tokio zugesagten Mittel der richtige Weg ist, um den notwendigen Reformdruck auf die afghanische Regierung aufrechtzuerhalten"). See also BMZ, 'Leitlinien', *supra* note 53, para. 25.

137 German Federal Government, 'Fortschrittsbericht Afghanistan 2014', supra note 13, 16.

138 *Ibid.*, 11–13.

and in the development law context, with differing nuances. According to the *Paris Declaration on Aid Effectiveness*, donor recipients are required to exercise effective leadership over their development policies and strategies and coordinate development measures. The term takes on a broader meaning within the UN's State and peacebuilding activities, where it is seen as generally requiring *bottom-up* localized processes.[139] Processes must be *demand-driven*, that is, based on the needs and preferences of local communities, as opposed to supply-driven, that is mandated by the political strategic agendas of foreign governments.[140] According to the *UN Secretary-General*:

> "We must learn as well to eschew one-size-fits-all formulas and the importation of foreign models, and, instead, base our support on national assessments, national participation and national needs and aspirations. Effective strategies will seek to support both technical capacity for reform and political will for reform. The UN must therefore support domestic reform constituencies, help build the capacity of national justice sector institutions, facilitate national consultations on justice reform and transitional justice and help fill the rule of law vacuum evident in so many post-conflict societies."[141]

Ownership features prominently in the Guidance Note of the *UN Secretary-General* on the UN Approach to Rule of Law Assistance. Ensuring "national ownership" according to the *UN Secretary-General* entails:

> "No rule of law programme can be successful in the long term if imposed from the outside. Process leadership and decision-making must be in the hands of national stakeholders. Rule of law development requires the full and meaningful participation and support of national stakeholders, inter alia, government officials, justice and other rule of law officials, national legal professionals, traditional leaders, women, children, minorities, refugees and displaced persons, other marginalized groups and civil society. Experience indicates that the rule of law is strengthened if reform efforts are focused on assisting the State to apply its international legal obligations, and are credible and adhere to

139 For a conceptual analysis of the concept, see H. Reich, 'Local Ownership in Conflict Transformation Projects–Partnership, Participation or Patronage?', *Berghof Occasional Paper* No. 27 (2006).

140 Cf. Tondini, 'Justice Sector Reform in Afghanistan, *supra* note 3, 667.

141 UNSC, *The Rule of Law and Transitional Justice in Conflict and Post-Conflict Societies: Report of the Secretary-General*, UN Doc S/2004/616, 23 August 2004 [UNSC, Rule of Law].

> the principles of inclusion, participation and transparency, facilitating increased legitimacy and national ownership. Meaningful ownership requires the legal empowerment of all segments of society."[142]

In short, the principle of local ownership straddles the gap between sovereignty and interdependence because it allows the receiving State, while not retaining its complete political independence, to at least dominate and control the transformative process. This covers both the development of overall strategies as well as the programming and implementation of specific rule of law projects. *Dann* and *Riegner* argue that local ownership entails a duty of donors to adhere to nationally-formulated strategies and projects, even if they clash with their own political priorities.[143]

What is the status of local ownership under international law? While it cannot be said to amount to a general principle of international law (yet), it can be identified both in the Preamble and in Article 2 (3) of the UN Charter, and references to it are frequent and becoming more numerous.[144]

There is a conceptual tension between local ownership and the output-focused development law principle of managing for results.[145] This tension is further aggravated by an increasing push to align development strategies with the *2030 Agenda for Sustainable Development* with its output-related imprint and focus on economically measurable achievements. There is an even stronger clash with conditionality.

Has local ownership been adequately realized in Afghanistan? Many Afghans and outside observers are doubtful.[146]

Significant efforts have been undertaken to increase local ownership since the end of the transition process, as reflected in the 2006 *Afghanistan Compact* and all subsequent national development strategies and international agreements. Noteworthy is the inclusion in the *Rome Communiqué* of the intention to strengthen local ownership through consideration of the particular Afghan context, especially the Islamic influences on the justice system, and the aim to "strive towards international standards and [a] strengthen[ing] [of] respect for human rights as provided for in the Afghan

---

142 UN Secretary-General, 'Rule of Law Assistance', *supra* note 18, para 5.
143 Dann & Riegner, *supra* note 11, 740–741.
144 Some consider it a structural principle, see *ibid*. See also GA Res. 41/128, UN Doc A/RES/41/128, 4 December 1986; BMZ, 'Leitlinien', *supra* note 53, para. 12.
145 See also Dann & Vierck, *supra* note 125, para. 18.
146 See Section B. IV.

Constitution".[147] There is also a clear preference for capacity-building over service-delivery. However, serious shortcomings remain.

The understanding of what local ownership entails is strongly influenced by the development context. The drafting of national development strategies is seen as proof of local ownership – ownership in program implementation, on the other hand, does not appear to be a central issue, though some donors, especially the UN but also Germany, try to incorporate ownership also at this level.

Further, real local ownership is hampered by limited local capacities. International actors have sought to fill the gaps. In accordance with the preference for capacity-building, in an attempt to increase local ownership for the future, numerous experts have been seconded (i.e. assigned for a limited period) to work in ministries and other government offices, at times replacing national officials. Section B. III. and IV. of this paper lists examples of such secondments. In some cases, serious doubts have been raised as to whether the work carried out can still be attributed to the Afghan Government. Replacement instead of on-the-job training, which is more burdensome and time-consuming, is but a reallocation of service delivery and there is a risk that the seconded staff will, even inadvertently, pursue their employer's preferences rather than those of the recipient government.[148] In addition, the process of preparing national development strategies is pre-regulated through the *World Bank*'s and other guidelines, thereby limiting national policy space.[149]

Rule of law activities in Afghanistan, as overall state-building, are still highly internationalized. As *Suhrke* notes, "major donors exercise control over funding and related policy agendas by channeling their assistance through international organizations or national subcontractors rather than through the Afghan Government or the multilateral [ARTF]."[150] The Afghan people have been relegated to a stakeholder in the process – the novel approach in the CAPD to anchor ownership with the Afghan people and not the government, as typically done, still has to be tested on the

---

147 Rome Conference on the Rule of Law in Afghanistan, *Joint Recommendations*, 2–3 July 2007, 1-2. Also, a novel institution, the Provincial Justice Coordination Mechanism, was to be set up to improve coordination of assistance to the justice sector and rule of law reform in the provinces.

148 See also the critical self-assessment by Germany, German Federal Government, 'Fortschrittsbericht Afghanistan 2014', *supra* note 13, 57.

149 Dann & Riegner, *supra* note 11, 752.

150 Suhrke, *supra* note 18, 226, 237-238.

ground.[151] At best, the current model can be described as a mixed ownership regime.

5. The International Rule of Law

As shown, the UN early on endorsed a thick, comprehensive understanding of the rule of law; and while it sought to promote the rule of law globally, it acknowledged that it felt itself bound by the principle: "The rule of law applies to the United Nations and should guide all of its activities."[152] What the UN requires of its members would then become applicable to itself; in the assistance context, notably the requirements of accountability, fairness, participation in decision-making, and transparency.[153] The principle of the international rule of law as a control standard for UN activities is as yet unexplored but offers interesting avenues for further research.[154]

II. National Legal Standards

In addition to international law, rule of law assistance may be also guided by the respective State's national laws. Violations of these standards will generally incur responsibility under national law. Given the particularity of each legal system, this section will focus on the laws applying to German actors in rule of law assistance in Afghanistan.

151 Suhrke, *supra* note 18, 225, 242.

152 GA Res. 67/1, UN Doc A/RES/67/1, 30 November 2012.

153 *The Rule of Law and Transitional Justice in Conflict and Post-Conflict Societies*, UN Doc S/2004/616, 23 August 2004, para. 6.

154 On the international rule of law see comprehensively C. A. Feinäugle (ed.), *The Rule of Law and its Application to the United Nations* (2016); S. Chesterman, 'Rule of Law', in R. Wolfrum (ed.), *Max Planck Encyclopedia of Public International Law* (2007), available at http://opil.ouplaw.com/view/10.1093/law:epil/9780199231690/law-9780199231690-e1676?prd=EPIL (last visited 12 December 2018).

1. Afghan Laws

Laws guiding the activity of the international community in general are contained in the Afghan Constitution[155], which various international actors have affirmed as binding on them, as shown above. The relevant human rights obligations are binding on the Afghan State. However, in their commitment to support the Afghan Government in fulfilling its obligations, States and intergovernmental organizations should strive to design programs and their implementation to meet the standards of the Constitution. This includes, for instance, Article 6 which defines State principles and obliges the government "to create a prosperous and progressive society based on social justice, preservation of human dignity, protection of human rights, realization of democracy, attainment of national unity as well as equality between all peoples and tribes and balance development of all areas of the country." Further, Article 22 prohibits all forms of discrimination between citizens including on the basis of gender. In addition, when carrying out rule of law assistance, foreign actors need to take constitutionally established procedure into account, such as the ordinary legislation procedure in Article 97 of the Afghan Constitution.

Several Afghan laws regulate the activities of NGOs.[156] With the exception of the 2005 *NGO Law*, these laws do not contain any provisions on how to carry out development cooperation. The *NGO Law*'s scope of application is broad, in that it covers both domestic, foreign, and international NGOs, if they are "non-political" and "not-for-profit" (Article 5 (5)). NGOs are obliged to observe the Constitution and applicable legislation in the implementation of activities (Article 3), but are otherwise generally free to carry out lawful activities. Substantive limitations are set out in Article 8 entitled "illegal activities", most notably with regard to "[p]articipation in political activities and campaigns" (Article 8 (1)) and "[t]he use of financial resources against the national interest, religious rights and religious prose-

155 Islamic Republic of Afghanistan, 'The Constitution of Afghanistan' (2004), available in an unofficial English Translation at http://unpan1.un.org/intradoc/groups/public/documents/APCITY/UNPAN015879.pdf (last visited 12 December 2018).

156 Most importantly: Law on Associations, as published in the Official Gazette No. 1114; Law on Non-Governmental Organization, Official Gazette No. 857/2005; Regulation on Procedure of Establishment and Registration of Associations, Official Gazette No. 1138; Income Tax Law, Official Gazette No. 976/2009; Customs Law, Official Gazette No. 847/2005; and Labour Law, Official Gazette No. 966/2008.

lytizing."(Article 8 (7)) These prohibitions are vague. It would be advisable to provide further elaboration to clarify that public advocacy and legal advice are not included. The law is being revised as of writing.

2. *Domestic Law of the Donor Country*

Domestic regulations vary among the donor countries. German law establishes substantive legal restraints – both for the State and for non-State actors. Concrete substantive limitations are imposed by a number of administrative executive regulations (*Verwaltungsvorschriften*) that generally have no external effect.[157] External effect can be created through inclusion of specific rules in the donor agreements.

The *BMZ Leitlinien* establish rules for seconded experts. First, experts shall only be seconded if the cooperation partner lacks the human and financial resources.[158] Second, the *BMZ Leitlinien* formulate duties for the experts. Apart from technical duties, which are determined by the concrete task assigned, experts shall comply with the laws of the land and respect its traditions and customs. They shall refrain from intervening in the internal affairs of the cooperation partner outside their professional duties in connection with their cooperation measure. In addition, they are expected to engage in trusting cooperation with the public agencies.[159]

The *BMZ Leitlinien* further define the focal thematic areas of development cooperation for the German Government. These include democracy, civil society, and public administration, including human rights specifically those of women and children, justice reform, decentralization, and subnational governance. However, it does not seem that noncompliance with one of these themes in programming or program implementation is grounds for rejection of a proposal or blacklisting.

German ministries have issued further administrative guidelines and policy papers, which affect how German officials may program and implement rule of law measures. The most relevant of these is the BMZ *Strategy Paper on Human Rights in Development Cooperation* in which the German Government commits to the human rights approach in development assis-

---

157 For rules on development cooperation with global development partners, see BMZ, *Entwicklungspolitische Zusammenarbeit mit globalen Entwicklungspartnern*, BMZ Strategiepapier No. 4/2015 (2015) [BMZ, Entwicklungspolitische Zusammenarbeit].

158 BMZ, 'Leitlinien', *supra* note 53, para. 81.

159 *Ibid.*, para. 85.

tance.[160] The document contains binding rules for the German government ministries dealing with development cooperation and the implementing organizations including GIZ when planning and implementing development measures – including rule of law assistance on behalf of the BMZ. It serves as a nonbinding guideline for civil society organizations. Human rights are to be considered in programming and implementation, including through human rights impact assessments in bilateral development agreements.[161] This is further elaborated in a detailed *Manual for the Recognition of Human Rights Standards and Principles, Including Gender, in the Preparation of Project Proposals in German Government Technical and Financial Cooperation* of 2013. The manual details possible risks for human rights in specific cooperation areas, including judicial reform, and outlines how these risks can be mitigated. However, it does not seem that the strategy paper or the manual contain rules on how to address violations within project implementation. In addition, the strategy strongly emphasizes policy dialog over conditionality and thus pursues a less proactive approach than the EU.[162]

These concretized duties supplement the constitutional duties of German State officials, especially those imposed by fundamental rights guarantees enshrined in the *German Basic Law*. They are applicable through Article 1 (3) of the *German Basic Law* for activities regarding development cooperation and state-building that are carried out on German territory, such as programming and grant selection. These obligations are seen to contin-

160 BMZ, *Menschenrechte in der deutschen Entwicklungspolitik*, BMZ-Strategiepaper 4/2011 (2011) [BMZ, Menschenrechte]. For further analysis of the paper, see Dann, *supra* note 95, 233-242.

161 BMZ, 'Menschenrechte', *supra* note 160, 1, 15.

162 *Ibid.*, 13. This is not surprising in light of the EU's strong human rights duties in external action enshrined in Article 208 TEU and Article 21 TEU, as well as the *New European Consensus on Development – 'Our World, Our Dignity, Our Future', Joint Statement by the Council and the Representatives of the Member States Meeting Within the Council, the European Parliament and the European Commission*, Strategic Document (7 June 2017), and Regulation (EU) No. 235/2014 of the European Parliament and of the Council of 11 March 2014, OJ 2014 L 77/85, a thematic funding instrument for EU external action aimed at supporting projects in human rights, fundamental freedoms, and democracy in non-EU countries. It is also contained in the CAPD, as noted above. For an overview of European Development Law, see Müller, *supra* note 92, 677.

ue to apply to a limited degree when activities are carried out extraterritorially,[163] including to GIZ because of its fulfillment of public functions.[164]

Meinecke argues that it is rather unlikely that rule of law programs cause human rights violations given that rule of law assistance is of a predominantly advisory nature with overall decision-making power resting with the cooperation partner. However, the secondment of experts to carry out ministerial work might be one case where such violations are possible – although no such example from practice was found. Also, these obligations prohibit support for discriminatory projects – an issue that arose with regard to legal pluralist approaches to rule of law assistance in Afghanistan. Further, the *de minimis* obligations – such as those enshrined in Article 1 (2) of the *German Basic Law* – and the State principles listed in Article 20 of the *German Basic Law* might require the State, under its duty to protect, to withdraw funding where it realizes that human rights guarantees are not met. The strategy paper shows that Germany has embraced the positive human rights obligations – known as *duty to fulfill* – by requiring that the Afghan State adopt measures to build the institutional and legal framework to comply with human rights, especially the rights of women and children, as exemplified in its negotiations to include improvements in this area as indicators under the TMAF and in its development policy strategy for Afghanistan 2014–2017.[165] The latter contains a clear policy shift towards conditionality. Further support is conditioned on "substantial advances in rule of law and anti-corruption".[166]

In addition, most nongovernmental actors and GIZ have issued their own guidelines or acceded to codes of conduct. GIZ, surprisingly, has not issued best practice rules for rule of law assistance. The *Code of Conduct*,

---

163 The extent to which basic rights continue to apply abroad is disputed. German Federal Constitutional Court, Case No. 1BvL 22/95, Order of the First Senate of 28 April 1999, BVerfGE 100, 313, 363; M. Yousif, *Zur Anwendbarkeit der Grundrechte bei Sachverhalten mit Auslandsbezug* (2007), 32; O. Meinecke, *Rechtsprojekte in der Entwicklungszusammenarbeit* (2007), 121. Basic rights are seen as fully applicable to actions involving German nationals. A minimal standard of rights is seen to be owed towards foreign nationals abroad which is to be determined in accordance with Article 25 of the *German Basic Law*.

164 Meinecke, *supra* note 163, 127. GIZ in addition has acceded to the *Global Compact* and applies the *UN Guiding Principles on Business and Human Rights*, available at https://www.giz.de/de/ueber_die_giz/37500.html (last visited 12 December 2018).

165 Regarding the duty to fulfill in development cooperation, see Dann & Riegner, *supra* note 11, 745-746.

166 BMZ, 'Strategie Afghanistan', *supra* note 15, 5, 26.

which applies to all staff members as well as to integrated experts, *inter alia* requires compliance with contractual agreements and German and cooperation partner laws, as well as sets out clear rules on bribery and corruption. Notably, a rule is included on conflicts of interests. It acknowledges the risk of such conflicts and requires strict transparency on conflicts as well as exclusion from involvement in decisions with financial implications where such conflicts exist.[167] GIZ has, however, acceded to several sustainability instruments and to the above-mentioned human rights instruments. It further considers as guiding, among other, the *UN Human Rights Treaties*, the *European Convention on Human Rights*, the *BMZ Human Rights Strategy*, the *UN Women's Empowerment Principles*, the *International Labour Organization Declaration on Fundamental Principles and Rights at Work*, and the BMZ *Anti-Corruption Strategy*. Unfortunately, the information on quality and evaluation does not suffice to deduce the existence of a concrete evaluation standard on the qualitative success of a measure.

F. Conclusion

Rule of law reforms in a post-conflict society may be mandated by a peace agreement; they may be required as the result of the findings of a truth commission; they may become necessary so that legislation complies with the provisions of a newly drafted constitution; or they may be needed because the existing legal framework was destroyed, abused, or replaced by an authoritative regime.[168] Very often in such cases, the assistance of the international community is enlisted.

Afghanistan is no exception. The international community was called on immediately after the overthrow of the Taliban regime to assist in the reconstruction of the State, including extensive rule of law assistance. This contribution has considered the mandate and the laws regulating this process. It has shown that the process did not occur in a law-free zone. Afghanistan welcomed the international community through conclusion of international and bilateral agreements, which were endorsed by the UNSC, and complemented by international communiqués, policy guidelines

---

167 GIZ, 'Code of Conduct 2017', available at https://www.giz.de/de/downloads/giz2017-en-GIV.pdf (last visited 12 December 2018).

168 UN Office on Drugs and Crime, *Guide for Practitioners on Criminal Justice Reform in Post-Conflict States* (2011), 59.

of international organizations and donors and implementing organizations, and national laws, regulations, and policy strategies of donor States.

Despite the many different agreements binding actors in rule of law assistance, only few general standards could be extracted from them with regard to the content of rule of law programs and especially their implementation: international human rights law, effectiveness, conditionality, and local ownership. While acknowledged and emphasized repeatedly, normatively, these standards have remained abstract.

A more detailed normative framework seems necessary to ensure the success – and sustainability – of rule of law promotion in Afghanistan. Although the situation has strongly improved as compared to 2001, serious shortcomings in the rule of law persist, including an inability to curb largescale corruption, loss of legitimacy of the government, and mounting insurgency and destabilization.[169] The justice sector remains one of the key reform challenges.[170]

The rule of law activities described are ultimately compatible with the legal principles distilled: Even though one may find that Afghanistan's political self-determination has often fallen to the wayside in the onslaught of foreign donors and experts, rule of law promotion is firmly grounded in freely entered-into agreements between sovereign States and corresponding UNSC Resolutions.

Still, doubts remain as to the *legitimacy* of the process. While the dogmatic status of concepts such as local ownership and aid effectiveness in international law remains unclear, they have gained a firm foothold in international documents. Yet the analysis above has sought to show that the constant evocation of sovereignty, Afghan independence and ownership has not prevented the international community from overriding Afghan priorities, ignoring existing legal, cultural and institutional frameworks, drafting laws modelled on standard blueprints, and replacing in-house staff with external consultants rather than teaching staff the skills needed.

A code of conduct for rule of law advisors, for example, might help to give effect to the principles that have been established over the years, particularly to ensure that local ownership is taken seriously – and not overridden by aid efficiency considerations. As shown, the latter have become the central international legal framework binding rule of law promotion.

---

169 Difficult for any development initiatives to develop where "the gun, corruption, and short-term survival [are] the prevailing logic", Gaston & Jensen, *supra* note 1, 74.

170 Hartmann, *supra* note 31, 178; Ruder, *supra* note 72, 1, 7.

However, their focus on quantifiable success may actually impede lasting progress on rule of law, which often escapes short- and mid-term measuring and, if taken seriously, is highly time- and resource-consuming.

What would be useful are detailed and coordinated instructions to the personnel implementing rule of law assistance on the ground as to the goals and limits of their work. Such rules could not be found for any of the researched German governmental and nongovernmental entities engaged in rule of law promotion activities in Afghanistan.

The Rule of Law à la ICTY – What the ICTY Deemed Just Good Enough and How it Supported the Countries in the Former Yugoslavia to Become Better

Kei Hannah Brodersen[*]

Table of Contents

---

* Kei Hannah Brodersen, PhD candidate at the Faculty of Law of the Maastricht University. The author wishes to thank the anonymous reviewers, the editor of this volume, as well as Prof. Esther Versluis and Prof. André Klip for useful comments on earlier drafts. Special thanks also go to Dr. Paul Brodersen for improving the look of the graphs.

Abstract

The ICTY was established as a criminal tribunal that would conduct prosecutions and trials addressing international crimes committed in the former Yugoslavia during the wars in the 1990s. Next to this core mandate, the Tribunal increasingly placed itself in the context of rule of law promotion, the trigger being its completion strategy and the insertion of Rule11*bis* into its *Rules of Procedure and Evidence* (RPE). Rule 11*bis* foresaw the possibility to refer cases from The Hague to national courts. In order to help prepare national justice systems for receiving these cases, the ICTY initiated a number of rule of law promotion measures, albeit without having officially defined the rule of law for itself, let alone having formulated a policy for systematic rule of law promotion. Based on a comprehensive case law, discourse, and document analysis, this contribution, however, puts together a mosaic of rule of law elements recommended by the ICTY, effectively resembling a definition. This *definition* has a normative dimension that concerns the legislative framework of a country, an institutional dimension that prescribes rules for the functioning of its justice institutions, and a cultural dimension, requiring that the rule of law be ideologically embraced by people and State representatives. As the ICTY's rule of law promotion activities reflect what it deemed relevant in the rule of law at the respective time, it becomes clear that the Tribunal took this *definition* as a basis for its efforts in the countries of the former Yugoslavia. Three examples will demonstrate this. Overall, this piece contributes to understanding the legal and normative bases of the ICTY's efforts at strengthening the rule of law in post-conflict former Yugoslavia.

A. *The ICTY as a Rule of Law Promoter*

The *International Criminal Tribunal for the former Yugoslavia* (ICTY or Tribunal) was established by the *United Nations Security Council* (UNSC) in 1993 in the middle of the Balkan wars. Ever since, it has been asserted that the ICTY "instill[ed]"[1], "re-establish[ed]"[2], "advance[ed]"[3], "enhance[d]"[4], "strengthen[ed]"[5], "improve[ed]"[6], "shap[ed]"[7], "embrace[d]"[8], "promot[ed]"[9] (this list could go on for pages) the rule of law in the countries under its jurisdiction. At first, these claims are surprising as promotion of the rule of law is not defined as an element of the Tribunal's mandate – neither in the legal documents regulating its work, nor in the UNSC resolution that founded the ICTY.[10] While in that resolution, the UNSC proclaimed as goals to prosecute violations of international humanitarian law, to deter future crimes, and to restore and maintain peace,[11] it defined the ICTY's core competence as "to prosecute persons responsible for serious violations of international humanitarian law committed in the territory of the former Yugoslavia since 1991" in Article 1 of the Tribunal's Statute.

---

1 P. Akhavan, 'Justice in the Hague, Peace in the Former Yugoslavia?: A Commentary on the United Nationals War Crimes Tribunal', 20 *Human Rights Quaterly* (1998) 4, 737, 749.

2 United Nations Secretary-General, *The Rule of Law and Transitional Justice in Conflict and Post-Conflict Societies: Report of the Secretary-General*, UN Doc S/2004/616, 3 August 2004, 13.

3 J. Hagan & S. K. Ivković, 'War Crimes, Democracy, and the Rule of Law in Belgrade, the Former Yugoslavia, and Beyond', 605 *The ANNALS of the American Academy of Political and Social Science* (2006) 1, 129, 130.

4 J. Stromseth, 'Justice on the Ground: Can International Criminal Courts Strengthen Domestic Rule of Law in Post-Conflict Societies?', 1 *Hague Journal on the Rule of Law* (2009) 1, 87, 88 [Stromseth, Justice on the Ground].

5 ICTY, 'Achievements', available at http://www.icty.org/sid/324 (last visited 10 December 2018); D. F. Orentlicher, *Shrinking the Space for Denial: The Impact of the ICTY in Serbia* (2008), 42.

6 P. C. McMahon & J. L. Miller, 'From Adjudication to Aftermath: Assessing the ICTY's Goals beyond Prosecution', 13 *Human Rights Review* (2012) 4, 421, 422-423.

7 E. Simpson, 'Stop to the Hague: Internal versus External Factors Suppressing the Advancement of the Rule of Law in Serbia', 36 *Georgetown Journal of International Law* (2004) 4, 1255, 1257.

8 Stromseth, 'Justice on the Ground', *supra* note 4, 87.

9 L. A. Barria & S. D. Roper, 'Judicial Capacity Building in Bosnia and Herzegovina: Understanding Legal Reform Beyond the Completion Strategy of the ICTY', 9 *Human Rights Review* (2008) 3, 317, 319 [Barria & Roper, Judicial Capacity Building in Bosnia and Herzegovina].

10 Although some commentators argue that the UN Security Council hoped the ICTY would contribute to the establishment of the rule of law in the countries under its jurisdiction. See for instance: Judge *Fausto Pocar* in Frédéric Mégret, 'The Legacy of the ICTY as Seen through Some of Its Actors and Observers', 3 *Goettingen Journal of International Law* (2011) 3, 1011, 1030.

11 Cf. SC Res. 827, UN Doc S/RES/827 (1993), 25 May 1993, preamble.

As time went by, however, the ICTY began to place itself in the context of rule of law promotion. At least with the adoption of the Tribunal's *completion strategy*, designed to gradually wind down the Tribunal by 2010,[12] rule of law promotion had come to the forefront.[13] ICTY representatives increasingly mentioned it as a goal, or even as a task. It is unlikely that statements to that effect were always carefully thought through, or even less, that they were based on a clear definition of the *rule of law* or on an appreciation of how exactly the Tribunal contributed to the rule of law. Although the ICTY did take a few active and conscious steps in that regard, overall, its role in rule of law promotion was more a side-effect to its core mandate of prosecuting war criminals. As *John Hocking*, the last ICTY Registrar, observed with regard to the Tribunal's legacy: "I [...] see a larger impact, a spill-over effect in the strengthening in the rule of law, even beyond our direct or intended efforts."[14] Hence, when reviewing individual statements about the ICTY's effect on the rule of law, it is often difficult to grasp what is meant by *the rule of law*, to what part of the rule of law the Tribunal contributes, and in what way. Upon comprehensive analysis, however, a mosaic of elements that the Tribunal associated with this term can be put together. What emerges is a framework of minimum rule of law standards with which national justice systems must comply before the ICTY deems these systems – bluntly said – *good enough*.[15]

---

12 The completion strategy foresaw a "three-phase plan", with all investigations terminated before the end of 2004, all first instance trials completed by the end of 2008 and the completion of all of the ICTY's work in 2010. The deadline concerning investigations has been met, whereas the other two have been extended several times. The Tribunal has closed in 2017. The *Mechanism for International Criminal Tribunals* (MICT) will subsequently complete all the remaining work, including appeals, enforcement of sentences, and nonjudicial tasks.

13 Cf. ICTY, 'Completion Strategy', available at http://www.icty.org/en/sid/10016 (last visited 10 December 2018) [ICTY, Completion Strategy]; SC Res. 1503, UN Doc S/RES/1503, 28 August 2003, 2 [SC Res. 1503]; SC Res. 1534, UN Doc S/RES/1534 (2004), 26 March 2004, 3; see also Barria & Roper, 'Judicial Capacity Building in Bosnia and Herzegovina', *supra* note 9, 318; A. S. Canter, '"For These Reasons, the Chamber: Denies the Prosecutor's Request for Referral": The False Hope of Rule 11*Bis*', 32 *Fordham International Law Journal* (2008) 5, 1614, 1654.

14 J. Hocking, 'Opening Remarks, Legacy Conference' (2017), 4, available at http://www.icty.org/x/file/Press/Statements%20and%20Speeches/Registrar/20170622-john-hocking-opening-remarks-sarajevo_en.pdf (last visited 10 December 2018).

15 Necessarily, given the Tribunal's field of competence and activity, this framework remains narrow and focused on the criminal justice system, although at times, ICTY actors do adopt a broader perspective.

In the following section, the present article will outline the policy and legal mechanisms that brought rule of law promotion into the realm of the ICTY's occupation. It will be demonstrated that the Tribunal's understanding of the rule of law has changed over time, reflecting the changing standing of the ICTY. In the beginning, the Tribunal had to struggle to be recognized as an international law enforcer – a role of which it reminded its audience again towards the end of its operation in view of building up a legacy narrative. In public statements from those times, the Tribunal therefore emphasized the *international rule of law* (referred to as IRoL in the figures). In between, however, the turning point being the completion strategy, its focus shifted towards the *national rule of law* (referred to as NRoL in the figures). With the completion strategy, the ICTY's jurisdictional regime factually changed from primacy over to complementarity to national courts. This change is manifested in Rule 11*bis* of the RPE which were amended in 2002 in order to allow the referral of cases from The Hague to national courts. Rule 11*bis* triggered a number of rule of law promotion efforts by the Tribunal, effectively becoming the legal basis, or at least the legal vehicle, for the Tribunal's activities in that regard. Section C will present the ICTY's notion of the *national rule of law*, as it is deduced from case law, discourse, and document analysis. This notion can be divided into a normative dimension, an institutional dimension, and a cultural dimension. In the normative dimension, the necessity of a legislative framework that foresees the adjudication of international crimes and guarantees certain fundamental human rights, especially fair trial rights, is highlighted by the ICTY. This is the law that should rule. If the notion ended here, it would come down to rule *by* laws that foresee adjudication of international crimes under respect for fair trial rights. Yet, such a definition has no added value in practice. Hence, the ICTY identified principles that *ensure* or *support* this rule by law which can be attributed to an institutional dimension on the one hand and a cultural dimension on the other. The institutional dimension comprises independent and impartial judicial organs that work efficiently and in a transparent manner. Lastly, a culture of law is paramount to the functioning of the rule of law. According to the ICTY, ordinary citizens, as well as public officials, and representatives of the judicial sector must adopt an "ideology of legality"[16] – which only happens if people are aware of accountability proceedings for international crimes

16 T. Meron, 'Statement of Theodor Meron, President of the International Criminal Tribunal for the former Yugoslavia, Delivered at the Inauguration of the War Crimes Chamber of the State Court of Bosnia and Herzegovina', TM/MOW/945 e,

and therefore develop trust into judicial institutions again. It is remarkable that also within the notion of the *national rule of law* one can observe change over time, with different elements being emphasized at different moments. In section D, it will be shown through examples that the ICTY aligned its rule of law promotion efforts according to what it deemed relevant in the rule of law at the respective time. To be clear, the ICTY's main priority had always been to exercise its core mandate of prosecuting and trying perpetrators of international crimes in the courtrooms of The Hague. However, over the years, it extended its activities beyond that. With a conception of the rule of law, with which the former Yugoslav countries should comply, in mind, it took steps that were clearly geared towards supporting the domestic actors in approaching this rule of law ideal. Three main activities to that end will be presented before some concluding remarks will be made in section E.

B. *The ICTY's Shifting Rule of Law Notions Over Time*

In order to understand how the ICTY became an actor in rule of law promotion, it must first be understood what the Tribunal understood by the *rule of law*. The findings of this contribution are based on a discourse analysis of all accessible public statements of ICTY representatives[17] and on a content analysis of all available ICTY publications.[18] In a first step, the in-

---

9 March 2005, available at http://www.icty.org/en/press/statement-theodor-meron-president-international-criminal-tribunal-former-yugoslavia-delivered (last visited 10 December 2018) [Meron, Statement 9 March 2005].

17 Firstly, this concerned the 101 public statements and speeches given by the three ICTY officials (the ICTY presidents, chief prosecutors, and registrars), available at http://www.icty.org/en/press/statements-and-speeches-of-the-icty (last visited 10 December 2018). In addition, the opening statements of the prosecutor in every trial were considered.

18 Documents analyzed up until 21 December 2017: the Tribunal's 24 annual reports, available at http://www.icty.org/en/documents/annual-reports; 28 completion strategy reports, available at http://www.icty.org/en/documents/completion-strategy-and-mict; 2185 press releases, available at http://www.icty.org/en/press/press-releases-archive; the 161 ICTY Digests (a publication that was distributed as of 2006 in order to inform the public about the Tribunal's work), available at http://www.icty.org/en/documents/icty-digest; as well as the only three annual reports of the Outreach Program from 2011, 2012, and 2013, available at http://www.icty.org/en/outreach/outreach-annual-reports, as well as the *15 Years of Outreach at the ICTY* report, available at http://www.icty.org/x/file/Outreach/15-years-of-outreach/outreach-15_en_light.pdf; all last visited 10 December 2018.

quiry was purely quantitative; counting how many times the term *rule of law* is mentioned in connection to the work of the Tribunal. This was done with a simple electronic search (control+F "rule of law"). In a second step, the respective hit was closely looked at in order to study 1) in what context the term *rule of law* was used, 2) whether any precise clarification on the meaning of the term was given, or – in the absence of a definition: 3) what aspects are subsumed under the *rule of law* or considered to be part of it. What this analysis reveals is that the ICTY's rule of law notion changed over time, reflecting the changing standing of the ICTY.

I. The Beginning: Standing its Ground as International Law Enforcer

In the beginning, in the years 1996-1999, the Tribunal primarily placed its work into the context of the *international rule of law* (see figure 1 below), which refers to upholding and enforcing international law.[19] One line of references to the *rule of law* thus sounds like this excerpt from the press release that announced the commencement of the ICTY's first trial in the *Tadić* case:

> "The upcoming trial marks the first occasion for the implementation of international humanitarian law, a body of law designed to regulate the conduct of combatants and to protect civilians during wars. It is based on standards agreed upon by States. By implementing this body of law, the International Tribunal will give it its true meaning. This first trial is thus an exercise in the assertion of the rule of law over the law of the gun, as this war-torn century draws to a close."[20]

In emphasizing its role as the enforcer of universal international humanitarian and criminal law, the Tribunal sought to justify its existence and operation. This was particularly necessary in its early years for several reasons: first, the ICTY was the first modern international criminal tribunal that pursued to develop upon the legacy of the Nuremberg and Tokyo tribunals that had operated five decades earlier, but with the aim of providing fair

19 In total, there are 55 references to the "international rule of law" in official ICTY statements or publications, 292 to the "national rule of law", and for 18 references it was unclear whether the international or the national rule of law was meant.

20 ICTY, 'The Tribunal's First Trial: Another Step in the Fulfillment of the Tribunal's Mandate', CC/PIO/070-E, 6 May 1996, available at http://www.icty.org/en/press/tribunals-first-trial-another-step-fulfillment-tribunals-mandate_(last visited 10 December 2018).

trials and of avoiding to be labelled as exercising *victor's justice*. Second, the ICTY's establishment by the UNSC under a thereto unheard interpretation of its powers under Chapter VII of the UN Charter had been questioned, criticized, and challenged.[21] In order not to be perceived as a political organ, it needed to situate itself in a legal context and recall its judicial nature. Third, as if that had not been challenging enough, the ICTY had a somewhat slow start that made many observers doubt whether it would ever operate effectively: it was officially established in May 1993, but without a courthouse, without staff, and without facilities. The judges, together with first staff members, who arrived in The Hague shortly after that, had to keep themselves busy with designing the RPE until May 1996 when the first trial against the accused *Duško Tadić* eventually commenced.[22] In the absence of a police force that would arrest the Tribunal's defendants, the ICTY depended on States or other international organizations to arrest and surrender them. In the case of *Tadić*, for instance, the ICTY had ordered Germany to hand over the accused, so that it could finally start its core judicial work. Given these challenges during its first years, the ICTY pointed out the significance of its mandate – to address international crimes – which would be important enough as to heal all the criticism against it. Linking the prosecution of international crimes to the re-establishment of the *international rule of law* gave it the additional legitimacy that was needed to counter the criticism.

21 Most notably by its first defendant *Duško Tadić*: *Prosecutor v. Tadić*, Motion on the Jurisdiction of the Tribunal, IT-94-T, Trial Chamber, 23 June 1995, 2; for the Appeals Chamber's judgment, see: *Prosecutor v. Tadić*, Decision on the Defence Motion for Interlocutory Appeal on Jurisdiction, Appeals Chamber, IT-94-1-AR72, 2 October 1995, para. 9-48.

22 Cf. ICTY, 'Timeline', available at http://www.icty.org/en/features/timeline (last visited 10 December 2018).

Figure 1

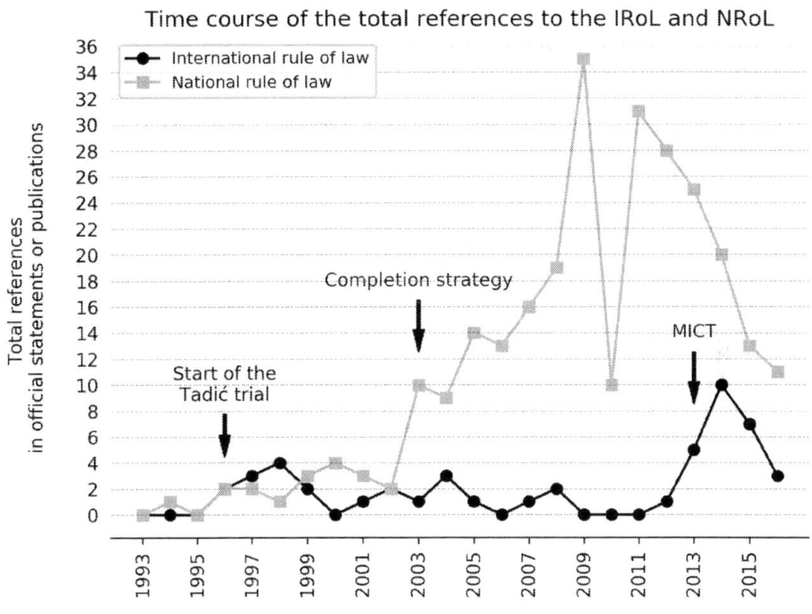

II. The Completion Strategy: Preparing the Ground for Rule of Law Promotion

Over the years, references to the *national rule of law*, the rule of law within a country, which commonly sets out rules that govern a particular society, increased dramatically (see figure 1 above). In 2002/2003, when the ICTY was at the height of its operation, with less than 20 out of 161 indictees remaining at large,[23] the ICTY judges – together with the judges of the *International Criminal Tribunal for Rwanda* (ICTR) – designed the completion strategy of their tribunals. The completion strategy was a plan to gradually terminate trials at the ICTY, although making sure that its work would be properly continued in the region was also increasingly seen as a *key aspect*

23 Cf. ICTY, 'Annual Report 2003', A/58/297-S/2003/829, 20 August 2003, 10, available at http://www.icty.org/x/file/About/Reports%20and%20Publications/AnnualReports/annual_report_2003_en.pdf (last visited 10 December 2018).

of the Tribunal's legacy.[24] The idea was that the ICTY "concludes its mission successfully, in a timely way and in coordination with domestic legal systems in the former Yugoslavia."[25] ICTY representatives even went as far as purporting that the Tribunal's own success depended on whether it would have rebuilt the rule of law in the countries under its jurisdiction – as expressed in the words of *Serge Brammertz*, the last Prosecutor of the ICTY:

> "[T]he completion of the Tribunal's mandate is not the end of war crimes[[26]] justice, but the beginning of the next chapter. Further accountability for the crimes now depends fully on national judiciaries in the former Yugoslavia. Thousands of cases remain to be processed, particularly many complex cases against senior- and mid-level suspects in every country. So ultimately, I believe that the ICTY's legacy is not simply measured by our own work, but by whether the countries of the former Yugoslavia build the rule of law and demonstrate they can secure meaningful justice for the victims of serious crimes during the conflicts."[27]

The completion strategy report from 2009 is even more explicit in this regard as it stated that:

> "The ultimate goal of the Tribunal's legacy strategy is entrenchment of the rule of law in the former Yugoslavia."[28]

In this spirit, the UNSC had already explicitly called upon the Tribunal to "strengthen [...] the capacity of [the national] jurisdictions"[29] in the for-

---

24 Cf. C. Garbett, 'Transitional Justice and "National Ownership": An Assessment of the Institutional Development of the War Crimes Chamber of Bosnia and Herzegovina', 13 *Human Rights Review* (2012) 1, 65, 65.

25 ICTY, 'Completion Strategy', *supra* note 13; cf. SC Res. 1503, *supra* note 13, 2.

26 This generic term is used to refer to the prosecution of all so-called international crimes (namely, those commonly found in the statutes of international criminal courts and tribunals). It will also sometimes be used in this contribution and will – unless made explicit otherwise – be synonymous with *international crimes*.

27 ICTY, '#ICTY24: Commemoration held at United Nations Headquarters' (2017), available at http://www.icty.org/en/press/icty24-commemoration-held-at-united-nations-headquarters (last visited 10 December 2018).

28 ICTY, 'Completion Strategy Report November 2009', UN Doc S/2009/589, 13 November 2009, 21, available at http://www.icty.org/x/file/About/Reports%20and%20Publications/CompletionStrategy/completion_strategy_13nov 2009_en.pdf (last visited 12 June 2018) [ICTY, Completion Strategy Report November 2009].

29 SC Res. 1503, *supra* note 13, 2.

mer Yugoslavia when it endorsed the proposed completion strategy in 2003, as this was considered "crucially important to the rule of law"[30]. At that same time, the political and legal systems in the former Yugoslav countries were consolidating, with Bosnia and Herzegovina (BiH) becoming a member of the *Council of Europe* in April 2002 and Serbia in April 2003.[31] The Tribunal more and more assumed the role of assisting this consolidation process, especially by contributing to rebuilding their national justice systems.

As one of the major instruments of the completion strategy, the ICTY judges proposed to transform Rule 11*bis* of the RPE into a legal basis for transferring cases to national courts in the former Yugoslavia.[32] Essentially, this case transfer system would be killing two birds with one stone: it would permit the ICTY to reduce its case load in view of winding down, and it would kick off and catalyze domestic war crimes proceedings, thereby strengthening the domestic rule of law. As will be shown in section D below, the case transfers brought about a series of rule of law promotion measures, effectively rendering Rule 11*bis* the mechanism behind the ICTY's rule of law transfer efforts.

The idea was to transfer cases concerning low- and intermediate-level perpetrators from the ICTY to national courts in the former Yugoslavia, and to concentrate on those crimes "most prejudicial to international pub-

---

30 SC Res. 1503, *supra* note 13, 2; the same was reiterated in operative part point 9 of SC Res. 1534, UN Doc S/RES/1534 (2004), 26 March 2004, 3.

31 Available at https://www.coe.int/en/web/portal/bosnia-and-herzegovina (last visited 10 December 2018) and available at https://www.coe.int/en/web/portal/ser bia (last visited 10 December 2018); Croatia had been a member since November 1996; available at https://www.coe.int/en/web/portal/croatia (last visited 10 December 2018).

32 Rule 11*bis* had been inserted into the ICTY's RPE as early as 1997, at the time providing the possibility to suspend an indictment at the ICTY if a national court could and would exercise its jurisdiction; Rule 11*bis* in its original available at http://www.icty.org/x/file/Legal%20Library/Rules_procedure_evidence/IT032_rev 12_en.pdf (last visited 10 December 2018) [Rule 11*bis*]. For amendments, see the different versions available at http://www.icty.org/en/documents/rules-procedure-evidence (last visited 10 December 2018); and generally M. Bohlander, 'Referring an indictment from the ICTY and ICTR to another court - Rule 11bis and the consequences for the law of extradition', 55 *International and Comparative Law Quarterly* (2006) 1, 219. Its current form was introduced in July 2004 with revision 32.

lic order"[33] in The Hague. A case would, however, only be referred if certain conditions were satisfied, most importantly, that the national court would be able to fully conform with internationally recognized standards of human rights and due process.[34]

Rule 11*bis*, amended accordingly in December 2002, foresaw the possibility to refer a case (whether with or without the accused already being arrested) to any State which could and would exercise jurisdiction over it:[35] either because the crimes had been committed on its territory (Rule 11*bis* (A) (i) RPE), or because the accused was arrested in that State (Rule 11*bis* (A) (ii) RPE), or because the State otherwise has jurisdiction and accepts the case (Rule 11*bis* (A) (iii) RPE).[36] A case could only be referred if the State's justice system was adequately prepared, if the accused would receive a fair trial, and if the death penalty would not be imposed or carried out.[37] Importantly, although the condition of the State being "adequately prepared" is mentioned only in Rule 11*bis* (A) (iii) and on a plain reading, one would therefore think that this condition only relates to those States otherwise having jurisdiction, it must in fact be met for any (of the three) jurisdictional scenarios. This follows from the system of Rule 11*bis* that requires reading paragraphs (A) and (B) together. The Appeals Chamber has held this view in *Stanković*:

> "as a strictly textual matter, Rule 11bis (A) does not require that a jurisdiction be 'willing and adequately prepared to accept' a transferred case if it was the territory in which the crime was committed or in which the accused was arrested. But that is beside the point, because unquestionably a jurisdiction's willingness and capacity to accept a re-

33 C. Jorda, 'Report on the Judicial Status of the International Criminal Tribunal for the former Yugoslavia and the Prospects for Referring Certain Cases to National Courts', annexed to the 'Letter dated 10 June 2002 from the President of the International Criminal Tribunal for the former Yugoslavia addressed to the Secretary General', annexed to the 'Letter dated 17 June 2002 from the Secretary-General addressed to the President of the Security Council' , 19 June 2002, 5, available at http://www.icty.org/x/file/About/Reports%20and%20Publications/CompletionStrategy/judicial_status_report_june2002_en.pdf_(last visited 10 December 2018) [Jorda, Report on the Judicial Status of the ICTY].

34 Cf. *ibid.*, 13-14.

35 A Referral Bench can decide to refer a case either *proprio motu* or upon application of the prosecutor (R11*bis* (B) RPE), *supra* note 32.

36 In the beginning, the amendments only comprised States that would have territorial jurisdiction, or where the accused would be arrested, but this was extended in July 2004. R11*bis* (A)RPE, *supra* note 32.

37 R11*bis* (B)RPE, *supra* note 32.

ferred case is an explicit prerequisite for any referral to a domestic jurisdiction [...]. Thus, the 'willing and adequately prepared' prong of Rule 11bis(A)(iii) is implicit also in the Rule 11bis(B) analysis."[38]

Apart from that, because high profile cases were to remain in The Hague, the Referral Bench also had to consider the gravity of the crimes at stake and the level of responsibility of the accused.[39] When a decision for referral of a case was taken, the accused, together with all necessary material supporting the indictment had to be transferred to the competent national authorities.[40]

An important element of Rule 11*bis* was the possibility for the ICTY Prosecutor to monitor the national proceedings.[41] If s/he deemed it necessary – for instance because of insufficient respect for fair trial rights – s/he could apply to the Referral Bench to revoke the referral.[42] This deferral mechanism was supposed to encourage national judiciaries to do particularly well in complying with international standards and to threaten them in case they would not.[43] A deferral would have meant for the national justice system to lose face both, towards their own population as well as towards the *international community* – a situation, which all countries of the former Yugoslavia wanted to avoid in order to rehabilitate their reputation as solid democracies operating under the rule of law. So, it was in the interest of both the ICTY and the national authorities to establish the conditions for a fair handling of these so-called Rule 11*bis* cases.[44]

---

38 *Prosecutor v. Stanković*, Decision, Appeals Chamber, IT-96-23/2-PT, 1 September 2005, para. 40.

39 R11*bis* (C) RPE, *supra* note 32; paragraphs (A) and (B) also set out procedural safeguards that must be met before referral is permitted: a case can only be referred back to the national judiciary if an indictment had been issued and confirmed already, but the trial must not yet have begun. The accused must have had the opportunity to be heard.

40 R11*bis* (D) (i) and (iii) RPE, *supra* note 32.

41 R11*bis* (D) (iv) RPE, *supra* note 32.

42 R11*bis* (F) RPE, *supra* note 32.

43 In the words of former chief prosecutor *Carla del Ponte*: "The mere existence of such a provision [that would enable the ICTY to defer back the case] should act as a strong incentive for the relevant domestic judicial authorities to handle the case in accordance with accepted international standards."; ICTY OTP, 'Completion Strategy Report May 2004', UN Doc S/2004/420, 24 May 2004, 45, available at http://www.icty.org/x/file/About/Reports%20and%20Publications/CompletionStrategy/completion_strategy_24may2004_en.pdf (last visited 10 December 2018).

44 Cf. ICTY OTP, 'Completion Strategy Report November 2017', UN Doc S/2017/1001, 29 November 2017, 76, available at http://www.icty.org/x/file/About/Reports%20and%20Publications/CompletionStrategy/171129-completion-strategy-r

At the same time, monitoring the adjudication of Rule 11*bis* cases provided the opportunity for targeted capacity building as it directly revealed deficiencies in the prosecution and adjudication of war crimes trials. Those deficiencies would then be addressed in tailor-made trainings for the local actors involved.[45] That way, "[t]he referral of [Rule 11*bis*] cases to national jurisdictions also served [...] to strengthen the capacity of those jurisdictions in the prosecution and trial of violations of international humanitarian law,"[46] "thus reinforcing the rule of law in these new States."[47] The monitoring was implemented by the *Organisation for Security and Co-operation in Europe* (OSCE) on behalf of the ICTY *Office of the Prosecutor*

eport-icty.pdf (last visited 10 December 2018); indeed, the State Court of Bosnia and Herzegovina sees the referral of six cases to its jurisdiction as a "recognition" of its professionality and its compliance with high standards in adjudicating war crimes: "*Priznanje profesionalnog rada i poštivanje visokih standarda u krivičnim procesima pred Sudom BiH ogleda se i u odlukama Međunarodnog krivičnog suda za bivšu Jugoslaviju, koji je, u skladu sa Pravilom 11 bis, Sudu BiH na dalje postupanje ustupio 6 predmeta sa 10 osumnjičenih. To su bile prve odluke o ustupanju predmeta jednom sudu u regionu, što je za Sud BiH bilo veliko priznanje.*" (in English: "The recognition that the SCBiH works professionally and respects high standards in its criminal trials is reflected in the decisions of the ICTY to refer six cases concerning ten accused to be adjudicated at the SCBiH. Those were the first decisions to transfer cases to a court in the region, which represents for the SCBiH a huge appreciation." (author's own translation)); Sud Bosne i Herzegovine, 'Istorijat Suda BiH', available at http://www.sudbih.gov.ba/stranica/86/pregled (last visited 10 December 2018).

45 Interview with representatives of the OSCE, Sarajevo, 2 February 2017; similar: ICTY OTP, 'Completion Strategy Report May 2007', UN Doc S/2007/283, 16 May 2007, 16, available at http://www.icty.org/x/file/About/Reports%20and%20Publications/CompletionStrategy/completion_strategy_16may2007_en.pdf (last visited 10 December 2018).

46 ICTY, 'Completion Strategy Report November 2011', UN Doc S/2011/716, 16 November 2011, 13, available at http://www.icty.org/x/file/About/Reports%20and%20Publications/CompletionStrategy/completion_strategy_16nov 2011_en.pdf (last visited 10 December 2018).

47 ICTY, 'Completion Strategy Report May 2012', UN Doc S/2012/354, 23 May 2012, 11, available at http://www.icty.org/x/file/About/Reports%20and%20Publications/CompletionStrategy/completion_strategy_23may2012_en.pdf (last visited 10 December 2018); see also ICTY, 'Completion Strategy Report November 2004', UN Doc S/2004/897, 23 November 2004, 3, available at http://www.icty.org/x/file/About/Reports%20and%20Publications/CompletionStrategy/completion_strategy_23november2004_en.pdf (last visited 10 December 2018); ICTY, 'Completion Strategy Report May 2005', UN Doc S/2005/343, 25 May 2005, 3, available at http://www.icty.org/x/file/About/Reports%20and%20Publications/CompletionStrategy/completion_strategy_25may2005_en.pdf (last visited 10 December 2018) [ICTY, Completion Strategy Report May 2005].

(OTP),[48] and the capacity building programme was developed in close co-operation between the two organizations.

Strikingly, the completion strategy *de facto* changed the Tribunal's jurisdictional regime from primacy and deferrals, to complementarity and referrals. Article 9 of the ICTY Statute stipulates a concurrent jurisdictional regime between the Hague Tribunal and domestic courts, with the Tribunal retaining primacy. This implies that the ICTY was never meant to prosecute *all* persons responsible for serious violations committed in the territory of the former Yugoslavia. In fact, when proposing to establish the ICTY, the *UN Secretary General* suggested that instead of precluding and preventing national courts to exercise their jurisdiction, they should be encouraged to prosecute and try perpetrators of violations of their national law.[49] For about a decade, this did not have any implications. Instead of advocating national prosecutions, the ICTY Prosecutor applied for deferrals under Article 9 (2) of the ICTY Statute and as a consequence, a number of cases for international crimes were taken away from national courts and deferred to the Tribunal in The Hague.[50] However, with the implementation of the completion strategy and the introduction of Rule 11*bis*, this trend was not only stopped, but reversed. As of then, the Tribunal gave back cases and it would only step in when they were not handled correctly at the domestic level. At the same time, the ICTY assisted domestic jurisdictions in living up to its standards through a broad capacity building programme.

Thus, while the completion strategy heralded the Tribunal's policy change regarding its jurisdictional regime, putting the *national rule of law* into the focus of the Tribunal, Rule 11*bis* became the vehicle for the ICTY's rule of law promotion efforts.

---

48 For the agreement and OSCE progress reports on each case, see ICTY, 'Status of Transferred Cases', available at http://www.icty.org/en/cases/transfer-of-cases/status-of-transferred-cases (last visited 10 December 2018). See also ICTY, 'Completion Strategy Report May 2005', *supra* note 47, 10.

49 Cf. United Nations Secretary-General, *Report of the Secretary General Pursuant to Paragraph 2 of Security Council Resolution 808*, UN Doc S/25704, 3 May 1993, 16.

50 The most famous deferrals are the cases against the ICTY's first accused *Duško Tadić*, which was taken from Germany, and against *Dražan Erdemović*, taken from Yugoslavia.

III. The End: Preparing for the ICTY's Legacy

Interestingly, as the Tribunal's closure approached and with the *Mechanism for International Criminal Tribunals* (MICT), the court that carries out the remaining functions of the ICTR and the ICTY since their respective closures in 2015 and 2017, preparing to operate as of 2013, allusions to the *international rule of law* became more prominent again (see figure 1 above). In public statements, ICTY officials again more often reminded its audience of its role as an international law enforcement mechanism and recalled its achievements in that respect, as exemplified by former ICTY President *Meron* observing in 2015 that "through hundreds of rulings addressing principles of international criminal, humanitarian, and human rights law, the ICTY has played a crucial role in strengthening international law and the rule of law and has made major contributions to the implementation of the purposes of the UN Charter."[51] It thereby sought to make sure that its pioneering role in upholding the *international rule of law* would not be forgotten.

In the remaining sections of this contribution, references to the *international rule of law* will be disregarded as it falls outside the scope of rule of law transfer and the focus will be on the *national rule of law* and the ICTY's promotion efforts.

C. The ICTY's Notion of the National Rule of Law

Clues about the Tribunal's *national rule of law* notion can be found in the jurisprudence rendered following referral applications by the OTP under Rule 11*bis*.[52] A system good enough for receiving a case would necessarily abide by the rule of law. Taken together, the factors the Referral Bench ex-

51 Adding that, in the years to come, the MICT (of which *Meron* is the current President) will carry forward the important work of the ICTY and the ICTR, thereby reflecting "the UN's continued commitment to justice and principled accountability"; ICTY, 'Tribunal and the Mechanism Commemorate 70 years of the United Nations', Press Release 20 October 2015, available at http://www.icty.org/en/press/tribunal-and-mechanism-commemorate-70-years-united-nations (last visited 10 December 2018).

52 Necessarily, given the Tribunal's field of competence and activity, this framework remains narrow and focused on the criminal justice system, although at times, ICTY actors do adopt a broader perspective.

amined before agreeing to refer a case,[53] constitute a framework of minimum standards with which national justice systems must comply before the Tribunal deemed them *adequate*.[54] This framework can be complemented through the discourse and document analysis of official statements and publications, deducing further elements that the ICTY views as being part of the *national rule of law*, or that it clearly links to the *national rule of law*. The list of elements is presented in figure 2 below; and the emerging mosaic, with its normative dimension, institutional dimension, and cultural dimension will be presented in the remainder of this section. It is remarkable that also within the notion of the *national rule of law* one can observe change over time, with different elements being emphasized at different moments. In section D, three main rule of law promotion activities, reflecting the Tribunal's current rule of law notion at the respective time, will be presented.

53 It might be worth noting that the Referral Bench was the same in all cases, consisting of Judge *Alphons Orie* (presiding), Judge *O-Gon Kwon*, and Judge *Kevin Parker*. The composition of the Appeals Chamber varied, however always involving the judges *Fausto Pocar*, *Theodor Meron*, *Mohamed Shahabuddeen*, *Mehmet Güney*, *Wolfgang Schomburg*, *Florence Ndepele Mwachande Mumba*, *Andrésia Vaz*, and *Liu Daqun*.

54 Necessarily, this framework remains fragmented: the general scope is determined by Rule 11*bis* (*supra* note 32) itself, which mentions some of the parameters to be appraised. What elements within these broad parameters the Bench specifically examines or what elements it analyses in depth depends on the questions at stake in each individual case, and often also on what the parties emphasize in their submissions. Consequently, the framework that emerges is more detailed on some elements (such as on impartiality and independence of national courts, the right to examine witnesses or humane detention conditions; see below) than on others. For instance, safeguards that an accused does not have to stand trial if s/he is mentally unfit (as part of the accused's fair trial rights) were only addressed in *Kovačević*, as this was not an issue in any other case.

Figure 2

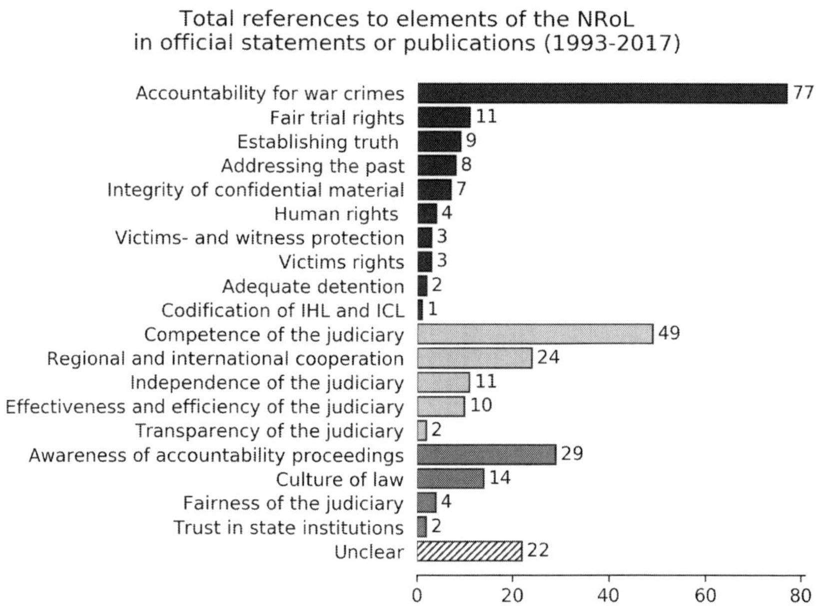

Normative dimension (black): accountability for war crimes, fair trial rights, establishing truth, addressing the past, integrity of confidential material, human rights, victims- and witness protection, victims rights, adequate detention, codification of IHL and ICL; institutional dimension (light grey): competence of the judiciary, regional and international cooperation, independence of the judiciary, effectiveness and efficiency of the judiciary, transparency of the judiciary; cultural dimension (dark grey): awareness of accountability proceedings, culture of law, fairness of the judiciary, trust in state institutions; "white and hatched": references to the national rule of law without any connection to a particular element, or where the reference is ambiguous

I. Normative Dimension

According to the ICTY, in order for the societies in the countries of the former Yugoslavia to function under the rule of law, they need to acknowledge the past,[55] learn from it, reconcile with it, and move on.[56] In this context, it is necessary that international crimes are addressed through criminal prosecutions. Perpetrators must be arrested,[57] brought to justice,[58] held

---

55 Cf. ICTY, 'Completion Strategy: Prosecutor Brammertz's Address Before the Security Council', Press Release, FS/OTP/1466e, 7 December 2011, available at http://www.icty.org/en/press/completion-strategy-prosecutor-brammertz's-address-security-council (last visited 10 December 2018); this and subsequent references to different rule of law elements are only examples. As has been explained, many references are repeated many times and it would be excessive to replicate all of them in the footnotes.

56 Cf. C. del Ponte, 'Address by Tribunal Prosecutor Carla Del Ponte to NATO Parliamentary Assembly: The ICTY and the Legacy of the Past', CdP/OTP/ PR1193e, 26 October 2007, available at http://www.icty.org/en/press/address-tribunal-prosecutor-carla-del-ponte-nato-parliamentary-assembly-belgrade-icty-and (last visited 10 December 2018); in the figures, these elements have been regrouped together under *addressing the past*.

57 Cf. G. Kirk McDonald, 'ICTY President Gabrielle Kirk McDonald addresses the "Dayton" Peace Implementation Council', CC/PIO/272-E, 9 December 1997, available at http://www.icty.org/en/press/icty-president-gabrielle-kirk-mcdonald-addresses-dayton-peace-implementation-council (last visited 10 December 2018); C. del Ponte, 'Address by Carla del Ponte, Prosecutor of the ICTY, to the UN Security Council', CDP/P.I.S./917-e, 23 November 2004, available at http://www.icty.org/en/press/address-carla-del-ponte-prosecutor-icty-un-security-council (last visited 10 December 2018); S. Brammertz, 'Completion Strategy Report: Prosecutor Brammertz's address before the Security Council', VE/CS/PR1571e, 12 June 2013, available at http://www.icty.org/en/press/completion-strategy-report-prosecutor-brammertz's-address-security-council-0 (last visited 10 December 2018).

58 Cf. F. Pocar, 'Address of Judge Fausto Pocar, President of the International Criminal Tribunal for the Former Yugoslavia, to the United Nations General Assembly', AH/MOW/1288e, 13 October 2008, available at http://www.icty.org/en/press/address-judge-fausto-pocar-president-international-criminal-tribunal-former-yugoslavia-united (last visited 10 December 2018).

accountable,[59] and punished.[60] On the one hand, trials would help to establish the facts about the violent past.[61] Moreover and more importantly, however, they are about establishing individual criminal responsibility.[62] Prosecuting and trying perpetrators of international crimes was reiterated over and over again throughout the existence of the Tribunal, with a noticeable high in the beginning of the 2000s. In that period, the ICTY started to envisage its own closure and therefore pointed out that prosecutions of international crimes would have to be continued by the national justice systems in the former Yugoslavia (see figure 3 below). Accordingly, it started to lobby and support these countries, especially BiH, to set up specialized institutions for that purpose. It also helped to kick off the work of these institutions by referring them low- and mid-level perpetrator cases, and scrutinizing and supporting the adjudication of these cases. This explicit rule of law promotion effort will be further explained in section D. I. below. The importance of accountability proceedings in order to reestablish the rule of law was again frequently recalled when the ICTY approached its closure, of which it was reminded when the MICT was preparing to operate and in its very final year of existence (see figure 3 below).

59 Cf. T. Meron, 'Statement by President Meron on the occasion of International Justice Day', 16 July 2015, 1, available at http://www.icty.org/x/file/Press/Statements%20and%20Speeches/President/150716-president_meron_international_justice_day_en.pdf (last visited 10 December 2018); G. Kirk McDonald, 'The International Criminal Tribunal for the former Yugoslavia: Making a Difference or Making Excuses?', JL/PIU/402-E, 13 May 1999, available at http://www.icty.org/en/press/international-criminal-tribunal-former-yugoslavia-making-difference-or-making-excuses (last visited 10 December 2018) [Kirk McDonald, Making a Difference or Making Excuses?].

60 Cf. ICTY, 'Annual Report 1994', UN Doc A/49/342 S/1994/1007, 29 August 1994, 12, available at http://www.icty.org/x/file/About/Reports%20and%20Publications/AnnualReports/annual_report_1994_en.pdf (last visited 10 December 2018); in the figures, these elements have been regrouped together under *accountability for war crimes*.

61 Cf. ICTY, 'Digest 52', 17 February 2009, 1, available at http://www.icty.org/x/file/About/Reports%20and%20Publications/ICTYDigest/icty_digest_52_en.pdf (last visited 10 December 2018); in the figures, this element is called *establishing truth*.

62 Cf. *Prosecutor v. Deronjić*, Closing Statement, IT-02-61-S, 231, available at http://www.icty.org/x/cases/deronjic/trans/en/040128IT.htm (last visited 10 December 2018).

Figure 3

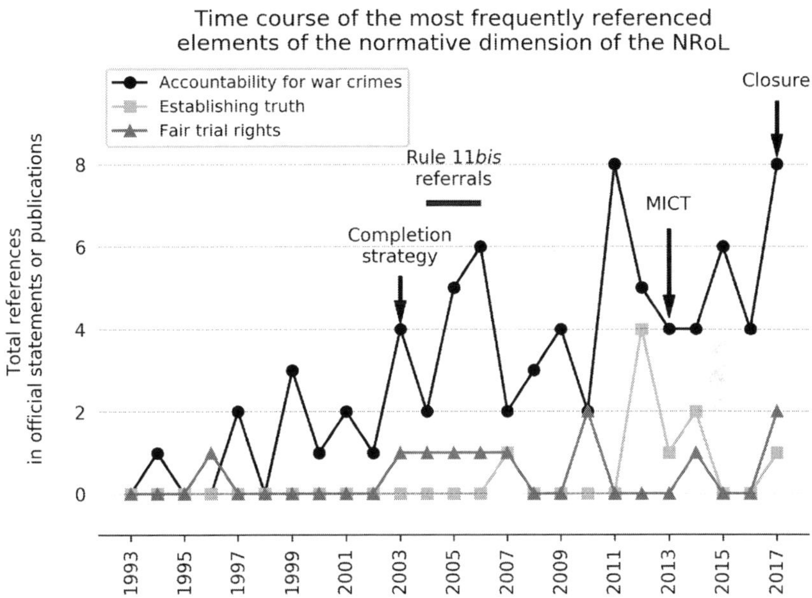

1. *Applicable Substantive Law*

The legal framework within which prosecutions and trials should be conducted was clarified in Rule 11*bis* cases, where the Tribunal verified whether the domestic law is adequate for prosecuting, trying, and eventually (if found guilty) punishing the defendant.[63] In general, the ICTY deemed that in order to hold international crimes trials,[64] the domestic le-

63 Cf. *Prosecutor v. Stanković*, Decision, Referral Bench, IT-96-23/2-PT, 17 May 2005, para. 37 [Cf. *Prosecutor v. Stanković*, Referral Bench]; see also W. W. Burke-White, 'The Domestic Influence of International Criminal Tribunals: The International Criminal Tribunal for the Former Yugoslavia and the Creation of the State Court of Bosnia & Herzegovina', 46 *Columbia Journal of Transnational Law* (2007) 2, 279, 323 [Burke-White, The Domestic Influence].

64 Cf. ICTY, 'OHR-ICTY Working Group on Development of BiH Capacity for War-crimes Trial Successfully Completed', Press Release, OHR/P.I.S./731e, 21 February 2013, available at http://www.icty.org/en/press/ohr-icty-working-group-development-bih-capacity-war-crimes-trial-successfully-completed (last visited 10 December

gal framework must entail provisions of international humanitarian and international criminal law.[65] This would be an "assertion of the rule of law over the law of the gun"[66], "breaking the cycle of impunity"[67]. The Referral Bench's focus, however, was whether the material elements of the crime are covered by the criminal law applicable at the time of the offense,[68] whether it provides for appropriate modes of liability to reflect the accused's conduct, and whether an appropriate punishment exists.[69]

Although the ICTY thus recommended codifying international criminal law, it was satisfied if the material elements of offenses underlying interna-

---

2018); T. Meron, 'Statement by President Meron on Establishment of Special War Crimes Chamber in Bosnian State Court', JL/P.I.S./761-e, 13 June 2003, available at http://www.icty.org/en/press/statement-president-meron-establishment-special-war-crimes-chamber-bosnian-state-court (last visited 10 December 2018); T. Meron, 'Address of Judge Theodor Meron, President of the ICTY, to the UN Security Council', TM/P.I.S./916-e, 23 November 2004, available at http://www.icty.org/en/press/address-judge-theodor-meron-president-icty-un-security-council (last visited 10 December 2018); ICTY, 'Annual Report 2005', UN Doc A/60/267–S/2005/532, 17 August 2005, 38, available at http://www.icty.org/x/file/About/Reports%20and%20Publications/AnnualReports/annual_report_2005_en.pdf (last visited 10 December 2018).

65 Cf. ICTY, 'Completion Strategy Report November 2009', *supra* note 28, 21; in the figures, this element is called *codification of IHL and ICL*.

66 ICTY, 'The Tribunal's First Trial: Another Step in the Fulfillment of the Tribunal's Mandate', Press Release, CC/PIO/070-E, 6 May 1996, available at http://www.icty.org/en/press/tribunals-first-trial-another-step-fulfillment-tribunals-mandate (last visited 10 December 2018).

67 G. Kirk McDonald, 'Address to the United Nations General Assembly by Judge Gabrielle Kirk McDonald, President of the International Criminal Tribunal for the former Yugoslavia', JL/P.I.S./445-E, 8 November 1999, available at http://www.icty.org/en/press/address-united-nations-general-assembly-judge-gabrielle-kirk-mcdonald-president-international (last visited 10 December 2018).

68 Cf. *Prosecutor v. Stanković*, Referral Bench, *supra* note 63, para. 46.

69 Cf. *ibid.*, para. 32. The exact same wording is also used in *Prosecutor v. Rašević and Todović*, Decision, Referral Bench, IT-97-25/1-PT, 8 July 2005, para. 34 [*Prosecutor v. Rašević and Todović*, Referral Bench]; *Prosecutor v. Mejakić, Gruban, Fuštar, Knežević*, Decision, Referral Bench, IT-02-65-PT, 20 July 2005, para. 43 [*Prosecutor v. Mejakić, et al.*, Referral Bench]; *Prosecutor v. Janković*, Decision, Referral Bench, IT-96-23/2-PT, 22 July 2005, para. 27 [*Prosecutor v. Janković*, Referral Bench]; *Prosecutor v. Ljubičić*, Decision, Referral Bench, IT-00-41-PT, 12 April 2006, para. 31 [*Prosecutor v. Ljubičić*, Referral Bench]; *Prosecutor v. Kovačević*, Decision, Referral Bench, IT-01-42/2-I, 17 November 2006, para. 25 [*Prosecutor v. Kovačević*, Referral Bench]; *Prosecutor v. Milan Lukić and Sredoje Lukić*, Decision, Referral Bench, IT-98-32/1-PT, 5 April 2007, para. 45 [*Prosecutor v. Milan Lukić and Sredoje Lukić*, Referral Bench].

tional crimes were covered by the applicable ordinary criminal law.[70] It was important, however, that the legality principle, especially its components *nullum crimen-* and *nulla poena sine lege* were respected and that no one was convicted or punished upon law that was not applicable at the time of the offense.[71]

In addition, the ICTY underlined the importance to have those modes of liability available that most accurately mirror the respective responsibility of accused in international crimes trials.[72] Most prominently, this concerned the notion of command responsibility as established in Article 7 (3) ICTY Statute.[73]

Lastly, it was necessary that an appropriate punishment was available. For international crimes trials, appropriate punishment would often entail a prison sentence,[74] but the Tribunal did not specify the proper length of sentences. Also concerning sanctions, the ICTY welcomed that the legality principle is cherished, this time the principle of *lex mitior* (that in the case of changes in the laws between the commission of the offense and its adjudication, the law that is more lenient to the accused shall be applied). It should, however, not impede the trial and punishment of a defendant.[75]

2. *Human Rights*

Publicly, the ICTY has always maintained that human rights need to be ensured at the domestic level.[76] Although this referred to all human rights as

---

70 Focus on the conduct means that it is not necessarily required that a particular offense is conceptualized as an international crime. It is sufficient that the conduct is covered by the law, whether as an ordinary crime or as an international crime.

71 Cf. *Prosecutor v. Janković*, Referral Bench, *supra* note 69, para. 40-41; *Prosecutor v. Milan Lukić and Sredoje Lukić*, Referral Bench, *supra* note 69, para. 55.

72 Cf. Jorda, 'Report on the Judicial Status of the ICTY', *supra* note 33, 19.

73 Cf. *Prosecutor v. Kovačević*, Referral Bench, *supra* note 69, para. 43-47; *Prosecutor v. Rašević and Todović*, Referral Bench, *supra* note 69, para. 51; *Prosecutor v. Ljubičić*, Referral Bench, *supra* note 69, para. 34-35.

74 Cf. *Prosecutor v. Stanković*, Referral Bench, *supra* note 63, para. 40 and 43.

75 Cf. *Prosecutor v. Milan Lukić and Sredoje Lukić*, Referral Bench, *supra* note 69, para. 55.

76 Cf. T. Meron, 'Address of Judge Theodor Meron, President of the ICTY, to the UN General Assembly', JP/ P.I.S/912-e, 15 November 2004, available at http://www.icty.org/en/press/address-judge-theodor-meron-president-icty-un-general-assembly-15-november-2004 (last visited 10 December 2018); T. Meron, 'Statement by President Meron on the occasion of International Justice Day', 16 July 2015, available

enshrined in the *European Convention on Human Rights* (ECHR) (including those that are not directly linked to prosecutions of international crimes, such as freedom of expression)[77], the focus naturally was on whether the criminal procedural law of a country would be human rights conform.[78] An evaluation of whether the human rights of the defendant are respected if a case is handed over to the national level has occupied a prominent place in all referral cases, and in the time period of referrals, the Tribunal frequently recalled the importance of respecting fair trial rights (see figure 3 above). In Rule 11*bis* case law, different aspects were emphasized, depending on the specific characteristics of the case. Most importantly, the Tribunal needed to be assured that the accused would not face the death penalty and that s/he would receive a fair trial[79] – but also that national law provided for decent detention conditions. In that respect, the Tribunal welcomed accession to the ECHR and the *International Covenant on Civil and Political Rights* (ICCPR) as this would constitute an additional layer of protection of fair trial rights, next to possible national constitutional law provisions or safeguards provided for in national criminal law.[80] Lastly, the ICTY stressed that the domestic legal framework must ensure victims and witness support and protection,[81] as well as the integrity of confidential materials.[82]

at http://www.icty.org/en/press/statement-president-meron-occasion-international-justice-day (last visited 10 December 2018); in the figures, this element is called *human rights*.

77 Cf. G. Krik McDonald, 'Statement by Judge Mcdonald, President of the International Criminal Tribunal for the Former Yugoslavia', JL/PIU/359-E, 5 November 1998, available at http://www.icty.org/en/press/statement-judge-mcdonald-president-international-criminal-tribunal-former-yugoslavia (last visited 10 December 2018).

78 In the figures, this element is called *fair trial rights*.

79 This is required by Rule 11*bis* (B), *supra* note 32.

80 Cf. *Prosecutor v. Mejakić, et al.*, Referral Bench, *supra* note 69, para. 69 and 79; *Prosecutor v. Milan Lukić and Sredoje Lukić*, Referral Bench, *supra* note 69, para. 74.

81 In the figures, this element is called *victims- and witness protection*, and *victims rights* when statements refer to their right to compensation.

82 Cf. ICTY, 'Vojislav Šešelj Charged with Contempt of Court', Press Release. NJ/MOW/1300e, 22 January 2009, available at http://www.icty.org/en/press/vojislav- (last visited 10 December 2018); ICTY, 'Completion Strategy Report November 2007', UN Doc S/2007/663, 12 November 2007, 10, available at http://www.icty.org/x/file/About/Reports%20and%20Publications/CompletionStrategy/completion_strategy_12november2007_en.pdf (last visited 10 December 2018) [ICTY, Completion Strategy Report November 2007]; in the figures, this element is called *integrity of confidential material*.

In *Stanković*, the Referral Bench laid out a list of minimum fair trial rights which largely replicated Article 21 ICTY Statute – which in itself is a reproduction of fair trial rights as recognized by Article 14 ICCPR from 1966 and by Article 6 of the ECHR.[83]

Firstly, all persons are equal before the court.[84] In the Balkan context, this especially referred to equality regardless of ethnic or religious background.[85] Secondly, everyone is entitled to a fair and public hearing by a competent, independent and impartial tribunal established by law.[86] This not only signifies that due process standards must be respected,[87] but also that several institutional safeguards need to be provided in order to in fact ensure a fair trial.[88] The third right entails the presumption of innocence until proven guilty according to the law.[89] Fourthly, the accused has the right to be informed promptly and in detail in a language which s/he understands of the nature and cause of the charge against him/her.[90] During trial, the accused has the right to free assistance of an interpreter if s/he cannot understand or speak the language used in the proceedings.[91]

---

83 Cf. *Prosecutor v. Stanković*, Referral Bench, *supra* note 63, para. 55; this list was reiterated in *Prosecutor v. Kovačević*, Referral Bench, *supra* note 69, para. 68; *Prosecutor v. Rašević and Savo Todović*, Referral Bench, *supra* note 69, para. 72; *Prosecutor v. Mejakić, et al.*, Referral Bench, *supra* note 69, para. 68; *Prosecutor v. Janković*, Referral Bench, *supra* note 69, para. 62; *Prosecutor v. Milan Lukić and Sredoje Lukić*, Referral Bench, *supra* note 69, para. 71.

84 Cf. *Prosecutor v. Stanković*, Referral Bench, *supra* note 63, para. 55.

85 Cf. ICTY, 'Joint Press Statement Visit to The Hague by Delegation from Republika Srpska', Press Release, CC/PIO/101-E, 31 July 1996, available at http://www.icty.org/en/press/joint-press-statement-visit-hague-delegation-republika-srpska (last visited 10 December 2018).

86 Cf. *Prosecutor v. Stanković*, Referral Bench, *supra* note 63, para. 55; ICTY, 'Trial Chamber II Hands Down its Decision on the Subpoena Issue: The Subpoena Duces Tecum Issued to Croatia and its Defence Minister in January 1997 Must be Complied with by 18 August 1997', Press Release, CC/PIO/230-E, 18 July 1997, available at http://www.icty.org/en/press/trial-chamber-ii-hands-down-its-decision-subpoena-issue-subpoena-duces-tecum-issued-croatia (last visited 10 December 2018) [ICTY, Press Release 18 July 1997]; Burke-White, 'The Domestic Influence', *supra* note 63, 323.

87 Cf. T. Meron, 'Address of Judge Theodor Meron, President of the ICTY, to the UN Security Council', TM/P.I.S./916-e, 23 November 2004, available at http://www.icty.org/en/press/address-judge-theodor-meron-president-icty-un-security-council (last visited 10 December 2018).

88 This will be elaborated further down under *Institutional Dimension*.

89 Cf. *Prosecutor v. Stanković*, Referral Bench, *supra* note 63, para. 55.

90 Cf. *ibid.*

91 Cf. *ibid.*

Fifthly, the accused's right to a defense comprises different elements that the Tribunal distinguished but that are somewhat related: first, it contains the right of an accused to have adequate time and facilities for the preparation of his/her defense and to communicate with counsel of his/her own choosing; second, the right to be tried in his/her presence, and to defend him/herself in person or through legal assistance of his/her own choosing; and third, the right to be informed, if s/he does not have legal assistance, of this right, and to have legal assistance assigned to him/her, in any case where the interests of justice so require, and without payment by him/her in any such case if s/he does not have sufficient means to pay for it.[92] It is accepted by the ICTY that the right to counsel of one's own choosing is not without limitation: it extends only to counsel who are entitled to appear before the respective court of trial and the accused must make his/her choice accordingly. In addition, it is also acceptable that in case the accused cannot pay for the counsel, s/he may choose from a list of available defense counsel – and if s/he does not, a counsel will be appointed by the court.[93]

The sixth fair trial right, the right to an expeditious trial,[94] grants the accused the right to be tried without undue delay.[95] Any possible delay in proceedings must not be undue, unreasonable or unnecessary.[96] It is accepted that a system that grants an accused the right to be brought before the court in the shortest reasonable time period and to be tried without delay and that requires that the duration of custody is reduced to the shortest time necessary, is in accordance with the right to an expeditious trial. In addition, it was lauded if incentives exist under the law to proceed without undue delay.[97]

Seventhly, an accused has the right to examine, or have examined, the witnesses against him and to obtain the attendance and examination of witnesses on his behalf under the same conditions as witnesses against him.[98] The Referral Bench indirectly related the issue of witness protection

---

92 Cf. *Prosecutor v. Stanković*, Referral Bench, *supra* note 63, para. 55.

93 Cf. *Prosecutor v. Rašević and Todović*, Referral Bench, *supra* note 69, para. 88; *Prosecutor v. Mejakić, et al.*, Referral Bench, *supra* note 69, para. 111; *Prosecutor v. Janković*, Referral Bench, *supra* note 69, para. 77.

94 Cf. ICTY, 'Press Release 18 July 1997', *supra* note 86.

95 Cf. *Prosecutor v. Stanković*, Referral Bench, *supra* note 63, para. 55; ICTY, 'Annual Report 2012', A/67/214–S/2012/592, 1 August 2012, 17, available at http://www.icty.org/x/file/About/Reports%20and%20Publications/AnnualReports/annual_report_2012_en.pdf (last visited 10 December 2018).

96 Cf. *Prosecutor v. Stanković*, Referral Bench, *supra* note 63, para. 77.

97 Cf. *Prosecutor v. Rašević* and Todović, Referral Bench, *supra* note 69, paras. 96, 102.

98 Cf. *Prosecutor v. Stanković*, Referral Bench, *supra* note 63, para. 55.

to the right of the accused to examine witnesses, as it may "promot[e] witness presence at trial by providing assurance to witnesses that legal measures exist for their protection."[99] Measures provided for in the laws of BiH were deemed sufficient in this respect: in criminal proceedings, both parties may request an order for protective measures, such as anonymity of a witness or the use of a pseudonym both, inside and outside of court. The *Witness Protection Programme Law* of Bosnia and Herzegovina regulates possible measures to take outside the courtroom, such as change of identity or issuance of cover documents.[100] Likewise, the Serbian *Law on Protection of Participants in Criminal Proceedings* – which is applicable to witnesses – provides for a protection program which can apply measures including physical protection of persons and property, change of place of residence, or the concealing or change of identity.[101] This was also conceived as sufficient.[102] While ICTY representatives repeatedly recalled the necessity of adequate victim and witness protection, the Appeals Chamber acknowledged in *Janković*[103] that "no judicial system, be it national or international, can guarantee absolute witness protection."[104] At the same time, the protection of witnesses can be somewhat detrimental to the right of the accused to properly defend him/herself as s/he might need to know who is testifying against him/her. In this respect, the Referral Bench welcomed certain safeguards so that "a proper balance will be struck between the rights of an accused and the need to protect vulnerable witnesses and witnesses under threat."[105] Thus, the application of protective measures must be carefully considered beforehand and only ordered after taking into account the views of the defense, and "sufficient details" should be released to the accused for him/her to prepare his/her defense.[106] In addition, in any case, the accused must be in the position to examine the protected witness by asking questions.[107]

---

99 *Prosecutor v. Stanković*, Referral Bench, *supra* note 63, para. 89.
100 Cf. *ibid.*; *Prosecutor v. Mejakić, et al.*, Referral Bench, *supra* note 69, paras. 105, 106.
101 Cf. *Prosecutor v. Kovačević*, Referral Bench, *supra* note 69, para. 84.
102 Cf. *ibid.*, para. 86.
103 And reiterated *Prosecutor v. Rašević and Todović*, Referral Bench, *supra* note 69, para. 65.
104 *Prosecutor v. Janković*, Referral Bench, *supra* note 69, para. 49.
105 *Prosecutor v. Rašević and Todović*, Referral Bench, *supra* note 69, para. 91.
106 Cf. *Prosecutor v. Mejakić, et al.*, Referral Bench, *supra* note 69, para. 100.
107 Cf. *ibid.*, para. 101.

As the eighth right enshrines the right not to incriminate oneself, the accused shall not be compelled to testify against him/herself or to confess guilt.[108]

Lastly, and although not mentioned in Article 21 ICTY Statute or in the list of fair trial rights the Referral Bench had reiterated since *Stanković*, the right not to stand trial in case of physical or mental unfitness was examined as a "fair trial consideration [...]"[109] in *Kovačević*.[110]

According to Rule 11*bis* (B), a case could only be referred if the death penalty would not be imposed or carried out. Case law has clarified that through the ratification of *Protocol 13 of ECHR*, which abolished the death penalty in all circumstances, this condition is fulfilled. That holds true even if national law applicable at the time of the offense foresaw the death penalty as punishment, since Protocol 13 would nonetheless preclude its imposition.[111]

In addition to these rights, the ICTY held that adequate detention "touches upon the fairness of [a] jurisdiction's criminal justice system."[112] There must be decent detention facilities for remand and convicted persons,[113] where their rights are respected by those responsible for detention pre-trial, during trial, and post-trial,[114] and where detainees are treated equally, no matter their nationality, political views, or religious beliefs.[115] Also the length of detention during pre-trial and trial periods must be adequate.[116]

---

108 Cf. *Prosecutor v. Stanković*, Referral Bench, *supra* note 63, para. 55.

109 *Prosecutor v. Kovačević*, Referral Bench, *supra* note 69, para. 50.

110 Cf. *ibid.*

111 Cf. *Prosecutor v. Stanković*, Referral Bench, *supra* note 63, para. 55; *Prosecutor v. Rašević and Todović*, Referral Bench, *supra* note 69, para. 56; *Prosecutor v. Mejakić, et al.*, Referral Bench, *supra* note 69, para. 66, 67; *Prosecutor v. Janković*, Referral Bench, *supra* note 69, paras. 47, 48; *Prosecutor v. Ljubičić*, Referral Bench, *supra* note 69, paras. 38, 39; *Prosecutor v. Milan Lukić and Sredoje Lukić*, Referral Bench, *supra* note 69, para. 62.

112 *Prosecutor v. Stanković*, Appeals Chamber, *supra* note 38, para. 34; in the figures, this element is called *adequate detention*.

113 Cf. ICTY, *Prosecutor v. Janković*, Appeals Chamber, Decision, IT-96-23/2-PT, 15 November 2005, paras. 69-76 [ICTY, *Prosecutor v. Janković*, Appeals Chamber]; ICTY, 'Completion Strategy Report November 2007', *supra* note 82, 11.

114 Cf. *Prosecutor v. Janković*, Appeals Chamber, *supra* note 113, paras. 69-76.

115 Cf. Jorda, 'Report on the Judicial Status of the ICTY', *supra* note 33, 25.

116 Cf. *Prosecutor v. Mejakić, et al.*, Referral Bench, *supra* note 69, para. 109; that the law of Bosnia and Herzegovina provided that the maximum period of pre-trial and trial detention does not exceed 1.5 years was mentioned as particularly suspect- and accused-friendly.

II. Institutional Dimension

Clearly, the ICTY's focus within the normative dimension of the rule of law is that a legislative framework exists that enables the prosecution and processing of international crimes, while effectively ensuring human rights, especially fair trial rights. However, as mentioned, this is not enough. The rule of law is only guaranteed if institutions exist that are capable of carrying out such proceedings. For that, in the ICTY's view, judicial institutions must be independent[117] and impartial, and – most importantly – legal practitioners, including judges, prosecutors, support staff, and defense counsel must be well-trained and competent.[118] These elements have been stressed a lot as of the moment that referrals of cases from the ICTY to the national judiciaries of the former Yugoslavia became a possibility (see figure 4 below).[119] Of course, these countries needed to be prepared to process these cases, and at the ICTY, one was most preoccupied due to possible lacks of independence and competence of the national judiciaries. In reaction, in an endeavor to support the national judiciaries (especially in BiH, Croatia, and Serbia) which all had set up specialized institutions for the prosecution and trial of international crimes, and whose work had been kicked off with the referred Rule 11*bis* cases, the ICTY engaged in enhanced capacity building, in particular between 2005 and 2011. This rule of law promotion effort will be further presented in section D. II. below.

117 In the figures, this element is called *independence of the judiciary*.
118 In the figures, this element is called *competence of the judiciary*.
119 As explained, this was first envisaged within the completion strategy in 2003.

Figure 4

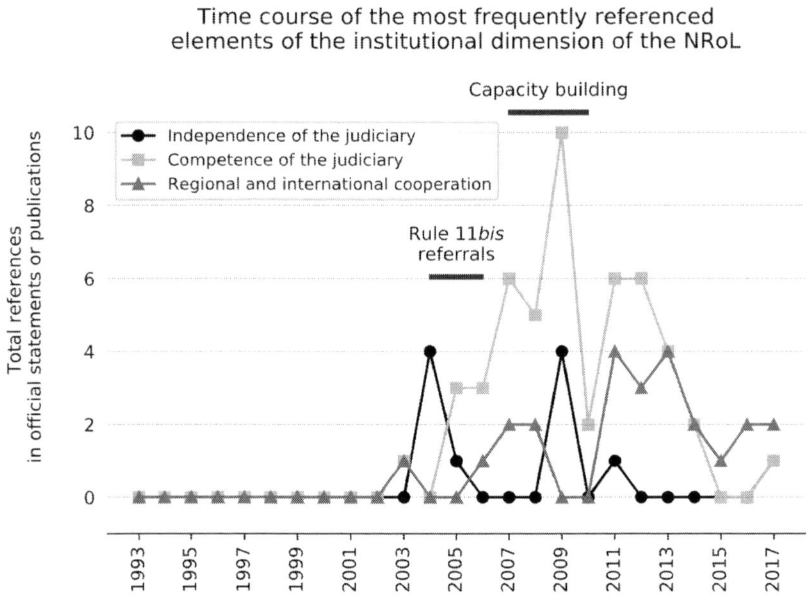

For the Tribunal, independence of a judicial system[120] first and foremost refers to the absence of anything that is not judicial, but political: the system as such must not be politicized,[121] political authorities should not be

120 Cf. *Prosecutor v. Stanković*, Referral Bench, *supra* note 63, para. 55; ICTY, 'Press Release 18 July 1997', *supra* note 86; ICTY, 'Digest 58', 2, available at http://www.icty.org/x/file/About/Reports%20and%20Publications/ICTYDigest/icty_digest_58_en.pdf (last visited at 10 December 2018); ICTY, 'Annual Report 2009', A/64/205–S/2009/394, 31 July 2009, 8, para. 16, available at http://www.icty.org/x/file/About/Reports%20and%20Publications/AnnualReports/annual_report_2009_en.pdf (last visited 10 December 2018); ICTY, 'Paddy Ashdown and Carla Del Ponte Call for BiH Parliament to Make War Crimes Chamber Operational by January 2005', Press Release, FH/P.I.S./903-e, 20 October 2004, available at http://www.icty.org/en/press/paddy-ashdown-and-carla-del-ponte-call-bih-parliament-make-war-crimes-chamber-operational (last visited 10 December 2018).

121 Cf. Jorda, 'Report on the Judicial Status of the ICTY', *supra* note 33, 19.

able to interfere in investigations,[122] and trials should not be used for political purposes,[123] or "pleas[e] political pressure"[124].

A judicial system, especially courts, also need to be impartial. Although impartiality has not directly been defined by the Tribunal, it entails several principles: firstly, in order to ensure the integrity of judges, i.e. that they are not corrupt, they must be "sufficiently remunerated and their independence guaranteed."[125] Secondly, a balanced composition of courts, particularly in ethnic terms, is helpful.[126] Impartiality heavily depends on appropriate selection standards and procedures for judicial personnel,[127] and on the availability of possibilities to disqualify a judge for lack of impartiality.[128]

Next to independence and impartiality, the ICTY also repeatedly highlighted judicial transparency,[129] efficiency and effectiveness,[130] and competence[131] as principles within the intuitional dimension of the rule of law. To ensure efficiency, sufficient financial and logistical resources are paramount.[132] To ensure effectiveness, the Tribunal demanded international and regional judicial cooperation,[133] which requires not only an adequate legal framework for the transfer of suspects and accused, evidence,

122 Cf. Jorda, 'Report on the Judicial Status of the ICTY', *supra* note 33, 25.

123 Cf. ICTY, 'Completion Strategy Report November 2004', *supra* note 47, 3.

124 ICTY, 'Completion Strategy Report May 2008', S/2008/326, 14 May 2008, 11, available at http://www.icty.org/x/file/About/Reports%20and%20Publications/CompletionStrategy/completion_strategy_14may2008_en.pdf (last visited 10 December 2018).

125 Jorda, 'Report on the Judicial Status of the ICTY', *supra* note 33, 25, fn. 24.

126 Cf. Jorda, *ibid.*, 19.

127 Cf. *Prosecutor v. Stanković*, Referral Bench, *supra* note 63, paras. 27-30; *Prosecutor v. Janković*, Appeals Chamber, *supra* note 113, para. 53.

128 Cf. *Prosecutor v. Mejakić, et al.*, Referral Bench, *supra* note 69, para. 86.

129 Cf. ICTY, 'Digest 63', 14 September 2009, 1, available at http://www.icty.org/x/file/About/Reports%20and%20Publications/ICTYDigest/icty_digest_63_en.pdf (last visited 10 December 2018); in the figures, this element is called *transparency of the judiciary*.

130 Cf. ICTY, 'Completion Strategy Report November 2007', *supra* note 82, 10; in the figures, this element is called *effectiveness and efficiency*.

131 Cf. Jorda, 'Report on the Judicial Status of the ICTY', *supra* note 33, 19; ICTY, 'Digest 52', *supra* note 61, 1; ICTY, 'Completion Strategy Report November 2009', *supra* note 28, 21; Burke-White, 'The Domestic Influence', *supra* note 63, 323.

132 Cf. Jorda, 'Report on the Judicial Status of the ICTY', *supra* note 33, 19.

133 Cf. ICTY, 'Annual Report 2011', A/66/210–S/2011/473, 31 July 2011, 15, available at http://www.icty.org/x/file/About/Reports%20and%20Publications/AnnualReports/annual_report_2011_en.pdf (last visited 10 December 2018); in the figures, this element is called *regional and international cooperation*.

or proceedings, but also compliance with relevant request.[134] Lastly, to ensure competence, members of the justice system need to be well selected and well trained in conducting the relevant investigations and judicial proceedings,[135] including war crimes proceedings.[136]

III. Cultural Dimension

Apart from principles that relate to the functioning of the institutional set-up of a national justice system, a legal culture is indispensable for the rule of law to be properly anchored in a society. A "culture of law instead of violence"[137], and an "ideology of legality"[138] should govern societies. This relates to everyone, including ordinary citizens. But the ICTY of course also stressed the particular necessity for justice institutions that "entrench the rule of law"[139] and that are an "articulation of shared values and moral imperatives"[140].[141] Thus, State organs, especially judicial institutions need to

134 Cf. ICTY OTP, 'Completion Strategy Report May 2012', S/2012/354, 23 May 2012, 34, available at http://www.icty.org/x/file/About/Reports%20and%20Publications/CompletionStrategy/completion_strategy_23may2012_en.pdf (last visited 10 December 2018).

135 Cf. Jorda, 'Report on the Judicial Status of the ICTY', *supra* note 33, 19; ICTY, 'Completion Strategy Report November 2009', *supra* note 28, 21; Burke-White, 'The Domestic Influence', *supra* note 63, 323.

136 Cf. ICTY, 'Completion Strategy Report May 2014', S/2014/351, 16 May 2014, 7, available at http://www.icty.org/x/file/About/Reports%20and%20Publications/CompletionStrategy/completion_strategy_16may2014_en.pdf (last visited 10 December 2018); ICTY, 'Press Release 21 February 2013', *supra* note 64; ICTY, 'Annual Report 2005', *supra* note 64, 38.

137 C. del Ponte, 'Address by the Prosecutor of the International Criminal Tribunals for the former Yugoslavia and Rwanda, Mrs. Carla del Ponte, to the United Nations Security Council', JJJ/P.I.S./709-e, 30 October 2002, available at http://www.icty.org/en/press/address-prosecutor-international-criminal-tribunals-former-yugoslavia-and-rwanda-mrs-carla-del (last visited 10 December 2018).

138 Meron, 'Statement 9 March 2005', *supra* note 16.

139 ICTY, 'Tribunal President Welcomes Support for Bosnia and Herzegovina's Judicial Institutions', Press Release, CVO/MO/1059e, 31 March 2006, available at http://www.icty.org/en/press/tribunal-president-welcomes-support-bosnia-and-herzegovinas-judicial-institutions (last visited 10 December 2018).

140 T. Meron, 'Address to the U.N. Security Council', 5 June 2014, 2, available at http://www.icty.org/x/file/Press/Statements%20and%20Speeches/President/140605_president_meron_un_sc_en.pdf (last visited 10 December 2018).

141 In the figures, these elements have been grouped together under *culture of law*.

work in a fair[142] manner and treat everyone equally, regardless of their ethnic or religious background.[143]

In order for citizens to develop faith in State institutions,[144] respect for the judicial process,[145] and trust in "judicial accountability"[146],[147] they need to be properly informed about the work of criminal justice institutions,[148] especially about international criminal proceedings that address a country's violent past.[149] The ICTY called for raising such awareness in the region, especially towards the end of its existence (see figure 5 below). But it also sought to contribute to it through its own outreach program, which was massively professionalized as of 2009. This particular rule of law promotion effort will be further elaborated upon in section D. III. below.

142 Cf. G. Kirk McDonald, *Prosecutor v. Tadić*, Opening Statements, IT-94-1-T, 9, available at http://www.icty.org/x/cases/tadic/trans/en/960507IT.htm (last visited 10 December 2018); Meron, 'Address to the U.N. Security Council,' *supra* note 140, 2.

143 Cf. ICTY, 'Press Release 31 July 1996,' *supra* note 85; in the figures, these elements have been grouped together under *fairness of the judiciary*.

144 Cf. Kirk McDonald, 'Making a Difference or Making Excuses?,' *supra* note 59.

145 Cf. S. Brammertz, 'Statement of the ICTY Prosecutor Serge Brammertz in Relation to the Gotovina and Markac Appeal Judgement,' 21 November 2012, 1, available at http://www.icty.org/x/file/Press/Statements%20and%20Speeches/Prosecutor/121121_prosecutor_brammertz_en.pdf (last visited 10 December 2018).

146 S. Brammertz, 'Address of Mr. Serge Brammertz, Prosecutor International Criminal Tribunal for the Former Yugoslavia and Mechanism for International Criminal Tribunals to the United Nations Security Council,' 8 December 2016, 3, available at http://www.icty.org/x/file/Press/Statements%20and%20Speeches/Prosecutor/161208_prosecutor_brammertz_un_sc_en.pdf (last visited 10 December 2018).

147 In the figures, these elements have been grouped together under *trust in state institutions*.

148 Cf. ICTY, 'Completion Strategy Report November 2009,' *supra* note 28, 21.

149 Cf. ICTY, 'Support from European Union to the ICTY,' Press Release, LM/P.I.S./547-e, 7 December 2000, available at http://www.icty.org/en/press/support-european-union-icty (last visited 10 December 2018); in the figures, these elements have been grouped together under *awareness of accountability proceedings*.

Figure 5

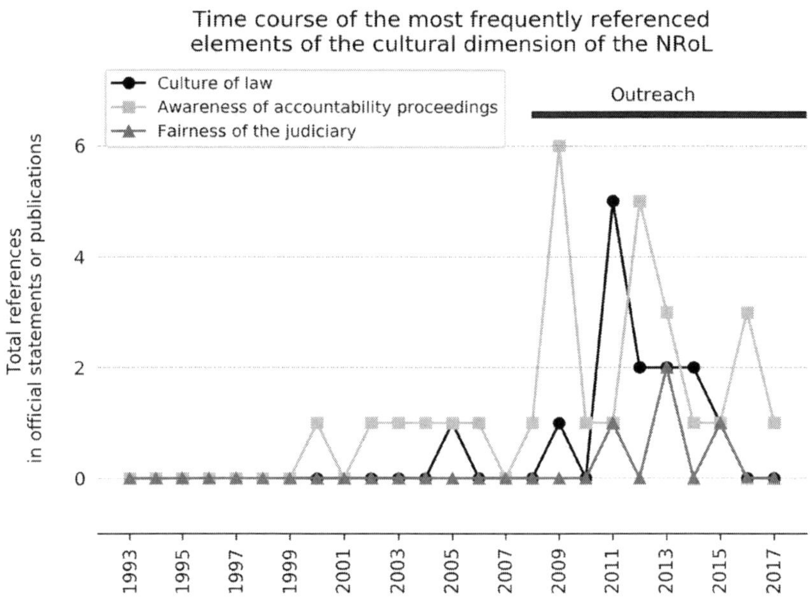

D. *The ICTY's Modest Rule of Law Promotion Efforts*

Although the ICTY is a criminal court with the main purpose of prosecuting and trying perpetrators of international crimes, the Tribunal clearly saw its own work in a broader – rule of law enhancing – context. Representatives frequently claimed that the Tribunal contributed to the rule of law, either to the *international rule of law* through its role of enforcer of international humanitarian and criminal law, or to the *national rule of law*. When analyzing official statements and publications of the ICTY, one gets a grip on what is meant by the *national rule of law*, although no official definition exists. At least with the adoption of the completion strategy and insertion of Rule 11*bis* into the ICTY RPE, it is obvious that the Tribunal undertook steps to enhance the *national rule of law* in the countries under its jurisdiction. While Rule 11*bis* did not require the ICTY to make an active effort (rather, the burden to comply with the rule's conditions for case referral is on the national justice systems), its existence nevertheless triggered a broad range of rule of law promotion activities, all geared towards preparing the national systems to meet the required standards. By virtue of Rule 11*bis* the Tribunal assumed the role of the rule of law promoter in the region.

Although the initiatives were many, the three main ones will be briefly sketched out here:[150] triggering national prosecutions and proceedings of international crimes, enhancing competence of national judiciaries, and raising awareness in order to build a culture of law. They directly relate to those elements that appear most frequently within each rule of law dimension (in the normative dimension, this element was conducting accountability proceedings for international crimes; in the institutional dimension, it was competence of the judiciary; and in the cultural dimension, this was awareness of accountability proceedings that address a country's violent past) in official statements or publications. Therefore, while Rule 11*bis* was the legal trigger for the ICTY to engage in rule of law promotion, the notion of the relevant national law the ICTY gradually developed informed the exact rule of law promotion steps to take.

I. Triggering Prosecutions: Building Institutions and Transferring Cases and Material

With the UNSC's call to strengthen the domestic justice systems in mind, the completion strategy and in particular, Rule 11*bis* prompted one of the most significant ICTY rule of law promotion initiatives: in order to trigger prosecutions in the region, the Tribunal lobbied the former Yugoslav countries to establish specialized institutions to prosecute and try perpetrators of international crimes, and advised them in this endeavor. The advantage of specialized institutions is mostly that they permit to concentrate resources and expertise,[151] which is particularly necessary in the context of adjudicating international crimes. These trials are complex, both in terms of the underlying substantive law and in terms of procedure, which poses a specific set of challenges. Subsequently, it transferred to these institutions Rule 11*bis* cases, ready to be tried, as well as further evidentiary material, out of which additional cases could be built. These cases and evidentiary

---

150 The focus will be on initiatives towards Bosnia and Herzegovina and Serbia, with BiH being the main target of the ICTY's rule of law promotion efforts and Serbia being the least important target. To compare those two countries hence gives an idea about the range of activities and their impact.

151 On advantages of specialized institutions and the Serbian experience, see M. Majić & D. Ignatović, 'Deset smerica zasnovanih na iskustvu Srbije vezanom za pitanja ratnih zločina', 9 *FICHL Policy Brief Series* (2012).

material were meant to kick off the work of the specialized institutions, with the help and under supervision of the ICTY OTP.

In 2002, the *State Court of Bosnia and Herzegovina* (SCBiH) was set up by a decision of the *High Representative* (OHR),[152] the institution responsible for overseeing implementation of civilian aspects of the *Dayton Peace Agreement* ending the war in BiH. At the same time, ICTY judges recommended the establishment of a specialized war crimes chamber within this court, staffed with both national and international judges.[153] While until 2005, trials for war-related crimes had been held only in the courts of the entities, the Federation of Bosnia and Herzegovina and the Republika Srpska, the most complex war crimes cases now take place within the new war crimes department at the SCBiH.[154] The corresponding BiH State Prosecutor's Office was established in January 2003,[155] and since March 2005 it also includes a special department for war crimes.[156] Overall, local actors report an overwhelming involvement of the ICTY in the establishment of these war crimes institutions in BiH. In fact, the war crimes department was set up upon an agreement between and as a "joint initiative"[157] of the OHR and the Tribunal. In addition, ICTY officials performed an important role with regard to the future work of the new court,[158] most impor-

---

152 Cf. Office of the High Representative, *Decision Establishing the BiH State Court*, 12 November 2000; the Law on the Court of Bosnia and Herzegovina had later been adopted by the two chambers of the BiH parliament as well; see: Sud Bosne i Herzegovine, 'Istorijat Suda BiH,' *supra* note 44.

153 Cf. Jorda, 'Report on the Judicial Status of the ICTY,' *supra* note 33, 25.

154 Cf. Y. Ronen, 'The Impact of the ICTY on Atrocity-Related Prosecutions in the Courts of Bosnia and Herzegovina,' 3 *Penn State Journal of Law and International Affairs* (2014) 1, 113, 124; see also: Government of BiH, 'Državna Strategija za Rad na Predmetima Ratnih Zločina' (*National War Crimes Strategy*), December 2008, 11-12, available at http://www.mpr.gov.ba/web_dokumenti/Drzavna%20strategije%20za%20rad%20na%20predmetima%20RZ.pdf (last visited 10 December 2018).

155 It was established by the *Law on the Prosecutor's Office of Bosnia and Herzegovina*, enacted by the High Representative in August 2002, and adopted by the Bosnian parliament in October 2003. The Law is published in the *Official Gazette of Bosnia and Herzegovina*, No 42/03.

156 Article 12 (3) *Law on the Prosecutor's Office of Bosnia and Herzegovina*; for more information, see the Prosecution Service's website: http://www.tuzilastvobih.gov.ba/?opcija=sadrzaj&kat=1&id=2&jezik=e (last visited 10 December 2018).

157 United Nations Security Council, 'Security Council Briefed on Establishment of War Crimes Chamber Within State Court of Bosnia and Herzegovina,' Press Release, SC/7888, 8 October 2003, available at http://www.un.org/press/en/2003/sc7888.doc.htm (last visited 10 December 2018).

158 Cf. Burke-White, 'The Domestic Influence,' *supra* note 63, 336.

tantly in preparing the SCBiH for receiving cases from The Hague.[159] In that regard, the Tribunal not only provided expertise in establishing these institutions, but also exerted pressure as it needed to make sure that there are domestic institutions equipped of receiving Rule 11*bis* cases.[160]

In Serbia, only a limited number of war crimes trials had taken place between 1991 and 2003. The serious concerns as to the proper conduct and fairness of these trials[161] considerably diminished with the establishment of specialized organs within the judicial system in 2003.[162] With the *Law on War Crimes*,[163] specialized institutions – the *War Crimes Prosecutor's Office*, the *War Crimes Department* within the *Belgrade High Court*, and the *War Crimes Investigation Service* within the Police – were established.[164] Contrary to the situation in BiH, in Serbia the establishment of specialized institutions were not instigated or brought about directly by the ICTY, but rather by regime change and external coercion.[165] However, prominent ICTY staff members participated in the expert group that assisted the Serbian government in the drafting of the *Law on War Crimes*, and their recommendations to establish specialized war crimes institutions were implemented.[166]

159 Cf. ICTY, 'Completion Strategy Report November 2004', *supra* note 47, 4.

160 Cf. Burke-White, 'The Domestic Influence', *supra* note 63, 335-344; interview with a representative of the Office of the High Representative, Sarajevo, 8 February 2017.

161 Cf. OSCE, *War Crimes Proceedings in Serbia (2003-2014) - An analysis of the OSCE Mission to Serbia's monitoring results* (2015), 21.

162 Cf. K. Michaeli, *The Impact of the International Criminal Tribunal for Yugoslavia on War Crime Investigations and Prosecutions in Serbia* (2011), 59.

163 The Law on Organization and Competences of Government Authorities in War Crimes Proceedings, Official Gazette of the Republic of Serbia, No 67/2003, and subsequent amendments.

164 For more information on the war crimes prosecution office, see: http://www.tuzilastvorz.org.rs/sr/ (last visited 10 December 2018), and on the war crimes department, see: http://www.bg.vi.sud.rs/lt/articles/o-visem-sudu/uredjenje/sudska-odeljenja/ (last visited 10 December 2018).

165 Cf. Michaeli, 'The Impact of the ICTY in Serbia', *supra* note 162, 59; coercion was exerted most notably through the *European Union* with its conditionality policy. I have elaborated on the EU's conditionality policy elsewhere: K.-H. Brodersen, 'The ICTY's Conditionality Dilemma', 22 *European Journal of Crime, Criminal Law and Criminal Justice* (2014) 3, 219.

166 Cf. L. Rüedi, *War Crimes Trials in Bosnia and Herzegovina: Selected Aspects of Transitional Justice Mechanisms* (2015), 86.

In the following, the ICTY transferred eight Rule 11*bis* cases involving 13 accused to the countries of the former Yugoslavia:[167] ten to BiH, two to Croatia, and one to Serbia.[168] In addition, the Tribunal has provided professional advice on reforming relevant legislation, especially in areas such as command responsibility and witness protection, so that these cases could be properly adjudicated.[169]

The calculation was that Rule 11*bis* cases would be a "catalyst for the strengthening of competent national judicial systems"[170] and that once they would be completed successfully, prosecutions and trials for international crimes would become the norm.[171] Opinions about the success of this rule of law promotion initiative are split, with the ICTY viewing it as very positive,[172] and while in BiH some actors agree,[173] other are more

167 Cf. ICTY, 'Transfer of Cases', available at http://www.icty.org/en/cases/transfer-cases (last visited 10 December 2018).

168 Although Serbia strived for receiving cases from the ICTY (cf. Michaeli, 'The Impact of the ICTY in Serbia', supra note 162, 67), only one case was referred to Serbia under Rule 11*bis* (cf. ICTY, 'Vladimir Kovacevic Declared Unfit to Stand Trial', Press Release, OK/MOW/1069e, 12 April 2006, available at http://www.icty.org/en/press/vladimir-kovacevic-declared-unfit-stand-trial (last visited 10 December 2018)). While the Bench declared it was satisfied that the Serbian legal system met the fair trial requirement, the fact that the *Kovačević* case was the only one referred to Serbia was not a source of pride considering the opposite conclusion reached by the Bench one year prior: in the *Mrkšić* case (the Vukovar Three case), Serbia's bid for referral was rejected (just as Croatia's) by the Referral Bench on the grounds of fair trial concerns (cf. ICTY, *Prosecutor v. Mrkšić, Radić, Šljivančanin*, 'Decision on Prosecutor's Motion to Withdraw Motion and Request for Referral of Indictment under Rule 11*bis*', IT-95-13/1-PT, Referral Bench, 30 June 2005). Serbia was also denied referral of the *Mejakić* case in April 2006, albeit on grounds that BiH possessed a stronger nexus with the case; cf. ICTY, *Prosecutor v. Mejakić*, Decision on Joint Defense Appeal against Decision on Referral under Rule 11*bis*, IT-02-65, Referral Bench, 7 April 2006.

169 Cf. ICTY, 'Completion Strategy', *supra* note 13.

170 *Ibid.*

171 Interview with a former international prosecutor in the Bosnian State Prosecution, The Hague, 7 December 2016.

172 Interview with a representative of the ICTY Office of the Prosecutor, The Hague, 25 November 2016; interview with an ICTY judge, The Hague, 2 December 2016.

173 Interview with a former international prosecutor in the Bosnian State Prosecution, The Hague, 7 December 2016; interview with a prosecutor of the Bosnian State Prosecution, Sarajevo, 9 February 2017; interview with a SCBiH judge, Sarajevo, 1 February 2017.

skeptical.[174] The ICTY especially emphasized that the threat of taking back the case if it is not dealt with properly – and the OSCE monitoring would provide proof for that – would have made national actors to be particularly cautious in handling these cases. In addition, Bosnians praise the tailor-made training provided by the OSCE, which directly addressed the needs of the local judiciary, which were observed and assembled in the OSCE's trial monitoring of Rule 11*bis* cases.[175] However, what is for sure is that the international community, the ICTY included, was watching how BiH dealt with the Rule 11*bis* referrals. People who were involved at the time claim that everyone was therefore doing their very best to "do it right".[176]

In addition to the referral cases, the OTP transferred evidentiary material to national judiciaries and granted them access to electronic databases and archives.[177] In the first place, case files were transferred regarding suspects investigated by the OTP but where no indictments were ever issued. Here, national judiciaries were enabled to bring these investigations to a conclusion on the basis of the evidence received from the ICTY and to raise indictments where appropriate. In a second place, several mechanisms in view of collaboration on evidentiary issues were put in place.[178] Similar to transferring ready-made Rule 11*bis* cases, these initiatives had

174 Interview with a Bosnian defense counsel, Sarajevo, 31 January 2017; interview with a representative of an international organization, Sarajevo, 2 February 2017; in particular, they maintain that too few cases were referred, and the threat to revoke the referral was too unrealistic to actually make a difference.

175 Interview with representatives of an international organization, Sarajevo, 2 February 2017; interview with a SCBiH judge, Sarajevo, 2 February 2017.

176 Interview with a former staff member of the Bosnian State Prosecution, 2 February 2017; interview with a former international prosecutor at the Bosnian State Prosecution, The Hague, 7 December 2017.

177 Cf. ICTY, 'Completion Strategy', *supra* note 13.

178 For instance, the OTP responds to specific requests from national prosecutors for information relating to their investigations; national liaison prosecutors sent to The Hague by the domestic judiciaries have direct access to the ICTY OTP databases and can directly use the material found there for investigations and prosecutions at national level; the ICTY is producing transcripts of its key proceedings in Bosnian, Croatian and Serbian (BCS) with the aim of improving the ability of national legal practitioners to access and search through testimony given before the ICTY for the purpose of their domestic proceedings; and also the Tribunal's Appeals Chamber Case Law Research Tool, which contains a compilation of summaries of the most important Appeals Chamber decisions, is being translated into BCS. In addition, specially tailored trainings are provided to lawyers in the region in order to assist them in accessing the Tribunal's records; cf. ICTY, 'Working with the Region', available at http://www.icty.org/en/about/office-of-the-prosecutor/working-with-the-region (last visited 10 December 2018);

the aim of enabling domestic legal actors to initiate investigations and prosecutions on their own, but still be supported by the ICTY.

II. Enhancing Competence: Capacity Building

In light of serious concerns about the state of the judicial systems in the former Yugoslavia,[179] in particular in terms of independence and competence, the 2002 ICTY completion strategy proposal already entailed recommendations about a number of reforms to be carried out in BiH. In particular, the judges advised incorporating all international crimes into the country's substantive penal law, to strengthen fair trial rights,[180] to improve detention conditions, to abolish the death penalty, to ensure the independence and impartiality of the judiciary, and to adopt a code of professional conduct for the judiciary.[181]

Despite this early engagement in advice on legal reform, capacity building had not been on the ICTY's priority list for long. Interaction between ICTY judges and their local counterparts was very difficult in the beginning, especially with Serbia. Apart from the political conditions which made such interaction difficult, the mutual mistrust between the judiciaries and the prevailing opinion amongst ICTY judges that this was not part of the mandate of the Tribunal contributed to the professional disconnect between the two systems.[182] In 2002, *David Tolbert*, former Senior Legal Adviser to the President of the ICTY, wrote about the ICTY's failure to build domestic legal capacity as "catastrophic" since "outside the relatively small number of accused who have faced or will face trial in The Hague", the local mechanisms "to bring to justice the scores of other perpetrators who committed serious violations of international humanitarian law in

---

ICTY, 'Capacity Building', available at http://www.icty.org/en/outreach/capacity-building (last visited 10 December 2018).

179 Cf. Jorda, 'Report on the Judicial Status of the ICTY', *supra* note 33.

180 In particular that public proceedings must be guaranteed, that the accused must be tried within a reasonable time, that the principle of the presumption of innocence and the equality of arms must be respected and that the victims and witnesses must be duly protected; cf. Jorda, 'Report on the Judicial Status of the ICTY', *supra* note 33, 25.

181 Cf. Jorda, 'Report on the Judicial Status of the ICTY', *supra* note 33, 18, 25.

182 Cf. Michaeli, 'The Impact of the ICTY in Serbia', *supra* note 162, 49-50.

the territory of the former Yugoslavia"[183] were ineffective. He deplored the irony of the "legacy of the rule of law"[184] that the ICTY would leave behind: despite the millions spent on building a judicial infrastructure in The Hague, virtually no effective enforcement of these laws persisted in the courts that ultimately matter most: the region's domestic courts.[185]

As late as 2008, there was a shift in thinking with the Tribunal beginning to develop a program on its legacy which put special emphasis on enhancing the capacity of domestic systems in the region. Consequently, the Tribunal intensified the interaction with the local judiciaries, studied their needs and responded to them directly.[186] Today, the ICTY describes supporting legal professionals and institutions in the region as a "key aspect of the Tribunal's work"[187]. Since 2010, the ICTY *Outreach Program* is responsible for capacity building by organizing working visits, training seminars, workshops and other activities, in order for the Tribunal to transfer its expertise to local counterparts in a wide range of areas, ranging from legal jurisprudence to courtroom techniques and witness protection.[188]

Although over the years the ICTY managed to cultivate a positive working relationship with Serbian institutions entrusted with war crimes prosecutions,[189] contact between the ICTY and the Bosnian judiciary was much more regular and intensive than with actors from the Serbian judiciary.[190] Amongst other reasons, this was due to the fact that most Rule 11*bis* cases had been referred to BiH and the ICTY consequently geared its capacity building efforts towards that country in order to address the shortcomings

---

183 D. Tolbert, 'The International Criminal Tribunal for the Former Yugoslavia: unforeseen Success and Foreseeable Shortcomings', 26 *The Fletcher Forum of World Affairs* (2002) 2, 7, 12.

184 V. Hussain, 'Sustaining Judicial Rescues: The Role of Outreach and Capacity Building Efforts in War Crimes Tribunals', 45 *Virginia Journal of International Law* (2005) 2, 547, 562.

185 Cf. Tolbert, 'Unforeseen Success and Foreseeable Shortcomings' *supra* note 183, 8.

186 Cf. Michaeli, 'The Impact of the ICTY in Serbia', *supra* note 162, 57; an overview on the activities can be found under ICTY, 'Overview of Capacity Building Activities', available at http://www.icty.org/en/outreach/capacity-building/overview-activities (last visited 10 December 2018).

187 ICTY, 'Capacity Building', *supra* note 178.

188 Cf. ICTY, 'Overview of Capacity Building Activities', *supra* note 186.

189 Cf. Michaeli, 'The Impact of the ICTY in Serbia', *supra* note 162, 5.

190 See, amongst others, the project's calendar of activities under OSCE, 'War Crimes Justice Project – Calender of Activities', available at http://www.icty.org/x/file/Outreach/capacity_building/wcjp_activity_calendar.pdf (last visited 10 December 2018).

within the institutional dimension of the rule of law that were observed in the course of these local trials. In BiH, one can also observe greater impact:[191] for instance, the SCBiH regularly uses ICTY case law concerning the interpretation of different international crimes or modes of liability, or in order to fill gaps in their criminal procedure.[192]

III. Raising Awareness in order to Build a Culture of Law: Outreach Program

As mentioned in section D. II., the beginning of the Tribunal's work was marked by a virtual absence of contact between the local judiciaries and actors in The Hague. Likewise, in its early years, the ICTY was reluctant to communicate with the citizens of the former Yugoslavia about the objectives and goals of the Tribunal.[193] Consequently, in the region, people sensed that the primary audience for the ICTY was the international community, that it mainly sought to further develop international humanitarian, human rights, and criminal law, and that it was rather an enforcer of the *international rule of law*,[194] than contributing to the *national rule of law*. It was viewed as remote and disconnected from the population. Also the fact that there was little information available about and from the ICTY (at least in local languages) was frequently used and abused for propaganda purposes by its opponents. And indeed, only when the ICTY realized how poorly it was perceived in the region and that this negative perception impacted its work, it began thinking about communicating with the local au-

191 For a critical review of capacity building initiatives in BiH, see A. Chehtman, 'Developing Bosnia and Herzegovina's Capacity to Process War Crimes Cases: Critical Notes on a 'Success Story'', 9 *Journal of International Criminal Justice* (2011) 3, 547.

192 The author has elaborated on this elsewhere: K.-H. Brodersen, '"We learnt that from The Hague" – How the ICTY influenced the fairness of criminal trials in the former Yugoslavia', in C. Stahn *et. al.* (eds.), *Legacies of the International Criminal Tribunal for the Former Yugoslavia: A Multidisciplinary Account* (forthcoming 2019); while local actors both in Bosnia and Herzegovina as well as in Serbia appreciate the close collaboration with the ICTY, they do insist that initiatives from other partners, such as the OSCE, were more useful; interviews with national prosecutors (Belgrade, 19 January 2017 and Sarajevo, 9 February 2017).

193 Cf. N. H. Pentelovitch, 'Seeing Justice Done: The Importance of Prioritizing Outreach Efforts at International Criminal Tribunals', 39 *Georgetown Journal of International Law* (2007) 3, 445, 451.

194 Cf. Hussain, 'Sustaining Judicial Rescues', *supra* note 184, 561-562.

dience.[195] ICTY President *Gabrielle Kirk McDonald* then initiated the *Outreach Program* in 1999, six years into the Tribunal's existence. In hindsight, it is described as "a milestone in the Tribunal's progression to maturity"[196] and "a sign that the court had become deeply aware that its work would resonate far beyond the judicial mandate of deciding the guilt or innocence of individual accused."[197] With the establishment of the *Outreach Program*, the Tribunal had recognized that it had a role to play in the process of dealing with the past in the former Yugoslavia, and that it could contribute to raising awareness about the accountability proceedings taking place in The Hague, and to spreading the truth that had been found in the course of these proceedings.

The *Outreach Program* was therefore effectively designed as a massive public relations and information spreading initiative. It consisted of several components, with particular emphasis on reaching out to the youth.[198] The first, and arguably the most important, step was to regularly translate ICTY materials into BCS, including the website. Also, live broadcasting of the proceedings on the internet commenced. Since 2000, offices had been opened in Belgrade, Pristina, Sarajevo and Zagreb, responsible for communicating with the media, the political, and the legal community, governmental and nongovernmental organizations, universities and high schools, victims associations, and diplomatic representatives.[199] According to the ICTY, thousands of people came into direct contact with the Tribunal through a variety of activities every year. These activities included work with the younger generation, grassroots communities, and the media; visits to the ICTY; and the production of a variety of information materials, multi-media website features, and social media outputs.[200] At least as of the moment that all fugitives had been arrested in 2011, the Tribunal yet again enhanced and methodologically revised its outreach efforts, as it saw the

195 Cf. S. Darehshori, 'Lessons for Outreach from the Ad Hoc Tribunals, the Special Court for Sierra Leone, and the International Criminal Court,' 14 *New England Journal of International and Comparative Law* (2007) 2, 299, 301.

196 ICTY, 'Outreach Programme,' available at http://www.icty.org/en/outreach/outreach-programme (last visited 10 December 2018).

197 *Ibid.*

198 For Youth Outreach, see http://www.icty.org/en/outreach/youth-outreach; for a list of activities, see http://www.icty.org/en/outreach/activities-archive; for the annual reports, see http://www.icty.org/en/outreach/outreach-annual-reports (all last visited 10 December 2018).

199 At the time of writing, only the offices in Belgrade and Sarajevo were still operating.

200 Cf. ICTY, 'Outreach Programme,' *supra* note 196.

"definitive opportunity to work with the communities in the region to reflect on the Tribunal's achievements and carry that legacy forward."[201]

Arguably, although many observers feel that the effort was too limited in scope and came too late to have any real effect,[202] through its outreach program the ICTY contributed to "shrinking the space for denial"[203] in the former Yugoslavia, which is the basis for a culture of law – the cultural dimension of the rule of law. In addition, thanks to lessons learned from the ICTY, outreach has now become a key component of international criminal justice.[204] Many of its initiatives, especially accessible publications on the prosecutors' investigations, the courts' trial work and their procedures, as well as outreach to the youth has been taken up in BiH, and even Serbia.[205]

E. Conclusion

The goal of the research this contribution is based on was to shed light on what made the ICTY engage in a promotion of the rule of law, what the ICTY understood by the *rule of law*, and how this understanding influenced its – very indirect – rule of law promotion efforts. The analysis presented here permits several conclusions.

First, the discourse and document analyses reveal that the ICTY's notion of the rule of law changed over time. Very early and very late references highlighted its role in promoting what has been termed the *international rule of law*. In between, the *national rule of law* was much more prominent in the ICTY's discourse. Clearly, this shift in notions reflects the changing standing of the ICTY over time: in its early and late years it sought to justify its existence and underline its achievements and it did so by emphasiz-

201 ICTY, 'Outreach Programme', *supra* note 196.

202 Cf. Hussain, 'Sustaining Judicial Rescues', *supra* note 184, 563; Tolbert, 'Unforeseen Success and Foreseeable Shortcomings', *supra* note 183, 14.

203 A phrase that became prominent with the book of Orentlicher, 'Shrinking the Space for Denial', *supra* note 5.

204 Cf. Darehshori, 'Lessons for Outreach', *supra* note 195, 299.

205 Interviews with national prosecutors (Belgrade, 19 January 2017 and Sarajevo, 9 February 2017); although it should be noted that while the SCBiH publishes all its decisions and judgments online, the war crimes chamber at the Belgrade High Court has a very restrictive policy towards access to court materials: they are not available online and one must ask for permission to access them, which is given only concerning particularly mentioned judgments, which makes a comprehensive search impossible.

ing its role as the enforcer of universal international criminal and humanitarian law. Around the 2000s and beyond, the completion strategy required the Tribunal to rethink its role, in particular because it realized that the domestic justice systems in the former Yugoslavia needed assistance in preparing for receiving Rule 11*bis* cases from The Hague. What followed was a range of measures aimed at contributing to the consolidation of the domestic justice systems in the region, which effectively rendered Rule 11*bis* the legal mechanism the ICTY's rule of law promotion efforts were rooted in.

The analysis further reveals that the *national rule of law* as understood by the ICTY has a normative dimension, an institutional dimension, and a cultural dimension. In the normative dimension, emphasis was put on the necessity of a legislative framework that foresees the adjudication of international crimes and guarantees certain fundamental human rights, especially fair trial rights. This is the law that should rule. The institutional components of a justice system that ensure that it *actually* operates under the rule of law comprise independent and impartial judicial organs that work efficiently and in a fair, nondiscriminatory, and transparent manner. Lastly, the ICTY recognized that a culture of law is paramount and that ordinary citizens, as well as public officials, and representatives of the judicial sector adopt an ideology of legality.

A third revelation is that within the ICTY's notion of the *national rule of law*, its emphasis on different elements also changed over time. Mostly, this reflected the current challenges the Tribunal or the countries of the former Yugoslavia faced at the respective time. Interestingly, the Tribunal reacted to these events and adapted its rule of law promotion efforts accordingly. For instance, in the early 2000s emphasis was placed on the necessity to conduct national war crimes proceedings and to conduct them fairly and without discrimination. This related to the normative dimension of the Tribunal's rule of law conception. It hence started to actively lobby and advise on the setting up of specialized domestic institutions that would deal with international crimes, and facilitated their start by transferring ready-made cases and other material. As of 2008, when the ICTY reflected upon the legacy it would leave behind, it enhanced its capacity building to strengthen domestic competence and efficiency to prosecute and adjudicate international crimes cases, as this was determined to be one of the major obstacles to successful international crimes trials in the former Yugoslavia. These initiatives sought to consolidate the institutional dimension of the rule of law. Around the same time, bearing in mind its impending closure, the ICTY called upon national judiciaries to raise awareness of international crimes trials so that the local population would develop trust that impunity is no longer accepted. It was hoped that this would strengthen the culture of law – the cultural dimension of the rule of law. In order to contribute to this awareness raising and to serve as an example for similar local initiatives, the Tribunal rendered its *Outreach Program* more robust.

It has been shown that the ICTY engaged in rule of law promotion on the basis of its completion strategy and, in particular, Rule 11*bis* of its RPE. Although these initiatives were not based on an explicitly expressed definition of the rule of law, a mosaic of elements the Tribunal associated with this concept emerges from its case law and public statements. It was demonstrated that the Tribunal's rule of law promotion efforts directly related to this rule of law conception. This piece, therefore, contributes to understanding the legal and normative bases of the ICTY's rule of law strengthening efforts in the post-conflict former Yugoslavia.

International Investment Law and the Rule of Law

Peter-Tobias Stoll[*]

Table of Contents

---

* Prof. Dr. Peter-Tobias Stoll, Full Professor for Public Law and International Law at the Georg-August-University Göttingen, Director at the Institute for International Law and European Law and holder of the Jean Monnet Chair for European Union and Global Sustainable Development through Law.

Abstract

International investment law appeals to a lawyer's appetite for the rule of law by disciplining the exercise of power between States and foreign investors through legalization and judicialization. Originally supposed to serve as a fix to promote foreign investments in developing countries in times of legal uncertainties, now, thousands of bilateral investment agreements exist, and the number of cases in investment arbitration has exploded in the last decade. Further, there is a tendency of generalization, as investment protection now features as a standard element of international trade agreements, far beyond the original focus on developing countries. A number of flaws and shortcomings of the rules and procedures became apparent in the course of the more frequent use of the system and resulted in much discussion within the expert community, which resulted in some changes. Furthermore, the long neglected possibility became apparent, that investment claims could be directed against industrialized countries and that the conduct of their authorities could be subjected to review by international arbitration tribunals. This sparked heated public debates, particularly so in the EU. These two developments have in common, that they implicitly as well as explicitly raised the issue of the rule of law. This paper will assess the system of international investment law as it stands, its critique and its reform, through the lens of the rule of law. It will also make a highly idealistic proposal on the further development of international investment protection. In concluding, it will reflect on the proper use of the rule of law in legal analysis, by setting out the different perspectives in which the term may be employed, and the methodological consequences.

A. The Emergence of International Investment Law

From the very beginning, international law contained rules on the treatment of aliens and their property, and recognized a right of the home States of such individuals to exercise diplomatic protection.[1] The modern treaty-based international investment law stands for an updated continuation of this practice. The most significant updates to international investment law in modern times are the detailed rules on expropriation and

---

1 For more detailed information on historical origins of International Investment Law see A. Newcombe & L. Paradell, *Law and Practice of Investment Treaties: Standards and Treatment* (2009), 3-18.

compensation payments, as well as direct procedural capacity of foreign investors on the international level. International investment law in the modern sense emerged as a reaction to various events that occurred in the first half of the twentieth century. *Calvo*, a diplomat and scholar of quite some influence, particularly in Latin America, pleaded that foreign investors should be treated equally to domestic investors under domestic law, rather than enjoying a separate international law standard of treatment.[2] Much more radically, a strong movement in the *United Nations* and particularly so in the *General Assembly* called for a sort of absolute sovereignty, including full independence to regulate economic activities, in an attempt to establish a *New International Economic Order*, which was meant to bring justice to developing countries after the end of colonialism.[3] These contestations went beyond academic debate and diplomatic activity. They also encouraged countries to legislate and to act accordingly in practice. A number of expropriations[4] and the ongoing debates severely affected the investment climate and the actual flows of foreign direct investments, which were urgently needed to promote economic development.

In this situation, the two pillars of contemporary international investment law were established. First, the contested customary international law standards were seconded by treaty-based standards incorporated in bilateral agreements, which also gave some more detail in order to respond to the needs of modern investment realities. As is well known, the first of these bilateral investment agreements was concluded between Germany and Pakistan in 1958. As for today, more than 3000 of such agreements have been concluded, and over time further developed to embrace more standards and rules for the pre-investment stage.[5]

Second, a forum for investor-State arbitration was set up in the framework of the *World Bank*. The *International Centre for the Settlement of Invest-*

2 C. Calvo, *Le droit International théorique et pratique: précéde d'un exposé historique des progrès de la science du droit des gens*, 4th ed. (1887), 138, para. 1276.

3 See GA Res. 3201 (S-VI), UN Doc A/Res/S–6/3201, 1 May 1974.

4 For instance, the large-scale nationalization in Russian Socialist Federated Soviet Republic following the Revolution in 1917; in Mexico in 1917 following the Agrarian Reform; furthermore, the nationalization of the Anglo-Iranian Oil Company in 1951 in Iran and the nationalization of the Universal Suez Maritime Canal by Egypt in 1956.

5 United Nations Conference on Trade and Development [UNCTAD], 'World Investment Report 2017: Investment and the Digital Economy' (2017), available at http://worldinvestmentreport.unctad.org/world-investment-report-2017/#key-messages (last visited 13 December 2018).

ment Disputes (ICSID) and its establishing agreement[6] provide for investor-State arbitration, drawing from established rules and practices in international commercial arbitration. The procedure furnishes the investor with an international legal remedy (Article 1 of the Agreement) and consequently forecloses the investor home State from exercising diplomatic protection (Article 27). Furthermore, in general, the procedure is detached from domestic remedies as it does not require the exhaustion of local remedies (Article 26). On the other hand, and in order to secure its effectiveness, the awards of ICSID arbitration enjoy an exceptionally strong enforcement, see Articles 53 (1), 54 (1).

B. *International Investment Law: Challenge, Contestation and Reform*

This combination of treaty-based substantial standards of protection and the unique arbitration procedure has proven to be quite successful over the years, as the growing numbers of bilateral investment treaties (BITs) and the increasing caseload in investment arbitration may signify.[7] This extensive practice revealed certain weaknesses of the system, which gave rise to far-reaching criticism and demonstrated a need for reform in detail. This reform of international investment law is currently under way. Three strands of discourse and development can be seen, which took place at different times and levels, and were interconnected.

A first line of development took place in the 1990s, and responded to the increasing caseload in investment arbitration. With investment arbitration becoming a frequently used and standard element of international economic law, the relatively few cases, which involved manifest flaws and errors became significant in number and called for action. While in accordance with the very character and purpose of arbitration, the awards are final (Article 53 (1)), the provisions of the ICSID Convention on annulment of awards (Articles 51 and 52) were extensively interpreted in order to allow for a correction of the award in exceptional cases of manifest error.[8]

6 *Convention on the Settlement of Investment Disputes between States and Nationals of Other States*, 18 March 1965, 575 UNTS 159 [ICSID Convention].

7 See UNCTAD's Overview of Investment Agreements, available at https://investmentpolicyhub.unctad.org/IIA (last visited 13 December 2018) and the ICSID Caseload Statistics, available at https://icsid.worldbank.org/en/Pages/resources/ICSID-Caseload-Statistics.aspx (last visited 13 December 2018).

8 *CDC Group plc v. Republic of Seychelles*, Decision on Annulment, ICSID Case No. ARB/02/14, 29 June 2005, para. 36.

The extensive interpretation of the annulment provisions developed in actual procedures, and was seconded by the wider investment law community. Today, it is a widely accepted and established practice, that an annulment procedure can take place for a number of reasons and many observers agree, that in terms of functionality, this move goes into the direction of an appellate procedure.[9] Also, the increasing caseload and the relatively small group of arbitrators preferred by parties resulted in cases of doubts as to their impartiality and independence. A code of conduct was elaborated and adopted to address this problem.[10] Lastly, in responding to criticism against the former confidentiality of the procedure, transparency became an issue and a practice developed to make available awards as well as submissions of parties to the public. Recently, hearings were also streamed.[11] A more systematic approach to transparency is now pursued with the *Mauritius Convention*.[12]

However, this reform of investment law did not only address its procedural parts, but also substance. From 1990 onwards, in a second move, a more general trend to mainstream sustainable development, environmental protection, human rights and labor standards into international econo-

9 C. Tams, 'An Appealing Opinion? The Debate About an ICSID Appellate Structure', *57 Beiträge zum Transnationalen Wirtschaftrecht* (2006) 5, 9; R. Dolzer & C. Schreuer, *Principles of International Investment Law*, 2nd ed. (2012), 302.

10 International Bar Association, 'IBA Guidelines on Conflict of Interest in International Arbitration' (2014), available at https://www.ibanet.org/Publications/publications_IBA_guides_and_free_materials.aspx#Practice%20Rules%20and%20Guidelines (last visited 13 December 2018); Comprehensive and Economic Trade Agreement, 30 October 2016, EU and Canada, Annex 29-B, available at http://ec.europa.eu/trade/policy/in-focus/ceta/ceta-chapter-by-chapter (last visited 13 December 2018) [CETA].

11 C. Trehearne, 'Transparency, Legitimacy, and Investor-State Dispute Settlement: What Can We Learn From the Streaming of Hearings?' (09 June 2018), Kluwer Arbitration Blog, available at http://arbitrationblog.kluwerarbitration.com/2018/06/09/transparency-legitimacy-investor-state-dispute-settlement-can-learn-streaming-hearings (last visited 13 December 2018).

12 *United Nations Convention on Transparency in Treaty-based Investor-State Arbitration*, 10 December 2014, 54 ILM (2015) 4, 747.

mic regulations emerged, which was promoted by the public[13], by NGOs[14] and a number of governments.[15] Soon, international investment law came into the focus of such developments and these aspects were taken into account in arbitrations in view of the legitimate policy space to be afforded to host States.[16] Even more significantly, chapters and articles on sustainable development, environmental protection, human rights and labor standards became a standard element of recent investment agreements and model agreements around the world.[17]

A third line of criticism and development concerns the interrelationship between international investment law and domestic legal systems. It marks

13 International Institute for Environment and Development, 'Rethinking Investment Treaties, Laws and Contracts' (2018), available at https://www.iied.org/rethinking-investment-treaties-laws-contracts (last visited 13 December 2018); Columbia Centre on Sustainable Investment, 'Five-Pillar Framework for Sustainable International Investment', available at http://ccsi.columbia.edu/about-us/five-pillar-framework-for-sustainable-international-investment-2/ (last visited 13 December 2018).

14 OECD, 'Guidelines for Multinational Enterprises' (2011 Edition), available at http://www.oecd.org/daf/inv/mne/48004323.pdf (last visited 13 December 2018); UNCTAD, 'Investment Policy Framework for Sustainable Development' (2015), available at http://unctad.org/en/PublicationsLibrary/diaepcb2015d5_en.pdf (last visited 13 December 2018).

15 See the much discussed Norwegian draft model BIT, Kingdom of Norway, 'Agreement for the Promotion and Protection of Investments' (2007), available at https://www.italaw.com/sites/default/files/archive/ita1031.pdf (last visited 13 December 2018), with cover letter, available at https://www.italaw.com/sites/default/files/archive/ita1030.pdf (last visited 13 December 2018) and commentary, available at https://www.italaw.com/sites/default/files/archive/ita1029.pdf (last visited 13 December 2018). However, the project was eventually abandoned after a public hearing.

16 *Marvin Roy Feldman Karpa v. United Mexican States*, Award, ICSID Case No. ARB(AF)/99/1, 16 December 2002, para. 103; *Técnicas Medioambientales Tecmed, S.A. v. United Mexican States*, Award, ICSID Case No. ARB(AF)/00/2, 29 May 2003, para. 121.

17 See, *South Korea-Peru Free Trade Agreement*, 14 November 2010, South Korea and Peru, Ch. 18, available at http://www.sice.oas.org/TPD/PER_KOR/PER_KOR_Texts_e/18_KPFTA_Labor.pdf (last visited 13 December 2018); *Agreement Between Japan and the Kingdom of Cambodia for the Liberalization, Promotion and Protection of Investment*, 14 June 2007, Japan and Cambodia, Article 24, available at http://www.meti.go.jp/policy/trade_policy/epa/pdf/epa/J-CAM_English.pdf (last visited 13 December 2018); *Agreement Between the Government of the Republic of Korea and the Government of Japan for the Liberalisation, Promotion and Protection of Investment*, 22 March 2002, Korea and Japan, Articles 11, 16 (1), 21, available at http://investmentpolicyhub.unctad.org/Download/TreatyFile/1727 (last visited 13 December 2018).

a departure in the way international investment law has been looked at thus far. Whereas so far, international investment law and its developments were driven by an international law perspective, now domestic constitutional aspects became key. In this perspective, the potential interference of international investment law with the proper domestic system of the exercise and control of public authority by way of legislation, administration and judicial review came to the forefront.[18]

This latter kind of criticism came up as the consequence of a paradigm change, which will very likely change the landscape of investment protection in the years to come.[19] Investment law originally was intended to protect investors from the North in their operations in developing countries, while not significantly affecting industrialized countries themselves. While bilateral investment treaties were drafted so as to oblige all sides to afford protection on equal terms, this protection was hardly expected to materialize. It was understood, that it would be the countries in the North, which would export capital and benefit from investment protection. The possibility, that the *developing* parties to the agreements could turn into capital exporters, as in reality happened later with countries such as India and China was hardly taken into account.[20] Also, in Western industrialized countries the view prevailed, that protection under the domestic legal order was superior to investment law standards and that accordingly, international investment law would not be relevant.[21] As claims initiated against Canada

---

18 See, in detail on the German constitutional law perspective, P.-T. Stoll, T. P. Holterhus & H. Gött, *Investitionsschutz und Verfassung* (2017).

19 See generally on international investment law's "shifting paradigm" S. Hindelang & M. Krajewski (eds), *Shifting Paradigms in International Investment Law* (2016).

20 On the European roots of BITs and their purpose to safeguard existing investments in former colonies see J. W. Salacuse, *The Law of Investment Treaties*, 2nd ed. (2015), 100-101; criticised as neo-colonalism by K. Miles, *The Origins of International Investment Law: Empire, Environment and the Safeguarding of Capital* (2013), 120; M. Sornarajah, *Resistance and Change in the International Law on Foreign Investment* (2015), 10-44; cf. also the observation by O. de Schutter *et al.*, 'Foreign Direct Investment, Human Development and Human Rights: Framing the Issues', 3 *Human Rights and International Legal Discourse* (2009) 2, 137, 168 who consider the strengthening of provisions on human development provisions in BITs more likely as developing countries conclude BITs among another while remaining sceptical of its actual realization in practice.

21 P.-T. Stoll & T. P. Holterhus, "The 'Generalization' of International Investment Law in Constitutional Perspective", in Hindelang & Krajewski, *supra* note 19, 339, 342-343.

and Germany indicate,[22] this expectation did not withstand a reality test. Investors took advantage of investor-State dispute settlement in a number of cases and arbitration panels on occasion found measures failing to meet minimum standards of protection. This raised a sometimes heated debate in some countries, which particularly put into question the legitimacy of the system as such and investor-State dispute settlement more specifically.[23]

This debate came at a time, when new actors, approaches and formats emerged in the international investment system, pointing in different directions. First, there has been a tendency to expand the system. A number of newly capital-exporting States such as China became active, concluded a number of treaties and this way mutated from being rule takers to rule exporters.[24] In 2008, the Lisbon treaty furnished the EU with an exclusive competence in the field of *foreign direct investment* as part of its commercial policy powers.[25] This came in time for the EU to engage in the negotiation and conclusion of a large number of new and innovative trade agreements, for instance with the US, Canada, Singapore, Vietnam and others, which include investment chapters as a standard.[26] In contrast to earlier practice, where investment rules were mainly agreed upon with developing coun-

22 Canada has been subject to investment arbitration claims especially under NAFTA, see i.e. *S.D. Myers Inc v. Government of Canada*, UNCITRAL Final Award, 30 December 2002; the most prominent case against Germany in recent times related to the country's nuclear energy phase-out, see *Vattenfall AB and others v. Federal Republic of Germany*, ICSID Case No. ARB/12/12, pending at the time of writing.

23 Best coined as the "backlash" against international investment arbitration, see M. Waibel *et al.* (eds), *The Backlash Against Investment Arbitration: Perceptions and Reality* (2010).

24 See for example on China's policy to conclude BITs with African countries in preparing acquisitions of large-scale land leases by A. Telesetsky, 'A New Investment Deal in Asia and Africa', in C. Brown & K. Miles (eds), *Evolution in Investment Treaty Law and Arbitration* (2011), 539, 545-547.

25 *Treaty on the Functioning of the European Union*, Article 207 (1); see further CJEU, *Opinion Pursuant to Article 218(11) TFEU*, Opinion 2/15, 16 May 2017, ECLI:EU:C:2017:376, paras. 81-87.

26 CETA, *supra* note 10, *Free Trade Agreement between the European Union and the Republic of Singapore*, currently in the signing process, EU and Singapore, available at http://trade.ec.europa.eu/doclib/press/index.cfm?id=1437 (last visited 13 December 2018); *Free Trade Agreement Between the European Union and the Socialist Republic of Vietnam* [EU-Vietnam FTA], currently in the signing process, EU and Vietnam, available at http://trade.ec.europa.eu/doclib/press/index.cfm?id=1437 (last visited 13 December 2018); as to the USA, the EU aimed for concluding the *Transatlantic Trade and Investment Partnership* [TTIP], however the project came to a halt after a policy change by the US government, the EU textual proposal can

tries, this tendency, in the sense of a *generalization* saw investment protection as a standard element of international economic relations.[27]

At the same time, international investment law is under challenge. A number of States in Latin America and Africa did drop out of the system, are considering doing so or are engaged in developing alternative means.[28] At the same time, the system is severely criticized by sections of the public in the EU and elsewhere.[29]

To comfort these trends, investment treaty language nowadays accommodates the need to clarify major standards used and explicitly acknowledges a right to regulate.[30] Furthermore and in response to criticism as to the legitimacy of dispute settlement through arbitration and its predictability, the EU has proposed, and in some cases has already agreed up-

---

still be accessed at European Union, 'EU Negotiating Texts in TTIP' (2016), available at http://trade.ec.europa.eu/doclib/press/index.cfm?id=1230&serie=866&langId=en (last visited 13 December 2018). For an overview and current state of EU FTAs and other trade negotiations see European Commission, 'Overview of FTA and Other Trade Negotiations' (2018), available at http://trade.ec.europa.eu/doclib/docs/2006/december/tradoc_118238.pdf (last visited 13 December 2018); on the policy strategy see European Commission, 'Trade for All: Towards a More Responsible Trade and Investment Policy' (2015), available at http://trade.ec.europa.eu/doclib/docs/2015/october/tradoc_153846.pdf (last visited 13 December 2018).

27 Stoll & Holterhus, *supra* note 21, 342-343.

28 For example, South Africa, Indonesia, Bolivia and Ecuador terminated many of their BITs. The BITs concluded and their status is listed by the UNCTAD's Investment Policy Hub Website, see UNCTAD, 'International Investment Agreements Navigator' (2013), available at http://investmentpolicyhub.unctad.org/IIA/IiasByCountry#iiaInnerMenu (last visited 13 December 2018); on denunciation in general see A. Tzanakopoulos, 'Denunciation of the ICSID Convention under the General International Law of Treaties', in R. Hofmann & C. Tams (eds), *International Investment Law and General International Law: From Clinical Isolation to Systemic Integration?* (2011), 75. Other states did not terminate their BITs but changed their international investment protection policy. For example, Brazil continues to approve international investment treaties but rejects any provisions on international investment arbitration since its 2015 Model BIT, Federal Republic of Brazil, 'Model for a Cooperation and Facilitation Investment Agreement' (2015), available at http://investmentpolicyhub.unctad.org/Download/TreatyFile/4786 (last visited 13 December 2018).

29 See for example Greenpeace, 'From ISTS to ICS: A Leopard Can't Change Its Spots' (2016), available at http://www.greenpeace.org/eu-unit/Global/eu-unit/reports-briefings/2016/2016_02_11_Greenpeace%20Position%20Paper%20ICS_Final.pdf (last visited 13 December 2018).

30 On the changes in investment treaty design see the analysis by C. Henckels, 'Protecting Regulatory Autonomy Through Greater Precision in Investment Treaties: The TPP, CETA, and TTIP', 19 *Journal of International Economic Law* (2016) 1, 27.

on, a replacement of arbitration by a two-tier investment court system, including an appeals procedure.[31] Actually, efforts are being made to develop this into a *Multilateral Investment Court*.[32]

C. International Investment Law and the Rule of Law

Protecting foreign investors against measures of a host State appeals to the lawyers' senses for the rule of law. And indeed, in various forms to be seen in detail, international investment law can be seen as promoting it. However, also the critiques of this particular area of international law might point to the rule of law in calling for reforms. As will be seen, however, the full implications of looking at international investment law through the lens of the rule of law only become apparent, where a proper line is drawn between the international and domestic dimensions of the rule of law.

I. The Obvious: Investment Law to Promote the Rule of Law

1. Legalization and Judicialization for International Peace and Security

First of all, the development of international investment law can be seen as an important achievement for the international rule of law. Both, the legalization of investment protection by BITs and *investor-State dispute settlement* (ISDS) – seen as judicialization – put rules and procedures in place, where power play and uncertainty reigned before.[33]

---

31 CETA, *supra* note 10, Article 8.27-8.28; EU-Vietnam FTA, *supra* note 26, Ch. 8 Part II Articles 12-13. The EU's approach is also suggested as a general international model, for example by the International Institute for Sustainable Development [IISD], 'A Sustainable Toolkit for Trade Negotiators: Trade and Investment as Vehicles for Achieving the 2030 Sustainable Development Agenda' (2017), para. 5.5.3., available at https://www.iisd.org/toolkits/sustainability-toolkit-for-trade-negotiators/ (last visited 13 December 2018).

32 See most recently Council of the European Union, *Negotiating Directives for a Convention Establishing a Multilateral Court for the Settlement of Investment Disputes*, 20 March 2018, 12981/17 ADD 1 DCL 1.

33 Supported for example by U. Kriebaum, 'Foreign Investments & Human Rights', 10 *Transnational Dispute Management* (2013) 1, 1; S. W. Schill & V. Djanic, 'International Investment Law and Community Interests', SIEL Working Paper 2016/01, 8-9, available at https://papers.ssrn.com/sol3/papers.cfm?abstract_id=2799500 (last visited 13 December 2018).

To fully appreciate the relevance of this, it should be recalled, that one of the basic tenets of the development of modern international law is to promote peace through the development of international rules and the establishment of means for the peaceful settlement of disputes.[34] Given the number of State-to-State disputes concerning the treatment of foreign investors in the past, amounting the use of force even in some cases[35], the establishment of international investment law surely is an achievement. This is so, because investment disputes are settled through legal means. Further, in engaging the investor and the host State, ISDS prevents or better still, excludes a potentially difficult confrontation with the investor home State. This is because Article 27 ICSID Convention explicitly prevents an investor home State from exercising diplomatic protection.

2. *Strengthening the Role of Law by Empowering the Individual*

Another obvious and impressive effect of international investment law is that it enables an individual to stand up against a State. As has been rightly observed, ISDS is one of the few areas, where international law, which in general is for States, stretches out to an individual.[36] In this regard, it comes close to the logic of human rights.[37] Indeed, human rights are often and rightly considered a core element of an international rule of law[38] and the same is certainly true for investment law in this perspective.

---

34 International dispute settlement as a means to promote international peace has its modern roots in the *Hague Convention for the Pacific Settlement of International Disputes*, 29 July 1899, 187 CTS 410 and *Hague Convention for the Pacific Settlement of International Disputes*, 18 October 1907, 205 CTS 233; for a contextualization of the role of international arbitration in international dispute settlement see for example P. Abel, 'Comparative Conclusions on Arbitral Dispute Settlement in Trade-Labour Matters Under US FTAs', in H. Gött (ed.), *Labour Standards in International Economic Law* (2018), 153, 156-158.

35 On the violent history of foreign investment protection see for example Miles, *supra* note 20, 19-121.

36 A. Peters, *Beyond Human Rights* (2016), 282-338.

37 See N. Klein, 'Human Rights and International Investment Law: Investment Protection as Human Right?', 4 *Goettingen Journal of International Law* (2012) 1, 179.

38 See for example *Universal Declaration of Human Rights*, 10 December 1948, UN Doc A/RES/3/217 A, Preamble, para. 3: "Whereas it is essential, if man is not to be compelled to have recourse, as a last resort, to rebellion against tyranny and oppression, that human rights should be protected by the rule of law"; UN Human Rights Council, *Human Rights, Democracy and the Rule of Law*, UN Doc. A/HRC/RES/19/36, 19 April 2012, para. 16 (d)-(j).

It has to be highlighted, that this marks a departure in the understanding of the rule of law. The traditional core of the rule of law is to establish rules, procedures and institutions, where power play prevailed.[39] The point at issue here is, that it is not just rules, procedures and institutions, but their content that counts as well.[40] The protection and respect for individuals as provided for by international investment law can be seen to reflect such a substantial dimension of the rule of law. By including such dimensions, the rule of law can be said to embody fundamental values.

3. *Strengthening the Rule of Law at Domestic Level?*

As is often observed, international investment law may promote the rule of law at the domestic level.[41] This is certainly true in that investment law standards of treatment relate to the conduct of public authorities within the domestic legal order of host States. However, it is worthwhile to look at this effect in some more detail and to contextualize it.

In a detailed perspective, first, this effect very likely depends on the level of the rule of law existing in the host country at hand. Indeed, where the reputation and stability of a legal system, including legislation, administration and jurisprudence are in question, the effect of international investment law may be substantial. However, where a stable and reliable legal system already exists, the effects of international investment law may be largely affirmative only, or minimal, or – as we will see later – even problematic.

Second, the extent and scope to which international investment law informs domestic legal systems is worth considering. This becomes particularly clear, if international investment law is seen in context with human rights law. Both come close in that they assign rights and legal protection to individuals and discipline States to that end. However, they differ in how this is to be achieved. Human rights law is much concerned with di-

---

39 On the genesis of the principle of the rule of law, see T. P. Holterhus, 'The History of the Rule of Law', in F. Lachenmann & R. Wolfrum (eds), 21 *Max Planck Yearbook of United Nations Law* (2018), 430.

40 *Ibid.*

41 See M. Sattorova, *The Impact of Investment Treaty Law on Host States*, (2018), 58; S. W. Schill, 'System Building in Investment Treaty Arbitration and Lawmaking', 12 *German Law Journal* (2011) 5, 1083, 1085; R. Dolzen, 'The Impact of International Investment Treaties on Domestic Administrative Law', 37 *NYU Journal of International Law and Politics* (2005) 4, 953, 971.

rect effect, proper implementation and access to justice and strives for being effective on the ground and to inform domestic legal systems to this end. Of course, international investment law may also produce a persuasive effect in view of domestic legal reform. In the sense of a spill-over effect, the related effects may well go beyond benefitting foreign investors and produce advantages also for national individuals and businesses. However, international investment law is much less explicit than human rights law at this point and hardly reflects a similar intention in view of the domestic legal order. Probably, the reason for this relates to the purposes of investment law. It is destined to specifically protect foreigners and relies on international dispute settlement.

4. *Development Dimensions of International Investment Law*

In connection to its contribution to the rule of law, international investment law is often said to be about development.[42] Indeed, the history, ambitions and real world effects of investment protection largely support this claim. It has been no accident, that the *World Bank* initiated the establishment of ICSID as a hub for ISDS in times of serious uncertainties about the legal security of investors under international law.[43] The facilitation of foreign direct investments has been seen as a necessary component of the Bank's mandate to promote economic development and as an essential complement to its own lending activities.[44] And indeed, with some caveats as to a proper quantification, the emerging international investment law system and ICSID as a core part of it have a substantial part in the promotion of foreign direct investment flows around the world.[45]

Even more, international investment law explicitly addresses the development concern in order to make sure, that protection is only afforded to those investments, which in a way contribute to the economic develop-

42 N. Monebhurrun, *La fonction du développement dans le droit international des investissements* (2016), 65; Y. Radi, 'International Investment Law and Development: A History of Two Concepts', in S. Schill, C. Tams, R. Hofmann (eds), *International Investment Law and Development: Bridging the Gap* (2015), 69, 74.

43 ICSID Convention, *supra* note 6, Preamble. See also A. R. Parra, *The History of ICSID* (2012), 11, 21-22.

44 *Articles of Agreement of the International Bank for Reconstruction and Development*, 27 December 1945, Article I, 2 UNTS 134.

45 UNCTAD, 'The Role of International Agreements in Attracting Foreign Direct Investment to Developing Countries' (2009), available at http://unctad.org/en/Docs/diaeia20095_en.pdf (last visited 13 December 2018).

ment in the host State.[46] The point at issue in this regard is the term *investment*, which is an essential precondition for protection in terms of substantial standards as well as of ISDS.[47]

However, improving legal security and protection to facilitate investment is just one way to see international investment law, the rule of law and development connected. Another way to look at it can build on the understanding that development builds on the rule of law and to ask, how international investment law can directly contribute in this way. Indeed, more recent economic research[48] and not least the writings of *Amartya Sen* have revealed, that the rule of law is a pertinent and critical element and driver of economic and social development.[49] From this point of view, however, the contribution of international investment law is likely to be less impressive for the reasons explained above in regard to the impact on the domestic legal order. While some spill-over effects can be expected to the benefit of domestic individuals and business operators, international investment law by large is focused on securing the rights and interests of foreign investors only.

II. Less Obvious: How the Rule of Law Informs International Investment Law

Asking for contributions of international investment law to the international rule of law is the obvious way to approach the relationship between the two. Yet, the opposite perspective is worth considering as well and arguably increasingly plays its role. This increasing relevance of the rule of law as a guiding principle in the development and practice in international investment law is more apparent, than it would appear at first glance.

46 *Salini Costruttori S.P.A. and Italstrade S.P.A. v. Kingdom of Morocco*, Decision on Jurisdiction, ICSID Case No. ARB/00/4, 23 July 2001, para. 52; *Joy Mining Machinery Limited v. The Arab Republic of Egypt*, Award on Jurisdiction, ICSID Case No. ARB/03/11, 6 August 2004, para. 53; *Malicorp Limited v. The Arab Republic of Egypt*, Award, ICSID Case No. ARB/08/18, 7 February 2011, para. 113.

47 See also M. Jezewski, 'Development Considerations in Defining Investment', in M. Cordonier Segger, M. W. Gehring & A. Newcombe (eds), *Sustainable Development in World Investment Law* (2011), 215, 219-221.

48 D. Kaufmann & A. Kraay, 'Growth Without Governance', World Bank Policy Research Working Paper No. 2928, 2002/11, available at https://ssrn.com/abstract=316861 (last visited 13 December 2018).

49 A. Sen, 'Global Justice', in J. Heckman, R. Nelson & L. Cabatingan (eds), *Global Perspective on the Rule of Law* (2010), 55.

1. Legal Certainty

An obvious first example for this is the issue of legal certainty. As has been seen, international investment law has been criticized for the rather general language of its substantive rules and the failure of investment arbitration to clarify those terms in a reliable way.[50] Foreseeability and predictability of the law and dispute settlement concern legal clarity and legal security, both of which belong to the core elements of legal certainty and the rule of law concept. A number of recent developments in international investment law address these points. The many efforts to clarify the concepts of indirect expropriation and fair and equitable treatment in recent bilateral investment treaties and in the investment chapters of trade agreements must be mentioned here.[51] Also and ultimately, the efforts to establish an international investment court are based on these grounds.[52]

A similar development concerns the earlier lack of means to correct errors in fact or law in arbitration, which was remedied by the extensive use of the annulment procedure and now shall be addressed by an appeals procedure, which is part of the concept of an international investment court.[53]

---

50 Dolzer & Schreuer, *supra* note 9, 35.

51 For instance, CETA, *supra* note 10, Art 8.12, 8.10 (2); *Treaty Between the Government of the United States of America and the Government of the Republic of Rwanda Concerning the Encouragement and Reciprocal Protection of Investment*, 19 February 2008, United States of America and Rwanda, Articles 5, 6, available at https://www.state.gov/documents/organization/101735.pdf (last visited 13 December 2018); *Agreement Establishing the ASEAN-Australia-New Zealand Free Trade Area*, 27 February 2009, ASEAN, Australia and New Zealand, Articles 6, 9, available at http://www.asean.org/storage/images/2013/economic/afta/AANZFTA/Agreement%20Establishing%20the%20AANZFTA.pdf (last visited 13 December 2018).

52 See C. Brown, 'The European Union's Approach to Investment Dispute Settlement' (2018), available at http://trade.ec.europa.eu/doclib/docs/2018/july/tradoc_157112.pdf (last visited 13 December 2018); United Nations Commission on International Trade, *Report of Working Group III (Investor-State Dispute Settlement) on the Work of Thirty-Fifth Session*, UN Doc A/CN.9/935, 14 May 2018, para. 12-18; European Commission Press Release, 'Commission Proposes New Investment Court System for TTIP and Other EU Trade and Investment Negotiations', available at http://europa.eu/rapid/press-release_IP-15-5651_en.htm (last visited 13 December 2018).

53 J. Ketcheson, 'Investment Arbitration: Learning from Experience', in Hindelang & Krajewski, *supra* note 19, 97, 118.

2. Consistency of the Law

Next to legal certainty, consistency is an issue at hand. In recent years, the interrelationship between investment law and other parts of international law, such as environmental law, sustainable development more generally, human rights and labor standards have been intensively discussed[54] and have been addressed in recent case law[55] as well as in recently concluded BITs.[56] Such questions of interrelationship between diverse regimes in international law have been the subject of a larger debate on the fragmentation of international law.[57] While that debate did not arrive at a complete understanding about the necessary coherence between such regimes and the norms which call for unity, it nevertheless became clear, that inconsistencies between different parts of international law put into question legal certainty and potentially also the idea of the consistency of law.[58] Both these principles form part of a more general understanding of the rule of law.[59] At least in cases of a manifest inconsistency such as coverage for investments, whose operation conflicts with human rights or labor standards, the rule of law can be said to be at stake.

---

54 J. E. Viñuales, *Foreign Investment and the Environment in International Law* (2012), 24-27; A. Kulick, *Global Public Interest in International Investment Law* (2014), 50, 69; G. Sacerdoti, 'Investment Protection and Sustainable Development', in Hindelang & Krajewski, *supra* note 19, 32-36.

55 *Urbaser S.A. and Consorcio de Aguas Bilbao Bizkaia, Bilbao Biskaia Ur Partzuergoa v. The Argentine Republic*, ICSID Case No. ARB/07/26, Award, 8 December 2016; *Burlington Resources Inc. v. Republic of Ecuador*, ICSID Case No. ARB/08/5, Decision on Ecuador's Counterclaims, 7 February 2017.

56 See, for instance: Canada, *Canadian Model Bilateral Investment Treaty* (2004), Article 11, available at https://www.italaw.com/documents/Canadian2004-FIPA-model-en.pdf (last visited 13 December 2018) [Canada Model BIT]; United States of America, 'US Model Bilateral Investment Treaty' (2012), Article 12, available at https://ustr.gov/sites/default/files/BIT%20text%20for%20ACIEP%20Meeting.pdf (last visited 13 December 2018) [US Model BIT].

57 Report of the Study Group of the International Law Commission to the Fifty-Eighth Session, Fragmentation of International Law: Difficulties Arising from the Diversification and Expansion of International Law, UN Doc. A/CN.4/L.682, 13 April 2006.

58 *Ibid.*, paras. 420, 465.

59 S. Chesterman, 'Rule of Law', in R. Wolfrum (ed), 8 *The Max Planck Encyclopaedia of Public International Law* (2012), 1014, 1014; B. Z. Tamanaha, *On the Rule of Law: History, Politics, Theory* (2004), 132; J. Orth, 'Exporting the Rule of Law', 24 *North Carolina Journal of International Law and Commercial Regulation* (1998) 1, 71, 81.

3. *Legitimacy*

Lastly legitimacy may be said to be related to the rule of law. It plays a major role in the recently raised doubts as to the appropriateness of settling investment disputes by arbitration.[60] Arbitration is a perfectly legitimate means of settling international commercial disputes between private parties, who agree to do so. However, and as has been increasingly made clear in recent years, arbitrators chosen by parties might fail to meet legitimacy criteria appropriate to dispute settlement, where complaints of individuals against the exercise of public authority are at stake.[61]

III. *International and Domestic Rule of Law: United or Conflicting?*

In the above assessment of the impact of international investment law on the rule of law, a distinction has been made between international and domestic levels. The need to draw such a line is not evident at first glance. Historically, the rule of law emerged at the domestic level and it took a while until the concept was transferred to the international level. As a result, quite a number of concepts from the national sphere were transferred to international levels and many of the concepts indeed can be said to exist in parallel. One might even discuss, whether such parallels reflect in part a conceptual unity between the two levels.[62] However, such similarity of concepts does not at once imply harmony in the actual working of the rule of law at international and domestic levels. Indeed, it is submitted here, that clearly separating international and domestic levels of the rule of law is not only useful for conceptual analysis but probably even more essential, when looking at how the rule of law is implemented at these levels.

---

60 K. Hobér, 'Investment Treaty Arbitration and Its Future -- If Any', 7 *Yearbook on Arbitration and Mediation* (2015), 1, 58.

61 See M. N. Cleis, *The Independence and Impartiality of ISCID Arbitrators: Current Case Law, Alternative Approaches, and Improvement Suggestions* (2017), 206-208; P. Sands, 'Conflict of Interest for Arbitrators and/or Counsel', in M. Kinnear *et al.* (eds), *Building International Investment Law: The First 50 Years of ICSID* (2016), 655, 664-665.

62 T. P. Holterhus, 'The History of the Rule of Law', *supra* note 39.

1. *International Investor-State Dispute Settlement and Domestic Adjudication – Local Remedies*

Indeed, a particularly clear line of conflict exists where international ISDS meets with domestic jurisdictions and adjudication by domestic courts. As has been seen, ISDS can be seen as a contribution to or an emanation of the international rule of law. At the same time and in domestic perspective, the rule of law can be seen to call for the adjudication of such cases through domestic courts. This potential conflict is a core issue in international investment law and its developments. It has been a major issue in the critics against international investment law[63] and forms the main argument underlying the *Calvo Doctrine*.[64] Furthermore, it has caused extensive discussion on the role of the exhaustion of local remedies,[65] has been at issue in a number of arbitrations,[66] is addressed by specific provisions in some recent agreements[67] and very recently has driven the proposal for the establishment of an investment court.[68]

The potential for conflict arises because domestic legal systems are equipped with their own proper dispute settlement systems, which are charged to see disputes arising within the respective jurisdiction exclusively. Such claim to exclusive adjudication rests on sovereignty and the rule of

63 In this vein for example G. van Harten, *Investment Treaty Arbitration and Public Law* (2007), 153-158.

64 P. Juillard, 'Calvo Doctrine/Calvo Clause', in R. Wolfrum (ed), 8 *Max Planck Encyclopedia of Public International Law* (2012), 1086, 1087, para. 6.

65 See for example M. Sattorova, 'Return to the Local Remedies Rule in European BITs: Power (Inequalities), Dispute Settlement, and Change in Investment Treaty Law', 39 *Legal Issues of Economic Integration* (2012) 2, 223-247.

66 For example, on the relationship of the protection against expropriation and prior adjudication on the matter by a domestic court, see *Waste Management Inc v. United Mexican States*, ICSID Case No. ARB(AF)/00/3, Award, 30 April 2004, paras. 174-175; see further A. van Aaken, 'Primary and Secondary Remedies in International Investment Law and National State Liability', in S. W. Schill (ed.), *International Investment Law and Comparative Public Law* (2010), 721, 735-739.

67 See for example CETA, *supra* note 10, Article 8.31 (2) which stipulates that the Investment Tribunal has no jurisdiction to determine the legality of the measure in question under domestic law, importantly including EU law, and that domestic law shall be dealt with as a matter of fact, following the prevailing interpretation given by domestic courts or authorities.

68 See for example the contextualization by N. Lavranos, 'How the European Commission and the EU Member States Are Reasserting Their Control Over Their Investment Treaties and ISDS Rules', in A. Kulick (ed.), *Reassertion of Control Over the Investment Treaty Regime* (2017), 309, 320-323.

law principle, which essentially calls for institutions and procedures to be in place to allow individuals to challenge measures of public authority and to claim compensation.[69]

In a similar way, the *European Union* claims the autonomy of its legal order, as a number of judgments of the *Court of Justice of the European Union* (CJEU) have indicated. This particular type of autonomy is primarily understood to entail that EU rules are exclusively interpreted by the EU courts and the CJEU in particular.[70] As is hoped, this might reduce the probability of a conflict, where investment law dispute settlement confines itself to adjudicating potential violations of investment protection standards defined by international agreement, without taking into account EU laws. It is to date an open question, however, whether this kind of a distinction is feasible.[71]

The relevance of such conflict can scarcely be denied by referring to a State's power to deliberately subject itself to international adjudication. Indeed, under their constitutional law, States have and do exercise this power in various ways and importantly also in the case of regional human rights courts. Just as is true for ISDS, human rights courts as, for instance, the *European Court of Human Rights* (ECHR) can hear individual complaints and adjudicate them with binding force for the respective States Parties, even including claims for compensation.[72] However, such adjudication differs considerably from the situation in ISDS. The ECHR procedure fully

---

69 See for example on German constitutional law Stoll, Holterhus & Gött, *supra* note 18, 151-154.

70 ECJ, Opinion 1/91, 14 December 1991, EU:C:1991:490, para. 30.; ECJ, Opinion 1/92,24 March 1995, EU:C:1995:83, para. 32; ECJ, Opinion 1/00, 18 April 2002, EU:C:2002:231, para. 13; CJEU, Opinion 1/09, 8 March 2011, EU:C:2011:123, para. 75; CJEU, Judgment of 3 September 2008, *Kadi and Al Barakaat*, C-402/05 P and C-415/05 P, EU:C:2008:461, para. 282; CJEU, Opinion 2/13, 18 December 2014, EU:C:2014:2454, para. 182; CJEU, Judgment of 20 April 2018, *Achmea*, C-284/16, EU:C:2018:158, paras. 32-37.

71 On this discussion see for example the recent contributions by C. Contartese, 'The Autonomy of the EU Legal Order in the ECJ's External Relations Case Law', 54 *Common Market Law Review* (2017) 6, 1627, 1661; C. Eckes, 'International Rulings and the EU Legal Order: Autonomy as Legitimacy?', in M. Cremona, A. Thies & R. A. Wessel (eds.), *The European Union and International Dispute Settlement* (2017), 161.

72 C. Tomuschat, *Human Rights*, 3rd ed. (2014), 277-286; on the individual complaint system in Europe, America and Africa in a comparative perspective see P. Abel, 'Menschenrechtsschutz durch Individualbeschwerdenverfahren: Eine regionaler Vergleich aus historischer, normativer und faktischer Perspektive', 51 *Archiv des Völkerrechts* (2013) 3, 369.

accommodates the interest of States Parties by means of requiring the exhaustion of local remedies before initiating procedures.[73] This comparison indeed is telling in view of a design of international investment dispute settlement, which may prevent a clash between the exercise of the rule of law at international and domestic levels. Indeed, a number of possibilities exist to secure that local remedies are exhausted in a way to accommodate a State's interest in seeing disputes being settled by its proper own adjudication before bringing them to an international body.[74]

2. *Is Arbitration a Legitimate Way to Adjudicate Issues Relating to the Exercise of Public Authority?*

Next to allowing for local remedies in the first place, human rights courts differ from ISDS in that they are designed as courts, whose judges are appointed by the States Parties and perform a specifically defined office as international judges.[75] In contrast, ISDS is performed in the way of an arbitration, where arbitrators are chosen by parties to a dispute and the third

73 *Convention for the Protection of Human Rights and Fundamental Freedoms*, 4 November 1950, Article 35 (1), ETS 5, 8 [ECHR].

74 There is nothing in international investment law that prohibits the inclusion of some sort of local remedies rule, as for example specifically mentioned in Article 26 ICSID Convention, *supra* note 6. There is a variety of different forms to ensure that domestic courts address a dispute first, for example: cooling-off periods which force the investor to wait a certain amount of time before raising an investment claim, for example provided in Article 24 USA Model BIT, *supra* note 56; fork-in-the-road provisions which allow an investor to raise either an investment claim or a lawsuit before a domestic court, for example provided *Agreement Between the Government of the Hellenic Republic and the Government of the Republic of Albania for the Encouragement and Reciprocal Protection of Investments*, 1 August 1991, Greece and Albania, Article 10 (2), available at http://investmentpolicyhub.unctad.org/Download/TreatyFile/15 (last visited 13 December 2018); and classic local remedies-rules which demand from the investor to bring a dispute to domestic courts before resorting to investment arbitration, for example provided in *Treaty Between the Federal Republic of Germany and the Argentine Republic on the Encouragement and Reciprocal Protection of Investments*, 9 April 1991, Germany and Argentina, Articles 10 (2) and (3) (a), available at http://www.wipo.int/edocs/lexdocs/treaties/en/ar-de/trt_ar_de.pdf (last visited 13 December 2018) which, however, allows for the filing of an investment claim if the competent domestic court does not issue a decision on the merits within 18 months of the initiation of domestic proceedings. See generally on these different clauses Aaken, *supra* note 66, 739-743.

75 ECHR, *supra* note 73, Articles 19-23.

and chairing arbitrator in a panel is chosen by its fellow arbitrators.[76] This differs considerably from the idea of a court. Having in mind the extensive practice of commercial arbitration at domestic and international levels, this might not look worrisome at first glance. Arbitration is provided for by most legal systems in the world as an alternative to court proceedings on the understanding, that it deals with disputes among private parties involving their private interest and that it is based on a consensus between those parties. ISDS has been intentionally tailored along the lines of the well-established forms of international commercial arbitration.[77] And indeed, some observers did conclude, that arbitration can make an investor-State-dispute look like or even transform it into a matter of private law with the aim of *depoliticizing* the matter at hand.[78]

It took some time for the view to emerge, that investor-State disputes are about individual rights as affected by the exercise of public authority and that, accordingly, public interest is involved in settlement.[79] This having said, the disputing party's *ad hoc* choice of arbitrators appears to be questionable in terms of legitimacy. There is quite some constitutional law reason to believe, that the public rather than individual disputing parties should have a say in selecting individuals to sit on a case involving public interest. For instance, this point has been made under the *German Basic Law* and in view of its Article 92 – (*Gesetzlicher Richter*) and Article 20 (3) – the rule of law principle.[80] This is an essential point in the upcoming criticism about investor-State arbitration and the main concern, which drives the proposal for an international investment court, where individuals to sit on a case will be picked from a list as initially set up by States parties. More generally, this issue clearly indicates, that the rule of law also has a legitimacy dimension.[81]

---

76 See further M. Sasson, 'Investment Arbitration: Procedure', in M. Bungenberg *et al.* (eds.), *International Investment Law* (2015), 1288, 1321-1335, paras. 78-108.

77 Z. Douglas, 'The Hybrid Foundations of Investment Treaty Arbitration', 74 *British Yearbook of International Law* (2004) 1, 151, 224.

78 See for example I. F. I. Shihata, 'Towards A Greater Depoliticization of Investment Disputes: The Roles of ICSID and MIGA', 1 *ICSID Review* (1986) 1, 1, 3-12, 24-25.

79 Van Harten, *supra* note 63, 54-58, 96-99.

80 Stoll, Holterhus & Gött, *supra* note 18, 139-143.

81 In this vein already van Harten, *supra* note 63, 167-175; on German constitutional law in this regard see Stoll, Holterhus & Gött, *supra* note 18, 151-154.

3. *Discrimination*

Another tension might occur, where the protection of foreign investors, a welcome achievement of the international rule of law, works to the disadvantage of domestic investors and raises questions as to discrimination and the domestic rule of law. International investment law initially has been developed to remedy a lack of effective protection for foreign investors. Probably in order to accommodate sovereignty concerns, this law never touched upon economic rights more generally at national level. In the situation of questionable levels of protection of foreigners, this worked well. However, in a domestic legal environment, where foreign and domestic investors enjoy effective protection, the additional international protection of foreign investors may cause discrimination.[82] The existence and extent of such discrimination very likely depends on the level of protection afforded by applicable international investment law as compared to the level of domestic protection. Many observers understand the level of substantive protection in most industrialized countries to easily exceed international investment law standards.[83] Whether this general statement stands a reality test in a given case, where complex legislation and adjudication meets the rather general terms of international investment law and the considerable variety of arbitral awards is an open question, particular when looking at details, such as the amount of compensation and its calculation.

When turning to the procedural side, the divergences become more obvious, as the international ISDS – a one-tier arbitration, which can be done in quite a short time stands against possibly lengthy litigation before a hierarchy of different courts at domestic level. Modern BITs or investment chapters put sophisticated conditions for the use of these two tracks alternatively or in sequence and prescribe certain conditions in order to prevent the parallel use of the two tracks and to give incentives to go to domestic courts first.[84] With all these complex regulations in mind, however, it is fair to resume, that a foreign investor enjoys more procedural options to remedy a measure by the host State as compared to a national.

---

82 For a more detailed analysis see Stoll, Holterhus & Gött, *supra* note 18, 135-136.

83 S. Hindelang & S. Wernicke (eds.), 'Essentials of Modern Investment Protection – Harnack-Haus Reflections' (2015), 10, available at http://www.jura.fu-berlin.de/fachbereich/einrichtungen/oeffentliches-recht/lehrende/hindelangs/Harnack-House/Harnack-House-Reflections-Investment-Protection-ENG.pdf (last visited 13 December 2018).

84 See, for instance US Model BIT, *supra* note 56, Article 24; Canada Model BIT, *supra* note 56, Article 26; CETA, *supra* note 10, Article 8.22.

In sum, it can be concluded, that international investment law may result in a discrimination against national investors at domestic levels. Certainly, the legality of such discrimination under domestic, regional and international law depends on applicable standards of non-discrimination and potential justifications. It is sufficient to conclude here, that discrimination might occur. Such discrimination may very well be a concern in view of the rule of law. This is so, because the rule of law can be understood to embrace the principle of non-discrimination as a separate element or as part of human rights more generally.

4. *An Utopian Proposal: Establishing a Global Human Right to Property*

In overview, international investment law may look as an important but yet insufficient step forward to promote the international rule of law. It suffers from its focus on protecting foreigners only, which roots back to the ancient international law of aliens and diplomatic protection but possibly results in a discrimination against domestic investors. It also suffers from employing arbitration as a dispute settlement mechanism, which, as has been seen, does not fully correspond to needs of legitimation.

Yet investment law importantly and effectively protects individuals and in this way comes close to the idea of human rights. At this point, it is worth recalling, that a human right to property has been part of the *United Nations Universal Declaration of Human Rights* but still today is only provided for at regional level.[85]

A human right to property could remedy the shortcomings of the investment law system. It would protect foreign and domestic investors alike and this way benefit social and economic development and prevent discrimination. It could come along with a human rights court-type dispute settlement and enforcement including compensation easing the legitimacy concerns of investment arbitration. Establishing such a right at global level indeed could be seen as the missing mile to go, to fully transform a useful but unsatisfactory legal construct, to present needs and realities of the

85 *Additional Protocol I to the ECHR*, 20 March 1952, Article 1, ETS 9, 1; *American Convention on Human Rights*, 22 November 1969, Article 21, 1144 UNTS 123, 150; *African Charter on Human and Peoples' Rights*, 27 June 1981, Article 14, 1520 UNTS 217, 248.

global economy and human rights development.[86] Of course, there have been reasons for not embodying a right to property in the global human rights rulebook to date and such reasons are likely to prevail. Thus, there is need to keep and further refine international investment law. However, this should not be used as an excuse to not demand for the elaboration of a human right to property. Such right to property could not only cure some of the deficits of investment law. It is also called for to complete the global human rights rulebook. Investment law and such human right to property could even be mutually supportive. A human right to property could take the lead, where it has been established and implemented effectively by a State Party. Otherwise, investment law would come to bearing. Its application would be particularly well acceptable from the point of the rule of law, if it is shown, that more appropriate forms of protection have failed to be effectively established.

Thus, the protection of property as a human right at global level could be linked to the existing system of international investment law: the application of international investment law with all its merits and shortcomings could be confined to cases, where States fail to agree on or the to properly implement a global human right to property. This way, an incentive would be created for States to accept and implement such a proposed human right to property. Where they fail to do so, the application of international investment law would look particularly well founded.

D. *Three Perspectives on the Rule of Law*

The above discussion of international investment law invites a more general reflection on the rule of law, the way it is understood and its conceptual underpinnings. As particularly the discussion of international investment law indicates, the rule of law is used in different ways.

I. *The Rule of Law as an Empirical Indicator*

Firstly, from a business perspective, but also with regard to the political, economic and social situation of certain countries, the rule of law is re-

86 On the global right to property see, for instance J. G. Sprankling, 'The Global Right to Property', 52 *Columbia Journal of Transnational Law* (2014) 2, 464, 465, 486, 504-505.

ferred to as an empirical indicator, which allows for comparing and even for ranking particular countries. A number of rule of law indices exist, including in publications of the *World Bank* or other entities and foundations.[87] They are mostly created by way of expert interviews and therefore reflect the personal opinion of a number of selected individuals rather than the result of an institutional or legal analysis. Those indices might be helpful as an orientation for businesses and for general policy-making. They are even welcome in providing us with an overall picture. However, it has to be kept in mind that such quantitative indicators do not build on, and do not reflect, a more detailed legal reasoning or normative judgement.

II. The Rule of Law as Lege Lata

Much to the contrary, we can – secondly – speak about the rule of law as part of applicable law – as *lege lata*. There is good reason to believe, that the rule of law, in spite of the rather general and abstract nature of the term, indeed forms part of the international and domestic legal orders as a general principle, from which even more specific rules and principles could be derived. Seen in this way, the rule of law has to be taken into account in legal analysis as applicable law.

Yet, while several substantive elements of international investment law such as the fair and equitable treatment standard as well as procedural issues such as the extended use of the annulment procedure suggest themselves as a manifestation of the rule of law principle, the principle is hardly ever applied in case law, treaty practice or more general reflections on the state of international investment law. Very likely, rather than directly and explicitly referring to the principle as such, positive rules, which reflect it, such as the aforementioned fair and equitable treatment standard or legal arguments based on certain elements of the rule of law such as the *bona fide* principle, have been employed. Where no positive rules or principles are at hand, however, the rule of law can come into play. Applying it in a given case would, however, require one to explore its legal foundations and meaning, which probably is a difficult and burdensome task.

---

87 For instance, World Justice Project, 'Rule of Law Index' (2018), available at https://worldjusticeproject.org/sites/default/files/documents/WJP-ROLI-2018-June-Online-Edition_0.pdf (last visited 13 December 2018); World Bank, 'Worldwide Governance Indicators' (2018), available at www.govindicators.org (last visited 13 December 2018).

III. The Rule of Law as an Analytical Concept

It has not been intended in this article, to extensively explore the impact of the rule of law as *lege lata*. Rather, the paper has been concerned with international investment law with the aim to explain its developments and challenges in international and domestic dimensions and to draw some conclusions *de lege ferenda*. Accordingly, it was meant to make use of the rule of law in a third sense, which may be described as a conceptual approach. Rather than striving for ascertaining the legal validity of the rule of law as a principle in some circumstance and spelling out its significance in the context of specific legal questions, it has been used as a normative orientation to analyze, compare and categorize and discuss legal developments. This approach builds on the understanding, that the rule of law can be seen as a useful concept for legal analysis, which goes far beyond its manifest positive legal significance. Such *conceptual* use of the term is driven by the purposes of legal analysis and has to conform to its rationale. Concepts need to adequately respond to research questions and purposes, be based on clear terminology, and be applied consistently.

E. Conclusion

The above discussion has manifested what was observed at the outset: investment law appeals to the lawyer's senses for the rule of law. Indeed, the concept of the rule of law brings together several pertinent issues, highlights interlinkages and thus provides us with a clearer picture of this particular, sometimes even peculiar part of international law. It has become clear, that a rule of law view on investment law must consider, that this law does not only contribute to, but might also be informed by the rule of law. It also turned out, that a dividing line has to be drawn between international and domestic levels, not so much in view of concepts but because conflicts may arise in the course of operation of the rule of law at different levels. Altogether, the rule of law concept will become significantly more relevant for the development of a part of international law, which emerged as some sort of a provisional fix for an economic problem and now has become a firm element of the international legal order. In substance, it has been proposed to establish a global human right to property to cure various shortcomings of international investment law. Such a human right could coexist and even be linked to international investment law in that the latter would apply only where the former has not been accepted and properly implemented.